Perfect Circles

(An exploration of faith and relationships with YHWH – (Yahweh) Our heavenly Father)

VOLUME ONE

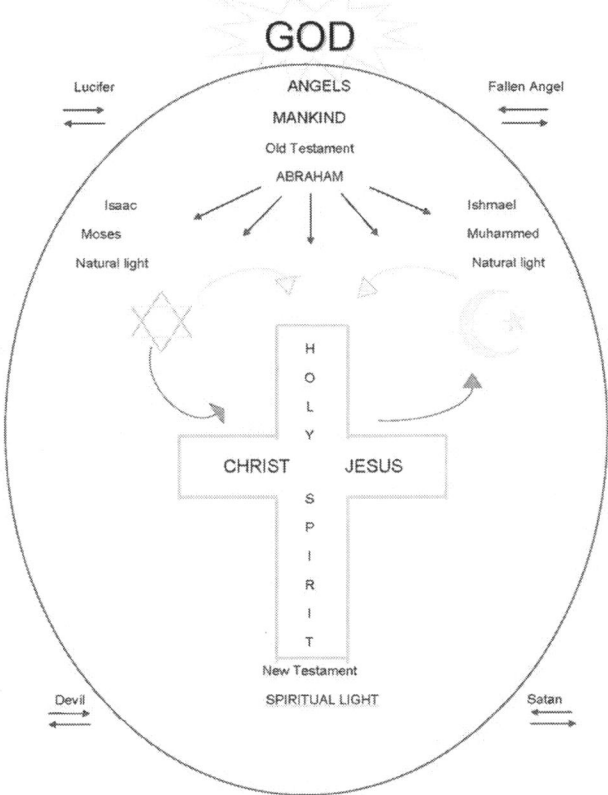

By Doreen Joseph (Khadija Omowale)

Illustrated by Safron Joseph

ISBN – 13: 978-1479396573

ISBN – 10: 1479396575

Proposed Contents For Volumes

Vol 1 – (an exploration of faith & relationships with YHWH (Yahweh) –our heavenly Father)

Acknowledgements

Main references: Holy Books cited

Preface

Introduction

Part One: The Purpose Of Life

Diagram 1: Perfect Circles

Diagram 2: Annotated Perfect Circles: Journey through "God's" circles

1. Alpha and Omega
2. Before Creation
3. In the Beginning
4. Man's pride knows no bounds
5. Proof's of "God's" everlasting love
6. The way forward back in time
7. Beware and be a winner

Diagram 3: 3 religions - 1 faith

Part Two: The Spirit of Conviction

    8. Satan stripped bare – part 1

Diagram 4: Table of Events – since birth of Jesus Christ

    9. Satan stripped bare – part 2

Epilogue & P. S: Author's comments

Vol 2 – (an exploration of faith and relationships with YHWH – Unveilings & further profound revelations)

    10. Imagine

    11. For all our souls

    12. Lift up the veil – see the Truth

    13. Unveiled – the lies of today

    14. Seek divine inspiration

    15. Black pride..... old and new

    16. Holy Trinity

    17. Dreams bring messages too

    18. From an acorn.....

Vol 3 – (an exploration of faith & relationships with YHWH – the faith that holds up our Saviour as Lord and King)

    19. Man in our Creator's image part 1

    20. Man in our Creator's image part 2

    21. Innocent Blood

    22. Faith

    23. Dilemma or not?

    24. End of the Great Controversy – the Final Victory

VOLUME ONE

Contents

Acknowledgements   (vii)

Main references: Holy Books cited   (ix)

Preface   (xiii)

Introduction   (xv)

Part One: The Purpose Of Life   1

Diagram 1: Perfect Circles   2

Diagram 2: Annotated Perfect Circles:
          Journey through "God's" circles   3

   1. Alpha and Omega   5

   2. Before Creation   9

   3. In the Beginning   13

   4. Man's pride knows no bounds   23

   5. Proofs of "God's" everlasting love   27

   6. The way forward back in time   31

   7. Beware and be a winner   33

Diagram 3: 3 religions – 1 faith   61

Part Two: The Spirit Of Conviction   **79**

    8. Satan stripped bare – part 1   81

Diagram 4: Table of Events – since birth of Jesus Christ   148

Diagram 5: Ten Commandments comparison   179

Diagram 6: Ten Commandments comparison   180

    9. Satan stripped bare – part 2   181

    Epilogue & Author's comments   379

(References are given throughout and at end of chapters)   355

Photos and pictures: near pages

The Hidden or Secret Garden – (my Eden)   19

The Waterfall   320

Heale House gardens – (the tree and river of Life)   401

Topical Index   403

Acknowledgements

Firstly I'd like to express my love and gratitude to Our Father, YHWH (Yahweh), who art in heaven, who first loved us enough to create us and the earth in which we inhabit.

I am also eternally grateful to Jesus Christ who loved Our Father and us enough to save me and set me free.

I thank the Comforter (Holy Spirit) who helps and guides me through this life and hopefully into the next, under whose inspiration I wrote this book, Perfect Circles.

Also I am hugely grateful to my children, Alithea, Chloe and Safron and my grandchildren, Matisse and Dillon, and my sister Betty, brother Desmond, and family members, and close friends, pastor Clive de Silva, and my SDA church family. They have given me encouragement and support, and were my purpose for persevering with this book against the onslaught of Satanic attack.

I especially thank and pray for Revd. Paul Grey, who divinely encouraged me this past year. May his ministry also be blessed, for our beloved Jesus Christ.

I also appreciate Chipmunkapublishing and publishers CreateSpace's help in bringing this publication to fruition. May their courage be rewarded with many blessings.

And again, I give glory and praise to Our Father in heaven, for whom it has been my desire, honour and privilege to love and serve. Bless His holy Name!!!

Main References
The Holy Books Cited

The Holy Bible: Revised Standard Version, Roman Catholic Edition, 1966, The Catholic Truth Society, London, UK.

Good News Bible, 1976, Today's English Version. The Bible Society. American, British, & Foreign.

Holy Bible (placed by Gideons), 1996 (1973), New International Version, Lutterworth, UK.

Holy Bible: New King James Version, Next Millennium Edition, (New HMS Richards Study Helps), Red Letter, 1982, (c. 1960-1990), Thomas Nelson Inc. Review & Herald Publishing Association, USA.

Holy Bible NKJV, 2008 (1982), The Amazing Facts, Prophecy study Bible, Thomas Nelson Inc. USA.

The Open Bible New living Translation NLT study Bible, 1998 (1966), Thomas Nelson Inc. USA

The Original African Heritage Study Bible, King James version, 1998 (1993), World Bible Publishers Inc. USA.

Holy Bible – Home Health Education Service – Authorised KJV, 1976, C.D. Stampley Enterprise Inc. USA.

The Sayings of Jesus, 1991, ed. Andrew Linzey, published by Gerald Duckworth & Co. Ltd., London. Used gospel extracts from Revised Standard version of Bible (1952 & 1971), and Division of Christian Education of the Churches of Christ, USA.

The Holy Qur'an, (Text, Translation and Commentary), by A. Yusuf Ali, 1975, The Islamic Foundation, Leicester, UK.

Licensed Permissions For Song Lyrics Used:

Preface

Perfect Circles – a book of Faith, Spirituality, Mental Clarity (or insanity?)

Part 1 of this book was written in May 1990, under the inspiration of the Holy Spirit, (also called my schizophrenic period; might be called in other cultures 'intense spiritual vision'). Part 2 was written in August and September 1990 after intensive research in my recovery period. Some twenty years later, they have been edited and added to, which with the benefit of history and experiences, have provided a more in-depth clarity.

It is only now, despite previous attempts, that the book has been come to be published, some 20 years later. Was it ahead of its time?

The book was written at a time when the Muslim world had a high profile in world news. Saddam Hussein had invaded Kuwait and the Western Allied forces were waging war against him. There were other incidents around the world such as the Muslim coup in Trinidad; and the siege and attempted kidnap of an Arabian prince at a London nightclub. The Kurds had been maltreated also.

In my personal life I had been exposed to other Muslim influences – friends, and in the teaching of Muslim children in a multi-cultural school. I came to appreciate the Muslim way of life, and researched into it further. It was a very intense time for me, and the urgency and need for inter – faith dialogue is expressed in this book.

Judge for yourself – is this book the result of 'madness' or 'visionary inspiration'? Though written through traumatic experiences, it takes the reader on a journey of discovery and faith – towards regaining 'Perfect Circles', or more accurately, 'Perfected Circles'. These allow our communion with our Creator, from Adam to Jesus, to us and future generations. May He guide you on your journey through this book.

Introduction

Perfect Circles

This Revelatory book spans time before Creation to the future. It explores perfect circles – the wholeness of being in one accord with our Creator YHWH (Yahweh), within Creation, beauty, love and life.

It tells how Yahweh reaches out to mankind to reconnect that idyllic relationship that was severed by the deceitful, destructive devil.

The book shows how to regain perfect circles. It explores how Jew, Moslem, Christian, anyone, can find joy, peace and fulfilment in Yahweh through Christ.

This book is a step into the wonderful worlds of Islam and Christianity.

It invites the reader to cross several bridges. These bridges cross over the chasm between the two religions, and acknowledge one faith in "God". It crosses the bridge linking earthly existence with the spiritual one. It sees Jesus as a bridge to complete personal circles to perfection.

This book challenges thinkers to take a new perspective on faith.

Part 1 introduces the idea of perfect circles – which is a wholesome experience of relationships with our Creator, YHWH.

Part 2 gives a more in-depth exploration of faith, and ways to achieve perfected circles. It seeks to stimulate inter-faith communication and dialogue.

The book explores faith, and the connections between Judaism, Christianity and Islam; ancient Egyptian mythology; former and current religious/ political power influences, media and music influencers. It points out man's inhumanity to man; and who is the most pervasive influencer in these Revelation Times.

It highlights the One who can help us through difficult and traumatic situations, and free us from mental slavery & oppression to have Life and have it abundantly.

PART ONE

THE PURPOSE OF LIFE

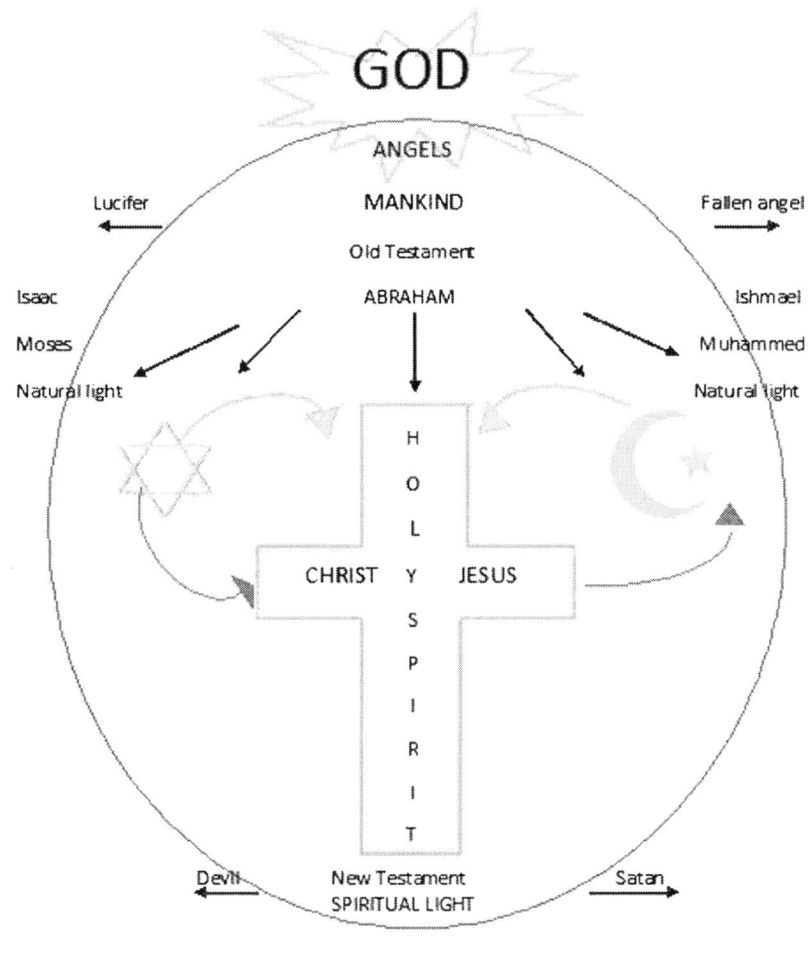

GOD

=

ALPHA & OMEGA/ Beginning & End/ Infinite:- Genesis to Revelation

Lucifer, denying God. disobedient, vain– glorious, disregarding God.

First Angel Lucifer, Arch angels & angels. Acknowledging & loving God, obedient, humble & God-fearing.

(Broken Circle)
The world created in 6 days.
Rested 7th day - Sabbath

Fallen Angel Satan/ Devil - False gods, multi-named, he is miserable & lonely.

Happy praising God, singing rejoicing & communicating-one language/ few words together, heavenly hosts.

Adam & Eve

In the garden of Eden-perfect

Exiled

Noah – Flood & rainbow-covenant

Imperfect = toil, suffering & death

Abraham –covenant of circumcision

son **Isaac** – Jacob/Israel – Joseph, Moses, David;   son **Ishmael** - Muhammed

Jews –

Chosen,

Stubborn,

Judaism

Egyptian, Arabs– Great, but warring nation, Islam

Egyptians

Unclean Gentiles –to- Acceptable
Christians.....

New Testament

Spiritual Light

(Christian Muslims)

Chose to worship Satan via Isis etc. Too proud, Scarlet woman on beast, harlot with every nation. Cleopatra. Rameses II vainglorious, jealous & fearful of Israelites & enslaved them, whom Moses freed. God showed Himself as the only living God. - scattered & punished, they can be redeemed through Coptic Holy Ethiopian church. African Belal, Muhammed, Khadija Omowale bring Muslims to Christ.

H
O
L
y
S
P
I
R
I
T

CHRIST   **JESUS**

(Messianic Jews)

Judgement Day - {Satan destroyed}

New Jerusalem – New heaven & new earth

For '144,000' elect & angels in communion

with GOD for all eternity – peace, joy, worship

The Devil

Satan

1

Alpha and Omega

We have come full circle. From the beginning to the end. From before creation and thereafter – into the timeless state of infinity.

Having passed through time and humanity, we return to that ephemeral state that existed before creation. Return to that time when God, the angels and pure spirits, alone were in full communion with each other. We return there. Yet with a difference. The difference that man, once perfect in the sight of God, brought upon himself. Self-inflicted through succumbing to temptation, through greed for knowledge and power. Through DISOBEDIENCE to God!

For God created mankind with free will, along with everything that could give contentment, peace and happiness. Yet man was not satisfied. He used his gift of free will to deny God's Truth. He chose not to accept the status quo, or God's Word that things were just so. He desired to find out for himself. He just had to.

He began the struggle for that state of communion between God and man. For that communion with Him that was there from the beginning in friendship and trust. But it was severed by dissatisfaction, which is one of the symptoms of vaingloriousness.

From Genesis to Revelation, let us look closer at the Bible and see how God in His mercy, ever-loving and forgiving, has struggled to repair the damage to restore harmonious communion with mankind. We will see how the ensuing mismatch occurs because of the intervention of confusion and dazzling images upon the free will of mankind.

Yet there is only one bright light. This is God's light shining through, to guide those who choose to follow its path through the confusion back to Him. The path is not straight, nor is it broad. Yet despite the challenges and temptations, those who seek Truth shall find it in God.

There is much help at hand, and many true examples to follow. To find the Truth seekers need only follow Christ's guiding light. They need to willingly submit to the Will of God (Prophet Muhammed), and need to offer total obedience to God in humility and piety (Virgin Mary). They, like Christ, must become totally unselfish, totally selfless, ephemeral and pure, living for, and loving only God. Thereby reaffirming, re-acknowledging the Truth of God, as ever-loving, all-powerful and all-knowing.

The disobedient, vainglorious fallen angel, Satan, will truly know who is all-powerful and all-knowing in his final destruction. Then the angels and archangels and the saved will join in unison to sing God's praises.

The circle will be complete, refreshed for having the knowledge of the world. Yet become so much wiser, by acknowledging that the created cannot be more knowledgeable than the one who made us, the Creator. And that having digressed, repented and asked forgiveness, receiving it, be welcomed back into the loving arms of the Father, just like the prodigal son was by his father.

The Lord God, our Father, will finally have reason to be well pleased with His work that He began in Genesis. Amen.

2

Before Creation

In the beginning was God. God was the Word, and the Word was God. (1).

There was an existence of God, for some unknown period of time, where He lived and still lives in Eternity. This could have been at least 3000 years in human time, according to the Zoroastrians (2). Though their interpretation of existence differs from that of the Bible, what is important to note is their belief in a spiritual existence of creatures before creation.

Indeed the Bible says God roamed the firmament before the idea of creating the world dawned on Him. It is said He lived with the angels and archangels, cherubims and seraphims, all singing His praises and glorifying Him (3). Indeed the guardian spirit of Zarathustra is said to have spent 3000 years proclaiming celestial mansions (4).

It must be understood that God is an entity in His own right. He is without shape or form. No man has seen His countenance (5). He is free to roam wheresoever He pleases, whether external to us, or within us; within and outside of human notion of Time. God just is.

To Moses God says: 'I am who I am....I am says' (6). In our human search for God we have come to know Him as: All-powerful, All-knowing, Ever-loving, Ever-merciful, and wrathful when appropriate, yet compassionate and forgiving. He is all-embracing, the essence of our being, central to our being, all of which are qualities of being, qualities of existence. These are qualities that make us like Him, though not equal to Him. For God made man in His own image, and breathed life into him. For centuries believers have taken image to mean literal human body. Yet it is possible here to conceive of God's image that He created as being these qualities, rather than physical attributes.

It is our concentration on image in the physical sense that has developed our consciousness, so that we strive to represent God as replicas of ourselves, according to our own racial features. So in former history we have images of a Black Madonna, and in Romantic European times we have a white interpretation of God. In our current time, the 1990s we see a resurgence of black images of Jesus Christ. By focussing on skin colour – one of the bases used for segregation and racism – we have been blinded to the other more probable interpretations of image, that is, qualities valued as humanitarian and divine (8).

God being the Word, was happy in dialogue or communion, that shared experience He had with the company of angels. They all existed together in perfect harmony, united in their contentment. God enjoying the conversation and communion with them, and they singing all praises and glory to Him (3).

If you can imagine a perfect circle, each point equidistant from the centre, with circumference smooth and unbroken. Then imagine their communal existence in Eternity. All at one, and in accord with God. Then imagine the circle wrenched open letting out all the goodness to be dispersed anywhere, whilst the broken segment stands aside and challenges the status quo. In the act of defiance, of breaking the circle, disruption, disharmony has already occurred. So that like a flower, once one or two of its petals have been pulled off, it is very difficult, almost impossible to stick it back together in the complete wholeness of its former self.

Then think of the disruption caused by one particular angel, who becomes so proud and vainglorious, as to think himself as equal to, if not greater than God (7). How can one who has been created be greater than his Creator? (18). Yet this is what he thought. This angel was so conceited that he defied and challenged God. He refused to bow down to Him as master. So he incurred God's wrath (14). For Satan's disobedience he was banished from the heavens.

Yet even then Satan was unrepentant. He grew evermore obstinate and conceited. The fallen angel, named Satan, Sheol, has many names. He was banished to his realm of Hell. No doubt he took some of his like-minded followers with him.

3

In the Beginning

However God, 'though wrathful at the time, does not stay angry forever. He delights in creating things. He enjoys beauty. So it is not long before, mindful of the hosts of angels who are faithful to Him, He glides across the firmament. It is then that He decides to create the world in His infinite wisdom. It took Him six days to form the world and create all living things in it. On the seventh day He rested, and made that day holy (20). At each stage He paused and delighted in what He created. He paused, admired it all, "saw that it was good", and decided to create even more.

He created light across the firmament to separate night from day. He separated the heavens and the earth. He created things, creatures and mankind. In six days He changed the nature of existence. From inanimate dust He created life forms. He created mankind, as He continues to do to this day and beyond.

He created the world out of His love for beauty. This love we can begin to appreciate if we pause to wonder about the stuff of life; about the essence of nature - the smallness and big-ness of plants and creatures; the exquisiteness of some and the plainness of others. The seven natural wonders of the world are proofs enough.

There are many more wonders in nature – the beauty of marine life, their serenity and various colours and shapes. The variety of life forms, from the tiniest ant or seed, to the ginormous whale or cedar and oak trees. The polyps, anthropods, humans and the beauty of creations made through them – fine art, music, poetry, scientific discoveries and innovations. All are wondrous and beautiful. As Louis Armstrong sang in 1968, and Sir David Attenborough recited in December 2011 following the final epi-sode of BBC nature documentary 'Frozen Planet',

'What a wonderful world'.

I see trees of green, red roses too,

I see them bloom for me and you,

and I think to myself what a wonderful world..

I see skies of blue and clouds of white,

bright blessed day, dark sacred night,

and I think to myself, 'what a wonderful world'.

The colours in the rainbow so pretty in the sky,

Are also on the faces of the people passing by,

I see friends shaking hands, sayin' 'How do you do?'

They're really sayin', 'I love you'.

I hear babies cry, I watch them grow,

They'll learn much more than I'll ever know,

and I think to myself, 'What a wonderful world!'

Yes I think to myself, 'What a wonderful world', oh yeah....' (18b)

(**"What a Wonderful World"** Written by George David Weiss and Robert Thiele (c) 1967. Renewed 1995 and Assigned to Quartet Music, Inc., Range Road, Abilene Music LLC c/o Larry Spier Music LLC, NY, NY. All Rights Reserved. International Copyright Secured).

(**"WHAT A WONDERFUL WORLD"** – Words and Music by George David Weiss and Bob Thiele – (c) 1967 Range Road Music, Inc., Bug Music – Quartet Music, Inc., and Abilene Music, Inc., USA. – Copyright Renewed – All Rights Reserved – Reproduced by kind permission of Carlin Music Corp. London NW1 8BD in respect of the 50% interest of Range Road Music Inc and Bug Music – Quartet Music Inc on behalf of Bob Thiele.)

Imagine the Lord God's delight at creating a being, brimming with life and beauty, whose company He can then enjoy. Every day, every minute, we experience the wonder of creation and re-creation. All that we need for life is contained within the earth. There is no need to go outside, extra territorially, for the earth is self-contained. The Lord's patience is sorely tested, will people never learn? Surely the astronauts cannot be hoping to find God, among other things in space? (23)

We are reminded of the Tower of Babel, where the people, having grown so successful, prosperous, talented and knowledgeable, desired to build a tower, a connecting bridge between heaven and earth (9). They wanted to reach God directly, but that privilege was severed with the disobedience of Adam and Eve. God, perceiving that they would not stop building this tower so long as they could communicate, decided to make them international. He made them each speak a different language, and they were so confused they had to abandon the tower. So they too suffered the consequences of their disobedience (21).

However, when God created Adam and Eve, in His own likeness, and in whom He was well-pleased, he gave them a special area to live – the garden of Eden. He provided them with everything. Through their inner spirituality they could converse with the animals, and were at peace with them, 'though they governed them. Through their inner spirituality they could converse in full communion with God. He delighted in their natural beauty, and in the conversations with them. Yet having given them a mind, free will, and a heart, they were content, and they delighted in the love of our Lord God (18).

The garden was perfect. It epitomised all that is appreciated as wonderful and beautiful in the world. For a close experience of it, imagine a beautiful serene garden, with peonies, the most beautiful flower, and walking through it whilst listening to Bach's cantata BWV 147, 'Jesu, joy of man's desiring' (choral) (18a). The music symbolises pure, peaceful and delightful conversation with God.

However, this idyllic setting was shattered by the intervention of the vainglorious one. Though banished to his own realm of endless torture and suffering, Satan was still insolent. He decided to spite God, through them – the very creatures that God most delighted in (22). Satan, knowing very well that God had forbidden them to eat from the tree of knowledge, first tempts Eve, and via her, Adam (11).

Then God recognised their disobedience. For suddenly they were ashamed of their nakedness in the sight of God. It must be understood that it is DISOBEDIENCE which most angers God (12). For He does not ask very much. Afterall He created all that exists – the angels, both true and untrue, this wondrous world and all that is in it. He gave life to so many plants, creatures and humankind. All that He asks is that we acknowledge Him, and praise His Holy Name. Surely we can do that?

We must not get too conceited ourselves. We must realise that when the first man and woman disobeyed God, it was part of a larger plan of things. It is part of the dispute between the Lord our God, and the conceited fallen angel, one who would call himself a god. In this light mankind can be seen as being like a piggy in the middle. The world is a testing ground for this battle to win over the allegiance and devotion of man.

The scenario is not a difficult one to imagine. If we remember Greek mythology that was adopted by the Romans – Zeus and Venus and all the other pagan gods that sat on Mount Olympus. From there, the Olympians watched and influenced the decisions and fates of their humans, Jason and the Argonauts, for instance. They intervened to change the fortunes of Jason, to present a challenge or to lend a helping hand. Yet in the end it was Jason's own skilful determination that won him through.

Modern man, like his ancestors, meets this same duelling of forces daily. However there can only be one winner for each personal battle. One cannot have two masters. So inevitably, with free will, man will determine to whom he pledges allegiance, and will get consequent rewards. To whom do we owe allegiance - to God our Creator, or to the devil, that Pretender? Know your Lord.

God's original plan for mankind was not sin and punishment. When He created Adam and Eve in His image, they were equal partners in their relationship, and having equal dominion over all the creatures of the world (40). They were perfect and had everything they needed in the garden. But the devil, jealous of God's love for them, the love he had lost from God because of his own vain-gloriousness, decided to be spiteful to God and to spoil His delight. He intervened and insidiously planted the seeds of discontent in their heads and sowed discord in their relationships between them and God, and between themselves.

The devil, through his skilful deceit, caused Adam and Eve to disobey God and eat the apple of the tree of knowledge. They, being innocent, too naive and even I would say, 'own-willed' (ie wanting their own way, like the devil), actually complied with his suggestion. They did not die, as God had pre-warned them they would. They did not die, as the devil had assured them they wouldn't. They did not die then. But they did die, eventually.

The Hidden or Secret Garden - (my Eden), tapestry by unnamed service user/person with lived experience of mental distress, that I purchased in autumn of 2010 in Derby UK.

God ever-merciful, ever-loving, spared them immediate death. He 'saved' them then, as Jesus came to 'save' humanity later. God did, however, put a curse on them – the man, woman and the serpent, that they would now become enemies, deadly to each other (in fact and intent). Man would still have dominion over the creatures of the earth, but now too, over his wife Eve, his former equal partner (40). This curse is often quoted, together with Ephesians 5 v 22, to get women/wives to submit to their husbands/partners that the men might have dominance over them, hence the inequality of the sexes the world over. And all too often, unfortunately abusers take this dominance to extremes in domestic violence.

However, since this curse was brought about, we have Ephesians 5 v 21-33, and1 Peter 3 v 1-7, that portray how husband and wife should live together. It involves the wife being submissive to her husband, yes, but also that the husband should respect, understand and honour the woman. Both require loyalty and fidelity to each other. For as oft- quoted 'those whom God has joined together, let no-one put asunder' as 'the two become one' and adultery is the only grounds for divorce that Jesus said was permitted because of the Jews' stubbornness on the matter (Matt. 5 v 27-32; Matt 19 v 4-9; Ephes 5 v 31). But note that 1 Peter 3 v 6, emphasises that the woman should NOT be afraid of, or fear her husband. So domestic violence is not condoned, and abuse should also be considered grounds for divorce.

The inequality of the sexes was caused through temptation and disobedience. But this was not God's original plan back in the garden of Eden. Ephesians 5 v 21 and 23, either side of that oft-cited quote, reveal the true status of the man-woman relationship as God intended it to be. They were meant to be equals. They were meant to live forever. Satan destroyed that idyllic scene, and brought the sin of disobedience, a curse and death into the picture. Adam and Eve did grow old and die, after a life of hardship, turmoil and no doubt, regret. But Jesus Christ came to 'save' humanity. When He died on the cross, death could not hold or keep Him, for He is God incarnate!!!! He rose again, was resurrected, and conquered death and showed us and the devil, that God has the ultimate control, and has the final say.

When Christ returns, when Armageddon is finally arrived, He will claim His own – the dead and living who have lived their lives for him. And after Satan is finally crushed, destroyed forever along with Hell, Hades and his demons and human followers, then God will create a new heaven and a new earth. He will create them for those who belong to His son, Christ, to share in His painfully earned, but glorious kingdom, where they will have peace, joy, happiness and ETERNAL LIFE!!! They will live in perfected circles, re-connected, and in full communion with God.

'To God be the Glory, great things He has done! For He truly is a wonderful, loving and marvellous God, whom I love immensely and with a heart full of love bursting with joy and happiness. Selah.

However, back to Eden where, for their disobedience God banished Adam and Eve from the garden of Eden. He denied them access to contentment in life. They were banished so that they might learn the meaning of struggle and toil. Through suffering they could begin to appreciate the contented life they had taken for granted. Today it is only through toil and suffering that we can gain a glimmer of the real image of God: those essential qualities of humanity (12).

4

Man's pride knows no bounds...

God, ever-loving and ever-merciful, still looked for redeeming features in mankind. Amongst the people He saw one man, Noah, who was faithful to Him. He protected Noah and his family from His ensuing wrath. Because He was not destructive by nature, he told them to take two of every land and winged creature into the ark with them (13).

Then He brought the floods upon the earth for forty days and nights. When the dove of peace returned with an olive branch Noah knew that the water was subsiding and soon there would be dry land. God in His remorse, having lost all those people, vowed to Noah that He would never again cause such complete and utter destruction. The rainbow would be a sign and reminder of this covenant and promise to mankind.

God had hope. And He waited. The people of Noah's sons multiplied their number, but again they grew away from God. God wonders whose is the greater struggle, the people in hardship, or God's in trying to reach their hardened ears? Even yet God's heart could be gladdened. There were those among the people who truly loved God.

God is ever-merciful. As mankind struggled and toiled, God showed them mercy and blessed them with success and prosperity. In Babylon, with the Tower of Babel (9), the people created villages and cities. They were successful in trade and commerce, achieved high levels of craftsmanship and had gained exceptional levels of knowledge.

Yet they knew they had a God, who they believed lived in the celestial heavens. They strove to reach Him though He forbad them to do so. They were still in the disgrace of original sin, and so were not worthy to have communion with Him. And they proved to be even more unworthy through disobedience. So they were given many languages and scattered throughout the world.

Yet God is ever-loving and ever-merciful. He could have destroyed them completely for their disobedience. He could have struck them dumb. But He wanted still to have communion and dialogue with His people. For though saddened, He was ever hopeful that they would come willingly to Him.

However, as soon as they became successful in managing the hard existence on the earth, they grew vainglorious and drew away from God. After all they could see that they were progressing as a result of their own efforts. They grew to forget God, who had created them. They turned instead to the easy living that Satan was offering them. Life was hard and difficult, and mankind can be weak. Many chose the easy option and blinded themselves to God.

God let them procreate and multiply. But they drew away from God and became wild. They created their own deities and gods. Truly they had deserted God, the One who made and loved them. His competitor, though no match for God, saw that for a while he could get the allegiance of the people, and so present an ever-present challenge to the power and knowledge of God. He encouraged the people to worship him. Paganism was rife.

5

Proof of God's Everlasting Love

God spoke to Abraham and asked him to prove his love for God. He asked him to sacrifice his only son, whom he loved so much, flesh of his flesh. God was only testing him. Abraham proved himself to be worthy of God's love. At the crucial minute God saved the son, and accepted a ram as suitable sacrifice instead. God was well pleased with him.

The sacrificial lamb recurs again in the scriptures. But this time there is a change. God has brought a new testament, a new way to prove love and devotion to God – through sacrifice of oneself on behalf of saving others. This time the sacrificial lamb was not spared. Jesus Christ agreed to offer himself as a sacrifice to save mankind. This means repairing the severed connections with God. He provided a human bridge, offering light among the pathway of personal sacrifice, to prove one's love and allegiance to God. So through this special kind of suffering man can once again hope to share in total communion with the Lord our God.

God spoke to Abraham. God spoke to Jesus. Each in turn proved his love of Him by willing submission to His will. Time and again God shows us many proofs of His love for us. Despite the many temptations and deceit away from Him, God, ever-loving, realising the strength that is needed to resist temptation, sent many prophets to help guide the people.

Though Abraham had two sons, the Lord God is seen to show his especial love for the Jewish house of the Semitic race, through his son Isaac. Time and again God lays His helping hand upon certain people who have shown especial qualities that are close to His image. The stories of Isaac, David, Solomon, are examples of God's intervention for us. The people are very trying, and the battle still rages. Sheol fights to claim his own.

So God, ever patient, ever-loving, sent Moses to His people. The 10 Commandments are laws to guide the people to live a Godly life. God who works in mysterious ways, sent Moses, a Hebrew, brought up in the royal Egyptian household of Pharoah's daughter. A slave raised in the most exalted house of the Egyptian conquerors. God blessed Moses with favours, valour and wisdom over and above the Pharoah's rightful heir, Rameses II. So much so that had he remained with the Egyptians, he would surely have ruled in Rameses' stead. At his peak, when he was right for leadership, God revealed Moses true birth and ancestry to him, and took him on a journey that would culminate in the rescue of the Israelites from the proud Egyptians; and the all-important 10 Commandments.

Yet people have short memories. They forgot the years of suffering and toil, and instead got used to the idea of immediate gratification. They raised up their own deities to Sheol, and the golden calf. For this disobedience, and their ingratitude for freedom from bondage, those who chose the calf were immediately destroyed. The remainder, like Moses, were not permitted to enter the promised land. But they suffered penance for forty years in the wilderness, until everyone of those who had been involved in the exodus had died. Even their condemnation to the wilderness can be seen as merciful of God, and redeeming for them, as it provided the opportunity to purify them in their search for Truth and Life.

Then came John the Baptist, Isaiah's prophecy incarnate, proclaiming "Make way! For the Messiah is imminent." And that people should prepare to meet him, and get baptised to cleanse away original sin.

The Virgin Mary was purest of all women. God could already see, before she was born, how pure she would be in nature and spirit, how humble, obedient and chaste. He took away her original sin so that the son of God, who Himself is sinless, could be born, untainted and free of sin (24).

There begins the New Testament, the new way of life, Jesus, who 'died' to save all mankind from perpetual original sin, having mercy on humanity. The Lord God has been long-suffering enough. He sent a code of law via Moses to guide the people in appropriate, God-fearing conduct. Yet this is not enough to convince them. So God, ever-merciful and loving, patience itself, sent Jesus Christ, His only son, whom He, like Abraham, is prepared to sacrifice. This sacrifice is to prove love of mankind for God's sake.

It is difficult to comprehend the enormity of the task in hand – the way of the cross. Anyone who has watched a son or daughter go off to war, not knowing whether they will return or survive even, can experience the immensity of the torment the Lord God had to endure. God watched and waited, to see His son, Jesus, tortured by the Jews and Romans, crucified and disappear to Hades, not knowing will He return.

Or, conversely, to appreciate the psychological turmoil of our Lord, Jesus Christ: His moments of doubt; moments when He felt unsure of His physical and mental ability to endure the tortures to come; His courage and fearlessness at the absurdity and cheek of the devil trying to tempt him with political power and riches on earth. His renewed courage and strength, which while suffering He felt would carry Him through, for the sake of all the lost souls who would be saved. They would be saved by His counteracting original sin, and whose paths to God will be more accessible should they choose to follow. Yet even as mortal man, still He has compassion for His fellow companions being crucified. And His suffering is so great and unbearable for Him to cry out for His Father: "My God, my God, why have you forsaken me?", and yet still almost immediately know that God is there for Him.

Any woman who has experienced the pain of childbirth (40) can have an inkling of, and idea of the pain Christ had to suffer. How many souls did He bear on His shoulders? Can we count them? I fear not. And yet dear mothers – what joy and bliss you enjoy and experience when after struggling so hard, you give birth to a new child! Bliss, as you open up the doors of new opportunity, new living. The same experience multiplied several times over is what one can imagine lay in store for the Lord on His third day, when He rose from the dead. The Lord God exalted Him and gave Him the name above all names: Immanuel, and put all nations and death under His feet.

For all His suffering – do we deserve it? I say yes. For at the end of it all, he could be supremely happy in the knowledge that so many people will have the opportunity to come to know God, and He is in His family, joining the angels in communion with Him (8).

However there is one condition – that one tries to be Christ-like: through long-suffering, endurance, tortures and turmoil, self-denial of riches and wealth of this world. Through so much love for mankind, that one could sacrifice oneself for the name of Christ, who is the Way, the Truth and the Light. And who is indeed the image of God, our Lord Creator. (17, 19).

6

The way Forward back in Time

We still have more suffering to endure. For some 2000 years Gentiles worldwide have been given God's blessing to come to Him first, through following the way of Christ. But Gentiles are not exclusive. Just like their fore-runners, the Jews, discovered they too, are not exclusive. Christ had come for all men, so that all men's sins might be forgiven. So that this is a world inclusive of anyone who has ears and wants to know God through Christ. (8)

Jesus left us the Holy Spirit to guide the apostles, the papacy, the high priests, saints and martyrs, who live a life of humility and sanctity, and so pleased God, they became recognised as saints. They were exemplars of God's way of life. But now their work is not enough. They need more help. They cannot do it alone. The Spirit is going to guide more ordinary folk, so as to get a wider dispersal, a quicker result to capture the people who wish to live God's way.

The Holy Spirit, God's Eternal Guide, is guiding ordinary folk who choose to live in Christ as examples of the qualities found in God's Image. They are teachers and new educators of the urgency and necessity to learn and follow Christ's way – the way of God the Father. The way that He intended we should live from the beginning.

7

Beware and be a Winner

There is still a big battle. Satan grows anxious. Revelation is at hand. And the Harvest is ripe for the picking. It is soon time to gather in. Oh and how the battle rages! (25)

Satan runs amok creating confusion, delusion, illusion everywhere. There is a resurgence of nationalities and old pagan cults and languages, tribalism. The callous, calculating, deceitful anarchists, lawless hell-raisers are his messengers. Separation, division, fragmentation, loneliness, isolation are apt. Satan delights in, and instigates disobedience, disharmony, envy, greed, jealousy, selfishness, cold and callous deeds. He has a myopic outlook. He advocates minute dispersal, like an atom bomb explosion, almost blown to nothing, which is his end.

Our Father in heaven sends out an army of ordinary, spiritual folk as guides and educators, with qualities of compassion, love, peace, harmony, endurance, patience. They guide the people more quickly back to Him, back to the oneness of Him, to the wholeness and warmth of family love. He delights in the beauty of all His diverse people. He does not encourage segregation or cultural separation. There is unity possible through shared language and the ability of multilingual communication, and also through spiritual communion and dialogue with our Father. He wants to gather us back into heaven, to experience that pure, self-less state, in ever-lasting love, and adoration of Him, all-powerful, ever-living, all-embracing Father. And there is more. It is not over yet.

Our Father in heaven knows the future...

Our Father has 'predestinated' this army of ordinary people. 'He chose' them 'in Him before the foundation of the world' and 'adopted' them 'to Himself as children in Christ, Jesus', those people whom He 'predestined to be conformed to the image of Jesus. They were to be likened to Jesus, and to be 'called', 'justified' and then 'glorified'. He foreknew them (26). This was possible because He knows the future.

Our Father is all-powerful (omnipotent). He is in all places at once (omnipresent). Even the devil can't achieve this. Our Father is all-knowing (omniscient). He knows everything – He can see what we do in the night darkness as well as in the daylight. He knows what we feel in our hearts. He knows what is in our minds. Only He can do this. The devil cannot read our minds. He can only make an estimated guess at our likely reactions, given what how we have behaved in the past. He repeats things that he has triggered that he knows has worked for him in the past, to bring about the results he wants to achieve. Our Father is all-loving (omni-benevolent). 'For He so loved the world, that He gave us Jesus, that whosoever (anyone) who believes on him shall have eternal life.' (27 :-John 3v16).

(Omni is an attribute of Our Father in heaven).

He knows the future. But does this mean He *forces* what is going to happen, that He *makes* it happen? NO. He gave us FREE will. We can CHOOSE. He gave us choices. We can choose to do what is right or what is wrong. But He is also 'longsuffering (patient) towards us, not willing that any should perish, but that all should come to repentance' (28). He gives everyone chances to change their minds, and repent and decide to do good things. Jesus said 'Behold, I stand at the door and knock. If anyone hears My voice and opens the door, I will come in to him and dine with him, and he with Me.' (29) Also 'let him who hears say "Come! ...let him who thirsts come. Whoever desires let him take the water of life freely.'(30). Note that the wages of sin is death. But the gift of Our Father is eternal life (31).

He had a plan. You may wonder: if our Father could see the future why did He let it run? Because the way we were created is in the 'image' of Him. We were created out of love. In love there is a choice to give of your own will. He knows there is a risk involved. A risk that if you give someone your love, that they might not return it. Loving involves a risk. He took that risk. He loved all His angels and even Lucifer. But the point came where Lucifer decided he would not return His love. (31a). There was a war in heaven, and Archangel Michael, who is Jesus, fought on our Father's side against the Lucifer (the dragon). The Great Controversy was the battle. (32). The issue was LOVE. Love. Put our Father first. Give Him your time. Respect Him and be content with your life. Because of this battle, when we love someone, there is a risk that we too, might not get it back – unrequited love. Our Father's plan was that in order to really love Him, we have to CHOOSE to love Him, and love willingly and freely. And conversely we also have to be free NOT to love. Therein lies the crux of the matter.

He does not force us, nor make us love Him. He did not make us to be robots. We don't have a chance to go 'back to the future', and there is no dress rehearsal. There is only one way and that is forward onto the end of time, and one life on this earth. We can choose to make a choice, to live the right way.

At present the people who choose to do wrong things live in the same world as those who choose to do the right thing. They will all have their deeds assessed, not now, but at Judgement Day. (... wheats and tares (weeds), let them grow together till the harvest day; then they will be separated and the wheat taken, and the tares thrown away) (33). If this is not our Father's plan A, this is probably His plan Z. (34).

I thank our Father He is omniscient. It's like watching the films, 'The Colour Purple' about the experience of life during African-American slavery times, and 'The Matrix' (1999) (93) about a surreal world where everything is not as it seems, and that humans are really plugged into machines that give them their dreams of a world 'reality' that is not real. I can watch the films, I can see what is unfolding, but I cannot change it , because it has been set. It is the same with our Father in heaven, who has already decreed what will happen at the end of Time. His word is true and cannot be undone.

You might ask: if He knows the future, then He already knows who will be saved, so why does He bother, why does He just not cut straight to the end, forget about the wicked and just spend His time on and with those to be saved? Because sometimes things that He says have to be seen to be believed. He is being watched by the angels and the fallen angel, Lucifer and company, who keeps testing His patience. For even the angels were worried (35) when Our Father told them that He was going to let man onto earth, for they had already witnessed the disobedience of Lucifer, and what happened to him, and feared the same for man. They were right to be worried as it turned out, but our Father lets history run its course.

Others are watching, and still challenging and testing the sovereignty of our Father. This is the point of the story of Job in the Bible, our Father had to let the devil witness for himself, that no matter what he did to Job, or how badly he treated him, he could not force Job to stop loving and being faithful to our Father, who as he said: 'the Lord giveth ,and He taketh away, let me praise Him and die'. In other words he is but clay, or the creation of our Father, whose prerogative it is to bless, or not, his people. He was content to just praise Him even unto death. Again the children's story about the dispute between the wind and the sun over who can make the man take his coat off. The wind blew with all his might, but the man grew colder and pulled his coat on tighter. However it was the sun who won, and the man grew hot and took off his coat. The sun knew he could gently persuade the man to comply with his wishes, whereas the wind had to learn that force does not pay.

So when the angels and people saw that Jesus was crucified as had been foretold in the scriptures (36), then they had proof that the word of our Father in heaven is true, that He can tell the future. They realised that what the devil had said were lies, and that he did not either know the future, nor did he have the ultimate say. He was seen to be a liar, and full of wind. His lies had no substance, and no matter how much he 'bigged him-self up' or boasted of his abilities, he could not deliver on his promises. This is why so many people, who've been misled or given false hope/ false promises, have been disappointed and disillusioned.

Our Father in heaven knows the future. Daniel chapter 2 in the Bible, explains a prophetic dream that the Babylonian king Nebuchadnezzar had, that his own 'wise' men and their sorcery could not see or interpret. He speaks of a statue that represents the kingdoms at the present time, and to come, which had relevance for the king then, and for the rest of humanity up to the end of Time. We are now at the 'latter days' of time, Revelation time, where, as he explained, the feet of the statue were made of iron and clay that could not adhere to each other - like oil and water, they keep separating. This also refers to modern times where the powers of Europe have tried to unite their countries to make them as strong as iron, like Roman Empire once was, - Napoleon Bonaparte, Hitler, used draconian measures, but failed. Queen Victoria tried to unite them through marrying off her children to various European princes and princesses, would-be kings and queens, but failed. Current governments have tried this through the EU, but are failing because the weaker countries like Italy, Greece, Ireland, have had to be bailed out and supported by stronger ones like Germany, France and England. Iron and clay cannot mix, and so these attempts have and will continue to fail, because our Father has spoken and His word is true.

But stop a minute and think. The idea of the righteous being chosen, of being predestined/predestinated, of having their footsteps ordered by our Father – does this really make sense? If we watch a film, even though we cannot change what we are watching, we are not powerless or without options. We can choose not to watch, and to get up and leave. If the footsteps were predestined, then we would not be able to change things, or our lives. We would either be the chosen ones (good ones) or the damned. There would be no point us even trying to improve the way we live. There would be no hope of a future that is way better than anything we see or experience on this earth, in this our present life.

No. We do have choices. We have free will. We can choose how we conduct ourselves, our attitudes to life, and to learn to love unconditionally, to learn to forgive those who hurt us, and to return to the love that our heavenly Father continually gives us. We are told that He knows the future, and says He doesn't want certain things in our lives. So He helps us make the right choices. However it is sometimes better for us to not know the future, so we can make the right choices, because sometimes knowing too much might be harmful to us (Adam and Eve). As humans, even after a day we get tired. Could we handle knowing too much? It would be like a small child, who is given all the knowledge of an adult at once – it would blow his or her mind! The Comforter(43) reveals bits of knowledge at a time, because we too couldn't handle it all at once. These bits of knowledge fit together like a jigsaw puzzle that once complete, gives us the bigger picture.

But we have the solution. Our Father is omniscient and He is omnipotent. At the end of the day (at the end of Time) He will win. The end is sure. He will succeed. The crux is: will we succeed with Him, or will we perish with the devil? We choose. Our Father is patient (long-suffering). But He will not wait forever.

Nothing else is predetermined other than the final outcomes at the end of Time, and Judgement Day has arrived. For as the prophets have shown and come to be proven to be right – the Lord our Father's word is true, and so is certain. We have seen prophecies fulfilled thus far: Isaiah, Ezekiel, Hosea, John the Baptist, all their predictions have come true. Jesus came, as our Messiah. He saved us from damnation in Hell and Death. He did rise up from death, and He will surely return in His full glory. For our Creator says; the wages of sin is death, and the wicked will surely be punished and die, if they do not repent and turn back to Him! But the reward of the obedient and faithful is Life in Eternity.

So what IS predetermined is this:-

Lucifer and the wicked will be punished and die, and perish into ashes in Hell.

Jesus will be (is already) victorious! He will have His glory, and praises, and His kingdom of faithful followers whom He redeemed with His precious, life-saving blood.

So rest assured. Our Creator has spoken. He asked 'Have you not heard, long ago I ordained it...and planned it?' (Isaiah 37 v26), and so it will be in the end.

The outcome for Lucifer is death for his disobedience. The reward for Jesus is victory and eternal LIFE, for His obedience and faithfulness and LOVE!

One – the devil – used his free will to hate and be disobedient.

The other – Jesus Christ – chose to love freely and willingly, and whole-heartedly obey the Lord Most High, our Creator, and has His wonderful reward:

LIFE, JOY, HAPPINESS, PEACE AND UNCONDITIONAL LOVE for all Eternity.

These are what are predetermined. Amen.

So there is a choice. Where are you in your choices? Moving towards our Father, allows Him to move in and through your life. Satan wants us to get to the point where we give up. But our Father knows your future, and what is for your benefit - peace and joy. He knows whatever the devil's plans are for you. So whatever his plans to ambush and destroy you, our Father can lead you away and protect you from him. However bad the circumstance is – glass ceiling in career prospects, failures, illness, blockages, barriers – our Father can help you.

So will you love and serve our Father who is omnipotent, omnipresent, omniscient and omni-benevolent? He who loves us so much that He is striving against sin, to keep us free from sin. Satan is after you and me (32a), discouraging, distracting, deterring you so you stumble and feel that you might as well end it all – your church life, your spiritual life, your physical life. But take heart. Our Father has this great plan - the Ultimate Destiny. His 'house with many mansions in it' (37) with the colour scheme and design just for us.

'My yoke is easy'...

But how do we get into our mansions within His house?

Jesus says 'Come to Me, all you who labour and are heavy laden, and I will give you rest. Take My yoke upon you and learn from Me, and you'll find rest for your souls. For My yoke is easy and My burden light.' (38). Now some may know that a yoke is certainly not light. It is a burdensome, heavy, controlling implement used in farming to hold cattle (mainly oxen) together to plough the fields. It is cruel and goes against the very nature of the animal, which is its desire to roam free and graze on the grass.

We too are 'yoked' under the burdens in our daily lives. For instance, problems in our work, relationships, marriages, friend-ships, financial worries, security issues around our homes, our poor health conditions, disabilities, and so forth. These burdens were not part of our Father's original plans for our lives. They were brought about through the first sin of disobedience to Him, from before Creation.

So what does Jesus mean when he says His yoke is easy and his burden light? What makes it easy and bearable is Love. He says 'learn from me...'. So we learn from not only what he says but also what he did. He loves his heavenly Father so much that he was prepared to do, not his own will, but do that of his Father. To prove his love for Him, he accepted our Father's mis-sion, and came down from heaven to live on earth, not as great and mighty king, but as a ordinary baby, who grew into a meek and lowly (quiet and humble) man. Then he completed his mis-sion, by getting baptised, by telling people about our Father and His love for us, by making disciples, and by agreeing to give up his life, to take on the 'sins' /burdens of us, the people, onto his shoulders and suffer and die on the cross at Calvary. He did not have to do this. But he chose to do so, because he loved his Father so much, and his fellow mankind, that he willingly obeyed our Father.

He calls us to do the same. We must learn to surrender our will, our selfish desires, and obey the will of our heavenly Father. We can do this if we have love, a selfless love for Him. The kind of love that He first showed us, when He created us and was 'well pleased' (39) and delighted with His creation. But we are still living hell on earth. We still have burdens, cares and worries. Yes we do, but these burdens become easier if we decide to do what Christ told us and showed us. If we bear our burdens/ crosses, and endure them, because we love our Father, and because we have our eyes on the prize of finding 'rest for our souls' in the 'house with many mansions'. Then our 'yoke will be easy and' our 'burden light'.

But Jesus when he left this earth, resurrected from death (41), to return to his Father in heaven (42), did not abandon us to just get on with life's burdens. He left behind 'the Comforter' (43) the Holy Spirit, to help us and guide the rest of us since then, now and to come, in how we take on this easy yoke and light burden. Unlike the rest of the slogans that tell you that 'you can do things by yourself', and 'yes we can' achieve all, alone or together - that have so far left us dissatisfied and confused. Jesus still gives us his love and helps us whenever we falter, encourages us when we feel down or alone, gives us courage to face the music or dangers, helps our resolve to soldier on through difficult times, helps us when we want to speak out about wrong doings. He is there for us every step of the way, if we accept his invitation.

How willing are you to learn from Jesus? How much do you want to, like Jesus, prove your love for our Father in heaven? Do you even appreciate the concept of how much He loves you? And that He is beside you every step of the journey, through your trials and tribulations and your burdens, if you just look to Him? Do you realise that we are nothing without Him, and that He is with us always, if we want Him in our lives?

To Our Father in heaven be the glory...for Jesus is truly merci- ful. I love Him so much that I have dedicated my life to follow- ing Christ's teachings and example. In my period of confused insanity, I loved him so much that I wanted to BE Jesus. But our heavenly Father in His infinite wisdom and mercy, grounded me, and showed me that it was okay to try to emulate Jesus, ie. be like him, but that I could never BE him. Jesus was called a rabbi, a teacher, and he asked us to listen to his teachings and follow his example if we want to attain the hope of a future. He did not order us to, but invites us and asks us to listen to him.

How will we see the transformation in us, if we follow Christ's ways?

We have become accustomed to the idea of transformation in religious teachings and now in popular culture. The Western film industry in particular has given us ideas of man being able to change himself into something better, or of supernatural or super human or alien transformations. We have such super heroes – superman, spider-man, wonder-woman, teenage mutant ninja turtles, Ben 10 with his Alien Force watch, to machines being Transformers aliens from outer space. I've even heard a young boy sing along to the words of a gospel song 'I'm a transformer'.

Since Adam and Eve bit the apple of the tree of knowledge (and death) they covered themselves up with fig leaves to try and hide the 'shame' of their bodies' nakedness.

It was not shame of nudity. It was shame that they'd realised they'd been deceived by the serpent, Satan, into disobeying their heavenly Father, who had created them out of love and made them beautiful. Now because they became blinded to this beauty, they perceived themselves to be as naked, ugly and unworthy. From this time, centuries and eons of time since, egged on by Satan, people still have this negative concept of themselves, and hence their pursuit of beautifying ourselves. The make-up, hair, nails, accessories, tattooing, body markings and cuttings and piercings (43a), obsessions over diet, health and fitness exercise regimes, drugs, plastic surgery, all are various attempts to get the 'body beautiful', or 'perfect body'. We think if we achieve these we will feel better about ourselves, corrupted by the shame of sin. Ultimate excesses

have led to disasters e.g. in plastic surgery or drugs some people have ended up 'freaks like me', as shown on TV as entertainment. Lucifer laughs at and mocks us as we debase ourselves and become ugly like him, ashamed because of the sin
of disobedience.

We were already beautiful at the time of creation, but we spoilt
our self-concept to bring about our low self-esteem. How can
we change our self image back to our heavenly Father's original concept of us, our inner beauty? By adopting characteristics
of Jesus, who was meek and lowly, self-respecting and respectful of others. He was not vain, but was willingly obedient and
humble, and was made worthy to be transformed to real beauty.

At present we may feel unworthy, or bad or hopeless. But our
heavenly Father does not see us as the world sees us. If the
world perceives you as weak, a criminal, a loser, a no-hoper,
a misfit, an unwed mother, a vagrant or whatever, and you are
uncomfortable with yourself, He can see that you may be struggling to do the right thing. That is why He gave you a conscience
so you could distinguish between right and wrong. And because
you do wrong things, it does not necessarily mean you are a
bad person. He hates the sin/wrong-doing, not the sinner (44a).

He can see that you want to do better, and become better, not
as the world sees in ambition, material wealth, possessions and
success. He can see that you may want what really matters,
in this life and the next, what is really valuable - that quality of
enduring love, our heavenly Father's love.

Who will be transformed?

We are not transformers, and we cannot transform ourselves,
by our own devices. We can be transformed, by our heavenly
Father after we have proved ourselves worthy of His love. And
don't get it twisted and think that by performing good deeds
and good works alone, that this will make us worthy (44b/c).

It is our change in attitude and intentions towards our Father, and to fellow human beings in the love we show them, from our hearts, that will make the difference. This is what it means to be made in the image of our heavenly Father, it is having the capacity for unconditional love for Him, others and even towards our enemies. We are to learn to have love without conditions attached, with no hidden agendas, no secret intentions, just holistic, genuine love.

How will He know if we are genuine in our love and want to be followers of Christ? We will be recognised by how we treat others – attending to the needs of the poor, the lonely, to widows and orphans, to prisoners; by those people who offer clothing and shelter, and support those who are weaker than ourselves. BUT these who would follow Christ, themselves need to repent of their sins, be baptised, AND be prepared to endure the 'fire' or 'trials and tribulations' that will 'refine and purify them' and make them fit and 'worthy' and be transformed to that beauty that is more enduring than external beauty. Their souls will be saved, and they will have their names entered in the Book of Life, along with all the people who have gone before and suffered likewise, and the prophets. They, like Jesus, will be transformed.

When will the transformation take place?

When Jesus died (44), and was resurrected from the dead, he reappeared on a few occasions to the people who knew and were close to him in life (45). He did not appear as a ghost. His body was real. But his body, underwent a process of transformation. When the women first saw him, he told them 'don't touch me yet as I have not yet been transformed (46). However by the time he met with the disciples, on a later occasion, he was able to allow 'doubting' Thomas to put his hands in his wounds (pierced side, and holes in his hands and feet from the nails of crucifixion) (47). He was not a ghost, because the disciples could touch him, and see him drink and eat with them. But he was also able to appear before them when he joined them, without entering the doors, for they were locked (48). Finally by the time Jesus ascended on clouds from the top of Mount Olive, to return to his Father in heaven (49), his transformation was complete. We know that the atmosphere has extreme coldness in the air, and heat from the sun, but Jesus was able to withstand these extremes because his body was transformed. The vision of victorious Jesus Christ transformed into his full glory, is depicted in Rev. 1 v 12-17. He is wonderfully beautiful shining in glory: 'One like the son of man, clothed in a garment down to the feet and girded about the chest with a golden band. His head and hair were white like wool, as white as snow, and His eyes like a flame of fire; His feet were like fine brass, as if refined in a furnace, and His voice as the sound of many waters; He had in His right hand seven stars, out of His mouth were a sharp two-edged sword, and His countenance was like the sun shining in its strength.'(49a).

Likewise when Jesus Christ returns on the Last Day, at the End of Time, those who have chosen to live their lives in a Christ-like way, will also be transformed. They will be transformed into a state or form that reflects our heavenly Father's original plan A in the garden of Eden, which will now become His plan Z. They will have been made fit and worthy, regained His trust, and once again be beautiful, so that He might delight again in His creation with whom He would be 'well pleased' (39).

When Christ returns this time, only the dead who have died and suffered for his sake, will arise from their graves, (50) along with the wicked who pierced his side and his accusers at his crucifixion – resurrected to witness the loud, noisy, bright glorious return of Jesus like a flash of lightening across the whole earth simultaneously, (51) that all who are living and those arisen dead, can be in no doubt that it is he come. On that day the reaction from the majority of the people will be great mourning and panic, but those who have died in Christ, will be rejoicing for the day they had been looking forward to, would have come (52).

However, after Armageddon, when it is time for the Day of Judgement, then everyone who has died from all time, or is still living at the time, will be raised up to face judgement, when their deeds shall be assessed and people dealt with accordingly (53). Only those whose names have been written in the Book of Life will remain with our heavenly Father and have immortality - immortality that was His original plan A for Adam and Eve, and mankind.

What will the transformed look like? They will be beautiful, perfect(ed), ageless, without sickness or infirmity, and they will not age. As time will no longer exist, they will be living in eternity, no one will grow old. They will exist just at the age at which they died (52a). However, only those who have been tested and endured as Christ did, will be among the '144,000' saved (54) . When Satan tempted Adam and Eve, and introduced death into the world, he was not concerned that countless people, and children would have to die. Because of the sin of disobedience, death was brought about, and so we are all born into sin, and so cannot be innocent. We can only have that sin removed when we follow Christ's lead, and that means some of us may not make it. This is the harsh reality, and this is why it is so important to teach children the right ways before they too perish (54a). Only children who do not have knowledge of good and evil can be excused. For even the Israelites could not escape punishment, and were made to wander for 40 years in the wilderness (54a), until all that disobedient generation had died out. Only the innocent who remained, were permitted to enter Canaan, the land promised to their patriarch and forefather, Abraham. Satan knows this, and starts on our children from a very early age. We must be vigilant and mindful.

For Satan is after our children from before they are even born (95), and as babies and young children and young people, our youth. He wants us to dedicate ourselves to him, pledging our allegiance to him. Solomon's Ecclesiastes 12 v 1, tells the youth to dedicate themselves to the Lord, whilst they are still young, so they can spend the rest of their lives under him.

But although Solomon was the wisest man of all time, he was also a fool. He disobeyed his Father's wishes(55), and went back into Egypt, the land his forefathers had been rescued from(56), literally, mentally and spiritually, by buying their horses and acquiring foreign wives and concubines, whose gods he then worshipped(57). His Lord was therefore not our Father in heaven, which was why he was despondent of life without purpose. He forsook the Lord, and did not know Jesus. Jesus asked us to be wise and wary. He spoke in parables- stories, to illustrate how much our Father in heaven loves us, and how cunning the devil is, and how we should live our lives to attain a future life of peace and joy and immortality. This is why disciples of Jesus are needed to teach us how best to save our lives (souls) and those of our children.

Would-be disciples of Jesus Christ...

We should not be discouraged in our mission as would-be disciples of Christ. Christ asks of us, the same as he did of Simon Peter: 'do you love me?' (i.e. how much do you love me?). Peter said 'you know I love you'. Jesus instructed: 'then feed my sheep' and again, 'feed my flock', (to prove that you do.) (58).

Jesus did not mean literally feed my sheep. He meant allegorically feed the people spiritual food, i.e. his teachings, because he felt they were 'lost' and mindless and aimless. The spiritual food - knowledge of his life, and teachings about our Father- would give the people encouragement and hope for their futures, if they make the decision to follow his example.

The devil wants us to be like mindless, lost sheep. He hoodwinks us, confuses us, and leads us astray through his tactics of mind control. Our mission as disciples is to unveil and expose the devil for who he is, and his agenda; and to lead the people back to the only true, living and loving Father in heaven.

How much do you love our heavenly Father? How willing are you to 'feed His sheep?' How much do you love your fellow 'brothers and sisters' (79) - humanity? Are you prepared to 'sacrifice' love of the embellished attractions of this world the devil has concocted to deceive us? Will you give these up so that you can gain your life in our Father's real and soon-to-be perfected New world and New heaven, with Jesus at the end of Time? Are you? Will you?

As disciples of Christ, we need not be afraid of anything the devil throws at us to try and put us off completing our mission. For if our Father in heaven is 'for you...who can be against you?...(No-one, nothing at all)....(59). It is our heavenly Father 'who holds your right hand. It is He 'who says to you – fear not, I will help you.' We need not fear harm as the Lord Himself will be our refuge (60), (60a). And moreover, very importantly to help you get through against your enemies, Jesus said: 'love, forgive and pray for those who persecute you...your enemies' (61). And again he instructs us to 'do good to your enemies....don't take revenge (for vengeance is mine says the Lord), but repay evil with good.' (62). For we can be certain that some very tough times are ahead, physically, mentally, emotionally, spiritually to challenge us in our mission, as the devil tries to force us to quit.

But as the apostle James says we are to 'count it all joy.... when you meet various trials, knowing that the testing of your faith produces steadfastness/ patience....(63). 'Blessed is the man who endures trials, for when he has stood the test, he will receive the crown of life which' our Father 'has promised to those who love Him.' (64). But we are to take heart because as apostle Paul says 'we are afflicted, but not crushed....persecuted but not forsaken...struck down but not destroyed.... (65). For 'these are transient things...'(66), whereas 'the things that are unseen are eternal...' and 'though we are wasting away, inwardly we are being renewed daily.' (67). According to apostle Peter 'our faith is to be tested by fire, but it is more precious than gold that perishes' (68). For 'he/she who turns a sinner away from sin, will save them from death and will cover a multitude of sins' (69), and there is great rejoicing in heaven amongst our Father and the angels for this success (69a). Like the prophets of old whose faith was tested (69b), we will be able to achieve great feats by faith (69c), turning others away from sin and Satan, and back towards our heavenly Father-refers to Luke 15 & the prophets. (Yahweh's Holy Spirit gave this to me in a dream, prior to the baptism of my 2 daughters, in 13 Aug 2011. That day was one of the happiest in my life, better even their births, or my own baptism! Bless.)

Jesus who rebuked the wind and calmed the storm (70) said 'don't be afraid. But 'in all things give thanks ....rejoice and pray without ceasing...(71). Paul tells us how we are to conduct ourselves as ambassadors (72) and disciples of Christ in 2 Corinthians 6 v 3 -10. We are to do so in such a way that does not cause offense or cause the ministry of Christ to be blamed or found wanting/faulty.

Apostle Paul was very aware of the perils that faced his life and said 'I die daily'(73). He endured physical beatings and torture and imprisonment as he conducted his mission for Christ. But he also referred to dying daily to the 'carnal' temptations, of his physical desires, surrounded by the licentious statues and behaviour of the people, especially Gentiles. Whatever wicked or sexual thoughts that entered his head, he had to fight to suppress these natural urges, and put his spiritual motivations first. Christ knew that our physical bodies have limitations, no matter how willing we are or how much we try. 'The spirit is willing, but the flesh is weak' (74)he said about the disciples who couldn't stay awake and keep him company in the garden of Gethsemane, the night of his betrayal by Judas Iscariot, and his subsequent arrest. Carnal weaknesses can be sleep exhaustion, frailties, illnesses, sexual and various temptations, evil intentions, and unacceptable behaviours that may put people off coming to Christ.

As ambassadors we must be careful how we conduct ourselves (75). For instance if gluttony, or if eating meat in front of a vegetarian, immorality, and aggressive or abusive behaviour, loud and lewd practices, selfish attitudes in kind or money, violent repression or speaking a way that wounds/hurts another, or discourages or prevents people from getting to know Christ, these attitudes and behaviours must be avoided. Remember that once we accept Christ in our lives, we become witnesses to others of Our Father in heaven's love and greatness and beneficence for us, in this life and the next. So our behaviour and words should reflect Christ's, and therefore reflect heaven, so that we can experience the joy of peace and heaven's bliss whilst we are yet here on earth. As disciples, witnesses and instructors, we are living proof of our love, rejoicing and testifying of Christ's effect on our lives, his promises realised already, and our hope for the future, so that others may be encouraged and inspired to come to know him, and ultimately our heavenly Father, better.

Indeed Paul says we must be 'steadfast....in the liberty by which Christ has made us free, and do not be entangled in a yoke of bondage, ..that is carnal sin' (76). Become free of bodily pleasures that the spirit fights against. Don't be enslaved in mental bondage or slavery that Christ has released us from. We can remain entangled, but at great cost – loss of your soul, which would then be enmeshed with Satan in his destruction. Christ can help us attain the salvation of your soul, and our ultimate goal – life eternal.

Have courage and be fearless....

Don't be frightened or discouraged by the fearful and evilous attacks from the devil, by people, things and images he puts in your minds, or by the sights and sounds he tries to frighten you with. Don't be scared by ghosts and ghouls and loud noises and the scare-mongering (of terror attacks), beatings, physical and mental and emotional tortures. Apostle Paul and others, and even Jesus were tormented and tortured, Himself blameless and sinless. How much more, will we be(63), who commit sins, knowingly or unwittingly? But if we are willing to put all these sins aside, and strive to do better, to do what is right in the sight of our Father in heaven, then we too, will face opposition, similar attacks and have our names and reputations scandalised, be falsely accused, and suffer tactics designed to put us off separating ourselves from the wicked and superficial, temporary things of this world. We are 'in the world, but we don't have to be of the world' (77). We can be different.

We can be champions of righteousness, justice and truth, like former and current courageous Davids fighting against giant Goliaths (77a), for the sake of the saving the people. Former champions include the Christian martyrs especially Joan of Arc, burnt at the stake; other 20th and 21st century defenders like Martin Luther King, Malcolm X, Angela Davis, Maurice Bishop, Steve Biko, Nelson and Winnie Mandela; and today, modern day 'Davids' are: Professor Griff (60a) exposing the Illuminati; Julian Assange, exposing the documents of the US and UK war crimes in Iraq and Afghanistan; and Jane Bergemeister and others exposing the scandal of Aids and Swine flu viruses in 'health' warfare (77b). The Holy Spirit of our heavenly Father is really moving, as the people they are fighting for rally round them and support them financially, and physically with food and shelter, and moral and spiritual encouragement, when they have been attacked by 'the powers that be'. Likewise, we can choose the right way and follow Jesus, back into our Father's protective arms. Fear not those who can kill the body, but rather fear the One who can destroy both body and soul - our Father YHWH (78a). And we can face opposition and even death like those martyrs who whilst suffering horrible deaths, sang out joyously giving praises, as they saw Jesus, the 'joy of man's desiring'(18a) welcoming them into heaven.

Be fearless, but not as children are, who don't yet know or realise the dangers they may face. 'Be wise as serpents'(78b) and 'cunning as a fox', and guard yourselves against evil onslaught. 'Put on the whole armour... of Truth and ...salvation....' (80).

Take courage and be fearless in the face of danger, in the full knowledge of what evil might be hurled at you, to prevent you defecting from your sinful ways and hence the devil. He wants to prevent us telling others the Truth, so that they too can turn away from the devils' ways, and turn back to our heavenly Father, through Jesus Christ. Take courage knowing that the battle will soon be over. And 'though hard fought, it will be won by Christ, and those who choose his way. Victory is His, ours and our Father in heaven (78a). And remember Jesus prays and intercedes for our protection: 'I do not pray that thou (Our Father) shouldst take them out of the world, but that thou shouldst keep them from the evil one' (80a).

'Go forth and feed my sheep'. We are advised to not be like the worker in one of Jesus' parables, who hid the coin his master had given him, rather than invest like the others' had. On his master's return, he only had the same coin to give him, and thus angered his master, who punished him, and took the coin and gave it to the one who had invested and produced the most profit (81). As disciples we are expected to go and spread the Good News of the gospels, and 'invest' what we have been freely given (the Good News) in the people and increase the number not only of disciples, but the number of those whose souls will be saved, if they choose to follow Christ's teachings and example.

For if you have taken Jesus into your hearts, don't hide this fact, as this will be like hiding a light/lamp under a bush (81a). Let people know that you have dedicated you life to following Jesus, for the love of the one who is 'good', our heavenly Father. It should be apparent not only in what you preach and tell people about Jesus, but evident in the way you conduct your life. And also remember, that however dedicated a worker or disciple you may be, eager to serve the heavenly Father, that you deserve your rest. Our Father rested on the 7th day after He created the world. He asks us to keep that day holy in remembrance of that fact, and to honour Him and to be a blessing to us. The Sabbath day is the same as traditionally has been for the Jews and early Christians – the Saturday, which we start to prepare for the evening before, sunset to sun-down of the Sabbath. He instructed us to keep this day holy. Can we not do this one thing for Him, who created the whole universe, the world and us? Remember it is an honour and a privilege to love and serve Him, our Father in heaven.

As disciples of Jesus we are instructed to go from place to place, lodge at someone's house who offers you hospitality, spread the gospels and work to earn your keep. You don't need to take huge luggage with you (82), and don't be concerned about amassing worldly comforts, eg houses, luxuries, and so forth. Only take with you the tools that will help you to easier convey Christ's messages. This may mean using public or personal transport, or using technologies, like the internet, notebooks phones etc. that help spread the Good News. As Jesus said 'don't store up for yourself treasures (acquisitions) on this earth that are only temporary and will perish' (83) and cannot enhance your soul's future. Don't worry about what you should eat tomorrow, or what clothes you should wear, for if the birds are taken care of daily, by Him who knows the exact number of hairs on your head, and cares for you more than the animals, , how much more will our heavenly Father care for you?(84). So don't worry about tomorrow, for today's cares are more than enough to contend with. Jesus says 'rather store up things in heaven for yourself' (77c) ie acquire qualities that are valuable in heaven and to our Father, love, kindness, forgiving nature, humility, obedience, loyalty, etc. If you put these as your goals, then the other things you need to live in this world 'will be added unto you'. For Jesus said 'fear not, little flock, for it is your Father's good pleasure to give you the kingdom' (83) which is such an important reward for us who faithfully follow the Lord. Do the best that you can do, for the love and honour of our Father in heaven who loves us.

'Feed the lost sheep' so that they can learn about Jesus' sacrifice for all our sakes, so that we can be 'reconciled' back to our

Father, and so attain true eternal life. Jesus is that bridge who links us back to our Father in heaven. He is the only way back into our Father's good books. Through Jesus we can be made worthy – perfected - to rejoin our Father's circle of love and have communion with Him, face-to-face. For not even patriarch and prophet Moses, was able to converse with Him face-to-face, but by a 'burning bush' that was not consumed (85). When Christ returns in all his heavenly glory, and we are transformed, then we will be able to see the face of our heavenly Father, commune with Him, enjoy each others' company, and that of the heavenly hosts of angels for all eternity. This is our hope of a possible future, if we 'believe on' Jesus Christ, our Saviour, the Messiah.

As a disciple of Christ you will not be the only one fighting against the devil and his followers. In these the latter days of Time, other disciples will be raised up, upon whom there will be a 'great out-pouring of the Holy Spirit' in the church. The Holy Spirit imparts spiritual gifts, one of which is the ability to prophesy. And in these last days there will be many prophets when they are needed most, because this will be a time of great opposition and warfare by Satan and his followers against Christ, our Father in heaven and those who are loyal to Them(85a). Fear not, our Father will not abandon you. He will provide help.

The real fear that we should have is not of Satan, who attempts to scare us away from loving our Creator, but it should be of our Father/Creator, who has the power to destroy not only the body, but also the soul in hell-fire!!!

This is Satan's problem. For all his bravado at not fearing our Father, and jeering Him for not punishing him thus far (85b), or for not bringing about what He threatened...yet. Yet, is the important word. Yes the devil has escaped, or managed to avoid his due punishment all these eons of time to date. But he will not escape forever. For he knows that of our Father in heaven, His words are true and reliable, and that He is faithful to His word, and to those who love Him.

He promised to deliver the faithful from evil and threatened that the wicked and evil will be punished and destroyed. As He said at the beginning, 'Let there be light!' and it was so. He parted the Red Sea for Moses and the Israelites in their escape from their Egyptian enslavers. He promised a Saviour to the people – a Messiah, and He sent Jesus Christ, who then promised to send a Comforter/Counsellor/Holy Spirit to help and guide us through these latter days before Christ returns in His full glory. Why then would our Father fail in His threat to destroy Satan and his wicked followers? His word is true. His word is faithful.

So Satan's end is certain. Our Creator of all, our Father in heaven, will have His vengeance against Lucifer and his followers, and he as Satan or whatever aliases he employs, will be destroyed, in hell, to oblivion! For there will be no hell left, 'not a root or a branch....but all evildoers will be trampled as ashes underfoot'.... so no evidence will remain that they ever existed (85c).

The disciples 'important commission:

The important significance of Jesus 'the good shepherd' for us as disciples is that:-We take care of and look after with love, the flock that Jesus has entrusted to us, as a prized and dear possession. For, they are costly and priceless, having been pur-chased by the very life–giving blood of Jesus on the cross at Calvary. He paid a very dear price to ransom the lost sheep from Satan's snares. We cannot therefore, be fickle or inatten-tive in the duty for our charge/responsibility of sheep. We have to earnestly, willingly, happily, endeavour to help and guide them in the way of the Lord, and by our own examples, so that they may grow and flourish in the Lord, and prosper in attaining eternal life. This is our task/commission as disciples, and we will be held to account for every one of those given to us, who are counted as lost, but are also beautiful in the eyes of the Lord. They are valuable to Him, and must also be to us, as we are entrusted to take care of/ pastor them, out of love for Jesus and for our Father in heaven.

To get an idea of how valuable Jesus' flock or sheep or mankind is to Him, we can look at the Scriptures for what Our Father has placed as having greatest or highest value. He has used material examples to help us understand and appreciate what value He wants us to place on Him, as our Creator, on Jesus Christ our Saviour, and on ourselves, His greatest creation.

The Scriptures showcase physical, allegorical and spiritual references. So for instance, when Solomon insisted on building a temple in honour of our Lord Almighty to demonstrate his love for Him, Our Father instructed him to use the best quality cedar wood, gold and silver and gems, and other materials in its construction (90a). The temple vessels and implements used for worship and sacrificial offerings were to be of the highest quality gold (90b); and the animals to be used in sacrifice had to be the purest, without blemish or injury (undefiled) (90c), and only the tribe of Levi (of the 12 tribes of Israel) the Levites (90d) were to minister and officiate as temple priests and vestal virgins and enter the holy places, especially the inner sanctuary – the holy of holies.

Similarly, when the three Magi, wise men/kings came to visit and worship the new born, baby Jesus, they brought gifts that were fitting for a king and for the high price He would have to pay later on, His death on the cross – gold, frankincense and myrrh(90e). The myrrh was expensive perfumes used to embalm His dead body, His life, the costly price He paid to redeem mankind, His own personal sacrifice for our sakes, out of love and obedience to our Father, and who is the only person deemed/considered worthy enough to open the 7 seals in the Book of Life on Judgement Day (90f). As faithful and obedient disciples of Christ, only those of us who choose to make the same personal self-sacrifices will be deemed worthy and fit enough to be His (the sacrificial lamb) 'bride', as the city of the new Jerusalem, His kingdom, in the new heaven and new earth, after the end of Time, in Eternity. Our father in heaven is too awesome, and is truly magnificent for offering us the highest valued prize for our sacrifices – that of joy, peace and immortality with Him forever and ever!

Make no mistake, when Jesus returns to claim His own, He will demand of us 'where are the flock that were given to you, my beautiful flock?' (90g). 'He that is found faithful will receive a great reward' –' he will receive a crown of glory that does not fade away' (90h).

We need to be dutiful, diligent, protective of, and love our flocks. Christ bids His ministers/ under-shepherds/ disciples to 'have the same interest that He manifested, and feel the sacred responsibility of charge as if a chief shepherd'. We are to be 'faithful, to feed the flock (with spiritual food), to strengthen the weak, to revive the fainting, and to shield them from devouring wolves (Satanic forces)(90h). We, like the high priests, will be held accountable to Jesus Christ, on Judgement Day. For those who lead the flock astray, or misguide them or falsely teach them, it will be worse for them than for Sodom and Gomorrah (90i).

Christ is not joking. This is serious business. Christ purchased our souls with His life blood on the cross. He was innocent and sinless, but He took on our sins so that we might have the chance of re-communing with our Father and Creator, who can offer us eternal life, if we are willing to make the changes and make personal sacrifices for Jesus' name sake. We will have earned our right to be the 'elect' (90j) and be His reward/ His bride/ His kingdom of the Holy city Jerusalem (90k) when He returns at the end of Time, has sat in Judgement of us all, and has selected His 'elect'.

I reiterate... yes there will be tough times ahead. But this is the road we must travel, if we are to prove to our Father, and to others who are watching (97) – people, angels, demons, and Lucifer – that we choose this path and are prepared to endure what is thrown at us, because we love Him, our Lord and Creator.

Note that we *choose* to love Him. And this is the sweetest love that He desires from us – Proof that He was right to give us free will, so that we can use it to choose to return the love He first gave us. In this mutually exchanged love we can be reconciled into communion with Him, as Adam and Eve once enjoyed, as patriarchs and prophets Noah, Abraham, Moses and His son Jesus, our Lord and Saviour also enjoyed. This is our hope, and the hope of our Father, the Creator, that He will once again come from heaven amongst us, and enjoy full communion with His beloved mankind – in Perfect Circles.

Back to business...

When the right time comes, then He will reveal His light to the brothers of the Jews, the house of Ishmael, the Arabs. The Jews will be even more jealous (86). However we must not think ourselves better than the spurned Jews. For if it were not for their stubbornness, we would still be suffering under pagan gods of Sheol, with no hope of salvation. And yet, our Father, ever-loving and merciful, will gladly welcome those Jews who can learn and adopt the Christian way. Their place is reserved.

Now the sons of Abraham's Ishmael, the Arabs, having been brought out of paganism to know our Father through Muhammed, are ready to receive the way of the cross, Christ, with our help. Let's jump to it. Be quick to guide our Muslim brethren to Christ. Through Islam they have learnt to submit to Allah. They have learnt to give willingly and unselfishly of their riches to the poor and needy. Now let us show them how to live and serve our Father in heaven, through Christ.

Soon it will be the turn of the Jews. Already those who have survived or descended from survivors of the Holocaust, are desiring to learn this ability for goodness. Fearlessness, in the midst of great danger. Love and happiness in the selfless love of mankind - the original Christian way.

Revelation has begun. (87) In that time man will see all manner of things. But fear not, for the Creator, our Father is good, and loves those who love Him. (88) Let us waste no more time in petty squabbles. They are wasters and thieves of Time. The battle is fierce and rages on. But the writing is on the wall for Satan.(89) Let us hurry so that all mankind can get to know our Father, through Christ, and so dispense with fear, problems and disharmony altogether. (90)

Shalom, Assalamu aleikum, Amen. (91)

(7a)   P36

3 religions - 1 faith

The Holy

Trinity

Just as God's faith in man

Is eternal in steadfast love

From the Holy Land

3 World Religions -

Judaism Christianity Islam

One faith in God.

For the struggle of

Humanity they brought:

1 God's law

Moses   star

Muhammed moon

Rules & regulations

2 God's son:

The way to live by example:

Christ cross

Brotherly love &

Purity of spirit.

3 The Holy Spirit:

Guides each individual on

GOD

Holy

CHRIST JESUS

Spirit

Omnipotent

MANKIND

FREE YOUR SPIRIT

Each individual must
choose, and if seeking
God, he must through self-
sacrifice, free his spirit
from turmoil and
confusion.

Proofs of Love for God.
Sacrificial Offerings:

1 Abraham –
to sacrifice his son,
offering issue of

His flesh- Obedient

2 Jesus Christ –

God sacrifices His only son – Christ who
accepts God's will –
makes personal sacrifice,
of his own Flesh & Blood
to save us.

3 Now **we** must
sacrifice treasures of this world.
Seek treasure of heaven,
in full Communion with God.
No more sacrifices on behalf of mankind.

Only one's own
personal sacrifices,
on behalf of one's soul.

REFERENCES
Chapters 2-6:

1Hebrews 11v3; Genesis 1; John 1 v1-2; Revelation 19 v13

2 Zoroastrians – of world religion of Persia, now represented by a small community in Parsis, India. They see life as a battle-ground between the forces of light and of darkness. As Mithraism it spread throughout the Roman Empire, but was ousted by Christianity. (The Times Atlas of World History, editor Norman Stone, (1978) 1989, 3rd edition, Guild Publishing, p72-73)

3 Revelations 4; Genesis 1; worship in heaven

4 extract from unpublished "Holy Mothers, Holy Child", p3.

5 Exodus 33 v20; 1Timothy 6 v16

6 Exod. 3 v14

7 Revs. 12 v 4-6, 7-9, 13-14, 17. Devil seeking to destroy Mary and child Jesus.

8 Revs. 7 v4-5, Twelve tribes of Israel...from every race and nation

9 Gen.11

10 Gen. 1-2

11 Gen. 3; 1 timothy 2 v14

12 Revs. 3 v14 – 22

13. Gen. 6 v9-22; Gen. 7 v 1-17

14 Revs. 12 v7-9 Devil cast out from heaven

15 Gen. 22

16 1 Timothy 6 v 3-5 warnings against false teachings. Genuine faith comes from love, a pure heart, and clear conscience, and no plots and schemes for financial gain

17 1 Tim. 6 v11 Righteousness, Godliness, faith, love, endurance and gentleness.

18 Isaiah 29 v16-17,clay and Potter; 2 Thessalonians 2 v1-12 Satan exalts himself as god.

18a Composer Bach's Cantata BWV 147, 'Jesu, joy of man's desiring' (choral).

18b Jazz musician Louis Armstrong achieved UK best selling record in 1968. Written by Bob Thiele (as George Douglas) and George David Weiss, as antedote to the increasingly racially and politically charged climate of daily life in USA, the song is also hopeful and optimistic for the future. It had a varied history of recording artistes and uses for film and recording industries internationally, even though it was not promoted in America. Armstrong's recording was inducted in the Grammy Hall of Fame in 1999. The publishing for this song is controlled by Memory Lane Music Group (http://www.memorylanemusic-group.com) and Carlin Music Corp., and Bug Music Inc., (http://www.bugmusic.com). In Dec. 2011 Sir David Attenborough aired an advertisement that consisted of a spoken-word rendition of the song, using nature images to illustrate the lyrics. It was aired following the final episode of the nature documentary 'Frozen Planet' on BBC TV, UK. Source: What aWonderful

World – Wikipedia, the free encyclopedia, on the internet. And www.lyrics007.com .

19 Revs. 14 v12

20 The 7th day our Creator kept and made holy. *THE* day to be used in contemplation of the wonders of creation, of nature, and of being, and of acknowledging and praising His holy Name. In so doing becoming more alive, allowing one's spirit to live in Him, and not die in Satan. We have the chance to refresh our spirituality. The number 7 is significant to many nations, as seen in the letter and sound of 's' in many languages. It is a testament to our Creator's creation of the world in 7 days, and the 7 lamps that are the Holy Spirits of YHWH- Rev 4 v 5.

21 Language and its usage: In the beginning people spoke one language with few words – Gen, 11 v 1-9. The Word is love and unity. The Tower of Babel brought about the many languages, removed even further away from perfect communion with God. When the apostles were sent out into the world, the Holy Spirit gave them the gift of languages to spread their testimonies, internationally. Yet we must be aware of Satan's divisive use of language to create confusion and lead to selfish national pride.

22 The devil tempts Adam and Eve. He lies to them. He says they will not die if they eat the fruit, and so introduces death to them. God is not responsible for introducing death into the world. Satan is. God loves life. Adam and Eve were not meant to die. They were to enjoy eternal life like the angels. But when they disobeyed, the tree of life was denied them. Satan told them they would have knowledge and become like gods. In fact they learnt to discern between good and evil. They became ashamed of their own beauty, their inner selves, themselves who were already God-like, - created in God's image. Satan taught them to think of themselves as intrinsically bad, and externally ugly.

So they felt themselves to be unworthy in the sight of God. In so doing they denied God's truth of their beauty. Disobedient, they had to learn new things. They acquired logic to survive in the physical world; with economics, the mastery of his environment; with biological procreation, and knowledge of love through humanitarian values. The spirit needs only the food of self-less love for mankind. It needs the cultivation of love in purity and devotion to get closer to God.

23 Surely it is morally perverse to persist in such extravagant expenditure on space exploration, with so many people in the world deprived of the basic necessities of life. In the third world, 40,000 (1990 figs.) children die of preventable diseases on a daily basis, and it goes unremarked.

24 "I am the first and last. I am the living one. I was dead but now am alive forever....I have authority over death." Rev. 5 v5-10; John 5 v 26-29.

Chapter 7:

25 Rev. 11 v 17. The heathens were filled with rage, because the time for God's anger has come.....the time for the dead to be judged.

26 - 'predestined' and 'adopted as children like Christ' Ephesians 1 v 1-6; God foreknew them, Roms. 8 v 28-30.

27 - John 3 v16.

28 - 2 Peter 3 v9.

29 - Revs. 3 v 20.

30 - Revs. 22 v 17.

31 - The wages of sin is death... Roms. 6 v 23.

31 a - Revs. 12 v 7-9.

32 - 'The Great Controversy' by Ellen G. White, (1888, ed 1971), in her 5-book series: The Conflict of Ages in Christian Dispensation. Publishers Pacific Press.

32a - Dragon persecutes the woman, her child and other off-spring - those who keep the commandments and have the testimony of Christ, Rev. 12 v 1-7, v 13-17.

33 - Matt. 13 v 24-30; v 36-43.

34 - Pastor Clive de Silva, SDA, UK. (2010).

35 - S.30in Holy Quran, by A. Yusuf Ali, 1975, (Text, translation and commentary). Publishers Islamic Foundation UK.

36 - Jesus crucified, Matt. 27 v 25-27; Matt 28 v 5.

37 - house...mansions, John 14 v 1-4. Also see 'To him who overcomes I will grant to sit with me on my throne, as I also overcame and sat down with my Father on His throne' Revs. 3 v21.

38 - Matt. 11 v28-30.

39 - Matt. 3 v 16-17; Matt. 17 v 5; 2 Peter 1 v17.

40 - Genesis 1 v 26-28, Adam and Eve were originally equal partners; Gen. 3 v16, Eve and women were not originally to have pain in conception or childbirth, but due to disobedience were cursed by Our Creator. He said 'I will greatly multiply your sorrows and your conception; in pain you shall bring forth

children. Your desire shall be for your husband and he shall rule over you.'

41 - Mark 16 v 6.

42 - 1 Corinthians 15 v 50-55

43 - The Comforter cited in E G White Patriarchs and Prophets, 1880+, introductory pages 2, 4; Counsellor/ the Helper/ the Spirit of Truth/ the Holy Spirit, John 14 v16-17, v25,26; John 16 v 13.

43a – Leviticus 19 v 28, 'Make no mark in your flesh for the dead, nor tattoo any marks on you. I am the Lord'. Yahweh abhors body markings, piercings or tattooing, especially if done in honour of the dead.

44 - John 20 v19-20.

44a - the Lord hates the sin, not the sinner, Matt. 21 v 31-32; Mark 2 v 14-17; Luke 5 v 27-32; Luke 19 v 1-9.

44b - Malachi 3 v 17-18. It's not enough to be a good person. We need to choose whether we want to be 'wicked and evil' or 'precious jewels' for our heavenly Father through being Christ – like.

44c - Romans 12 v 20-21, although by repaying evil with good, we 'will heap hot coals upon the head' of the evil doer. Burning like a purifying, cleansing agent., or just a prick of his/her conscience.

45 - Matt. 28 v 5, v 10; Emmaus, Luke 24 v13-49; John chap 21.

46 - John 20 v 17.

47 - John 20 v 26.

48 - John 20 v 25.

49 - Luke 24 v 51; 1 Corin. 15 v 50-55.

49a - Rev. 1 v 12-17.

50 - Rev. 1 v7, those who pierced his side; Isaiah 26 v 16 -21, those who suffered and were martyred for Christ' s name sake – the dead shall rise, and He will vindicate their spilt blood.

51 Matt. 24 v 27.

52 - 'wailing and gnashing of teeth' Matt. 13 v 49-50; separating righteous from wicked Matt. 25 v 31-46; 'elect' or '144,000' Matt. 24 v 30-31.

52a - 1 Corin. 15 v 50-58: transformed bodies, v 55 – 'death, where is your sting?,

1 Corin 15 v 57 – Jesus Christ has victory over sin and death.

53 - Judgement Day 2 Corin. 5 v 10.

54 - 144,000 saved, Revs. 7 v 1-5; Revs. 14 v 1-5.

54a - Children saved from perishing – Deut. 1 v 39 (unlike the adults consigned for 40 years in the wilderness, because of their disobedience, and golden calf/idol worship). The children who remained, innocent, were the only ones permitted to enter the promised land Canaan, because they, as little ones, had no 'knowledge between good and evil' ie innocent.

55 - Our Father's instructions to David, that his son Solomon disobeyed: 1 Kings 2 v4, 3 v 14.

56 - Exodus 14 v 30; Deuteronomy 16 v 1.

57 - Deut 17 v 16 – 17; 1 Kings 11 v 29-35.

58 - John 21 v 15 -19.

59 - Roms. 8 v31 -39.

60 - Isaiah 41 v 10. Psalm 23.

60a - google www.Prof Griff , whose life was endangered, and his house with extensive library was burnt down to warn him off exposing the Illuminati in the entertainment industry. But the very people he was trying to help, the ordinary Black folk in the slums, helped to get him back on his feet, in kindness, shelter and in money, (even putting their small impoverished change into his pockets as they met him on the streets). Our Father is truly merciful and our saviour.

61 - 'Love, forgive and pray for... your enemies', Matt. 5 v 44 - 48. 'Love your neighbour as yourself', Leviticus 19 v18. 'Love one another, even as I have loved you. By this all men will know that you are my disciples, if you have love for one another', John 13 v 34-35.

62 - Roms 12 v 19 – 21.

63 - James 1 v 2 – 4; Rev. 17 v 14; Rev. 3 v 18-19; Isaiah 38 v 17; Matt 24 v 9 {will be hated, delivered up for tribulation or killed for (Christ') name sake}.

64 - James 1 v 12; Matt. 16 v 24 -28. Psalm 24 v 3-5; 2 Thessal. 1 v 4-10.

65 - 2 Corin 4 v 8 – 9.

66 - 2 Corin 5 v 17.

67 - 2 Corin 4 v 8 -18.

68 - 1 Peter 1 v 6 -9.

69 - James 5 v 20 – 'he who turns a sinner from the error of his way can save a soul from death , and cover a multitude of sins'.

69a - there is great rejoicing in heaven when a sinner is turned away from sin, Luke 15 v 7, v 10, v 32. This is oft-quoted to concisely express all the messages Luke 15 is conveying. (includes prodigal son, lost sheep, lost penny, idea of joy of retrieving something precious that was lost; or was dead and is now alive!). Matt. 18 v 12-14, a man rejoices more over finding his 1 lost sheep than over the 99 that did not go astray, v14 'even so it is not the will of your Father who is in heaven, that one of these little ones should perish'. For He loves us so, thank you Lord Jesus and heavenly Father.

69b - Gen. 22 v 1-19; book of Job.

69c - Hebrews 11 v 33; Daniel 11 v 32.

70 - Mark 4 v 35 – 41.

71 - 1 Thessalonians 5 v 16 -22.

72 - 2 Corin 5 v 20-21.

73 - I die daily – physical persecutions Acts 14 v 19 -28; 2 Timothy 3 v 1-12; die to sin – 1 Thess. 4 v 3 – 7; 'dying' to/ 'crucifying' carnal lusts and passions, Gal. 5v24.

74 - Matt. 26 v 40 -41.

75 - 2 Corin 6 v 3 -10.

76 - Galatians 5 v 1; Romans chap 8, esp. v 15; Roms 12 v 1 -2.

77 - John 15 v19; John 17 v 11-15. We are in the world, but be not OF the world.

77a - David and Goliath, 1 Samuel chp 17.

77b - Julian Assange in USA, Wikileaks on the internet 24 Feb 2010 exposed the US defence war crimes, atrocities in Afghanistan and Iraq, and is consequently now facing sexual allegations and future indictment by US govt; Jane Bergemeister, in hiding in Europe, Youtube internet interview 8 Sept 2009, has been trying to bring a case against the Austrian govt. For crimes against humanity in programme of forced inoculations against swine flu, but are more detrimental than the flu because they have been contaminated with Aids Virus; also fellow scientist Dr. Alan Cantwell MD, 2009 USA,– Aids hoax, Trojan horse tactics, and Mexican flu hoax, exposed the deliberate contamination of vaccines intended to cure other diseases. (see refs in Chap 9 of this book for more details).

77c - Galatians 5 v 22 -23. Rather acquire for yourselves, qualities that are valuable to our Father in heaven, like kindness, humility, love, obedience, generous spirit, loyalty; that are fruits of the Holy Spirit. Deut 14 v 22-23, v27, we are to tithe (dedicate to Yahweh), *ALL* the increase or profit from our work/harvest, and NOT glean every scrap from our produce/harvest because we must leave some for, or provide for the 'Levite'/priest and his family, the fatherless, the widow and the stranger in our midst, for the needy. It is part of our almsgiving or charitable deeds. Indeed we must remember the stranger, for the Israelites were strangers in Egypt and were welcomed and given good treatment from famine, under Joseph, (the dreamer with multi coloured coat), notwithstanding their subsequent maltreatment and rigour under slavery, before Moses liberated them.

Deut 18 v 44, tithe the 'first fruits' of our 'grain'/crop/harvest/ profits, because we should not 'forsake'/ leave out or forget to look after the 'Levite'.. for he has no part in 'Israel's inheritance' unlike the remaining 11 tribes of Israel. Their portion is the tithes that the people dedicate to the Lord, as reward for their ministering in the service of the Lord. NB The priests are not to amass wealth and possessions for themselves, but the Roman Catholic Church has done exactly the opposite!

78a - fear the One who can destroy both body and soul – Matt. 10 v 27 -28; Rev. 1 v 18; Jesus Christ is the Alpha & Omega, Rev. 1 v 12-17, v 18 description of Jesus in His victorious glory when He returns. Luke 12 v 4-5, Jesus said 'I tell you, my friends, do not fear those who kill the body, and after that have no more that they can do. But I will WARN you whom to fear: fear Him, who after He has killed, has power to cast into hell; yes I tell you, fear Him!!! Also Isaiah 8 v 13 -14, 'Do not fear anything except the Lord Almighty. He alone is the Holy One. If you fear him, you need fear nothing else. V 14 He will keep you safe...'

78b - be wise... Matt. 10 v 16 - 17.

79 - Matt. 12 v 48 -50.

80 - Ephesians 6 v 13 -18.

80a - John 17 v 15. (The Sayings of Jesus, by Andrew Linzey, 1991, p 26). Jesus prays for our protection from the evil one.

81 - Matt 25 v 14 – 30.

81a - you are the light to the world, city on a hill, lamp under a bushel, Matt 5 v 14-16; Mark 4 v 21-23; Luke 8 v 16-18.

82 - Luke 9 v 3 – 4.

83 - Matt 6 v 19 – 21 and v 31 – 33; Luke 12 v 30 - 34 - seek first the kingdom of heaven and all the other things that are needed to help you bear this world more easily, will be given to you.

84 - Matt 6 v 25 -34.

85 - Exodus 3 v 1 -22.

85a – Ellen G White, Patriarchs and Prophets, p6-7 of her introduction. Rev. 12 v 17; Rev. 19 v 10; 1 Corin. 12 v 9-10. Gifts of
the Holy Spirit, 1 Corin 12 v 4-11; 14 v 1-4, and of the gifts faith,
hope and love, the greatest of these is love, 1 Corin 13 v13.

85b - Isaiah 5 v 19, 'Woe to those who say let God hurry...so
that we may see it'. Satanists jeer and mock God for His delay
in punishing them! Eccles. 8 v 11-13, 'because the sentence
against an evil work is not executed speedily (swiftly), therefore
the heart of the sons of men is fully set in them to do evil. V12
Though a sinner does evil a hundred times, and his days are
prolonged, yet I surely know that it will be well with those who
fear God, who fear before Him. V 13 But it will not be well with
the wicked; nor will he prolong his days, which are as a shadow,
because he does not fear before God'.

Satan mocks and jeers because he has escaped due punishment thus far. But make no mistake, he will not escape forever.
His judgement day WILL come, (and even I feel sorry for him,
but not for long, when I remember that his impudence and disobedience brought YHWH's wrath down upon himself. By his
own wilfulness and wicked sin he caused his and others doom.
His evil and causing others to follow him into sin and death, and
even causing children to turn against their righteous parents
in unbelievable rebellion, because of this I am not sorry, but
GLADLY REJOICE that Satan and his demons and agents, who
remain unrepentant, will get their long overdue punishments!

As for the rest of us, who have been sinners but have repented
and choose Christ as leader and role model, we will not have
our deserved wages of sin, namely death, but we will have the
gift of YHWH which is eternal life (Roms 6 v 23), when He,
thankfully, forgives us with his abundant, loving mercy. Praise

His holy Name forever and ever! For, if YHWH was not merciful and executed His punishments daily, in natural disasters such as tsunamis and earthquakes, like Noah's Flood, there would be hardly anyone left to 'fix-up' and populate and inhabit the earth, which He made for His purpose and enjoyment and delight.

No, YHWH is merciful and longsuffering, and daily begs, no, beseeches us, to come back to His loving arms, through accepting His son, Jesus' Way and Truth, to salvation and eternal Life. He is only waiting until the full number of His people have been born, and grown to accept Him, before He will permit Jesus to return to avenge all the saints and martyrs, and claim them back in the first resurrection, save them from Armageddon, and sup/ dine with them at His marriage feast in the new Jerusalem to come. His holy redeemed people, are His 'bride', His prize for giving up His life's blood on Calvary's cross. Halleluiah!!! That day is fast approaching. Are you fit, worthy and ready to greet Him? I hope and pray so.

85c - Malachi 4 v 1-2, v4, hell reduced to ashes.

86 - Romans 10 v19 - 20. Jews made jealous. Birthright/privileged position is taken away from the 'beloved' Jews and given to the Gentiles(& now Moslems), Matt 21 v 43, Jesus quotes Isaiah saying: 'the kingdom of God will be taken from you, and given to a nation bearing the fruits of it':- (Isaiah 8 v 14-15: 'The Lord Almighty...will keep you safe. But to Israel and Judah he will be a stone that causes people to stumble, and a rock that makes them fall. And for the people of Jerusalem he will be a trap that entangles them. Many of them will stumble and fall, never to rise again. Many will be captured'). John 10 v 16, Jesus said 'I have other sheep (Gentiles and now Moslems) that are not of this (the Jews) sheep pen. I must bring them in also. They too will listen to my voice and there shall be one flock and one shepherd'.

87 - Revs. 14 v6 -9.

88 - Revs. 13 v 10, endurance and faith.

89 - Daniel 5 v 5, and v 25-30. 'Mene mene Tekel Parsin' – the writing on the wall.

90 - Revs. 11 v 17-18. The 7th trumpet heralding destruction.

90a - 1 Kings chps. 6 and 7.

90b - Daniel 5 v 2-4. Defiling Yahweh's sacred vessels; and idolatry.

90c - Numbers 18 v17 -19; Numbs chps 28 & 29.

90d - Numbs. 18 v 1 – 10, v 23.

90e - Matt. 2 v 11.

90f - Rev. 5 v 2, 5-7, 9, 12-14.

90g - 'Vipers! Hypocrites!' - Matt 23 v 13-36; Matt. 12 v 34,-35; Matt. 15 v 7-9; Matt. 15 v 11-20; worse than for Sodom and Gomorrah, Matt. 10 v 14-15.

90h - Matt. 24 v 22, v 31.

90i - Rev. 21 v 2, v 9-27; Matt. 22 v 1-5.

91 - Muslims come to know God through Islam. They share the same name of two of their prophets, Rama and Krishna, with a certain Hindu group. Through this common link we can reach Hindus and Muslims who wish to become Christ – like. Hinduism is a conglomerate of pagan religions. But even there God stretched out his hand to reach the people through Rama and Krishna powerful against the demons. Holy Quran (H Q) Sura 2:37.

92 - Greetings: Judaism – Shalom, peace be upon you.

Islam – Assalamu aleikum – peace be upon you.

Christianity – Amen – so be it. The will of God.

93 - 'The Colour Purple' by Alice Walker, 1983, Book Club Associates/ The Women's Press; and the film 'The Matrix', 1999, whose original author, Sophia Stewart, successfully won damages against the film makers on Monday October 4th, 2004. Styled on the internet on Monday January 7th 2008, posted by Muhsana, USA, as 'Black woman wrote The Matrix and Terminator and wins law suit!, Stewart is hailed as a role model for African Americans. She won the Copyright infringement case in her 6 year dispute with film giants – the Wachowski Brothers, Joel Silver and Warner Brothers. The films The Matrix and Terminator and their sequels grossed over $2.5 billion. Her manuscript (copyrighted 1981) 'The 3rd Eye' was used by the film giants without her permission. After her victory, Stewart planned to involve a record label, Popsilk Records, and a motion picture production company, All Eyez on Me, 'in reference to God.' (I wonder who she is really serving – the Lord our Almighty Creator or Satan, as many of *her* references are based on Christ ('the One') and the Bible, (Apocalypse and Armageddon? But are devoid of reference to our Creator).

94 - 1 Timothy 2 v14. It was not Adam who was first deceived. It was Eve. But she will be saved through having children, if she perseveres in faith, love, holiness and modesty. However both sexes can have a chance to have original sin removed through baptism in Christ.

95 - Revs. 12 v 4 -6, 13-14, 17. Snake versus woman. 'The dragon sat waiting at the point where the woman gave birth so that he might devour it as soon as it was born'. Satan chases the Virgin and her offspring, those who keep God's command-ments, and have the testimony of Jesus Christ. In other words he chases and persecutes those who would be Christ-like, to destroy them. This must be so, so that what was done, can be

undone. Woman first brought original sin through listening to the flirtatious temptations of the serpent. Woman must erase this sin through piety and virginal purity. Just as Satan was proud and disobedient, woman and man must become humble and obedient to God.

96 - As a disciple and prophet, the point is NOT that so many people and myself will be hurt or even killed as a result of my exposing the devil and his pervasive influences over our lives. The point is that those people who are willing to be Christ-like, might have the chance to have their souls saved for the life after death, and not be destroyed along with Satan.

This is why I willingly carry out this mission, and primarily because I love our heavenly Father, who first loved us, and wants to help us to make the right choice for our salvation. I will not hold my peace (Rev 14 v 6-9; or 2 Chronicles 14 v14) and keep from telling people just who the devil is, and what he is doing, because like all the prophets who have gone before, and Jesus, I want to obey our Father in heaven, and enable the souls of the '144,000' people to be saved. They are surely worth my personal sacrifices and my commitment to our Father in heaven. To Him be the glory, and to no other. Amen.

97 - There are many interested parties in Creation who are watching to see if the Lord, our Creator, was right to create man with free will to obey or not; and to show the loyal angels, and the defectors – demons- and Lucifer/Satan, that He *is* Just, and True, and Faithful and Right. He is lawful and righteous. See E G White, Patriarchs and Prophets, 1958, chp 1, p41-43; Review & Herald Publishing Association, USA; Pacific Press, Publishing Assocn, Canada. Our perseverance is evidence that the Lord Yahweh *is* just, and His judgement *is right*, (2 Thess 1 v 1-10. May He rule forever. Halleluiah!

PART TWO

THE SPIRIT OF CONVICTION

8

Satan stripped bare – part 1

Now we come to the real root of the problem. The real cause of human suffering in the world, and torment in hell if we choose to disobey our Father in heaven, and worship the devil. Many moons ago, some time before the beginning of Creation, when the Word existed and was with Him, our Father, in His wisdom and delight for beauty, created the first angel. He was so delighted with His creation that He made more. And through all eternity, along with the Word, they kept Him company. They sang all praises and glory to Him, all the time, and were happy to do so. They were a host and company of angels, and delighted in our Father's company and each other, as did He.

However, this first angel saw how wonderful our Father's existence was, how happy He was, and decided that he would like to live the same way. After all, if our Father can do it, so can he. It can't be that difficult. He grew vainglorious and proud, fancying himself above all the other angels, because of his beauty and exceptional musical talent (a). And despite our Father's admonitions and cautions to calm down and behave himself, he refused to do so.

Instead he grew prouder. So that he thought being the first angel, he could be like our Father in heaven, and god-like, and in theory (though not in fact) that he could be His partner. But as Prophet Muhammed stated, to regard any creatures as partners of the Almighty, or as associated with Him, was intolerable infidelity.(1) So our Father's patience stretched, and His anger truly kindled, banished this first angel from heaven.

Now, in heaven Satan had been used to an existence in the company of creatures, angels, and archangels, with our Father and the Word, which he forgot about. The Word was our Father's first companion, not partner. It was the Word who created all things. (2) Satan was banished from the heavens, to live a lonely existence, wandering the elements, through eternity in punishment. And the further away from our Father he grew, the more ugly he got. He grew bitter and miserable, lonely and vengeful. After all, our Father no longer wanted him in His sight. He had had enough of his disobedience. So he was left in his aloneness. (3)

Our Father in heaven in the meantime, still creative and wonderful, decided after some time, to create the world, as revealed in the Holy Books. In 6 days He created all the elements of the Earth, and created out of dust, man Adam, and from his rib, woman Eve. On the 7th day He rested, and bad us keep that day Holy. So, the first, now fallen angel, Satan, grew jealous of the happiness he saw shared by our Father, Adam and Eve in the garden of Eden, (4) - blissful in communion with each other. And when our Father wanted He would join the host of angels in heaven.

After all why should they be so happy, and Satan be so miserable? So vengeful and spiteful, Satan decided to get his own back on our heavenly Father. He wanted to upset Him and His blissful existence. So he tempted Eve with lies about what she could easily gain from the tree of knowledge. Of her own free will, she chose an easy option. Out of greed for more than what our Father had already blessed her with, she ate of the tree of knowledge. And because she loved Adam she gave some to him. Or was it because in an instant she grew vengeful like Satan and spited her husband? Anything is possible.

Adam, on the other hand, could have refused the fruit. He could have said 'No.' He could have found our Father and reported Eve's disobedience to Him. But he too was greedy. He did not truly love our Father, or else he would have obeyed Him and been loyal, and refused to eat from the tree of knowledge.

Because of this, our Father, immediately knowing that something was wrong when they decided that they were now ugly, and their nakedness should be covered, grew angry and upset, and was sorry that the love He so willingly gave, was no longer willingly returned. They had chosen to follow someone other than Himself, who had created them. They had decided that the body that He created in His own likeness and image, was ugly, shameful and impure.

For their disobedience and disloyalty He decided to punish them too, like he had Satan. He banished them from the garden of Eden (5). Since they had been so greedy, and not satisfied with the blessings our Father had so readily given them, he decided to let them suffer. See if they can make out a similar existence by themselves in the harsh living in the world outside of Eden!

So the first hominids in Africa, prehistory millions of years ago, looked very basic, unbeautiful, almost beast-like creatures. Darwin's theory of evolution can be explored here (9). Our Father then began to soften in His heart, because He remembered how He delighted in human company. So He created homo-sapiens, in Africa, where they resemble the humans we are ourselves.

The people began to draw, then make symbols and write and communicate by word and 'pen' – which is when our heavenly Father instilled the word in them (7). Satan still miserable, though delighting in making mischief, is still very lonely. So many people around, yet still he had no-one to communicate with, and our Father definitely spurned him.

So when our Father brought the word to people Satan instantly tried to make friends with them. The Chinese had the first script, and the Egyptians had the hieroglyphs, which were lost to our understanding after the demise of the Pharoanic Egyptians, until recently 1799, with the discovery of the Rosetta Stone by a French soldier on an expedition in Egypt (1a) that they were able to be translated and hence the mystery of the Egyptians unravelled. Evermore vainglorious and confident, Satan was determined to make himself god-like. So he tempted people away from their search for our Father (8), and made them worship him through false gods, deities and wealth, which they soon discovered was deceitful and temporary. Egypt, in Africa – the home of creation, committed the first and most terrible sin against our Father. Like Satan, Eve and Adam, they turned away from our heavenly Father and loved Him not.

The Egyptians were so big-hearted they welcomed in all kinds to their homes and hearts. They were not particular who they made friends with. Satan was able to easily tempt them with wealth and success for them to completely deny our Father. Even though our Father gave them the ability to build pyramids, they too grew proud and conceited, loving every abomination and upsetting our Father. They made their lives in love and worship of goddess Isis, whom Cleopatra worshipped, and other gods Ra, Horus, Osiris, Anubis etc. The deities they worshipped were yet another disguise for Satan. Our Father in heaven said: 'Woe betide them!' for truly they had committed the first sin of disloyalty to Him. Isaiah chapters 18 – 19 show the extent to which our Father's wrath was kindled against them. They were carried off to foreign unknown lands – the Eastern and Western slave triangles, and would have all knowledge of their heritage and achievements taken away from the world (10). Only the pyramids would stand as a reminder of their former greatness, and as evidence of what can happen to the mightiest nations, who are idolatrous.

They were the first civilisation to break YHWH's sanctified Sabbath at the end of a 7-day week. Instead they intro-duced a 10 day 'week', with 3 weeks in a month (30 days), and a 360 days in a calendar year, adjusting for the 5 day, ¼ of a month extra. So they broke yet another of YHWH's laws essential for harmony and order on earth. Others did the same later, including Roman Catholic church in 321 AD, when Emperor Constantine re-introduced the 7 day week, but replaced Saturday Sabbath with Sunday as 'the most significant day of the week' (see later explanation in this chapter). (source: www.wikipedia.org/week; www.wiki-pedia.org/Egyptian_calendars;   www.dragonstrike.com/egypt~AncientEgyptiancalendar)

They were also punished because they enslaved and were cruel to our Father's chosen people, the Israelites (11). That is also why Moses was sent to them to show how useless their deities were, and as example of what can happen to idolators. And more importantly, so that our heavenly Father could show the world His glory, and that He is the only One to be worshipped.

However our Father in His mercy is ever-forgiving and lov-ing. Once Christ had come He extended His clemency to even the descendants of those idolators (12). Those who adopted Christianity in its fullness and purity kindled our Father's plea-sure. So that the high church in Ethiopia, of which Emperor Haile Selassi is important of our Christian Rastafarians, was seen as fit refuge for Prophet Muhammed when he was perse-cuted (6). His slave Belal, a tall, dark, gaunt black man, with-stood all persecution, and alone stood firm and steadfast in his love for Allah.

Thus it is that negro, black descendants of those proud, disloyal Egyptians can seek redemption and forgiveness from our
Father in this present day. Time is running out for Satan and his
followers (13). Our Father's patience is running low. And He is
about to destroy the disloyal and disobedient one.

Yet our Father wants to punish the Jews (Israelites) still further
for refusing to acknowledge Christ as the Messiah (14). He first
took away the chance for salvation from the Jews, His chosen
people, and gave it to their enemies, the Gentiles (15; chp7-
86). So we have Roman Catholic Christians, the first to adopt
the way of the cross of Jesus Christ.

Now to inflame the jealousy of the still stubborn Jews, our
Father is allowing their Semitic half brothers, the Muslims (15;
chp7 – 86), to come to understand Christ before His chosen
people (16). Yet He still awaits their return to Him. He still
loves them, and has saved a space for the handful of Jews,
the remnant, who finally come to accept the way of the cross,
to know and love Him through Christ. So let us not think that
we are better than the Jews, or become boastful (17), because
our Father allows us to know Christ first. For if it were not for
the stubbornness of the Jews, the rest of us would still be
heathen (18), in other words, 'not grafted in' or 'adopted' as
'brothers and sisters' of Christ, or as 'children' of our heavenly
Father (19).

So let us embrace our Father's command and prophecy, and
bring the Muslim people to know and understand the way
of the cross, through Christ Jesus, the Messiah. For just as
Adam and Eve displeased our Father by disobeying Him and
loving someone else, so it is that Jesus and Mary, counteract this, in their humility, love and obedience to our heavenly
Father. Just as Adam and Eve made themselves impure and
ugly, needing sex to procreate, Jesus was pure, beautiful and
virginal, just like his mother, Mary. Their sanctity is a blessing
upon all mankind.

So *who is in control?*

You may say this is all very well, but what is its relevance to you and your life today, in this current time? You may consider yourself to be a God-fearing person, who does not worship the devil, Satan or Lucifer.

Here I invite you to take the time to explore with me how unwittingly we may actually be doing this very thing – worshipping the devil – because we have fallen into his web of deceit and into his trap for our destruction. He has been able to do this without us even noticing it, and most people are unaware of how pervasive his presence is in our lives.

We, who are in the 'first' or 'progressive' world economies/ societies, are aware of and are exposed to the mass media. This is through cinema and music industries, TV, internet, written media e g newspapers, magazines, books etc. and various advertising media. We are influenced to varying degrees by it. But who controls this mass communication?

From time to time we hear rumours of 'conspiracy theories' about the world being controlled by just 7 top wealthy magnates; or the world being controlled by outside forces e g 'aliens', or by the Free Masonic Society, or the Illuminati and so forth. All seem to be fantasmagorical to be believed, or to be real. There is more fact behind these theories than fiction or imagination. And you will be devastated to find out who is the ultimate controller behind these factions, who are merely instruments or puppets for his designs and purposes. Become aware and be a winner....

Current influencers – the Illuminati...

In the modern music industry current influencers are some of the 'Hip – hop' artistes who are major players across the world. We are familiar with Dr Dre, Jay Z, Eminem, Kanye West, Beyonce,

Rihanna, Lady Gaga, Cheryl Cole, Simon Cowell, Black Eye Peas, Chipmunk, Christina Aguilera, and various others, who seem to be demon-possessed, or have allowed themselves to be possessed and used by Lucifer for his purposes. Their performances and music/videos are not from our Father in heaven, but are secular, hyper- and perversely sexual, seductive, degrading, violent and abusive/aggressive, and denigrating to our senses and to our humanity. Whether knowingly, willingly or not, they appear to have 'sold their souls to the devil' or even as Eminem says 'made a bargain' with him, and he feels he can't get out of it. (He could if he wanted to, but there is a cost, loss of fame and wealth, and possibly even one's own life. Others have broken free, and survived e g Donna Summer who turned to religion afterwards, and Ashanti, and Professor Griff - ex – member of Hip hop group Public Enemy) (20, chp7 -60a). Other music genres e. g. Heavy Metal, Hard Rock, Punk Rock, etc. have also been berated for demonic content and influences, especially upon the youth. Babies and toddlers can be seen to be attracted to the 'catchy' tunes and lyrics, and dancing/gyrating to the rhythmic beats, never mind the effect on the older generations. It is really infectious and *so* not good for our souls!

For Lucifer was talented as a great musician himself, given that gift in order to praise and worship our heavenly Father. But now disgraced and spitefully angry he uses that gift to influence mankind through every genre of music. Through it he can control the people, as music is pervasive everywhere, and even in external silence, he can enable us to hear music/songs in our heads. Music is a powerful tool that can affect our moods and emotions ranging from love to hate, calming or inducing/ reflecting rage, happiness to sadness and so forth. This has been a powerful and successful weapon that Lucifer has used to distract mankind from our Father and to the ruin of our souls. This is why we chase material success so much.

Everyone wants to be successful at what they do, but the younger generation, no longer aspire to be ordinary workers like nurses, bankers, teachers and other professions. Inspired by 'Pop Idol' and 'Big Brother' and 'I'm a Celebrity Get me out of here!' popular shows, the youth now want to be pop stars and celebrities with the goal to get 'Cribs' (houses) that are out of the reach of most of us, and represent the lifestyles of the rich and famous, and are prepared to do anything to get it.

Unfortunately the current trend for 'idol' worship is not new. In the post – World War Two, the successful moral boosters of 'pin –up' girls and movie stars, before the pervasive advent of the 'small screen' /TV, meant that the populace started to grow accustomed to celebrities and their unachievable lifestyles, which was continued in the music industry of the 1950's to present day. We've grown accustomed to celebrities influencing our lives, directly through film or music , but also through the advertisements and press (paparazzi and celebrity magazines). We crave fame, material wealth and life-styles beyond most of our reach. But the scriptures chide us to 'not be envious of evil men...or those who do wrong....or who appear to be living the 'good life'. For, they will 'wither and die'... and 'be cut off'... and will perish' (21). Instead Jesus advises us to store up riches that are NOT perishable on this earth (22, chp7 -83), like valuable love, and joy and eternal life. For then, 'if we commit our ways to the Lord' (21) our Father, who knows our heart and mind, 'will give us the desires of our heart' (21), and will bless us with Life for all Eternity.

The secular angle was more covert, and not so explicit. Subliminal demonic messages have been said to be almost undetectable/imperceptible in the acting, lyrics, dancing or videos of the various media or artistes. However since the advent of Hip hop we have witnessed an explosion of explicit, in – your-face, blatant sexual, gratuitous, violent, rebellious images and messages right into our own homes via the TV and the internet on computer, and 'porn' videos and magazines. There is little or no avoidance of it, nor protection for the young, who are very easily influenced, unless there is some parental or guiding control, and we are all subjected to it, even when we decide to not watch TV, or listen to music.

It seems that it might well be the so-called Illuminati, (meaning 'bearers of the light') who are an organisation that has infiltrated the Masonic Society. They are among those who believe in the New World Order, and seek to bring it about in the new Millenium. Professor Griff (60a) in interview of 4th September 2010, gives his 'Insight on Free Masonry in the Hip-Hop Game and claims that they control the media (defined by him as a) Multi-Ethnic Destruction in America, or b) Maniacal European devils in Action), whose deliberate racist plan is to degrade and disable Black people. Their agenda is about keeping Afro-Americans ignorant of moral and scientific principles and of their own history, through music that erodes said morals, and degrades humans to basic sexually- charged, hormonal and animalistic levels. Griff cites an American Naval Intelligence Officer, William Cooper who in his book 'Behold the Pale Horse' claims that music is the silent weapon used to degrade and confuse Afro-American people. The aim is to keep them ignorant, confused on gender, roles, and politics, and undisciplined, disorganised, (so they can't rise up and demand their human rights and seek justice on matters of scientific principles, politics, history, religion).

For if they are undisciplined and confused about their very gender and roles in the family, and therefore society, then as a 'race' they are kept de-stabilised and undermined and 'controllable' and 'containable' as they are incarcerated in the mental secure units and penitentiaries (in USA 1% of population are in prisons, and of them almost 90% are Blacks! Similar figures are being found in UK too, especially since the 2008 'supervised community treatment amendment to the MH Act, for 'mental' service users detained in secure hospitals). A US official, John Coleman discusses how to control the minds of the Black population through media in his book 'Tavistock Institute (London) on Human Relations', and how to basically keep them undermined and subdued as when they were slaves! Incidentally the US prison system is basically slavery by the back door, where the inmates service an industry propping up the country's economy and so keeping the use/need for immigrant Mexican labour down. Mega profits are made for businesses who 'employ' prison/slave labour as well as benefit, because the inmates also need to 'buy' /use so many products or services that the privately owned prisons provide, according to civil rights activist Angela Davis (23).

Our oppressors think that if we are made to be confused over gender (23a), over appropriate sexual behaviour and relationships, over the roles for men and women in the family and hence society, they can continue to undermine us and control us for their purposes -which ultimately is to keep them superior to, and have power over us. So Black people are fed lyrics that degrade or disrespect Black women as 'bitches and 'hoes'(whores), and the men as 'pimps'. Songs are spun that encourage men to 'hook up' with women who are rich – have an education, have money, house, cars, jobs or businesses- so they can 'leech – off' them in parasitical relationships. This is opposed to the norm of self-respecting, dignified, upstanding and law-abiding citizens, who are proud men in their own rights, with their own incomes – work or business, and have their own worth or value.

Unfortunately, induced behaviour from slavery still persists amongst Black people, where the men were used as studs to impregnate women to produce more slave offspring, without being allowed to raise them as their own responsibility. The families were separated deliberately, and so were destabilised and called 'dysfunctional' matriarchal or matrifocal families, as they were then left as headed by the mother/ or other caring woman(relative or friend). Joseph (1983; 1985; (24) stated that this history has left a legacy of single parenting and generations of 'baby mothers' and 'baby fathers' in recent decades amongst the Black populace, a situation which, for various reasons, is not getting better as time progresses (although is not surprising given the 'diet' of immoral music they are being fed.).

However even the best made plans do not go as expected, and traces of the traditional family structure, men and women's roles as respected parents and leaders in the community/society are still evident amongst some Black families. The Black family is not completely eradicated or destroyed by racist ploys and tactics. Some Black men try to maintain their responsibilities, whether full or part-time fathers, whether working or unemployed, by supporting the mothers and children, in the best ways they know how, and actively participate in the upbringing of the children. Such men refuse to be devalued as human beings, or treated as though only their sexual organs or prowess are worth note. They are men in all aspects of the role attributed to partners/husbands and fathers. Unlike European family structures that place the onus on the father at best, and both parents secondarily, to be responsible for the children; according to African tradition 'it takes a whole village to raise a child', ie it is not just the nuclear family's concern, but is that of the whole 'village'/community or society. Therein lies the strength and unity of a family, community and civilisation. And this strength has underpinned the survival of Black people through slavery, colonialism, 'lynching' and racist attacks of various kinds, and oppression to the present day. But evil is still lurking....

It is therefore the Illuminati, who are controlling and influencing our artistes and what they put out there for our 'entertainment'. The artistes are contracted to do certain performances, produce so many songs, videos and films and promotions and concerts etc. Only a few artistes have some personal influence or control over what they do (Michael Jackson, (MJ) was one of them). But this means the messages and signals they send out are not their own, and when I listen to some of the lyrics, I wonder if the artistes themselves even know what they are saying or singing? Some don't even make sense, especially if they do not seem to be practising what they preach: eg. Rihanna singing with Eminem about 'liking the way you lie' or 'burns' or that she may be a 'masochist' in their song 'Love the Way You Lie' -2010/'11. If this were true, why did she not remain with her boyfriend Chris Brown after he beat her up for humiliating him with her slack behaviour, kissing Kanye West at a public event, (or has she kept him in secret, as rumoured)?

We can see here many examples of freedom of speech and expression gone too far beyond extremes. Where is the Mrs Mary Whitehouse of the 1970s -90s equivalent today? There is no public censorship, and the 9pm watershed is a joke, with many adult content and perversions and abominations and violence readily exposed everywhere on every medium 24/7! No wonder the children are so hyped up and easily aggravated. Too much too soon, that little minds cannot handle or develop resistance against. Parents we need to step up to the plate to protect our children.

It seems as though the artistes have contractual obligations to perform certain degrading acts or lyrics in order to gain the fantastic success and wealth and fame they seem to crave. All kinds of sexual, homosexual (diverse ?/ perverse), violent, degrading and debasing and even murderous activities seem to be expected of them and indeed they are pushed so hard and so far, that I wonder if there is no limit to what they will do for fame? From dressing in apparel of the opposite sex, gender bending, and homosexual activity to the extremes of e.g. Lady Gaga publicly performing wearing a dress made out of raw meat!, (25). Or more disturbingly, the latest music video by Kanye West, Jay Z and two others, 'Monsters' which shows hanged, scantily clad young women and cannibalism, whilst the artistes sing that they know people will say they are from the devil, but *they don't care!*

Professor Griff, (20, chp7 -60a) at great risk to his own life, has exposed in detail the various celebrities who seem to have made 'bargains' with, and are leading people towards 'worshipping

the devil' indirectly through 'pop' idols, and directly in their public performances. Some artistes have publicly said they feared
for their safety and their lives (and may even have lost it) from
those who control the music industry who don't seem to care for
their well-being e.g. MJ, Left- Eye formerly of girl hip hop group
TLC, Beyonce formerly of girl group Destiny's Child, (26), but
care only the money they can generate, or more sinisterly, the
control they(and the devil) can exert over the masses of people
world-wide.

But fame costs. There is a price to be paid either by yourself or
someone close to you. We know of the tragic losses to members of their friends or families, for people like, the Tennis champions, Venus and Serena Williams, Damian Dash, Kanye West,
Jennifer Hudson, 'Shug' Knights, and others who've 'sacrificed'
their loved ones eg Aliyah, Tu Pac, Biggie Small, and others in
exchange for the fame and success and wealth they craved (20,
chp7 – 60a) and are encouraging the populace to also crave.

These are subtle and almost imperceptible attempts to 'control
the minds' of the people, by the devil, through the Illuminati,
and via using the artistes as their 'puppets'. Why is the devil
using mind control on the masses? It is because he is still in
the business of rebelling against our heavenly Father, and trying to spite Him for banishing him from heaven. He still wants
to be same as Him with all the power and glory and adoration
that accompanies His greatness. Through his various puppets
and devices, the devil entices the people to worship his very
ugly and ignoble, vainglorious self. He is doing his damndest
to turn the people away from our Father, and to steal and so
destroy our souls, and thereby upset and deprive our Father of
His delight and joy in us - His creation. But remember the devil
is a liar, a deceiver, a thief of time, and of lives and souls.

From the earliest times, the devil has 'instilled' in the minds of
the priests, moguls, Illuminati and various others, the idea that
symbols, (our means of communication), have significance and

hence power, to control others. His symbols are everywhere, but we are 'blinded' to them under his 'veil' of deception. The most influential of all time were the Egyptian symbols and concept of the 'all-seeing eye' or the 'evil eye'. This is seen variously as an eye within a triangle, or pyramid. This is basically the devil trying to convince and so control the people that he is omniscient like our heavenly Father. But he is a liar. He cannot read your mind, he can only read your behaviour, using his eons of gleaned knowledge of human behaviour. He can therefore orchestrate, provoke or trigger your reactions to give his desired effects, if you are not aware of it; plus he has myriads of armies of spiritual and physical spies, and accomplices everywhere- demons and human agents, to aid his agenda. Neither can he predict or tell the future; and he does not really bless us, since our blessings and gifts and talents come from one source, our Creator, YHWH. Only the Creator is omniscient and He understands that we have been deceived, and that when we worship unwittingly, that some of us mean to worship Him, and not the devil. Only our Creator can read us, the content of our minds and our hearts, and knows if we truly and genuinely love Him. But the devil, being vainglorious, likes to take credit for someone else's hard work, or in this case, take the glory away from our heavenly Father. But 'I will not give my glory to another', says our Father (27).

Satan's symbols can be seen in even the videos of the music artistes, Chipmunk's latest one even has him sitting in front of the Greek god Baphomet; in the films, in the buildings, on them and in how they are structured or even situated. (20, chp7 - 60a). Even in children's films like 'Prince Caspian in the Chronicles of Narnia' the devil so unashamedly shows himself in his full ugliness as the horned, hairy bison/beast standing upright on two legs, towering over the men. The disturbing thing is that the Illuminati and hence the devil, are so convinced that the majority of the people will not believe the various conspiracy theories, that they blatantly let us know what they are doing, concocted within lies and half-truths, and they seem to have gotten away with it. So the occult, voodoo, all devil-worship is openly depicted through various films like 'Dracula', 'The Exorcist' , 'Carrie', 'The Mummy', 'Harry Potter' , 'Charmed', 'Sabrina the teenage witch', even earlier 'Bewitched',and various others; and we, now de-sensitised, think it is natural and normal. But it is all part of Lucifer's cunning plan to steal the people away from our heavenly Father, and to make us miserable, 'rob us of our joy' and ultimately destroy us.

Illuminati means the 'torch bearers' or 'torch carriers' , 'bearers of the light'. Hence the significance of the Olympic torch bearers carrying a lighted torch from city to city around the world before the advent of the next Olympic sports event, every four years. In Christianity, Jesus is seen as 'the light of the world', come down to us from heaven, to save us from the peril of destruction. The 'light' of Jesus is said to shine and be apparent in those who have taken his teachings and cross seriously in their lives, and who therefore stand out as beacons (torches) as his witnesses, and to show the way for others to follow suit. The devil, always trying to associate himself with goodness and wanting to take credit for what is not his, has 'cleverly' adopted the light and torch ideas in his symbology, as seen in the 'Illuminati'. But don't believe the hype. Remember the devil can appear as if he were an angel of light (goodness) (28), in one of his many disguises. (He is a fallen angel, now demon, devil, Lucifer). NB Rev 12 v 9 'So, the great dragon was cast out (of heaven), that serpent of old, called the devil and Satan, who deceives the WHOLE world; he was cast to the earth, and his angels were cast out with him'.

Don't believe me? A prime and very real of this kind of deception can be seen with the megastar Michael Jackson. He 'Bobby dazzled' the whole world for over 45 years with his amazing talented singing, and electric fantasmagorical dancing, the 'moon walk', and videos, and personal ranch and theme park, Neverland, designed to give children a happy childhood experience with him. He enthralled and had the whole world under his spell from a child of 5 to his unexpected sudden death aged 51, in June 2009. But all the 'razzle dazzle' that was so bewitching belied the sinister truth behind his so very popular image. He deluded/ deceived the WHOLE world with his feigned/ pretended innocence.

This 'angel of light' hid a secret paedophile deception. For in 1979, a clue came from a young man who claimed he had received an indecent phone call from Michael Jackson. It was not followed up by the police. But several years later, in 1993, and up to 2003, a boy Jordan Chandler, who had been one of the many children who regularly visited Neverlands, alleged that when he slept over in M Js bed, Michael had touched him inappropriately (sexually). In the outrage and scandal and disbelief that ensued, and pending a court case, Michael Jackson settled out of court, paying the boy's family a huge sum, to drop the case and effectively shut them up. However the damage was done, and no matter how M J tried to portray himself whiter than white and squeaky clean, even going so far as to appear in same guise as Jesus Christ Himself !!!!, he was never able to shake the soiled image associated with his name. MJ died June 2009. Chandler's father, who had been pursuing MJ for years to extort money for this, committed suicide October 2009. Jordan and his mother June, have not spoken for 11 years. Had Michael been innocent, he would have held out, no matter how ill the scandal made him, to declare and prove his innocence. Instead he bribed the family, and spent $millions on the court case, in effect perverting the course of true justice!

A few years before his inopportune death, M Js theme park/ ranch was shut down by the FBI, his assets of his vast wealth were seized, and he fled abroad, to Saudi Arabia, awaiting his fate. Among the riches and treasures he possessed, were found some very disturbing paintings and statues, that pointed to the true nature of his character. Notwithstanding that he had been caught out several times, speaking in his natural deep voice, when he forgot himself and his infamous high pitched tone, as if alluding to the childhood innocence and Peter Pan youth that he was reluctant to lose sight of. Some of his paintings, that he had commissioned artists to paint for him, of himself as prince and angel, and also with hoards of children surrounding and following him like the Pied piper of fairy tales, on closer inspection revealed very different meanings and significance.

Among them were references to Greek god Pan, half man, half beast, whose infamous statues portray him as an 'dirty' old man, having immoral sexual relations with young men/ boys – homosexuality and pederasty; and in other statues he sexually molested animals, like a deer/antelope (?) – bestiality. Now the Greek and Romans, with their gods Zeus, Deus, etc., had a prevalent pederast culture, which encouraged what we now call paedophilia, (since criminalised by the emergence of Christianity). Young men and boys were trained to become sexual partners for old wealthy men. Today we have young children, little boys and girls, being trained to bounce up and down on bottles, to prepare them for paedophiles who flock to the Philippines, notably Thailand for that very purpose!!! And you wonder why they had the terrible tsunamis there; and recent floods in the North and Midlands UK.

In Cambridgeshire and Lincolnshire, child sex pornography and paedophilia was highlighted in 2002, when 2, 10 year old girls, friends Holly Wells and Jessica Chapman were murdered by sex offender Ian Kevin Huntley, convicted and imprisoned for life in 2003. Importantly the case exposed irregularities and tardiness in the police investigation, including the deleting of data that could have more quickly identified that Huntley was a serial offender of underage and teenage girls, raping 3 of them, one only 11 years old! Police corruption emerged as 2 of the officers, one a detective, involved in the murder case, turned out to have been charged for, and one convicted of child pornography offences. Even whilst holidaying in Great Yarmouth, the year before the Soham case, I was alerted to police cover-up in child sex assaults, by a woman and her teenage daughter, who had been a victim, and was the investigation was 'hushed up', and rightly they were enraged and felt let down by those supposed to protect and defend them. As a result the Criminal Records Bureau (CRB) checks was instituted on prospective people over 16 year olds, who wanted to work with children and vulnerable adults, in a bid to protect them.

This week, ('Mail' on-line,28th Sept 2012) questions are being asked for accountability from the authorities –the Crown Prosecution Service, the police and social services, and the Asian community for failing to protect girls as young as 11 from being sexually groomed and trafficked by men in a sex ring. The Mail asks 'who'll take the blame over rape gangs? Not a single social worker sacked over teenage grooming scandal'. After years of reports to the police and social services, including from the NHS, and after the Times newspaper exposed 'Rochdale sex trafficking gang' in 2011, and TV documentary that followed leading to the investigation and criminal conviction of a group 9 men, (more were charged, but acquitted), in May this year (2012). The young victims, some were repeated raped, or gang raped by up to 20 men at a time, two forced to have abortions – one as young as 13; a mother had to put her child into social services care to get her away from the sex gangs! Can you imagine their torment and distress and feeling vulnerable and let down by those who were supposed to protect them?

Excuses circulating for appalling negligence given are 'lack of training and procedures'; other suggest fear of being called racist, (most of the men were Asian Pakistanis,), I suspect fear of triggering terrorist attacks on British soil again, may be a motive; but even more likely is the cover-up of culture of corruption and paedophilia within the areas, including the authorities. Although it has only been cases of Asian men who have come to public attention at the moment, it has been noted that the practice of 'grooming' occurs solitarily or in gangs from other races also (eg white men in the North solitary; networks in the North and Midlands many have been British Asians; in Devon it was white men; in Bath and Bristol, Afro-Caribbeans; in London, all ethnic mixes, whites, Iraqis, Kurds, Afghans, Somalis. – source Child Exploitation and Online Protection Centre and Barnardos childrens' homes, 2011). But as Nazir Afzal, newly appointed chief crown prosecutor, who brought the case to trial, said the key issue is that 'there is no community where women and girls are not vulnerable to sexual attack and that's a fact'.) This is a very sad state of affairs and indictment on mankind, today, and as in Noah's time – deplorable depravity and degradation. You can be sure that YHWH is sorely vexed with such perversions and abominations!!!

PS Sadly and disturbingly, last night (1st Oct '12), a little 5 year old girl, April Jones, was abducted and driven away in a car, in Machynlleth, mid-Wales, whilst she played with a friend, on her bike, outside her home around 7pm. We pray for the little ones safety, and empathise with her worried parents.

Unbelievably this week beginning Oct 2012, yet more sickening scandals have emerged with mega-celebrity and knighted, Sir Jimmy Saville as a paedophile and pederast spanning more than his 50 year music and TV career and UK –wide. Now deceased, he leaves social services, the NHS, the BBC and parliament to answer pertinent questions as to why their cultures would allow him, (and others) to get away with it for so long. Not even his many victims, alleged up to 400, vulnerable, and sick children and teenagers (groupies), from children's homes, hospitals, and his TV shows reported him to the police. His halo shining from his celebrity and charitable fundraising activities shrouded his true abusive character, betraying the trust of his victims and of those who knew him. Even now many find it hard to believe that such a generous and loveable 'rogue' character could be capable of such evil. A, MJ 'Bobby dazzler' scenario all over again. Up to five other celebrities, including comedian Freddie Starr and Gary Glitter (already a convicted paedophile), are also under investigation in this scandal.

Only in the past year one or two women were brave enough to be interviewed for a BBC 'Newsnight' programme, the shelving of which in favour of 3 more popular (and lucrative TV ratings) shows for Christmas 2011, was highlighted to this month's public outrage, demanding answers for this BBC decision. This has blown up into a humungous scandal, affecting several of British societies major establishments, and the fall out of which is still occurring almost daily. Yesterday (11/11/12), following 2 others who've stepped down pending the inquiry, the head of BBC resigned after 54 days in post, and was awarded 1 year's severance pay, £450,000 or equivalent of 3,000 fines for not paying TV license, for his future help with inquiries. People are livid! We wait with keen interest to see if indeed perversion and 'injustice (will) shut her mouth' (Job 5 v 8-16), and commonsense and compassion for the child abuse victims will prevail.

And last week PM Cameron warned that he didn't want this investigation to turn into a 'gay witch hunt', following a false implication of an MP as a paedo. It seems that gays are to be given more sensitive consideration, than the victims of the paedophiles!!!! What happened to the old adage 'women and children first' to be saved from a sinking ship? And is not the motto of the government's social services department to 'put the needs of the child as paramount'?

What allows this pederast/paedophile culture to pervade societies worldwide? From Chinese elite allowing 7 year old girls to be given to senile men, or notorious child prostitution in Thailand, or enshrined in Jewish law of Talmud where sex with 3 year old girls, or sodomy with boys over 9 years old are not illegal? Certain cults also encourage under age sex with adults, eg Mormon Christians, and no doubt many other less publicised child sexual abuses occur in other countries and religions; and even within the very sanctuary of the home. Indeed pederasty was only criminalised into paedophilia after Christianity outlawed it, but it is still widely practised and children are still not

safe. These are major offenses against YHWH's beautiful innocent children, and He is mighty angry about it!!!!

Yahweh is fuming with wrath! So now wonder there are so many
disasters worldwide – the tsunamis, floods and earthquakes and
hurricanes/ tornadoes! Mankind has sunk to depraved depths
as in Noah's Time before the Flood. Surely YHWH will send
Christ back to avenge the innocent victims very soon! Watch
out! YHWH know s what you are about! So stop your wickedness and repent, before it's too late. Yes it may already be too
late, and the Books written up complete, for the close of probation, (Rev 10 v 6; EG White Story of Redemption, chp 59 pps
402-403). Better hope and pray your sins have been 'blotted
out' of the book of Transgressions, and entered into the Book of
Life in YHWH's mercy!!!

So, back to MJ's paintings where covert references to god Pan
were made, as images of him hidden in the tree foliage, or as an
angel playing a pan-flute. Others, show children gaily coloured
and gaily playing, dancing, happy and freely. Yet in one picture
an older girl has her dress lifted up, exposing her naked but-
tocks, by a dull grey younger boy, with an evil SINister, and
very wrong facial expression. Another showed a little blonde
haired, blue-eyed girl with a garland of flowers on her head, this
was reference to the the god Baphomet (aforementioned connection with hip-hop artists Beyonce and Chipmunk). Also por-
traits of MJ with similar flower garland around his head, as he
imitated the god Pan's pose with reed sceptre, actually invites
the viewer to idolise him, and sexualise him (and the little girl!).
And the innocent blue, and yellow and pink balloons that the
children play with, refer to the Free Mason's flag colours!!! So
although the paintings at first glance seem innocent in themselves, imperceptibly hidden are references to paedophilia,
Masonic allegiance and all which take away the innocence of
children. (Perhaps MJ was a victim as well as perpetrator of
pederasty/ paedophilia?). That whitened face masked more
than his racial identity.

No wonder he was so easily able to charm the whole world and sway their concepts of 'bad', 'wicked' over to being perceived as good things – inversion of concepts and meanings! This has been continued today with young people describing something they value or appreciate as good, by calling them 'sick'. Really? Since when has vomit been a good thing? 'Woe to those who call evil good, and good evil....for they have rejected the law of the Lord Almighty, and spurned the word of the Holy One of Israel... Therefore the Lord's anger burns against His people...and their land will be (desolate) in darkness and distress', (Isaiah 5 v 20-30).

This has been the pervasive and subtle overpowering ability of the Illuminati and Masonic Society to influence and pervert the natural order of things. MTV (Music Television), formerly called CTV, was originally owned by the head of the Masonic Society, Grand Master and High Priest of the Free Masons (Lodges)!!!! Does MTV perhaps really refer to the Masonic Temple in which its Headquarters reside, ie Masonic Television??? One of their influencers was Aleister Crowley, occultist and celebrated magician/ sorcerer, who was also a pansexual. This 'pan-' idea means sex with anyone and anything, -no boundaries, no morals. So pederasty, paedophilia, sodomy, homosexuality, Olympics, bestiality, adultery, fornication, ALL DEGRADATION, was okay with him. BUT remember it led to the destruction of Sodom and Gomorrah, Tyre and Sidon, by an incensed Father in heaven, who did not create our bodies for such abuse and perversion and abomination!!!

Led by 1950s philosophy, concerning the existence of 'Dark Matter' in outer space, they alleged it existed and had power by inference, with reference to the things that we can see with the naked eye. They claimed Dark Matter, no matter the sophistication of the telescope, could not be fathomed or 'seen', and that no amount of light could penetrate it, but would be absorbed in it; but the fact that matter was suspended within it, then it must have matter itself, because of its gravitational properties!!

Really? I thought that the planets were held on their own axes because the Almighty Creator put them there, and ensured they were held there. I did not know that Dark Matter, that does not need an instrument to see it, (it is clearly visible with the naked eye), could have that capacity. Yet again Satan's agents discredit and destroy our Father's capabilities! Instead he tries to attach importance to something (Dark Matter) that did not have it before, or from the Beginning, so as to give it some credibility of being powerful (Rev 12 v9). As prince of darkness, with his all-seeing eye (ancient Egyptian), Satan is still trying to 'big himself up', and delude himself and others that he is so great and important. But he is a liar, full of hot air!

(Sources a)http://en.wikipedia.org/wiki/1993_child_sexual_abuse_ accusations_against_Michael_Jackson; b) PreachingPlace.com/:- 'Dark Matter – Exposing the Dark Secrets of Hollywood', sermon by Michael Dantzie, published 1st Sept. 2012.)

So this thinking/philosophy sparked the entertainment industry, and its pervasive influence over mankind. And Michael Jackson falls into this framework, that states, that their concept of the image of for instance, a witch as romanticised, good, and beautiful, will prevail, (because they said so, and they are all powerful!). So Sabrina, the teenage witch, Charmed, 'Wizards of Waverley Place', Harry Potter's young friends are all beautiful or attractive or youthful, and convey the idea of innocence, and so cannot possibly be harmful or evil for children, and society. Really? And we have all been hoodwinked and bewitched and charmed and spells cast on us, either through dramatic films/ TV or real life shows that give actual magicians (sorcerers/tricksters) a platform and enter our homes through the screen, and therefore influence our perceptions, and so control our minds. Have we become mindless puppets, monkey see, monkey do, imitating fiction that we see, practising it in our real, not virtual, daily lives? Are we being groomed and primed to be soldiers in Satan's army, along with the kings and princes and leaders all arrayed to oppose Christ when He returns, at the battle of Armageddon? Far-fetched? I think not.

For Lucifer was once a stunningly beautiful angel, but soon fell from our Creator's grace and favour because of his sinful flaw – pride and vaingloriousness- that led him to rebel and contend against the Almighty, who is the Most High Entity in all of the universe. Once created beautiful, Lucifer is now the master of deception, using sorcery, magic, trickery and other occult devices to deceive and destroy mankind. He is jealous and rages relentlessly and violently aggressive against our Father, in his bid to conquer all. He wants to be master of all that he surveys/sees – of everything that he did not himself create, but takes credit and glory for. He is a liar and a thief. (Rev 12 v 9) – THE Great Controversy that began in heaven, when the Devil, meaning the Adversary, or Satan, meaning the Accuser, as Lucifer originator of sin, stood against YHWH, and accused Him of being unjust, with therefore no authority to rule the Universe(s) and heaven and earth!!!! Imagine! The impudence!!!

(Lord have mercy! 'Pull down strongholds and arguments against You'! 2 Corin 10 v 4-6).

Satan is so deluded that he believes he is omnipotent, and does not want to realise or remember that the power he has, is only permitted to him by our Creator, temporarily (28a) when He cast him out of heaven for his rebellious pride and disobedience. He conveniently forgot this when he tried to tempt Christ whilst he was enduring 40 days and nights without food or water in preparation for his ministry that followed. Satan offered Christ power to rule over all that he surveyed – 'the whole world' if he would just bow down and worship him. He really thought Jesus would be stupid or so confused (deprived of nutriments) that he'd be desperate enough to succumb to Satan's dazzling temptations. Satan, full of delusion, thought he could ensnare Jesus to give up all the power, his divine power, that He already possessed over the whole world and universe, and bow down

to him, Lucifer, who was so far beneath Him, that even our merciful and forgiving Father, our Creator, did not want him, anywhere near. What a fool Satan is! He really is a deluded idiot.

Similarly, in his symbology, the devil has parodied Jesus, the
'son' of man (or our Father in heaven), and substituted 'sun' for
his own worship. The Illuminati, following the ancient Egyptian
mythology worshipping Horus, (and Greek Zeus , Roman Deus)
and other pagan gods (Freyr, Anglo-Saxon/ Norse sun-god of
fertility, and Thor god of Thunder)(29), were, and are 'sun' –
worshippers ie worship the devil. Unfortunately the Roman
Catholics reverted back to their 'sun' worshipping after Jesus
died, and inter-mingled the pagan beliefs with the new Christian
one (30 -p76, p100 -101) (31 –p3/51). This was to make followers more easily convert to Christianity, by making it seem
more like their own. This is still current practice in attempts to
convert other nations worldwide. Paganism is in even the very
concept of 'transubstantiation' that the R Cs claim, ie. That the
Eucharist - the Holy Communion of bread and wine - is the *real*
substantial transformation into the body and blood of Jesus
Christ, and is not merely symbolic, as I had always believed.
How can that be? We are not cannibals!!! We do not eat Christ's
body and drink his blood, cannibalism, as practiced by heathen/
pagan peoples! To suggest such is a sacrilege and an abomination to the sanctity of the new covenant between our Father
and mankind, and a defilement of Jesus' sacrifice! Yet there
is more impudence and disrespect by so-called respected religious leaders.

In A. D. 364, the Council of Laodicea, passed a law (Cannon
XXIX) that instructed people to not Judaize the Saturday, ie
keep the Saturday holy as did the Jews, but 'to work on' it, and
anyone 'found Judaizing, they shall be shut out from Christ'
(30 -p102 ibid) (31 p6/51). This is why we have Sunday as the
Christian Sabbath, as the last day of the week, and the Monday
being the first, which is contrary to the original Sabbath as des-
ignated by our Creator, when He rested on the 7th day, and

instructed the Israelites/ Jews to keep it holy (30 -p100 -102 ibid; Exod. 20 v8 -11,

Exod. 31 v12-17). And now, having been developed over the past few years, a new Sunday Law is due to be passed, (agreed June 2009 between American President Obama and Pope Benedict XVI), which will compel all Christians (and others) to worship on only a Sunday, with consequences for those who refuse to comply. This has serious implications for the original Sabbath day keepers. Obama also went on to sign the NDAA (National Defence Authorisation Act) Dec 31st 2011, which gives the right to detain indefinitely American citizens, a la Guantanamo Bay style imprisonment, which is contrary to the fifth Amendment, thereby stripping American citizens of their statutory rights to citizenship and freedoms therein, (if they pose a threat to national security in 'the war on terror').

This is why the RC church is so antithecal to the Seventh Day Adventist Christian church which adheres to the original Sabbath (30 -p104 ibid) (31), and has exposed the corrupted version of the 10 Commandments that the Catholics preach, which is not the original Moses Commandments (30)(31). The R C church 'expunged' (removed) Moses 2nd commandment: 'to not make and worship graven images or other thing as gods', thus contravening our Father's instruction to hold no other person or idol, before Him, ie in His place. They substituted it by dividing the 10th commandment into 2 separate ones – 'you shall not covet your neighbour's house' and 'you shall not covet your neighbours wife'- to make the numbers up to 10 again (30). They openly admit to this in their commentaries. This why they can revere the Pope as the head of the RC church, as virtually god on earth, a travesty, rather than as a servant of the Lord Jesus, equal to the status of any of Jesus' disciples where Christ taught that not any one be master and servant, but equal as brothers and sisters. For Jesus deigned to wash their feet, to show how they must serve one another on a level playing field (32).

As for celebrating Christmas on the 25th December, that too is a travesty! The R C church openly admits that they deliberately decided to put it on the same day as the pagan worship of: 'dies natalis solis invicti (birth of the invincible sun-god) (33). Christmas was adopted in AD 354, by Liberius, Bishop of Rome, on the December 25th, on the birthday of Mithra, the Iranian 'god of light' (31 p4/51). It is also celebrated as the birthday of the sun (31 –p4/51). A few other churches celebrate the approximate date of Christ's birth, (estimated from the arrival of the Magi (wise men) at Bethlehem, as January 6th (33). The birth date of Jesus Christ is not recorded in the Bible anywhere at all. And even the celebration of birthdays was a pagan ritual.

Even Easter, the celebration of Christ' death and resurrection has been corrupted by pagan influences. It originated with the Jewish Passover, which is the commemoration of Yahweh, delivering the enslaved Israelites out of Egypt through His instrumental leader, Moses. However it became merged with the Anglo-Saxon goddess of spring, Eostre. In her honour, sacrifices were offered at the vernal equinox, or spring. She is also known as the Babylonian goddess Ishtar or Astarte. By the 8th century, church leaders applied 'Eostre' to Christ's resurrection. Later, Passover began to be eradicated and replaced as Easter in some Bibles, (31 –p3/51).

Although it is important that Christ was born, and to lowly, humble circumstances, perhaps, it is more important to mark the fact that he willingly, did his Father's bidding, and took our sins upon his shoulders, and died on the cross to give us the chance and hope of life in eternity, thus cancelling death which the devil brought upon us. If any day is to be celebrated for Jesus, it is the day of his resurrection, more so than his birth! For, His resurrection means that a whole new situation has arisen for the rest of mankind. We now have a chance to be reconciled with our Creator, after the disconnection caused by the disobedience and disloyalty of Adam and Eve. Christ repaired that disconnection with His precious, life-saving blood, and *this* is what is true cause for celebrations! He enables us to reconcile with our Father, who created us out of love, is willing to forgive us if we repent, because He still wants us to be in His family. *This* is worth making a song and dance about, because in our sinful ways, we do *not* deserve the Lord's love and mercy.

Ironically as we progress, in the UK, if not elsewhere in the West, Sunday has been declining as a day of holy observance, and has become more secular. For many it has become just another business day for recreation and leisure; shopping and pub lunches take precedence over attending church. This turn of events works even more in favour of the devil, as people no longer seem to prioritise church and religious observance. Even Christmas is more about St. Nicolas aka Santa Claus and exchanging gifts, rather than about the birth of Christ. This practice derives from the legend of Saint Nicolas, Bishop of Myra in Lycia, in AD 300. The belief that he enters a house through the chimney, originated with Norse (pagan) legend, who believed that the goddess Hertha appeared in a fireplace, and brought good luck to the house, (31 –p4/51).

There are other ways in which the devil has deceived us, by enticing us to worship him instead of our Father the Creator. There are other days that he has led us to change from our Father's holy days to pagan ones. The Druid festival of Saturnalia, after the winter solstice on 21st December, to mark the rebirth/rejuvenation of the sun emerging out of the darkest and shortest day of the year. It is named after Saturn and remembered on the Saturday, (named from the Roman Julian calendar) and is pre-Christian and hence pagan.

Yet this day, Saturday, has been given to the very day of the week, the 7th, that is commemorated by the Jews, and was given by our Father in heaven as HIS holy day – Shabat' or Sabbath. The Sabbath is our reminder that our Father rested on this day after creating the world and all in it in 6 days. It is *His* holy day, and has special blessing and reverence in it. As Shelton and Quinn,

(2004) state 'there is only one reason the 7th day (Saturday) Sabbath is holy – God *blessed* and *sanctified* that particular day and called it *His 'holy day'* (30 –p76-77). He instructed us to keep it holy, doing no work on that day, and especially so that we remember Him. This should be good enough reason for all of us to devote that day to worshipping Him.

The Sabbath existed from the 7th day that Creation was made and Time began, before any religion was thought of. Yet it is *this* very sacred and holy day of our Father, that the devil has taken it upon himself to denigrate and diminish to a pagan, ordinary day of the week. Such incredible disrespect and defiance to our Creator! Does the clay really think itself better than the potter who made it? (34). Surely he cannot escape punishment for this!

Even Jesus, who is Lord, and his disciples/apostles, always worshipped on the Jewish Sabbath (Saturday) as they them-selves were Jews. (Evidence of the apostles' weekly obser-vance of the Sabbath is in Acts 13 v 14, v44; Acts 16 v 13; Acts 17 v 2; Acts 18 v 1, v4).

But in the 2nd century, the church at Alexandria and Rome began Sunday worship. About AD 130, Barnabas of Alexandria, refers to the 7th day Sabbath as representing the 7th millennium of earth's history. He then says that the present Sabbaths were unacceptable to God, who would make:

> 'a beginning of the 8th day (Sunday), that is the beginning of another world. Wherefore, also, we keep the 8th day with joyfulness, the day on which Jesus, rose again from the dead'. (31 –p5/51).

(NB see my comments on the actual day that Christ was resur-rected later on).

By the 5th century there was a social change as both days were observed. This continued until the state legalized Sunday as the day of rest. The faithful still observed Saturday as Sabbath, as according to 5th century writer, Sozomen, a contemporary of Socrates, wrote:

> 'The people of Constantinople, and almost everywhere, assemble together on the Sabbath, as well as on the 1st day of the week, which custom is never observed at Rome or at Alexandria.' (31 p-5/51).

Apostolic constitutions of the same period also wrote:

> 'let the slaves work 5 days, but on the Sabbath (Saturday) and the Lord's day (Sunday) let them have leisure to go to church for instruction and piety'. (31 –p5/51) (Possible origins of weekends off work?)

Finally the nail was hammered into the coffin when in AD 364 the council of Laodicea (Cannon 29) forbad 'Judaizing on the Sabbath (Saturday) on pain of being 'shut out from Christ'. 'In effect they had REVERSED the 4th commandment by saying Christians shall not Judaize and be idle on that day, but shall WORK on that day.'

Not only content to change the day of worship, and forcing people to honour this new day (Sunday), they took steps to 'dishonour the true Sabbath and to ensure that people broke the Sabbath'!!! (31 – p6/51). This is utter sacrilege, disrespectful and disobedient to our Creators' 4th commandment! Misled, the people then unwittingly, fall into condemnation from our Creator, for disobedience to His sacred commandment.

'In a master stroke of marketing, the church started referring to Sunday as the "Lord's day", urging believers to honour the resurrection. At the same time they distanced themselves from the Sabbath by actively encouraging prejudice towards Jews and all Jewish customs'. The Roman Catholic church has admitted to this change in doctrine, because it claims it has the right to make such changes. 'The Cathecism of the Council of Trent 1829 says:

> 'But the church of God has in her wisdom ordained that the celebration of the Sabbath day should be transferred to the Lord's day'.

This is because, as 4th century Christian historian, Eusebius wrote:

> All things whatsoever it was the duty to do on the Sabbath, these we have transferred to the Lord's day, as more appropriately belonging to it, because it has a precedence and is first in rank, and MORE honourable(!!!!) than the Jewish Sabbath'.

I ask you, is Sunday/ sun-god/ devil –worship more honourable than worship of our Creator??? Surely they cannot be serious! Please also note that the Lord referred to here is not our Lord Jesus Christ. It is the Lord's ie emperor's day. Sunday was the day the Roman emperor received his treasury payments (MONEY – Mammon, the motivation). And sun-worshippers had Sunday as the venerable day of the sun, (30 –p76).

> The Roman Catholic church even mock the other Christian churches, the Protestants, for still following RC doctrine and worshipping on the Sunday, instead of reverting back to the Saturday Sabbath. As Peter Geierman wrote in 'The Convert's Catechism of Catholic Doctrine', 1951, p 60, in answering the question 'Why do we observer Sunday instead of Saturday (for the Sabbath)?

> 'We observe Sunday instead of Saturday because the Catholic Church transferred the solemnity from Saturday to Sunday'. (31 –p7/51).

Others write about the contradictions and 'inconsistency of Protestants who refuse to accept all the other feasts and traditions commanded by the (RC) church, yet keep Sunday holy'. Henry Tuberville states in 'An Abridgment of the Christian Doctrines', 1833, p58, his reply to the question:

> 'Q. How prove you that the Church has power to command feasts and holy days?
>
> Ans. By the very act of changing the Sabbath into Sunday which Protestants allow of,
>
> And therefore they fondly contradict themselves, by keeping Sunday strictly, and breaking most other feast commanded by the same church.' (31 p7/51).

The churches are guilty, by breaking this 4th commandment alone, of disobedience, disloyalty and disrespect of our Father Most High, our Almighty Creator, never mind the other commandments. But rather than mocking and rejoicing at the Protestants' deluded demise, the RC church should beware. For Jesus admonished the scribes and Pharisees, the Jewish religious leaders of his day: 'You serpents! Brood of vipers! Hypocrites!'... Woe to you' for leading the people astray and preventing them from coming into their salvation. 'For you shut up the kingdom of heaven against men, for you neither go in yourselves, nor do you allow those who are entering to go in. Woe to you.....'. (35 – 1).

For them the judgement will be the same as for those who 'cause one of the little children to sin' when their minds and hearts are for Jesus Christ, it would be better for them 'to tie a milestone around (their own) necks and be cast into the depths of the sea' (35 – 2). In fact the judgement for even wicked Tyre and Sidon, and for Sodom and Gomorrah would be easier/more lenient, and they would fare better (35 – 3) than these 'false prophets'/ 'hypocrites' aka religious leaders, with their false teachings, who purport to know, and be better than us, the ordinary folk. Christ calls them 'blind guides, who strain out a gnat and swallow a camel' who are more concerned about picking out the speck in another's eye rather than remove the log that is in their own, (36 – 1). As He asked them 'can the blind lead the blind? Will they not both fall into the ditch?' (36 – 2). In other words will they both not be ensnared into hell? I assure you, it is not a good look.

Other people, ignorant of the special significance and *sanctified blessing* attached to that day, the Sabbath (Saturday), argue that 'it doesn't make any difference which day we choose, (to set apart to worship our Creator), as long as we rest. What a slap in the face this must be to our Creator YHWH!' (30 – p81). The Sabbath is a reminder that He is our Creator and Redeemer (through Christ), (30 – p87). That day is holy and should be kept wholly for the worship of Him in His honour and glory (30 –p89), and as the least act of thanks and gratitude for His not CONSUMING us even as we breathe, as we still constantly defy and disrespect Him!!! For our Creator patiently restrains His anger 'for the sake of His praise, that He may not cut us off' as we deserve! (40 - 1).

Truly it is the *day* itself that is *blessed and sanctified*, that we are to keep *holy*, not the resting, or the ability to rest on that day (30 – p105). The 'ignominious' teacher and 'mother of abomination', namely the Catholic church (30 –p107), defies YHWH Himself, 'despite the most terrible threats pronounced' by Him 'against those who disobey the command, "Remember to keep holy the Sabbath"' and are Apostate – contradicting and contending against the Almighty Lord Most High. Let it be known that, according to the Bible, 'Sabbath – breaking is an apostasy' (30 – p109). And you can be sure it shall not go unremarked or unpunished by our Omnipotent Creator, YHWH!!!

But other groups such as Christians in Ethiopia and the Waldenses (Protestants) never forgot the true Sabbath observance.' (31 –p6/51). Today the Seventh Day Adventists also honour the original Sabbath, worshipping on Saturday. They give reverence and the time of day, and dedication to our Lord Most High, who is our Creator on a Saturday – from sunset Friday to sunset Saturday. Thank you Lord Jesus for your mercies!

Now, again we see the repeated emergence of pagan sun-worship aka the devil/Satan/Lucifer/the Anti-Christ. But hold fast, for we must remember our Creator commanded the Israelites – His beloved Jews- (and also Christians) to:

> 'take care to yourself that you are not ensnared to follow them....do not enquire after their gods, saying: How did these nations serve their gods? I will do likewise. You shall NOT worship the Lord your God in that way.... Whatever I command you, be careful to observe it.' (Deut. 12 v 29-32;)

> So 'do not learn the way of the Gentiles (pagan Romans) for the wisdom of the people is futile (in vain)',(31 -p 3/51)...

...for, they cut out from trees and fashion (make) for themselves gods, which they decorate with silver and gold and bow down to worhip them. These gods which cannot move by themselves, that they need to prop up and which do not breathe, because they are not Living, (40 - 2). This is idolatry, worship of graven images, which is against our Creator's 2nd commandment, that is just below the 1st solemn decree that we should worship and honour Him only, as He is the only true and living God, and put no other gods before Him.

How futile is it for the people, deceived by 'a deluded mind' (40 - 3) - Satan, to worship anything other than the Lord our Creator? For in a section of the Bible that is in R C standard version 1966, in between Daniel 3 v 23 and v 24, but is omitted in other Bibles:

> Insert v 37: 'Bless the Lord, all you angels of the Lord, sing praises to Him and highly exalt Him forever....v 38

> Bless the Lord all waters above the heaven (clouds), v40
> Bless the Lord, sun and moon... v 41 Bless the Lord stars
> of heaven... (and all celestial and earthly elements, such
> as water, cold, rain and dew, wind and snow)...(v 1 – 68)
>
> ALL are to 'Bless the Lord, and praise and highly exalt
> Him.' (ref. 40 -4)

So if even the sun, moon, stars etc., are to praise and exalt the
Lord Most High, why should man, the Lord's most prized and
beloved creation (after His first beloved angel, fallen from His
grace and favour due to pride, and so become the devil), why I
repeat, should man take it upon himself to bow down and worship the elements, that were also created by our Father, such
as the sun and moon, and which themselves are incapable of
being creators? Surely this is futile! Surely this is foolishness!

Is man that stupid, or so debased and thinks so little of himself, who once was created a beautiful and prized possession,
highly esteemed by the Lord, that he now has to worship created things and elements and idols that are beneath him (41)?
Is he so far removed from the face of our Creator, and from the
first image of himself as made in the Father's image, that is
now corrupted and defaced and displaced by sin and disobedience (Adam and Eve right up 'til today)? Is he so desperate to
seek that which is better and more superior to himself, that he
will worship *anything* that seems 'good' to him? It seems to not
matter how base or repugnant this thing is – wood, tree, sun; or
even the devil/Satan/Lucifer – who has blinded them by his dazzling veil of deceit over their longing and desperate eyes. How
low has man stooped!!!

One area of R C doctrine that particularly disconcerted me for
years, even when I was a teenage devout Catholic, and puzzled me because it did not make sense, was the celebration
of Christ's resurrection on Easter Sunday. I don't have issue
with the resurrection or Easter. It is the *day* of the week that

disconcerts me. Jesus told the Jewish priests that He would 'tear down this temple and rebuild it in 3 days' (37). They mocked Him saying it had taken men years to build it, and He says He can do the impossible? But Jesus was referring not to the bricks and mortar of the building, but to the temple that was His body, which He prophesied would rise up to life again in 3 days from His death on the cross.

By my calculation, 3 days from 'Good Friday' when He was cru- cified and buried, is not a Sunday, but a Monday! Whether it is 'after 3 days' (38) or on the 3rd day (39) according to the differ- ent gospels, it still is not Sunday! Now given what we have just outlined about the corruptions in the church and the Bible, was this a deliberate *mis-* calculation by those in the R C church, who were under the corruptive influence/spell of Lucifer, to have the feast day celebrated on the same pagan day, the Sunday, to keep the observance to the 'sun'-god alias himself?

To make matters worse the dates for the celebration of Easter is shifted to accommodate the celestial moods rather than for the commemoration of Jesus Christ's death and resurrection! This year (2011) Easter has had dates allocated to it from 'Good Friday, Easter Saturday and Sunday and bank holiday Monday' the 22nd to 25th April, three weeks later than the usual March dates. It is rumoured that it has something to do with the moon. What? Surely this cannot be correct!

The celebration of Christ's resurrection from the dead should be in line with when the Jews celebrate their Passover. The Passover a remembrance of when our Mighty Creator delivered them out of bondage/slavery in Ancient Egypt, led to the prom- ised land of Canaan by prophet and patriarch Moses (Exodus). The feast of Passover started from the night that the Lord Most High, reversed Pharoah Rameses II curse on the Israelites, and struck dead the first born of every household in the land, both human and livestock in Egypt instead. The Israelites were only saved from the pestilence of destruction by obeying our

Creator's command to sacrifice a lamb, cook and eat it with unleavened bread, the night before, and daub/put the lamb's blood on the lintel of the doorpost of their homes for protection. That night was to become known as when the Lord 'passed over' their homes and spared their lives (42). The next morning there would be no time to allow yeast/ leaven bread to rise, in the Israelites' haste to depart from Egypt; and thence after Exodus reveals more of the Might and Power of our omnipotent Creator, YHWH, whose sacred name means simply and greatly : 'I AM that I AM' (43). Amen.

So why have the dates allocated to Easter changed this year? Again I reiterate, it was explained as having something to do with the moon. Yet again we see that pagan worship is given precedence over the commands and dictates of the Almighty and the holy sacrifice of His son, our most precious Jesus Christ. Lord have mercy!

Are there no depths to which the devil and his agents will stoop to defy, degrade and deface our Lord and Creator Most High, so that *he* takes precedence over our Creator's most remarkable feat – the RESURRECTION from, and thus defeat of death, and so have the VICTORY? Lucifer's impudence and insults beggar belief!

In order to explain further just how the Roman Catholic church has become the prime agent of Satan, we need to look at the Biblical verses to provide the context and understanding of the meanings of the allegories and prophecies in regard to these, the last days before Christ's second coming. Francis Njau (2010) in Prophecy Explained book 3 – Daniel and Our Destiny (102)... is very enlightening in this respect. He argues that Daniel chapter 2 is further developed in Daniel chapter 7 in regard to the political and religious world situation today. Daniel 7 v 24 talks about 10 horns which indicate 10 political kingdoms, out of which one grew bigger and plucked out 3 of the other horns. This bigger horn was more than a political kingdom. It represents the Roman Catholic church which is also a religious kingdom, that had its roots in Judaism, but whose political and religious seat derived from pagan Rome from around the 4th century AD.

It began with a Roman Catholic priest, Arius, very influential in Alexandria, who taught 'an unorthodox doctrine, that Christ was not fully God, nor was he an eternal being, having been created by the Father way back in Eternity' (102 -1). Although he was excommunicated and later died in exile, his ideas spread and in retaliation, the then still half pagan emperor Constantine, fearing his vision of a united empire via a united church would be put in jeopardy, he convened the first church ecumenical council at Nicea, in AD 325. BUT though Constantine attempted to right the wrong by re-establishing the deity of Christ, the church then overstretched the doctrine right back into reverse 360 degrees!

Because the church was concerned about the divinity of Christ who was sinless, it could not have him born of a sinner. They created the idea of Mary as being sinless and having an immaculate conception. But Njau shows that Psalm 51 v 5, affirms that like the rest of mankind, Mary was also born a sinner. By claiming that Mary was the 'mother of God' they inferred that she was the mother of his divinity, but really she was merely the mother of his humanity. Not content with this, they gave Mary her own divinity, which triggered worship and veneration of her.

Furthermore 'they created a belief in the Assumption of Mary in 1950, that she was miraculously resurrected and taken to heaven bodily and enthronement as Queen of heaven,' (102 -2). In 1965 Pope Paul VI declared Mary as Mother of the Church, and since then her maternal care has replaced 'God' the Father's paternal care of the Catholic Church. Further yet , she has been given a redemptive role alongside our Saviour. Some of the church's faithful have even petitioned the Pope to officially declare her as co-redeemer and co-mediator with Christ, ostensibly helping Christ to do his work of redemption and dispense blessings and grace to believers! According to

Catholic doctrine, she is the queen of heaven from which she co-rules with her son!!! But Njau explains that the only queen of heaven known to us is the IDOL Jeremiah saw being given offerings by Jewish women and which ignited the destruction of Jerusalem and the temple (Jeremiah 7 v 18; Jerem 44 v 15). This is the idol worship that was transferred to the Catholic church and proclaimed as truth. He also writes 'from a simple attempt to protect the deity of Christ, the Catholic church has developed the monstrous doctrine of Mariology, which has shifted the attention of the Catholic faithful from Christ to Mary. This is how Satan hijacked the Catholic church's endeavour to fight Arianism and made it serve his purpose'. (102 -2).

The Roman Catholic church has quite clearly kept its people ignorant and led them astray. It vigorously and aggressively discourages its laity from reading and studying the Scriptures to prevent them discovering the anomalies and discrepancies that exist between what is written in the Bible and the Catholic doctrines (102 -3). This church is doing Satan's work for him, and together they have turned the situation around 360 degrees, back to pagan idol worship of himself as god or gods! We see how still today, long after being cast out of heaven and down to earth, Satan, by inciting mankind, is still challenging, opposing and defying our Creator and stealing His glory, and robbing Him of His joy in His beloved creation, humankind.

Unfortunately Satan still has dominion over the world and its greatest instrument and agent is the Roman Catholic church. This has held sway for over 1500 years, and persecuted the faithful believers in Christ during 1260 years of Apostasy from 538AD, when the Pope took political control, until 1798 when Napoleon arrested Pope Pius VI and abolished the Papacy for a while. This period of 1260 years was prophesied as 'time, times and a half' in Revelation 12 v 6, v14. Adventists have calculated from the prophetic years written in Numbers 14 v 34, Ezekiel 4 v 6, and Daniel 4 v 23, where '7 times' prophesied for Nebuchadnezzar's madness was 7 years. So, a time = 1 year (360 days), times = 2 years (720 days) and a half time = 6 months (180 prophetic days). Noting that there were 360 days in a Jewish calendar, these add up to 1260 days, meaning 1260 years. (Time, times and time and a half also reoccurs in Rev 12 v 14, where the woman – Mary, and her child – Jesus, are given sanctuary and nourishment as they are hidden from the serpent – Satan, who waited to devour them and was thwarted by divine intervention). As the Creator spoke, it came into existence. He prophesied 1260 days of tribulation for the church, and history evidences 1260 years of Apostasy.

However the R C church resumed its sovereignty worldwide – religiously and politically and financially, emanating from Rome, throughout the Western world –Europe, United Kingdom, North and South America, the Australias and tentacles in Africa, Asia, Middle East and Far East. In short – worldwide to the present day. As Njau says ' the Catholic church therefore plays a double role in every country it operates in – a religious and political one. No other religion or Christian denomination, ancient or modern, has ever had such a privilege. It is a MYSTERY of history how a church maintains a political agenda worldwide with NO political power asking why' (102-4).

But it is not so much of a mystery for it was prophesied (103 -1) that many nations (kings) will be 'drunk with the wine of the wrath of her fornication' – her being the 'scarlet woman' or 'harlot', who is namely the R C church. 'On her forehead a name was written: MYSTERY, BABYLON THE GREAT, THE MOTHER OF HARLOTS AND OF THE ABOMINATIONS OF THE EARTH' (103 -2). This woman has deceived many by her sorcery, and is found to be drunk and full of the blood of the saints and martyrs she has killed, and she sits regally on the waters of the sea, which is the peoples and multitudes and nations and 'tongues' (languages) (103 – 3). The drunken nations and kings will weep and lament that 'Babylon is fallen is fallen,' when they see what has become of 'that great city' when her judgement time arrives, and she is made desolate by the hand of the avenging Creator (103

-4). Her outcome will be ruin and desolation, but we must not be sad. Instead all 'heaven and you holy apostles and prophets must REJOICE over her for (God) for our Father has avenged you on her' (103 -5). So we are urged to 'come out of her my people,' so that we do not share in her fate, 'for her sins have reached heaven, and (God) remembers her iniquities (wickedness)'(103 -6).

It was also prophesied that Satan will be released to rise up once more, and will deceive many (104) and also muster up armies from the various kingly and princely allies, to challenge and oppose Christ our Saviour and Sovereign Lord, in the last days, which will culminate at the battle of Armageddon (105). But the outcome of that battle will be that Satan 'the beast' will be captured and together with the 'false prophet' will be 'cast alive into the lake of fire burning with brimstone. And the rest (their wicked allies) will be killed with the sword which pro-ceeded from the mouth of Him who sat on the horse.' He, is Jesus Christ, who will avenge the blood of the saints and mar-tyrs. 'And all the birds were filled with their flesh' (106). So it is no mystery. It was prophesied, so it will happen. And already we are witnessing the proof of prophecies as they come to pass.

The R C church that started so well and was devoted to fol-lowing Jesus Christ, has been corrupted by pagan influences, and has since further corrupted and misled and misguided, mis-treated, exploited, abused, tortured, and murdered those who want to be faithful devotees of Christ our Living Saviour and Redeemer, heaven have mercy! But the religious leaders, the hierarchical and higher echelons of the RC church will not be held blameless for this. They will asked to account for the blood and souls of every one of the 'lost sheep', 'the beautiful flock' that Christ entrusted into their pastoral care. Rest assured, they will NOT escape due punishment for their heinous crimes, and their flouting of our Father Yahweh's eternal and righteous laws.

As we shall see later, the devil has tainted and corrupted other areas of reverence, including holy books, hymns and gospels songs and even evangelical TV broadcast programmes, which have affected so many religious teachings/doctrines. But he has not succeeded in corrupting everyone, and our Creator helps us yet. For example the New and old King James versions of the Bible mark the words Jesus spoke in red, to more easily distinguish them from any other possible devilish corruption elsewhere in the scriptures.

However, our modern, secular decline into decadence has taken over. We are more concerned about gaining money, wealth, fame (for nothing, or for notoriety), and conducting sinful, degrading and debasing lives. These unsavoury qualities are promoted and pushed by the controlling Illuminati through various means, so that even babies and toddlers gyrate to the rhythms of sexy and violent music videos, as well as the rest of us who are exposed to them. We are pushing the self-destruct button on our lives and souls, whilst being manipulated by 'powers that be', and ultimately the devil.

One increasingly pervasive medium that is dominating our lives is the internet through governments promotions in their determination for every home to have a computer. This may seem like a good thing and progress, but there are hidden agendas at play. The push for people, especially young people to use the social networking sites, like face-book, twitter, and various others, is more than encouraging the sharing of knowledge and socialising. It derives from the 'concept of collective intelligence, which is a catholic/New Age/ Evolutionary idea. It is about trying to harness a collective consciousness of groups of individuals into one mind and one thought, on the road to human progress and enlightenment' (44).

This is the latest in mind control, which teaches men to rely on the wisdom and science of men, by the merging of human minds, rather than seek wisdom and learning from our heavenly Father. Yet another tool by which Satan aims to draw people away from our Creator. The propaganda that smoke-screens the 'powers that be' hidden agenda, fuelled by increased prof-its that can be generated from businesses and users of the medium, is that it helps in the war-on-terror. Since 9/11 and 7/7 the governments around the Western world have pushed for computer prevalence in our homes, because they can 'hack' into and access any information that a consumer may hold on their computers or even their mobile phones, even material that has been deleted. Big Brother's Totalitarian State (45) looms ever nearer.

Man's seemingly insatiable urge for world domination comes from none other than the angry, bitter, vainglorious, disrespect-ful, hateful and hating, jealous Lucifer. He still wants to be God and challenges our Father, who is in heaven (46). He disrespect our Father by undermining His credibility amongst the people, and shaking the people's faith in Him. Even suggesting that He does not exist, and that belief in Him is merely superstition and myth, as in the ancient pagan mythologies. Could he get more disrespectful towards the One who created him and all that exists?

Imagine that if you are a parent, and you are challenged by your child who defies your authority, wouldn't you be angry at the total impudence and disrespect from the child you conceived, brought into the world, raised and cared for? (46a) This very child who now turns around and tries to tell *you* what to do, and that you must obey, bow down and give reverence to *him or her*, wouldn't you be mad? Perhaps we can now understand how our Father in heaven must feel - hurt, incredulous and angry at the Lucifer's impertinence, a jumped –up nobody, created from His hands, who now demands to be His equal? Why should He allow the devil to bully and over-power Him? For He is a jealous being, who will 'share His glory with no other' (46b). He has no partners (47), and *He* is the Supreme Being.

The Usurper, and fallen angel Lucifer, disgraced and exiled, does his utmost to spite our Father by taking as many people onto his side, and making them give their allegiance to him and worship him, and so steal them and their souls away from our Creator. He lies, cheats and deceives, bullies, confuses and controls our minds to achieve this aim. He also tries to frighten us into believing that he can read our minds. He cannot. He can put ideas in, but he can only read your reactions, and predict what you might do, based on what he has successfully pro-voked before. Only our heavenly Father can read what is in our minds and hearts. Only *He* is omniscient. He knows us better than we know ourselves, and because He is our Creator and loves us, He understands what we are going through and sends us help.

There is no help for Lucifer however. He is not stupid. He knows he has no chance to get back into our Father's good books, because he refuses to bow down to, and accept His authority and sovereignty over him. He is stubborn, no worse, obstinate. This is not a good look. Determination is okay in moderation, everything in balance except the love of and for our Father. *That* we can do in abundance, to our Father in heaven be the glory!

Allegiance to, worship and love of anything or anyone above our Father in heaven is idol worship, and is contrary to the first of Moses Ten Commandments as written on the stone tablets by the finger of our Father. It doesn't matter if we love the constel-lations – sun, moon, or stars; or make demigods of a lead figure or personality, a loved one – partner, child, parent, best friend; or pets or other 'sacred' animals; or nature or plant; animate or inanimate objects –trees/wood, stone, mountains, the weather forces like wind or thunder (Thor); fame, wealth or money or any other thing. It becomes a problem if it supplants our natural spiritual inclination to give love and adoration that is due to our Father in heaven, our Creator first and foremost. This is unac-ceptable to Him. He 'shall not give His glory to another' and why should He? Without Him none of us would exist, and so we should be glad that He has given us life and a beautiful world to live in, in all of the Universe.

And conversely we should berate and condemn the Usurper, Satan, for corrupting it and us, so that for many of us the world has become a living hell! Please don't blame our Father for the way things have turned out. Lay the blame squarely and appropriately where it belongs – with Lucifer/Satan/ the devil and his various aliases. Idol worship is the ultimate sin, or rebellion to Our Creator. So don't be deceived and let Satan drag you down to destruction in hell with him. His end is coming and is certain. And your fate will be the same as his, if you don't 'wise up' and 'fix up', i.e. change your ways.

But we can't change on our own. (Unlike President Obama's slogan; 'yes we can' (said backwards means– 'thank you Satan – (48/ chp 7 – 60a). We need help. And this comes from the Holy Spirit, the Helper (49) in today's world. He can gently, but firmly and assuredly guide us back to our Father, through us acknowledging and following Jesus Christ's teachings and example of how to best live for now and our future.

Symbology and all the other ways of control our minds and bodies for our deception, ruin and destruction are not the only ways the devil is at work. As mentioned earlier films and videos that portray persons possessed by demons or evil spirits are not a new phenomenon. Demon possession existed long ago, and even Jesus cast out demons from persons possessed by them (50). But demon possession can take more subtle forms, and in ways that are even fleeting and can be noticeable only to the one it is targeted to scare – usually people who are resisting or exposing the evil influences of the devil.

As stated elsewhere, Satan instils ideas into people's minds, so that they may act out of character, to do his will, whether it be harmful to themselves, or to others. So sometimes a person may be deemed to be 'mad' 'crazy' or 'demon-possessed' especially if harmful, and these days that person would be consigned to mental hospital and 'medication'. However sometimes, it is the very people we trust, our family or friends or priest/pastor/imam, who may in fact be used by the devil to scare us out of taking a course of action that he feels is contrary to his purpose. If we choose to resist, desist, expose wrong-doing and ultimately not fall into his traps, he will come after us and use whatever means or persons necessary to stop us. But fear not, because our Father sees our plight, and our true and genuine hearts and helps us through the encouragement and support of Jesus and the Holy Spirit.

Even when the devil uses props to enable his malevolent powers to work, the Lord will protect us. Whether Satan uses symbols, objects – voodoo dolls, locks of hair, etc. for his sorcery, magic, obeah, hexes, witch-craft and other devinations – these can all be cancelled and their effects vanquished by the power of the Almighty, who can turn curses and spells into blessings for the intended victims, those who believe and love Him. So we must be wary and 'wise as serpents' (51) so that we become aware of the very many traps the devil has devised for our ruin and destruction.

Influencers further back in time...

Before the pervasive influence of the media and entertainment industry, power and influence over the people was exerted through religion and ideology, and more recently, science. Right from the beginning Satan acculturised the people to his way of thinking and perverted/corrupted our concept of our Creator as God. He was well aware of the existence of the Book of Life (52), in which all the names of those people who devoted and dedicated their lives to our Father in heaven and followed Jesus would be written for eternal life. So he conjured up the ancient Egyptian Book of the Dead, which we can still see depicts their idea of what the journey to and in the After-life would be like, especially for the Pharaohs. Our obsession with the life after death (brought about through Satan) has continued throughout the Ages.

Currently the Roman Catholics still say mass and pray for the dead, and have feast or holy days such as All Saints day and

All Souls day. These are really a waste of the deceived people's time as we can't help the dead once they are gone. It's too late for them. The time to pray and intercede for them, advise and correct them was when they were still alive. Once dead they can't hear or see you, so it's no use to you or them, praying for them and constantly visiting their graves etc. The 7th day Adventists reading the scriptures, believe that the deceased are just waiting there, waiting for the End of Time for the return of Jesus Christ in all his glory. At that time, only those who have died for Christ's sake will be resurrected, plus those who accused or killed him (the Jewish religious leaders) so that they can witness his return that was foretold (53, chp7 - 50), and realise that he *was* the so-longed-for Messiah (54). The rest of the dead will remain so until the Day of Judgement, when everyone will be held to account for their lives on earth, and the good will be separated and rewarded, from the wicked who will be punished and destroyed.

This is why it is important to understand what Jesus meant when he said 'let the dead bury the dead' (55). He meant those who are dead spiritually, because they were lost in the dark ignorance under the deception of Satan; and were being led into practices that were contrary to our Creator's will for life and the living. This is not to discount our grief – yes we are sorry for losing our loved ones, but we have our memories of them which comfort us (56). However attending to their graves, praying for them etc. will not bring them back, and cannot help them in death. They had their chance for betterment whilst they were still living. How they will fare on Judgement Day will go according to how they lived their lives. You can't help the dead. You can only help the living and yourself.

Unfortunately man's reliance on outward symbols to express ourselves has been exploited by the devil as he continues to deceive and confuse us. In recent decades the impact of racism is still very apparent on Black peoples' lives. The attempts to combat this, following on from the liberation struggles from emancipation from slavery to civil rights movement and the independence of many African and Caribbean countries from direct colonial oppression, are still ongoing. However the attempts to improve the self esteem of Black people, who for so long have been everywhere oppressed and treated as the scourge and dregs of the earth, through slogans like 'Black is Beautiful' and 'Black pride' generated from discovering our great historic achievements and ancestral roots, is taking a dangerous turn for the worse.

More and more Black people, especially the youth, turned off Christianity by what they see as promoted by racist white oppressors, are turning to Islam and Egyptian mythology. But beware, as this reliance on symbology which is one of the devil's tools - his strength, is the route to our downfall. 'Conscious' Black people are currently promoting the use of the Egyptian 'ank' symbol for life, but this comes from their Book of the *Dead.* They are rejecting the Christian 'cross' as to them it represents oppression from racist European white people, as well as reminds us of the kind of *death*, that Jesus Christ underwent at the hands of his persecutors. And the 'crescent moon'(57a & b) of the Moslems (who ironically, also enslaved Africans predating the trans-Atlantic slave trade of the European Christians) was mentioned in the Bible, where YHWH('I am that I am') warned the Israelites against mingling with the heathens (58). And when they disobeyed He punished them by giving them under oppressive attacks and rule by their enemies, heathens and gentiles. One of their enemies was the Midianites also called Ishmaelites, whose men wore ear-rings and hung crescents around their camels' necks (59 - Judges 8 v 21 -28; differing Bible translations – crescents or ornaments). The crescent symbols were left over from the pagan Zoroastrian religion with its many gods, which Prophet Mohammed turned the Arabs away from, but which crept back into Islamic traditions.

The early Christians, under great persecution unto death by lions in the Roman amphitheatres etc, used the code: two halves of a 'fish' in remembrance of Jesus' miracles of loaves and fishes – (60) by which to safely recognise each other in those dangerous times. It was only later that the Roman Catholics changed the symbol for Christianity to the 'cross' or 'crucifix' as reminders of the huge price Jesus paid for mankind – the sacrifice of his life, his death on the cross. Some Christians are returning to using that earlier Christian symbol – the fish. However, because symbology is the devil's weapon against mankind, in his various means of corrupting us, perhaps it is better to NOT use symbols or graven images to express our faith in our Father and Creator. It is better to have faith mentally and spiritually, and to express it in words and actions as Jesus showed us, and in our praises to the Most High, and Almighty Father, who created *LIFE!*

Some of the worst examples of Satan's corruption have been conducted in the name of Christianity and other Holy religions – Judaism and Islam – from the miniscule and almost imperceptible 'doctoring' of the scriptures and doctrines to devilish, abusive and oppressive practices over the people and children. The practices of usury (charging interest, in our modern day, to the extreme – including exorbitant taxation to fuel the excesses, and drunken brawls and incapacitated decision-makers in parliament!), cruelty to the poor and needy, neglect of widows and orphans, impoverishment, child abuse, domestic violence and adultery, the excessive accumulation of material wealth in the churches(, to warfare against other religious people in the fight to convert others, and home-grown oppression of those who reject their religions eg Roman Catholic Apostasy and the Spanish Inquisition of Protestants, Judaic and Islamic fanaticism), all work in favour of Satan's plan to destroy mankind, and to rob our Father in heaven of His joy over His creation.

Unfortunately for us, the devil has his agents working against us even within the religious leaders, doctrines and even through scribes who write the Holy books or hymns or gospel songs, whether they knowingly collude or not. After Jesus' return to heaven after his resurrection, he sent the Holy Spirit to visit the frightened and bewildered apostles as they huddled in a secret room. By the Spirit they were able to speak in 'tongues' (meaning all the languages that were spoken in that region and the world at that time), so that they could take the message of the gospels to the people (Gentiles/heathens /non-converted) everywhere they went. This was so that what our Father decreed and desired: that all peoples could have the chance of salvation throughout the world, and hope of Jesus Christ' return, and eternal life, could be realised.

However the Roman Catholic church delivered its 'mass' to the people in Latin, descended from the Greek and Roman translations from early Christian times, which meant that the majority of ordinary people, who were not versed in Latin, were excluded from really benefitting from the gospel messages. The Papacy was then able to introduce practices like encouraging the people to 'buy' pardons for their souls' forgiveness; told them that they still had a place called 'purgatory' to cleanse their sins after death; and various other doctrines by which the church amassed great wealth and possessions, which we still can see they hold onto today.

The R C church sold Jesus out. By selling their relics, beads and rosaries, crucifixes and various artefacts, memorabilia and papal 'indulgences'- for the pardon of sins, they are making money out of Jesus. They are profiting out of His very death and thus profaning the sacred, and denigrating the very sanctity of the Lord Most High's grace and favour – His forgiveness, which He gives freely and without price, to those who humbly and contritely seek His face. With the church's greed and total disrespect, she mars and disfigures the Lord's beautiful and loving act of forgiveness – that extension of His loving arm to those who were once lost in sin and wickedness, who repent and oft-turning towards Him, seek His help for the salvation of their souls and their very lives, for all eternity. How can these perverse corrupters who say they represent God, be saved from our Lord's condemnation and punishment for leading the people astray and denying them access to heaven (61). Their fate is surely worse than that of Sodom and Gomorrah, suffering the wrath and vengeance of the Lord - 'Vengeance is mine, says the Lord... I will repay.' (62). The R C church and other hypocritical religious leaders shall not be found 'blameless' (63) for the grooming of innocents, when Christ Jesus returns in vengeance.

And our Father will remember those who have suffered and died at the hands of evil-doers, for His name's sake. He will avenge and vindicate those who cry out 'how long must we wait Lord?' (64). He will deliver His final justice at the end of Time. The End is nigh. It will not be long now until Christ returns to claim His loyal devoted followers. Satisfaction and justice will be given to them. The Lord does not take back His word (65), for His word, sworn in righteousness, shall not return (66). He will do it. (67). So we can take comfort in His Word.

Unfortunately, even the modern day evangelists – the Billy Grahams in their popular crusades, and the rise of radio and TV broadcasts - seem to have lost *their* way. Ostensibly they seem to be doing the very thing Jesus instructed us to do - that is: preach the Good News to all corners of the earth, so that everyone may have a chance at attaining eternal life. But in their increased appetite for fame and wealth, they seem to mislead the masses who listen to them, in some of their messages.

For instance, a popular incentive to entice the people to part with their hard-earned money, and give to their coffers is to quote: 'give and it will come back to you, in full measure, pressed down shaken together and running over' (68 - Luke 6 v 37-38). However Jesus was also referring to *forgiveness,* when he made this statement. He meant that we must forgive, and do so with generosity of heart, so that our loving Father will also forgive us our wrongdoings in full measure. He did not mean give our *money* generously so that we can build up the treasury of the religious leaders and evangelists, who purport to be working on His behalf!!! Their behaviour is contrary to the concept and accepted practices of the original priesthood – the Israelite Levites. (69a). Levites were not to accumulate wealth for themselves! Their portion is tithes and offerings (69b -Numbs 18 v 9-21, v24). However, not only do current religious leaders rob the people financially, but also spiritually, as keeping them in ignorance, they lead them astray. In fact YHWH told Moses' brother Aaron, that the service of the priesthood of himself and his sons at the sanctuary and altar was a *gift,* and the Levites were specially chosen to aid in this service, (Numb 18 v 1-10, v 23). So it is a privilege and a gift to serve the Lord Almighty, and not to be profited on!

Even the symbols and very words used in the Holy Books, especially the Bible, the songs of praise and worship have been susceptible to corruption by the devil, despite the warning that apostle John declared at the end of the book of Revelation, that if anyone adds to or takes away from the prophecy therein revealed, that 'God' our Creator will 'add to him the plagues that are written in this book,...and shall take away his part from the Book of Life...' (70 – Rev. 22 v 18-19). For instance one gospel song we sing currently 'Rejoice and be glad.. For the steps of a righteous man are ordered by God,...and rejoice for the marriage of the lamb has come, and the bride has made *himself* ready' supposedly quoting Biblical reference (71 - Rev 21 v 2). However why is the bride represented as male? Surely a bride is female? Even the Christmas carols are not safe (given that it is celebrated during pagan Saturnalia, it is hardly surprising). But in the carol 'Oh come all ye faithful,'...I saw two corruptions of the original concepts or were they typo' errors? You decide. There was: 'Jesus, *sun* of God', (which should be 'son'), and elsewhere: 'come all ye citizens of heaven above' was replaced by 'come bright....' and didn't even make sense in the sentence. Fortunately the congregation stuck to the original version of the carol. As stated earlier, the Usurper, Satan, corrupts the words to deceive us into praising him and to 'big himself up' / make himself grandiose and take the credit and praise that is due to Christ or to our Creator, for himself.

As Christ told the scribes and Pharisees when they accused him of blasphemy – saying that He called himself the 'son of God' – he denied it and said 'it is you that say that I am'(72). He called himself the 'son of man', and as we shall see later, he could never call himself son of 'God' when we analyse who God really is. Again the typo' error 'bright' alludes to the bright sun light – as referred by the Illuminati and pagan sun worship. It is also the devil usurping the idea of Jesus Christ being the spiritual 'Light' who came into the world to save us and give us hope. Like Apostle John at the end of the book of Revelation, Jesus too called for punishment upon those who led the people astray. He called the leaders of the synagogues at the time, 'you brood of vipers and hypocrites!' (73/chp 7 -90g). They were too busy condemning the people for their lesser sins, that they could not see the 'log'(74) in their own eyes that stopped them seeing clearly who really was at fault.

Jesus said it would be worse for them than the perpetrators of wrong-doing, or even the wicked people of Tyre and Sidon who repented, or Sodom and Gomorrah who would have repented had they seen the 'mighty works' witnessed by the Jews,(75), because they gave the people false teachings, and practiced wickedly themselves against the vulnerable in society. With righteous indignation Jesus upbraided the cities and people who refused to listen to his warnings and refused to repent (75a).

He berated his beloved Jews because they had all the prophets come to warn them, up to John the Baptist, yet they refused to heed their words, and they cursed, accused, stoned, assaulted them and killed the Baptist (75b). Yet, he announced something 'greater than ...the temple,... greater than the prophets and John the Baptist is here' amongst them (75c). Who was that greater person? Jesus answers thus: 'for this is he of whom it is written:

"Behold, I send My messenger before Your face,

Who will prepare Your way before You' (75d).

It is none other than 'The son of man' who 'is Lord of the Sabbath' (75c) Amen! Again the Lord Jesus says that sinners will enter the kingdom of heaven before the religious leaders, because they believed him and repented. 'For John the Baptist came to you in righteousness, but you did not believe him, but tax collectors and harlots believed him, and even when you saw it (the sinners repenting), you (*still*) did not afterward repent and believe him (75e). He berated the scribes and Pharisees: 'you search the scriptures because you (mistakenly) believe that in them you will (assuredly) have eternal life, (but) it is (these very scriptures) that bear witness to me; yet you REFUSE to come to me that you may have life...for I know that you do not have the love of God in you', (75f). And again Jesus said

'well did Isaiah prophesy of you hypocrites, as it is written: "this people honour me with their lips, but their heart is far from me. In vain do they worship me, teaching as doctrines – the precepts of man. You leave the commandments of God, and hold fast to the traditions of man,'(75g). Not only does this refer to the Jewish scribes and Pharisees, but also the Roman Catholic church leaders, who change God's laws to suit themselves, including making their own Sabbath. The religious leaders of the Holy Books should know better, but they mislead the people (76), and further advance the devil's cause. So they too, ultimately, will share his fate and destruction in hell. Jesus bemoaned the fate of the people in the world 'because of the things that cause people to sin' and its results, but worse, he warns 'WOE to the man through whom they/sins come!' (76a).

The message for us from Jesus, if we are to be his disciples, that 'unless our righteousness exceeds the righteousness of the scribes and Pharisees , we will by no means enter the kingdom of heaven' (76b). For if the righteousness is not genuine, but hypocritical, then it is like false prophets, leading the people astray. So our righteousness needs to be better than theirs. It needs to be right, real and TRUE.

I grew up thinking there was only one Bible. But over the last few years I've come to realise there are many versions – authorised or not, and editions, in addition to the various translations. There are over 30,000 different Christian denominations, sects or cults in the world today (2011)!!! (107). They have different emphases and doctrines. Yet they are emanating from just ONE man, Jesus Christ, whose teachings culminate in the messages of Good News of hope and salvation and eternal life for all mankind. How is it then possible to have so many variations, with so many versions of the Bible?

Part of it is due to error and nuances attributed to the various translations, but that is not all of it. This alone cannot account for and explain the discrepancies. Muslims criticise and discount the Bible for its many contradictions within it. For our Father does not contradict Himself, otherwise He could not stand for Truth. But there are many discrepancies within Muslim religion also. They have fundamentalists, traditionalists, also separate sects or factions, Sunni, Shia, and also have various versions and translations of the Q'uran. Likewise the Judaic religion has different factions – Sadducees, Pharisees, with different emphases in the Torah.

How is it that these Holy Books - the Torah, Bible, Q'uran - all Holy Scriptures, that stemmed from one founding father, the Patriarch Abraham, whom Yahweh promised as reward for his obedience and faithfulness, to give him descendants as numerous and countless as grains of sand or the stars in the sky, should be so different and hostile to each other? Truly our Father has honoured his promise to Abraham, not merely by blood descendants - the Israelites/Jews, and Ishmaelites/Muslims - but 'children adopted in' to Yahweh's family – those Gentiles and heathens, people of all nations and languages, who have converted to following Christ, *the* most perfect seed of the house of Jesse, and son David.

Abraham was favoured because he chose to recognise that there is only one true Creator, out of all the other false gods that his contemporaries were worshipping. Yahweh was 'well pleased' with him. The Jews, Muslims, and Christians are all Abraham's seed, all descend from him, and come from every race, nation in the entire world. So our Father kept his promise to Abraham and is still fulfilling it today.

However the 3 religions are diverse, and they argue, fight, war against each other, and within themselves, over religion, faith, doctrines, teachings, laws etc. Why is this happening? For surely if they are from the same, one source, are all inspired by the Holy Spirit, sent by our Father, why then are there so many discrepancies and variations, even up unto the point of bloody and devastating killings? Why? Because there is not only one force in the world.

Remember Lucifer, the most beautiful covering guardian angel, when he disrespected our Father, he was cast down to earth, way back when, and was demoted to Satan, because he was vainglorious, disobedient, challenging, and evil. He and the other fallen angels, now demons, that he had convincingly deceived to follow him, along with his human agents, are busy, and surreptitiously active at instilling their lies amidst the truths in the Holy Scriptures. Lies and deceptions are rife, hidden and secreted within these various Books, with subtle variations and nuances, sometimes almost imperceptible. Because most of the Scriptures are true, Satan has skilfully and craftily linked and attached his lies, even a small percentage, to recognisable truths, and presented them as whole truths. In addition, man's own imaginations and wilfulness, aided by Satan's insidious planting of his ideas into the mind, makes further discrepancies. Remember he was once an angel, and can make himself appear as an angel of light (28) though he has become the most ugly demon, the devil. Not even the 'elect' are safe from attempts to deceive them, 'for many shall join with them by intrigue' (108).

So Satan has done a very good job at deceiving mankind, and setting man against each other, so that they have no time to regard and reverence our Father and Creator. They are so pre-occupied that they have no time to love or care for Him, or, there-fore each other. BUT we do have someone who is able to rescue us and redirect our attention to our heavenly Father, Yahweh. That person is none other than our loving Saviour, Jesus Christ. Thanks be to Him for His willing sacrifice, for all our sakes!!!

Some Bibles have included or excluded certain sections of the Bible, depending on the denomination, or developments or updates into more modern languages. For instance the Roman Catholic Standardised version, Catholic edition, 1966, has 74 books, whereas the New King James Version (NKJV) of the Holy Bible, 1982, has only 66 books, which the Seventh Day Adventists recognise as being written by those inspired by the Holy Spirit. This Bible has an omission of a section that is present in the RC Bible: a section that appears between book of Daniel 3, after verse 23 and before verse 24. This omitted section has 68 verses which elucidate the praises the 3 young friends of Daniel - Shadrach, Meshach and Abednego (given Babylonian names, instead of their Jewish names of Hananiah, Mishael and Azariah, Dan. 1 v 6-7). They exhort the elements and every created thing and being to exalt and praise the Almighty Creator, whilst they, together with a guardian angel, stand and dance and sing amidst the raging flames of the fiery furnace into which they were condemned, because they refused to bow down and worship the golden statue, idol of the Babylonian king, Nebuchadnezzar. Faithful to the Lord Creator, they are saved from death, and the king decreed everyone in his king-dom thereafter should worship their God. I have included this section at the end of this chapter, after the references, as an extract or exposition A (from ref 40 – 4).

Another example of a corruption or discrepancy in translation, is in Isaiah 14 v 12. The RC Bible has 'O Day Star, son of Dawn, How you are cut down to the ground.....',

But the SDA NKJV Bible has 'o Lucifer, son of the morning! How you are cut down to the ground. You who weakened the nations!...'

Again I ask is this simply a mistake, or a deliberate attempt to disguise the true identity of the person being cursed by the Lord our Father and Creator? For verses 13 to 15 explain that Lucifer's arrogance, and selfish, egotistical and deluded ambition is to ascend back into heaven and sit on the throne seeking to 'be like the Most High. Yet (he) shall be brought down to Sheol, to the lowest depths of the Pit (of Hell/Hades)' the Lord says. We are reminded that now is Revelation Time, and the truth shall come out.

Yet another discrepancy between different versions shows how the meaning can be totally different depending on the words used and the context. Isaiah 30 v 18 – 22 in the RC Bible has:

'v 18 Therefore the Lord waits to be gracious to you;

Therefore He exalts Himself to show mercy to you.

For the Lord is a God of justice; blessed are all those who wait for him.

V 20 And though the Lord give you the bread of adversity and the water of affliction yet your Teacher will not hide himself any more, but your eyes shall see your Teacher

V 21 And your ears shall hear a word behind you, saying, 'This is the way, walk in it', when you turn to the right ...or left.

V 22 Then you will defile your silver-covered graven images and your gold-plated molten images. You will scatter them as unclean things; you will say to them, 'Be gone!'

However the SDA NKJV Bible has v 20 '..Yet your teachers will not be moved into a corner anymore. But your eyes shall see your teachers.'

Which version is correct? It makes more sense to me to use the first, (RC) version, as the 'Teacher' I understand refers to the Lord Almighty Creator, who is our guide, redeemer and saviour, omnipotent and omni-benevolent, and ever merciful and gracious, as revealed in earlier verse 18. Substituting teachers for Teacher reduces and demeans the magnificence and benevolence of our Creator, altering his good intentions to us completely. It discredits Him and does Him an injustice.

Those who are entrusted by Jesus Christ, who claim that they would follow his teachings and example, and would do his bidding- 'feed his lost sheep' with good wholesome Christ-like principles for 'right living' and give them his promises and hope of salvation of their souls, these religious leaders have a huge responsibility and are accountable to him on Judgement Day. When Pontius Pilate was concerned about condemning the innocent Jesus to death, Jesus reassured him that Pilate 'would have no power over him unless it was given him from above (heavenly Father)'(77), so 'though guilty, he need not worry about having Christ's blood on his hands (Pilate washed his hands symbolically to absolve himself from this guilt(78)). However Jesus did continue and say that it was the one who had delivered Jesus to Pilate who had the greater sin (77). Who was that person? It was the High Priest Caiaphas, who was the religious leader of the beloved Jews (Israelites). Therefore the shedding of Christ's blood and his death falls upon Caiaphas and all those who were against the Lord our Saviour.

Judas was not the only one to be blamed. Judas betrayed Jesus and brought him to the Jewish priests (sold him for 30 pieces of silver (79)), and led the soldiers to the Garden of Gethsemane to arrest him. But it was Caiaphas and the elders who plotted against Jesus, and wanted to capture and kill him, and so manipulated the Roman Governor Pilate into allowing his crucifixion. Whilst Pilate, a Gentile and considered 'unclean', had less blame, the Jews, then beloved and 'righteous' further compounded their guilt of turning away from, and denying the Creator, by crucifying His son, Jesus, their Messiah, whom, to this day, most refuse to recognise as such.

Yet back then, just a week earlier, the Jewish people had welcomed and hailed Jesus, riding on a donkey into Jerusalem, as their king and Saviour. Barely a week later they nailed him to the cross under the auspices of the Roman governor, who proclaimed on a sign above his head, 'King of the Jews' in the prominent languages of the time: Latin, Greek and Hebrew. Enraged, the religious leaders demanded that it be altered to '*he said* I am king of the Jews', but Pilate refused saying 'what I have written, I have written' (80) – thus reinforcing the magnitude of what they had done, and ensuring that the world knew their guilt, and thus ensured that they would be held accountable.

The 'reward' or *punishment* for betraying and delivering Jesus Christ up for death, will be worse than for Sodom and Gomorrah, and this fate is for the religious leaders of that time and also these latter days/ End Times, and for all those who profess to be Christian, yet lead the people, his flock, astray. False teachings, misleading doctrines, false prophets, all are doomed to meet the same fate – death and destruction, in Hell and Hades cast into the lake of fire and brimstone for eternal torment (81).

When Lord Jesus returns, having taken off his priestly robes in which he prayed and interceded on behalf of the saints/ the elect, and replaced them with clothes for vengeance, be sure that 'the Lord will smite the wicked (Assyrians) to the sound of timbrels and lyres. He is stoking up hellfire for them, for a burning place has long been prepared' (82). 'He does not call back his words, but will arise against ....evil doers, and against the helpers of those who work iniquity'(83). For His words sworn in righteousness shall not return (84). When the Lord stretches out his hand, the helper will stumble and he who is helped will fall, and they will all perish together. So the devil is the one who has caused the people to sinfully create graven images (85) and to worship idols –of whatever shape or form. He has confused them so they don't know they are foolish in bowing down to idols, and that it is futile activity. For the devil has blinded and deafened the people to sin. Isaiah asks: 'shall I fall down before a block of wood? Is there not a lie in my right hand, ie an idol, an Abomination –NOT the living One who created me? (86). Man cannot see with his 'deceived soul', his deluded mind, that he is very far from wor-shipping the true being who is his Creator.

BUT all is not lost! Thank you merciful Father. For the Lord says 'turn to Him whom you have deeply revolted, O people of Israel, for in that day (when Jesus Christ returns), everyone shall cast away his idols of silver ...and gold, which your hands have sin-fully made for you (87). Because 'the fear of the Lord' will be their 'treasure' (88), if they are righteous and of 'humble and contrite spirit, and tremble before the Lord' (89). And behold there will be great rejoicing! We shall be glad when the Lord judges on that day – those elect and righteous shall be happy for they will at last be rewarded for their faithfulness, endurance and perseverance in their love of the Lord and *obedience* to Him:

'You shall have a song as in the night when the holy feast/fes-tival is kept;

And gladness of heart as when one sets out to the sound of the flute in going to the mountain of the Lord, the Rock of Israel'. (90).

So if we want to be amongst those who are rejoicing at the end of Time, let us REPENT of our wicked and evil ways, and be oft-turning to the Lord for forgiveness and mercy. And the Lord will be 'well pleased' with us for so doing. For 'there will be more joy in heaven over one sinner who repents, than over 99 righteous persons who need no repentance'. 'There is joy before the angels of God over one sinner who repents' (91)

Even the criminal on the cross beside Jesus, repented and asked to be where Jesus was going, and was blessed with the reply 'Truly, I say to you, today you will be with me in paradise' (92). It is still not too late to repent and say sorry for offending and disobeying the Lord's commands. Probation is still open. Do not be like the antediluvian (93) people in prophet Noah's time, who mocked and rejected his warnings, and left it too late to go into the Ark and were confused and confounded and panicked when, the doors had shut tight and only after 7 days passed did the rains begin and the flood waters rise. Be warned the flood is coming again, not literally, since the Creator promised in His covenant of a rainbow sign that He would not obliterate the earth with waters again. BUT it is coming in the spiritual form of Jesus Christ. *He* is the Flood - the water of Life - who is due to return to us, very very soon from now. He comes to reclaim his own faithful overcomers (94) of trials and sufferings for his name sake, *and* to pass judgement on the righteous and the wicked, and deal with them accordingly.

Will you be amongst the overcomers/the righteous, who have earned their 'robes washed white in the blood of Jesus', and have earned their place in the Book of Life, and who will be 'granted to sit down with' Jesus 'and His Father on His throne' in heaven? Or will you suffer the fate of Satan and end up in the place where 'there will be groaning and gnashing of teeth' and unbearable misery forever more?

I thank Jesus for his mercy and love that he is saving us and will not abandon us, but will come back to take us to where he is, as promised, to be in the mansions in his Father's house, to be with him forever and ever, if we so choose to follow him and heed his words. So hurry! Jesus bids you to waste no more time pursuing sinful pleasures and conceits. Repent now, and return to him, before the door of probation closes tight shut, and you are left to rot in the hell of your own making because you refuse to heed his warnings and you reject his life – giving invitation. Behold Jesus stands at the door and knocks. Will you be wise and let him into your life?

Give the Lord praise all the earth! 'For even have you, (scribes and Pharisees and Roman Catholic church) not read: "out of the mouths of babes and sucklings thou hast brought a 'perfect praise' (95). Praise that is due to the Lord Most High, Almighty Creator, 'who will not give His glory to any other' (96) or allow anyone else to take credit for His works, and certainly not to the Usurper who is the devil/Satan/Lucifer. The evil one will certainly burn in Hell in the lake of fire and brimstone (97) for his unbelievable impudence and disobedience. For assuredly, 'the devil is to be cast, along with the beast and the false prophet, into the lake of fire and brimstone to be tormented forever and ever' (98). This is the fate of them and anyone else who gives their allegiance to them. I warn and beg you, do not be deceived any longer. Open your eyes to the truth, and REPENT and turn to the Lord, before probation is over.

Take heed also that it is not only the Christian Holy books that have been subjected to corruptions from what Muhammed originally dictated in the Qu'ran. It has transpired recently, that those who do not want the people to convert to Christianity which they consider as a corrupt religion, have made serious errors in their translations, and in their claims about what is said about Jesus Christ in the Qu'ran. The Moslem religious leaders speak negatively about Jesus, and like the Jews, they will not acknowledge Him as the son of the Creator, but only as a prophet, a messenger of God. But for instance S.3.45 where Muqurrab is used to describe him as 'near to God', a newer translation interprets it as 'nearest' ie standing shoulder to shoulder with God. Jesus is mu'ayyad, which means 'aided by the Holy Spirit' (99). But nowhere else in the Qu'ran is said that anyone else is aided by the Holy Spirit. And the commentaries that are given in the Qu'ran to 'explain' the text are not always reliable and may in fact be misleading too. There was a new translation due out in the summer (2011) which is a more literal translation of the Qu'ran from the beautiful Arabic language into English. This may give more clarity and light on the truth of what Muhammed said about Jesus Christ (according to pastor Bahadur.).

During the European period of Enlightenment, emerging out of the Dark Ages of confusion and decline in religious influence, the ideology of modern Science arose to take over the peoples' minds. Darwin's Theory of Evolution, Science of Race and racism overtook religious 'conversion' and persecution and indoctrination for exploitation through enslavement of Africans, the effects of which are felt in the descendants today, especially through the new religion – Psychiatry. Many Black people are constrained under mental slavery of psychiatric 'treatments' and drugs (100) that cruelly torture, restrain, deform and weaken the physical and mental resolve of the descendants of ancient Egyptians. (Notice how the devil did not defend them against our Creator's wrath, and how he actually increases the punishments their descendants suffer, and mocks us in our ignorance of what happened to us before).

However, unlike the devil, our Father in heaven has not abandoned us to the devil's cruel tyranny of psychiatry. He sends us help out of our mental slavery, through Jesus Christ and the Holy Spirit guiding prophets to show them the way out. For yes, He is mighty, truly Awesome, forgiving and merciful. Praise and thank Him for His love for us.

Our Father is truly awesome and has a great sense of humour. For no matter what His word, once He speaks it, it does not return to Him. Jesus said that the gospels should be preached everywhere, to all nations and tongues (Mark 13 v 9-11), until the time of His return, so that everyone might have a chance of salvation in the time left – this, our probation period. And it seems that despite themselves, even false prophets and false preachers, egged on by Satan, cannot help but do our Father's command. For they do still preach the gospels, the word of our Lord, no matter their motives, but the word IS preached throughout the world. According to Philippians 1 v 15 – 18:

> 'Some preach the gospel out of envy and strife, preaching Christ from selfish ambition, not sincerity, and seeking to add "affliction to his (apostle Paul's) chains", (ie. Cause him more harm than good). Others preach out of goodness and love. But "what then"? Only that in every way, whether in pretence or in truth, (v 18) CHRIST IS PREACHED, and in this we rejoice!'

Yes, so even the money-grabbing evangelists (not all of them are), - from the campaigners and crusaders to the TV and radio evangelists – ultimately they are still serving the Almighty's purpose in ensuring that the gospel is preached to the ends of the earth. Everyone will have a chance to hear it, have a chance to Repent and to Return to the Lord before Christ returns, in his 2nd Advent. Halleluiah! For some *will* turn to the Lord, as I have, and be blessed, and I pray, be saved by discerning through the Holy Spirit, the truths out of the misguiding information and doctrines. For those who seek the Almighty Father will find His truths.

'Ask and you shall receive. Knock and the door will be opened' (Luke 11 v 9).

The door will be opened, as will your eyes and minds and hearts be, to our Saviour be glory!

Concurring with Phil. 1 v 23 – 24, 'being hard-pressed/ torn between the two, I desire to die and be with Christ, which is far better', having already seen a glimpse of heaven in July 1990. And before this, as a 14 year old, almost suicidal teenager, victimised, and abused/oppressed and isolated within my own home. But was told in that vision, by Virgin Mary, a pupil at a R C convent school then, that I couldn't go to heaven (as yet, I was to understand years later); and that I would grow up and leave home, so hold on, be patient. And again, Phil. 1 v 29 'for to you it has been granted on behalf of Christ, not only to believe in Him, but also to suffer for His sake' if we wish to be his disciples. It is a personal favour from Christ as His believers and his disciples. We must be prepared to carry our crosses to victory in His liberty that He so painfully won on Calvary. We can do nothing less, and there is NO other way to salvation in eternal Life, than through the Way, the Truth and the Light, that is Jesus Christ.

Thank you, loving and gracious Jesus, for your sacrifice for us all. Selah.

Diag 4: Table of Events since the birth of Jesus Christ (blood-line and spiritual descendants from faithful Abraham,
as numerous as grains of sand, or stars in the universe:)

DATES:

AD00   Christ Jesus born, line of Israel, David, into Judaism – Old Testament

0030-33   Christ preached the Good News – New Testament – Christianity.
             Was crucified, died and resurrected. Apostles spread the gospels.

538   Christianity went into the wilderness of Apostasy – Dark Ages of
             spiritual darkness and confusion.

570   Muhammed born, line of Ishmael, - Islam.

             The Golden Age of Islam. Moslems saved a few Bibles from burning in
             the Christian Apostasy (ref 101).

1517   Luther posts writ protesting against the Roman Catholic corruption in
             Christianity. Spanish Inquisition of those who protested and turned
             from Roman Catholicism.
             Renaissance, Reformation and Bibles become more accessible in
             translations and availability to the masses.
             Protestantism becomes more diverse and popular.

1844   The great disappointment of those who calculated when Christ would
             return.
             Birth of Seventh Day Adventist church awaiting the 2nd Advent of Christ
             .

21st cent.   More prophets emerging. Some Muslims and later, remnant Jews
             convert to Christianity.

Future: 2nd Advent of Christ at the End of Time (Date only known to our Father,
             our Creator)

             3rd Advent of Christ & The Final Battle Satan wages against Our Father
             in Armageddon /Rapture.   OUTCOME: Satan and his followers
             defeated, and cast into hell - destroyed completely.

             Judgement Day – books opened and only the faithful whose names are
             written in the book of Life, will be saved and live for eternity.

Living in the New heaven and New earth, in full communion with Our Creator, Jesus
Christ and Holy Spirit – completed and sealed Perfect Circles

Diagram 4: Table of Events

EXTRACT:-

See ref. 40 -4 (verses 1 – 68 in between Daniel 3 v 23 and 24, of Roman Catholic Revised Standard Version, 1966).

Dan. 3 v 23: And these three men, Shadrach, Meshach, Abednego, fell bound into the burning fiery furnace.

1.'*And they walked about in the midst of the flames, singing hymns to God and blessing the Lord. 2. Then Azariah (Abednego) stood and offered this prayer, in the midst of the fire he opened his mouth and said:*

3. "Blessed art thou, O Lord, God of our fathers, and worthy of praise; and thy name is glorified forever.

4. For thou art just in all that thou hast done to us, and all thy works are true and thy ways are right, and all thy judgements are truth.

5. Thou hast executed true judgements in all that thou hast brought upon us and upon Jerusalem, the holy city of our fathers, for in truth and justice thou hast brought all this upon us because of our sins

6. For we have sinfully and lawlessly departed from thee, and have sinned in all things and have not obeyed thy commandments;

7. We have not observed them or done them, as thou hast commanded us that it might go well with us.

8. So all that thou hast brought upon us, and all that thou hast done to us, thou hast done in true judgement.

9. Thou hast given us into the hands of lawless enemies, most hateful rebels, and to an unjust king, the most wicked in all the world.

10. And now we cannot open our mouths; shame and disgrace have befallen thy servants and worshippers.

11. For thy name's sake do not give us up utterly, and do not break thy covenant, 12. and do not withdraw thy mercy from us, for the sake of Abraham thy beloved and for the sake of Isaac thy servant and Israel thy holy one, 13. to whom thou didst promise to make their descendants as many as the stars of heaven and as the sand on the shore of the sea.

14. For we, O Lord, have become fewer than any nation, and are brought low this day in all the world because of our sins.

15. And all this time there is no prince, or prophet, or leader, no burnt offering, or incense, no place to make an offering before thee or find mercy.

16. Yet with a contrite heart and a humble spirit may we be accepted, as though it were with burnt offerings of rams and bulls, and with tens of thousands of fat lambs;

17. Such may our sacrifice be in thy sight this day, and may we wholly follow thee, for there will be no shame for those who trust thee.

18. And now with all our heart we follow thee, we fear thee and seek thy face.

19. Do not put us to shame, but deal with us in thy forbearance and in thy abundant mercy.

20. Deliver us in accordance with thy marvellous works, and give glory to thy name, O Lord! Let all who do harm to thy servants be put to shame;

21.Let them be disgraced and deprived of all power and dominion, and let their strength be broken.

22. Let them know that thou are the Lord, the only God, glorious over the whole world."

23 Now the king's servants who threw them in did not cease feeding the furnace fires with naptha, pitch, tow and brush.

24. And the flame streamed out above the furnace forty-nine cubits,

25. And it broke through and burned those of the Chaldeans whom it caught about the furnace.

26. But the angel of the Lord came down into the furnace to be with Azariah and his companions, and drove the fiery flame out of the furnace,

27 and made the midst of the furnace like a moist whistling wind, so that the fire did not touch them at all or hurt or trouble them.

28 Then the three, as with one mouth, praised and glorified and blessed God in the furnace, saying:

29 "Blessed art thou, O Lord, God of our fathers, and to be praised and highly exalted for ever;

30 And blessed is thy glorious, holy name and to be highly praised and exalted for ever;

31 Blessed art thou in the temple of thy holy glory and to be extolled and highly glorified for ever.

32 Blessed art thou, who sittest upon cherubim and lookest upon the deeps, and to be praised and highly exalted for ever.

33 Blessed art thou upon the throne of thy kingdom and to be extolled and highly exalted for ever.

34 Blessed art thou in the firmament of heaven and to be sung and glorified for ever.

35 Bless the Lord, all works of the Lord, sing praise to him and highly exalt him for ever.

36 Bless the Lord, you heavens, sing praise to him and highly exalt him for ever.

37 *Bless the Lord, you angels of the Lord, sing praise to him and highly exalt him for ever.*

38 *Bless the Lord, all waters above the heaven, sing praise to him and highly exalt him for ever.*

39 *Bless the Lord, all powers, sing praise to him and highly exalt him for ever.*

40 *Bless the Lord, sun and moon, sing praise to him and highly exalt him for ever.*

41 *Bless the Lord, stars of heaven, sing praise to him and highly exalt him for ever.*

42 *Bless the Lord, all rain and dew, sing praise to him and highly exalt him for ever.*

43 *Bless the Lord, all winds, sing praise to him and highly exalt him for ever.*

44 *Bless the Lord, fire and heat, sing praise to him and highly exalt him for ever.*

45 *Bless the Lord, winter cold and summer heat, sing praise to him and highly exalt him for ever.*

46 Bless the Lord, dews and snows, sing praise to him and highly exalt him for ever.

47 Bless the Lord, nights and days, sing praise to him and highly exalt him for ever.

48 Bless the Lord, light and darkness, sing praise to him and highly exalt him for ever.

49 Bless the Lord, ice and cold, sing praise to him and highly exalt him for ever.

50 Bless the Lord, frosts and snows, sing praise to him and highly exalt him for ever.

51 Bless the Lord, lightnings and clouds, sing praise to him and highly exalt him for ever.

52 Let the earth bless the Lord; let it sing praise to him and highly exalt him for ever.

53 Bless the Lord, mountains and hills, sing praise to him and highly exalt him for ever.

54 Bless the Lord, all things that grow on the earth, sing praise to him and highly exalt him for ever.

55 Bless the Lord, you springs, sing praise to him and highly exalt him for ever.

56 Bless the Lord, seas and rivers, sing praise to him and highly exalt him for ever.

57 Bless the Lord, you whales and all creatures that move in the waters, sing praise to him and highly exalt him for ever.

58 Bless the Lord, all birds of the air, sing praise to him and highly exalt him for ever.

59 Bless the Lord, all beasts and cattle, sing praise to him and highly exalt him for ever.

60 Bless the Lord, you sons of men, sing praise to him and highly exalt him for ever.

61 Bless the Lord, O Israel, sing praise to him and highly exalt him for ever.

62 Bless the Lord, you priests of the Lord, sing praise to him and highly exalt him for ever.

63 Bless the Lord, you servants of the Lord, sing praise to him and highly exalt him for ever.

64 Bless the Lord, spirits and souls of the righteous, sing praise to him and highly exalt him for ever.

65 Bless the Lord, you who are holy and humble in heart, sing praise to him and highly exalt him for ever.

66 Bless the Lord, Hananiah, Azariah and Mishael, sing praise to him and highly exalt him for ever; for he has rescued us from Hades and saved us from the hand of death, and delivered us from the midst of the burning fiery furnace; from the midst of the fire he has delivered us.

67 Give thanks to the Lord, for he is good, and his mercy endures for ever.

68 Bless him, all who worship the Lord, the God of gods, sing praise to him and give thanks to him, for his mercy endures for ever".

(end of extract verses 1 – 68, between Dan. 3 v 23 and 24).

In similar vein psalms 148 and 150 of David give exuberant praise:

(taken from The Holy Bible, The Amazing Facts Prophecy Study Edition, NKJV, 2008, Thomas Nelson, Inc. (The Holy Bible, New King James Version, 1982, Thomas Nelson, Inc.)

Psalm 148: PRAISE the LORD!

Praise the LORD from the heavens;

Praise Him in the heights!

2   Praise Him, all His angels;

Praise Him, all His hosts!

3   Praise Him, sun and moon;

Praise Him, all you stars of light!

4   Praise Him, you heavens of heavens,

And you waters above the heavens!

5   Let them praise the name of the LORD,

For He commanded and they were created.

6   He also established them forever and ever;

He made a decree which shall not pass away.

7   Praise the LORD from the earth,

You great sea creatures and all the depths;

8   Fire and hail, snow and clouds;

Stormy wind, fulfilling His word;

9   Mountains and all hills;

Fruitful trees and all cedars;

10   Beasts and all cattle;

Creeping things and flying fowl;

11   Kings of eh earth and all peoples;

Princes and all judges of the earth;

12   Both young men and maidens;

Old men and children.

13   Let them praise the name of the LORD,

For His name alone is exalted;

His glory is above the earth and heaven.

14   And He has exalted the horn of His people,

The praise of all His saints -

Of the people of Israel,

A people near to Him.

Praise the LORD!

And also Psalm 150:

PRAISE THE LORD!

Praise God in His sanctuary;

Praise Him in His mighty firmament!

2   Praise Him for His mighty acts;

Praise Him according to His excellent greatness!

3   Praise Him with the sound of the trumpet;

Praise Him with the lute and harp!

4   Praise Him with timbrel and dance;

Praise Him with stringed instruments and flutes!

5   Praise Him with loud cymbals;

Praise Him with clashing cymbals!

6   Let everything that has breath praise the LORD,

Praise the LORD!

(extracts from psalms 148 and 150 are quoted in E. G. Whites' 'This Day with God', June 20, p180, 1979, c The Ellen G. White Estate, Inc. USA, of special importance for me in June 2012).

Truly, who would worship anything or anyone other than the Lord Most High, our Father and Creator YHWH , after this? Bless His holy name and sing praise to Him and highly exalt Him forever and ever for all Eternity! Halleluiah forever!!!

REFERENCES chap 8

(a) – beautiful Lucifer, covering cherub, guardian angel, later became Satan. Ezekiel 28 v 13-17; E G White, ibid Patriarchs & Prophets, 1958, Review & Herald Publishing Assocn, USA, Pacific Press Publish. Assocn, Canada, (see also chp7 ref 97).

1 Mahomet and Islam by William Muir, 1886, Darf Publishers ltd., London, p37. The Word was the Creator, John 1 v1-5.

2 Only the devil created the saying 'partners in crime', for he is deceitful, disobedient and destructive.

3 Alone-ness is his domain and element. He is used to it, which is why when people spend protracted time alone, the devil and his demons come to tempt and torment them.

4 Yahweh and the Jewish star; Allah and the Muslim crescent; God and the Christian cross. The three come together to God in Isaiah 19 v 23 -25: 'Blessed be Egypt my people, Assyria the work of my hands, Israel my heritage'. And Acts 3 v 25 -26.

5 Now barren and mysteriously hidden, because God forbad anyone else to see it after banishing Adam and Eve.

6 ibid Mahomet and Islam p38-39. Muhammed took a handful of followers in his hagira to Abyssinia/Ethiopia, and was given refuge by king Negus the Christian.

7 Writing is a distinctly human ability of all God's creatures.

8 Zoroaistrians.

9 There is no missing link despite Darwin's theory. God in His mercy decided to recreate humankind as He had originally made Adam and Eve, in their beauty.

10 Isaiah 19 v 18 -22. Rev. 17 and 18, describe the harlot, scarlet queen, of Babylon, how she corrupted all the nations with her wine and fornication and idolatry. But note 'Babylon has fallen' as the queen who sat so proud and glorious, falls and is burnt in the fire of the wrath of justice and will have double portion of woes and torments to what she meted out to the saints and martyrs. The saying 'O how the mighty have fallen' applies to the great Ancient Egyptians who defiled themselves with pride, conceit and idolatry and fornication and incest, and consequently fell into disgrace and destitution, and became enslaved themselves later down the centuries.

11 Isaiah 19 v 16 -17, the Lord will make Judah (Israel) a terror to Egypt. Deut 7 v 6-10, the Israelites are a 'holy' and 'special people' to the Lord 'God'. He swore to their forefathers an oath which He kept when He took them out of slavery in Egypt. Deut 30 v 6, v19, the Israelites were set apart by circumcision of their foreskins. But now the Lord will 'circumcise their hearts' and their descendants, not physically but spiritually, so that they will love the Lord, 'God'. He called heaven and earth to witness this solemn blessing and cursing, life and death, and tells them to choose life for them and their descendants. That was what the Lord told them after he had delivered them from slavery in Egypt. He reminded them that they came to Egypt under Joseph as merely 70 persons, yet when they left, they numbered multitudes. Thus His promise to faithful and obedient Abraham was honoured and fulfilled, for they numbered as stars in the heaven and grains of sand on the sea shores.

12 Is. 19 v22.

13 Is. 25 v 7 -12. Revelation of the Truth, and death is to be swallowed.

14 Jews refuse to acknowledge Jesus Christ as the Messiah, Matt 26 v 63 – 66; the stubborn refusal of a wicked and adulterous generation Matt 12 v 38 -42; brood of vipers who persecute and kill prophets and wise men Matt 23 v 33 -39.

15 (also chp 7 ref 86) To make Jews jealous of Gentiles and now the Muslims. The Jews' Semitic brothers , the Muslims are to come to Him first, through Christ, Rom. 10 v 19 – 20. It is the turn of the descendants of Abraham's other son, the Ishmaelites /Muslims to learn to love our Father, Allah/Yahweh/ The Great I AM that I AM, through the Way who is Jesus Christ.

16 Remnant Jews – Roms 9 v 27; Roms 11 v 1 -5; 'remnant by grace'.

17 We should not boast over, or think ourselves better than the Jews, Roms 11 v 18.

18 Roms 10 v21, stubborn, disobedient Jews.

19 Those ' grafted in' are now 'adopted children' Roms 11 v 19 -24. They have become brothers and sisters in Christ. They have become sons and children of our Father, Roms 9 v 25 -26; 1 John 3 v 1, those who keep the commandments of God, and have the faith of Jesus. Those who pursue endearing qualities are to be His children 1 Timothy 1 v 5, 6 v 11. Beloved qualities e.g. love, faith, kindness, endurance.

20 The discovery in 1799 by a French soldier on Napoleon's expedition in Egypt of the Rosetta Stone, that was originally decreed in 196BC by Ptolemic Pharoah V, with tri-lingual inscriptions of Greek, hieroglyphs and demotic Egyptian, afforded the translations into Greek and Roman languages (Latin) of a similar time period. (google: www. Rosetta Stone). Black Guyanese historian of South America, Dr. Ivan van Sertima, (1980s) claimed that an African-American man was only one of two people who was able to translate and speak hieroglyphics and made the link between

the hieroglyphs on the Egyptian pyramids with those on the Aztec/ Inca/Mayan pyramids and Olmec monuments in Pre-Columbian Americas from Mexico to Peru and Chile in South America. Van Sertima showed that the Egyptians must have travelled to the Americas long before the 15th century transatlantic slave trade activated by Europeans, and they were not then slaves, but masters of theirs and others destinies - a mighty world power.

The Egyptians were served and aided by the Semitic Phoenicians of Tyre and Sidon, who were originally pale-skinned and straight -nosed, but through interracial mixing by the time of Hannibal of Carthage, had become dark-skinned (black) and broader nose, as evidenced on coins and skeletons of his period. The Phoenicians aided the Egyptians against the warring Assyrians (Western Asiatic/Middle Eastern power), and helped them in trading, and sea-faring explorations to the Americas. Dr van Sertima contends that the Egyptians sailed from North Africa, west down the Mediterranean, and by accident(?) via sea currents, ended up in Central America circa 948 – 680BC. This led to contact of Nubian(Black) Egyptian and Phoenician visitors/invaders who influenced the Olmec and Mayan developments into the greatest central American civilisation of AD250 – 900. They were ruled by Black/Nubian Egyptian terrifying kings for blood thirsty gods, like the god of de-capitation, who required much blood letting and blood sacrifices as surety for plentiful harvests and peaceful and successful empire. (ref notes p 14,-81 of ibid 1992).

Refs. They Came Before Columbus: The African Presence in Ancient America, 1977, Random House, and African Presence in Early America, edited by van Sertima, 1992, Journal of African Civilisations Ltd., Inc. VHS?DVD : Time Life's *Lost Civilisations* – MAYA The Blood of Kings, 1995, Time Life Video and Television, Ottho Heldringstraat 5, 1066 AZ Amsterdam, The Netherlands. Also VHS/DVD: Time Life's *Lost Civilisations* – EGYPTIANS Quest for Immortality, 1995.

21 Psalm 37 especially v 4 -6; psalm 73 v 27.

22 (chp 7 ref 83) Matt 6 v 31 – 33. It is pointless 'storing up riches/treasures' on earth that are perishable.

23 Angela Y Davis, 2003, Are Prisons Obsolete? Open Media Series, Seven Stones Press, New York, UK & Australia.

23a Confusion over gender and sexuality - see Deut 22 v 5 ' a woman shall not wear anything pertaining to a man', nor vice versa. 'It is an abomination to the Lord'. This extends to cross-dressing, gender-bending, trans-genders, trans- , and homosexuals. Levit 18 , Levit 20 v 13-16, Deut 7 v 26, for abominations and perversions.

24 Doreen Joseph, 1983, 'What happens when Baby-Father is Absent or Part-time?' article in West Indian Digest magazine, pp 21 -33, of Caribbean Times, London, Hansib Publications; D. Joseph co-author (1987)of Black People in Brent - 'section 3: some explorations in the perceptions, attitudes and activities among a group of Black Single Mothers' pp 81 – 116, A Pilot Study conducted for the Black Workers Support Group (Brent) BWSG, Hansib Publications Ltd., London.

25 Lady Gaga performed in a dress made of raw meat at the MTV MusicVideo Awards in Los Angeles, 13 Sept 2010. She had been criticised the previous week (8th Sept) for wearing a bikini version of raw meat for a Japanese magazine photo shoot. Animal Rights Activists protested.

26 Beyonce, 24th Nov 2010, interview about her personal film documentary showing the lonelier side of fame – where she broke down in tears, questioning why she had been given her talents and fame when she felt so lonely in such a heavily populated place as China - whilst she was on her alter-ego world tour 'I am Sasha Fierce'.

27 'I will not give my glory to another' says the Lord our Father and Creator, Isaiah 42 v 8; 'I am the Lord, that is my name, my glory I give to NO other; nor my praise to graven images', Is. 43 v 10-13, Is. 44 v 6 – 8, Is. 45 v 5, Is. 46 v 9 – 11, Is. 48 v 9 – 11.

Is. 43 v 11 'I, even I, am the Lord, and besides Me there is no Saviour'; Is. 45 v 22, 'For I am (YHWH), there is no other god'. YHWH does not take back His word/ His word does not return to Him once spoken in righteousness', Is. 45 v 23 -25.

28 For the devil can transform himself into an angel of light, 2 Corin. 11 v 14.

28a Devil causes war in heaven and is cast down to earth as punishment, Rev 12 v 7 – 9, v 12.

29 Freyr, the Anglo-Saxon Norse sun-god. (Thor, god of thunder). www. About.com – ancient and classical history, sun gods and sun goddesses by N S Gill.

30 Danny Shelton, Shelly J Quinn, 2005, Ten Commandments Twice Removed, Remnant Publications Inc. USA. (pp 76, p100 – 101); Judaizing p102; Seventh day Holy Sabbath p101 – 102; Exodus 20 v 8 -11, Exod 31 v 13; ibid p104; ibid inside cover – 10 commandments, p65 -66 God's laws. (see end of chp 8 for full comparison).

31 Laverna Patterson, 2001, History of the Church – Prophecy. www.teachinghearts.org/dre04historynotes.html

32 John 13 v 3 -20, Jesus washed his disciples' feet to show them they must treat each other as equals, (no one superior to the other). Luke 7 v 37 -48, Mary Magdalene washes Jesus' feet with her tears and dries them with her hair, embalming them with very expensive perfumed oils.

33 Why do Christians celebrate Christmas day on December 25th? By Mary Fairchild. About.com. http://christianity.about.com/od/Christmas/f/christmashistor.htm (Dec. 2010)

Why do we celebrate Christmas on December 25th? By W. John Walsh; and by President David O. McKay. (Dec. 2010). www.Lightplanet.com/mormons/daily/holidays/celebrate_christmas.html

34 (chp 2 ref 18) Potter – clay, (Is. 45 v 9 -10, Is. 29 v 16 – 17; 2 Thess. 2 v 1-12, Satan exalts himself as God.

35 1) Matt 23 v 13; 2) Matt 18 v 6-7; 3) Matt 1 v 20 – 24.

36 1) gnat/camel, Matt 23 v 24; speck/log , Matt 7 v 3 -5, Luke 6 v 41 -42; 2) Can the blind lead the blind? Luke 6 v 39.

37 Jesus says He will tear down the temple and rebuild in 3 days – He means His body that is a temple, John 2 v 19 -22.

38 After 3 days: Matt 12 v 39 -40, sign of Jonah in the belly of the whale 3 days and 3 nights, Jesus will be in the heart of the earth as long; Mark 8 v 31; Mark 9 v31, Mark 10 v 34.

39 On the 3rd day: Matt. 16 v 21, 20 v 19; Luke 18 v 33, 24 v 7.

40 -1:Isaiah 48 v 9, YHWH restrains His anger. He is patient and long-suffering and merciful. He is NOT murderous like Hitler, Hussein, or Satan and his fiercesome gods. -2: Futility of worshipping idols: Is. 41 v 7 as idols can't stand by themselves and have to be propped up 'by pegs' 'like helpless scarecrows', Jerem 10 v 2-5;

idols are 'useless', 44 v9 -20, 45 v 20 -22, 46 v 5 -7. For only He is the Creator and there is none like Him, Is 46 v 8 – 10; Jerem 10 v 6 & v 10, 'He is the everlasting King... the whole earth trembles at His anger. The nations hide before His wrath'.

-3: idol block of wood an abomination if worship it, Is 44 v 18 -19.;

-4: Daniel 3 v 23 -24 (in-between this verse is the Roman Catholic inclusion verses 1 -68 of praise and exaltation to the Lord our Father, by Shadrach, Meshach and Abednego, - see full extract at end of chapter 8). Is. 2 v 1-3, all nations and many people will come to the house of the Lord, that shall be exalted above the hills.

Is 2 v 11& v 17, the Lord alone shall be exalted on that day. Is 2 v 20, 'in that day man will cast away his (man-made) idols.'

41 Isaiah 40 v 18 – 25, idol/graven image –worship is against our Creator; Is. 41 v 21 -24, idols are worthless and their worshippers are 'detestable'.

42 Exod. 12 v 1 -20.

43 I AM that I AM, Exod 3 v14.

44 www.mk.co.uk/article/2010/1/6/collective-intelligence-semantic-systemsandsocialmedia-the-bermuda-triangle

45 George Orwell's book '1984', published in 1949 by Secker & Warburg.

46 Satan lied to the other angels, saying that 'God's' laws are not just, and so God did not deserve to be worshipped or have their allegiance still, E G White ibid Prophets and Patriarchs, chp 1, pp 35-39. Satan challenges the authority of Yahweh. But, the Lord waits patiently for the devil to be exposed by his own hand, so that those who are watching will see that indeed the Lord's laws and statutes are true and just and honourable. Is 42 v 21, 'the Lord is well pleased for His righteousness sake; He will exalt the law and make it honourable. Take heed, the Lord *will* be exalted.

46a Cain from the off inherited the sin of disobedience from his parents, Adam and Eve, and harboured unbelief, rebellion and disregard for the laws and will of Yahweh, sinking into degradation by killing his brother Abel out of jealousy, E G White ibid, Patriarchs & Prophets, chp 5, pp 71-74. Gen. 4 v 1-16.

46b Isaiah 42 v 8; 43 v 10-12; 44 v 6-8; 46 v 9; 48 v 11.

47 No partners – Isaiah 40 v 25; 47 -1 = Is. 40 v 28 'the Lord is the Everlasting One, Creator of the ends of the earth'; 47 – 2 = Is 40

v 21-25, our Creator 'sits enthroned about the circle of the earth... he brings princes and rulers of the earth down to nothing..., and He has no equal'. YHWH brought down to their knees once great rulers like Pharoah Rameses II, and He will do so again with modern state and church leaders who have united and joined forces in Satan's army, and in the battle of Armageddon to come, His son the rock, Jesus Christ will crush them to nought, and be victorious for all Eternity. Halleluiah!

48 (chp 7 ref 60a) google Professor Griff, exposes the Satanic Illuminati organisation behind the Music and film entertainment industry, at great risk to his safety.

49 (chp 7 ref 43) Holy Spirit/ Helper/ Comforter, E G White Patriarchs and Prophets, Introduction pgs 2,4; John 14 v 16 -17, v 25 – 26; John 16 v 13.

50 Jesus cast out demons in 'Legion' into herd of swine, Mark 1 v 23 -27, v 34; Luke 8 v 26 – 36.

51 (chp 7 ref 78b) Matt 10 v 16-17, 'wise as serpents'.

52 The '144,000' are 'those whose names are written in the Book of life' – Rev 21 v 27, who 'shall enter the Holy city of Jerusalem' –Rev 21 v 10, which is beautifully decorated with gems and beautiful flora/vegetation, from which 'anything that defiles or causes an abomination or a lie (Rev 21 v 27) shall not be permitted to enter in'. 'And anyone not found written in the Book of Life was cast into the lake of fire – the second death' – Rev 20 v 14-15.

53 (chp 7 ref 50) Rev 1 v 7 – 'Behold, He is coming with clouds, and every eye will see Him, even those who pierced Him'. 1 Thessalonians 4 v 15 – 18 – 'the dead in Christ will rise first' v 16, then we who are alive and remain shall be caught up together with them in the clouds to meet the Lord in the air. The dead who were Christ's accusers will also rise first so that they

may witness and see for themselves, that what was prophesied will have come true ie. that Jesus will have returned.

54 Christ's birth foretold and who He will be, - Is. 9 v 6-7: 'His name will be called wonderful, Counselor, mighty god, Everlasting Father, Prince of Peace, whose government and peace will increase and have no end'; and Isaiah chp 11 details more about Him. Luke 4 v 16 –'the longed for, and long awaited Messiah, Jesus Christ, of whom Isaiah spoke: Isaiah 42 v 1-4. Luke 4 v 27 ' today the scriptures have been fulfilled in your hearing' Jesus said to the religious leaders. Luke 1 v 32- 33 – Jesus Christ as 'son of the Most High'. Also Isaiah is quoted in Matt 12 v 15-21. John 4 v 25 -26, describes the woman at the well who said to Jesus: 'I know the Messiah is coming (who is called Christ). When he comes he will tell us all things. V26 Jesus replied to her: ' I who speak to you am He'. However Christ knew he would not always be popular – Luke 4 v 24 'no prophet is acceptable in his own country', Matt 13 v 57; & Luke 6v 1-5, Jesus is foretold – Is 42 v 1-7, 'Behold my servant...my Elect in whom my soul delights.'

55 Let the dead bury their dead, Luke 9 v 57 -62, esp v 60. Because once you have a glimpse of the prize or treasure, or have tasted honey, why would you go back to dross or salt? It shows that you do not appreciate or value what you have been privileged to experience, nor the commission given to you, so you do not then deserve the kingdom of heaven. Also Matt 8 v 22, 'Let those who are spiritually dead care for their own dead' (NLT).

56 Matt 5 v 4, memories of deceased loved ones will comfort us.

57 Significance of crescent moon pendants - Moslem 'crescent' pendants hanging around camels' necks and earings, were Ishmaelite (also known as Midianites) custom – Judges 8 v 21-28; (various translations describe as 'crescents' – R C

revised standard version, as 'collars' and 'ornaments' – Good News Bible, as 'ornaments and chains' – Gideon Bible, as 'crescent ornaments' in NKJVs. This text also shows how the Israelites melted gold into idols, which afterwards became a 'snare' for prophet Gideon and his family into idolatry. I discovered on June 25th, 2012, that ancient Egyptian goddess Isis, favoured the horns of the cow, because lying on their backs, they looked like the crescent moon, THE pagan origin of the crescent moon symbol!

57a www.About.com. 'The crescent moon – is it a symbol of Islam? By Hurda, about.com guide (21 Feb 2011). It is the internationally recognised symbol of Islam, for several Muslim countries. However the crescent moon and star predated Islam by several thousand years, and it is difficult to ascertain origins. Most sources agree that these ancient celestial symbols were used by peoples of Central Asia and Siberia in worship of sun, moon and sky gods! Also reported to have been used to represent Carthaginian (Hannibal – North African) goddess Tanit, or Greek goddess Diana – hence PAGAN! Notably great Babylonian king Nebuchadnezzar's goddess Tiamat, according to mythology, 'created' man from a corpse (ie. Dead body??? Where did it come from? Who was its originator? Before death comes life!!!). This myth is the opposite and counterfeit of YHWH's Biblical Creation Story in Genesis 1v 26-28, where He created Adam from dust, and Eve from Adam's rib, and blew the breath of life into their nostrils. Who do we believe, pagan gods and goddesses, or YHWH, our Life –giving Creator?

The early Muslim community did not have a symbol. During prophet Muhammed's time Islamic armies and caravans flew simple solid coloured flags –black, green or white. Not until Ottoman Empire (Mogul Turks –Islamic) was the crescent moon and star affiliated with the Muslim world, when the Turks conquered Constantinople (Istanbul) in 1453. According to legend, Osman the founder of the Ottoman empire, had a dream where the crescent moon stretched from one end of the earth to the other, which he took as a good omen/sign. Unfortunately it is possible that the devil instilled this dream/omen as it brought pagan elements into a pure religion. Fortunately many Muslims reject the crescent moon as a symbol that represents Islam. Islam historically had no symbol prior to Osman's adoption of it.

58 YHWH (Yahweh) – I AM that I AM (Exod. 3 v 14-15), the name that He is to be remembered from generation to generation – the 'God' of the Israelites' fathers, Abraham, Isaac and Jacob – warns the Israelites not to mingle/mix with the (heathens) the other nations, whose land He conquers for them, nor take their spoils lest they be tempted to fall into a) idolatry and b) sin, as happened with prophet Gideon and family, who then had disharmony and difficult times ahead thereafter.

59 Judges 8 v 21-28, other warnings. b) sIn: Covetousness Exod 20 v 17, 10th commandment: 'thou shall not covet (be envious) of thy neighbour's wife, house or possessions. Now Achan, son of Zerah, stole silver coins and gold and clothing from the spoils of the Babylonian enemy and hid them, and so brought an 'accursed thing to defile the Lord's covenant with Israel, who could not be victorious until it was removed and the guilty party and all his family and possessions were stoned to death and burnt in the fire to cleanse Israel from the sin of covetousness, that was of disobedience to His law – Joshua 7 v 11 – 26. For surely the wages of sin is death – Roms 6 v 23. The place of their burial, marked by a heap of stones, is called the Valley of Achor.

Relatedly the story of Ananias and his wife, Sapphira, who withheld part of their proceeds of their property's sale from the apostles intended use for the poor and needy. The Apostle Peter exposed their deceit saying 'You have not lied to men, but to God', and with that Ananias fell down and died, as did his wife when she came in later also repeating the lie, and she was buried next to her husband –

Acts 5 v 1-11. The witnesses in the whole church and surround-ing hearers felt great fear when they learned of their outcome. Yahweh does not joke about His laws, and He will not take back His word once spoken, (see refs 65 -67 below).

60 Fish code – from loaves and fishes used by Jesus to feed the 5,000 and 4,000 peoples plus, - Matt. 14 v 16-21; 15 v 32 -38; Mark 6 v 37-44; Luke 9 v 13-17; John 6 v 1-13.

61 Matt 23 v 13, Scribes &Pharisees leading the people astray and denying them access to heaven.

62 Roms 12 v 19-20, 'Vengeance is mine, I will repay' says the Lord.

63 let the elect/faithful be sure they are found 'blameless' and still faithful, doing what they were commanded /instructed, when Christ returns. Pray and work as required that 'your whole spirit, soul and body may be preserved blameless at the com-ing of our Lord Jesus Christ – 1 Thess 5 v 23. Phil. 1 v 10, may live pure and blameless lives; Phil 2 v 15 -16, blameless and harmless; Roms 12 v 1, be holy and acceptable to God; Pray 'that you may be counted as worthy to escape all these things (rapture/the woes in the last days and Armageddon) and stand before the son of man' Luke 21 v 31-36; 'Blessed is the servant who when his master returns he is found obedient and faithful', - blameless, 'Assuredly' Jesus 'will make him ruler over all his goods' , Matt 24 v 46-47.

64 Rev 6 v 9-11, crying out for vengeance.

65 Isaiah 45 v 23, the Lord does not take back His word sworn in integrity or righteousness.

66 Is. 45 v 23, His word does not return to Him, ('void' is NOT attached to Yahweh's statement!!! However Satan ever trying to pervert the truth, used his mouthpieces: my bestest friend

& even a woman pastor, to try to get me to attach it here. So that by adding 1% of a lie, it would discredit the 99% truth, so as to make me out to be a false prophet. But Yahweh's Holy Spirit of truth, made VERY sure, that I could discern their motives, and I corrected and ignored their attempts to pervert, and so delay, the inevitable course of justice, leading to Satan's DOOM!!!)

67 Is. 46 v 11, He *will* do it.

68 Luke 6 v38, give and it will be given back to you.

69 a) Levites in Exod 32 v 26-29; Deut 18 v 1-3, Levites were not to accumulate wealth for themselves. 'The Lord is their inheritance, as He promised them'.B) Their portion is tithes and offerings, Numbs 18 v 9-21, v24.

70 Rev 22 v 18-19.

71 as a bride of the Lamb, Rev 21 v 2.

72 Matt 26 v 63-64, 'It is you who say I am 'Christ, son of God', when Jesus was accused of blaspheming; Luke 22 v 70. Jesus calls himself 'son of man', Matt 24 v 36-37, v 44, and Matt 8 v20, and John 9 v 35-41;

but Matt 17 v 5, our heavenly Father calls him 'my beloved, with whom I am well-pleased'. Simon Peter tells him 'You are the Christ, the son of the living God

Matt 16 v 16; Mark 8 v 29; John 6 v 69.

73 (chp 7 ref 90g) 'You brood of vipers! Hypocrites!, Matt 23 v13-33; & 12 v34-35; Matt 15 v 7-9, v 11-20

74 log/speck – Matt 7 v 3-5; Luke 6 v 41-42; camel/gnat – Matt 23 v 24.

75 worse than for Tyre and Sidon, Matt 11 v 20-24, or for Sodom and Gomorrah, Matt 10 v 14-15, who repented.

75a Jesus upbraiding the cities: Matt 11 v 11-24.

75b Matt 11 v 7-10.

75c Matt 12 v 1-8, Jesus is greater than the temple...He is Lord of the Sabbath.

75d Matt 11 v 10 John the Baptist is the 'messenger sent before you'.

75e Matt 21 v 28-32.

75f John 5 v 39-42

75g Mark 7 v 6-8.

76 Matt 18 v 5-6 – if religious leaders cause even little children and others to sin, their punishment is to 'tie a rock around their own necks and drown in the sea'.

76a Matt 18 v 7, 'woe to those through whom sins come'.

76b Matt 5 v 20

77 John 19 v 11, who has the greater sin? 'The one who delivered me(Jesus) to you (Pilate)'.

78 Matt 27 v 24, Pilate washes his hands of the responsibility of Jesus' blood. He had been warned earlier by his wife's dream, to have nothing to do with this, Matt 27 v19.

79 Matt 27 v 9, Judas betrayed Jesus for 30 pieces of silver, as prophesied by Jeremiah: 'they took of silver , the value of Him who was pierced, whom they of the children of Israel priced,

and gave them for a potter's field, as the Lord directed me' –
Jerem 32 v 6-9.

80 John 19 v 19-22, Jews angrily tried to get Pilate to change
inscription to 'He said, he was king of the Jews'. Pilate refused.

81 Rev 20 v 10 – the devil , beast/AntiChrist and the false
prophet; and v 14, death and Hades shall also be cast into the
lake of fire and brimstone, to be tormented continuously forever
and ever.

82 Is. 30 v 32-33, the Lord (smote)dealt punishment accompanied by music of 'timbrels/tambourines and lyres/harps'.

83 Is. 31 v 2, , the Lord will rise against evildoers and their
helpers, He does not take back His word'; and Is 31 v 5, He will
rescue and shield Jerusalem.

84 Is. 45 v22

85 Is. 44 v 9-20, esp v 18, graven images.

86 Is. 44 v 19-20, is there not a lie in your hand, a block of
wood, - and would you bow down to it? Poor deceived soul, with
deluded mind.

87 Is. 31 v 6-7

88 Is. 33 v 6, the fear of the Lord is the key to his treasure.

89 Is. 66 v 2, him who has a humble and contrite spirit.

90 Is. 30 v 29, rejoicing in song.

91 Luke 15 v 7, v10 – Joy over repentant sinner.

92 Luke 23 v 43.

93 Antediluvian, in E G White's Patriarchs and Prophets, pp 90-92. At that time the human beings were giant in stature, beautiful and great in wisdom and skill. But they, like Satan before, grew vainglorious and conceited, and began to 'fix their affections upon the gifts instead of the Giver'. They forgot their Creator and worshipped creatures of their own imaginations and adorned idols of their own making, and so sunk into depravity , and became what they worshipped – base and sinful, wicked and inhumane and abominable. They became blood thirsty (eating of animal flesh) and murderous against each other, and so disrespectful of Life, that was our Creator's gift of love.

94 Pastor Paul Durairaj, preaching during Core Adventism May 2011, in London. Rev 21 v 7, 'He who OVERCOMES shal inherit all things. Rev 21 v 19, all the gems are the difficulties and trials and tribulations that Jesus will carry us through to triumphant victory. E G White Patriarchs and Prophets, chp5, p77 – CONQUERORS who OVERCAME Satan.

95 Matt 21 v 16. '...from the lips of children and infants you have ordained praise?'.

96 Is. 42 v 8, & Is 48 v 11.

97 Rev 19 v 19-20.

98 Rev 20 v 10

99 Sura. 2.87; S. 2.253; S. 5. 110.

100 Afiya Trust & ROTA (March 2011), A Response from race equality perspectives to the public health paper, 'Healthy Lives, Healthy People', re: Black people and psychiatry, (mental slavery), London UK;

and Jayasree Kalathil, and Beth Collier, Renuka Bhatkta, Odete Daniel, Doreen Joseph, Premila Trivedi, (March 2011),

Recovery & Resilience Report:- African, African Caribbean and South Asian Women's Narratives of recovering from mental distress. The Mental Health Foundation. (Survivor – Research – User-led perspectives – mental health).

101 Moslems saving Bibles during the Apostasy: sources Pastor Petras Bahadur (2008), Pastor John Bishop (2011), Laverna Patterson (2001), History of the Church – Prophesy, in 'Explore the Word, Change the world'. www.teachinghearts-org/dre04historynotes.html

As there were several periods when Bibles were burnt during the Dark Ages/Apostasy it has been difficult to categorically state when this incident occurred. I have narrowed it down from possible:

- AD 590 – 604, Pope Gregory I, The Great, banned literacy (p27/51 of L. Patterson cited)

- AD 1??? – 12th century, Pope Innocent III, passed law 'Deliberato' that forbad Bible reading in common language, (p 29/51)

- 13th century Council of Toulouse forbade laymen to possess the Bible if it was in the popular vernacular (layman's language) (p 34/51)

- AD 1234, Council of Tarragon ruled that Old and New Testament books (Bibles) may be burned if they were in the Romance (common) language, (p34/51)

- AD 1555-59 Pope Paul IV created the 'Index of Forbidden Books', (p28/51).

- Before Ad 1566, year of Pope Pius V who forbad the reading of the Scriptures by common people, (p35/51).

Referring to Bahadur's suggestion that it was probably Portuguese or Polish Christians to whom the Moslems gave the rescued Bibles, the possibilities are further narrowed. Muslim conquests took in the whole of the Iberian Peninsula in the 8th century, and then it took 700 years for the 'Reconquest' to complete the expulsion of Islam from that area. The Inquisition was then very active in that area – and a speciality of theirs was burning vernacular Bibles. Similarly, from the 13th century onwards there was a Muslim presence in Poland in the form of Tartars. Whilst in Portugal the Muslims were conquerors. In Poland, it is almost the opposite, in that they arrived often as merchants and as allies, and integrated with the class of the nobility. 'On the balance of probabilities, I am more inclined to turn to Portugal for the event rather than Poland' (Pastor Bishop 2011).

So a more likely period for the Moslems saving Bibles from burning during the Apostasy, is the 13th century and donating them to Portuguese Christians. Pastor Bishop adds that history showing peaceful or supportive interaction between Muslims and Christians is quite rare. Not because it didn't happen, but rather because it goes unreported, or can only be found in more obscure sources. However if the premise was that Islam protected and preserved the Bible, that would be easier to prove, - or at the very least, present a logical exploration of how it happened (2011).

In any event, Muslim – Christian relations have not always been antagonistic and hostile. It gives hope for more amicable and peaceful communications and understanding regarding faith and our relationships with the Creator. On such bases positive inter-faith dialogue can happen.

102 Francis Njau, 2010, Prophecy Explained Book 3:- DANIEL and our Destiny – God relocates to Babylon; Christian Research Centre, PO Box 819 – 00206, Ngong Hill, Kenya; Printed by Kijabe Press, PO Box 40, Kenya. 102 – 1) p 183-184;

102 – 2) p 184-185; 102 -3) p 206-207; 102 – 4) p189.

103 -1) prophesy of scarlet woman, kings drunk on the wine of her fornication,

Rev. 14 v 8, Rev. 17 v 1-2; 103 -2) MYSTERY, BABYLON... HARLOT. Rev. 17 v 3-5;

103-3) Rev 18 v 19 -24, Rev 17 v 6; 103 -4) outcomes for Babylon the harlot, Rev18; 103 -5) REJOICE! For the saints' and martyrs' blood will have been avenged! And the smoke of Babylon, the scarlet woman's eternal torment, will have ascended to heaven, where they can do no more harm or evil. Rev 18 v 20, & Rev 19 v 1-5. The smoke emanates from their torment in the lake of fire and brimstone, Rev 14 v 9-11.

103 -6).Come out of her (Babylon) my people, Rev. 18 v 4-5.

104 Satan will be released after a 1000 days, and will deceive many, Rev 20 v 7-8.

105 Satan will gather up armies of kings and allies to oppose Christ at battle of Armageddon, Rev 19 v19, Rev 20 v 8.

106 Outcomes for Satan, beast, false prophet and the wicked, Rev 19 v 20 -21.

107 30,000 Christian denominations - Pastor Paul Durairaj, Core Adventism London, May 2011.

108 Daniel 11 v 34.

See following pages for fuller ref 30, comparison of the Ten Commandments:

Moses commandments as written by the finger of 'I am that I am' / Yahweh, and the version changed by the Roman Catholic church.

Ref 30 chp 8 _ full comparison of 10 commandments. (see also Shelton &Quinn 2005 10 commandments twice removed ibid.)

The Ten Commandments

(Exodus 20 v 3-17)

I

Thou shalt have no other gods before Me.

II

Thou shalt not make unto thee any graven image, or any likeness of any thing that is in heaven above, or that is in the earth beneath, or that is in the water under the earth: thou shalt not bow down thyself to them, nor serve them: for I the Lord thy God am a jealous God, visiting the iniquity of the fathers upon the children unto the third and fourth generation of them that hate Me; and showing mercy unto thousands of them that love Me, and keep My commandments.

III

Thou shalt not take the name of the Lord thy God in vain; for the Lord will not hold him guiltless that taketh His name in vain.

IV

Remember the Sabbath day, to keep it holy. Six days shalt thou   labour, and do all thy work; but on the seventh day is the Sabbath of the Lord thy God; in it thou shalt not do any work, thou, nor thy son, nor thy daughter, thy manservant, nor thy maidservant, nor thy cattle, nor thy stranger that is within thy gates; for in six days the   Lord made heaven and earth, the sea, and all that in them is, and rested the seventh day; wherefore the Lord blessed the Sabbath day.

and hallowed it

The Ten Commandments

As abbreviated in Vernacular Roman Catholic Catechisms

"He shall think himself able to change times and laws"

Daniel 7 v25, Douay Version.

I

I am the Lord thy God. Thou shalt not have

Strange gods before Me.

II

Thou shalt not take the name of the Lord

Thy God in vain.

III

Remember thou keep holy the Sabbath day

IV

Honour thy father and thy mother.

The Ten Commandments	The Ten Commandments
(Exodus 20 v 3-17)	
V	V
Honour thy father and thy mother: that thy days may be long upon the land which the Lord thy God giveth thee.	Thou shalt not kill.
VI	VI
Thou shalt not kill.	Thou shalt not commit adultery.
VII	VII
Thou shalt not commit adultery	Thou shalt not steal.
VIII	VIII
Thou shalt not steal.	Thou shalt not bear false witness against thy neighbour.
IX	IX
Thou shalt not bear false witness against thy neighbour.	Thou shalt not covet thy neighbour's wife.
X	
Thou shalt not covet thy neighbour's house, thou shalt not covet thy neighbour's wife, nor his manservant, nor his maidservant, nor his ox, nor his ass, nor anything that is thy neighbour's.	X
	Thou shalt not covet thy neighbour's goods.

Satan laid bare part two: - his destructive agenda: 'hell-bent' on destruction...

The priests and religious leaders from earliest times have sought to control the people by putting the fear of God, or gods in their minds. But if we look back at history, it has not been the Almighty One who has done the most destruction or caused the most deaths in the world. Since Cain's disgruntled dissatisfaction with the Lord Most High's lack of appreciation of his 'first fruits' offering, he took his rage out on his brother Abel by killing him. This was the first murder, man against man, brother killing brother. And since this time it is man, probably egged on/urged and incited by Satan, who has carried on the killings, whether from 1 on 1, or up to huge massive scales in military warfare, germ warfare, or scientific experimentation or drugs, or whatever means. Rather than fear the Almighty, it is more the case of fearing 'man's inhumanity to man'.

Through our various selfish, greedy, discontented, disgruntled and evil actions men kill each other wilfully. (E.g Cain of his brother Abel in Gen. 4 v 1-16, especially v 7; EGW Patriarchs & Prophets, chp 5, esp p 74, where the brothers were 'tested'). And yes, there are some accidental deaths. Yes, the Lord Most High, our Creator, may wreak vengeance and punishments on the nations through natural disasters, pestilence and warfare and disease – BUT remember who instigated death in the first place. Death was a curse from our Creator, as punishment for the disobedience by Adam and Eve incited by Satan, in the Garden of Eden. Death was brought on because of Satan's deceptive behaviour, - whom I shall show later is known by another more pervasive and unsuspected name, in his 'usurpation' (1) of our Sovereign Lord, the Almighty Creator's place in the minds and hearts of the people. Satan is the great USURPER, called by a name that so familiar to us, yet he has deceived us with his false identity, using the Lord's credentials as his own. You will not believe it! Yet the Holy Spirit revealed this, and Satan him-self confirmed it, 24th Dec 2010, and had been told to me by my sister, in 1994, during another mentally distressing period in my life. I thought she was blaspheming, but these last few months have opened my eyes to deeper insight. Praise the Lord Jehovah for sparing me further deception, and enabling us to unveil the truths about Satan!

Corruptions and errors crept into to the early Christian gospels from around AD249, the beginning of the Dark Ages/Apostasy, under Emperor Decius, who instigated the 7th persecution against Christians (2a). By religious crusades, Inquisitions and persecutions, the Roman Catholic Church, infiltrated by dev-ilish ideas, has single-handedly perpetrated the most atroci-ties and murders and crimes against humanity than any other body or organised group. They persecuted the Jews, Muslims, Protestant 'heretics', and other people whom they considered to be alien to, or held beliefs that were contrary to their doctrines and traditions. Their Apostasy lasted until approximately the Reformation in 1517, when a German priest, Martin Luther, protested with his 95 theses, or writs, against the corruption in the Church and the exploitation of naive believers deceived into buying pardons and indulgences for forgiveness and salvation of their souls. Thereafter began another round of persecutions and Inquisitions, this time against fellow Christians, who were considered to be heretics or 'Protesters' /Protestants defecting from the mother Church – Roman Catholicism. The Church began to lose its power in the state, as revolutionary ideas abounded, and by the 1840s there came a 'Great Awakening' whereby Christians, led by calculations looked forward to the imminent return of Jesus Christ. However the date in 1844 arrived and went, with no second Advent, and there was a Great Disappointment. Many believers got disillusioned and many sects and factions broke out. But a young prophetess, Ellen G White began to have visions and prophecies that led to a new movement, the 7th Day Adventists, who have renewed vigour and excitement in anticipation of the unspecified date of Christ' second Advent – a date known only to the Ancient of Days, Yahweh/Jehovah, our Almighty Father.

Unfortunately many believers lost their lives during these persecutions. It is estimated that a total of almost 2 billion people were killed during the Apostasy (2b)! Laverna Patterson (2001) (2b) claims that during 600 – 1600 AD martyr estimates were 50,000,000, and from 1100 – 1600 AD heretic deaths were approximately 200,000,000 in 500 years! By Patterson's detailed calculations, the true figure of peoples killed are closer to 2 billion, added to which are the sufferings and tortures to those who did not die under persecution whose number can be multiplied several times over. The Roman Catholic Church fiercely disputes these figures, as it only admits to estimates of between 50 – 100 million deaths. But it simply does not add up, for there is a huge gap in accounting for the shortfall in what the world population was during the Middle Ages and what it should have been. If you allow for the great persecutions of the Crusades and Inquisitions, then the shortfall would make more sense, and the true extent of the murders would be evident (2b). It is almost a total wipeout of humanity! Regardless whatever the figures are, the reality is that too many people suffered and died at the hands of religious leaders who professed to be working on behalf of Christ. The same Christ who reaffirmed the 6th commandment 'do not kill anyone', and said 'love thy neighbour as thyself', and would in no wise agree to what was done in his name. Rather instead of following Christ, they are serving the Anti-Christ, Satan, and advancing his agenda!

The religious leaders were so pompous and arrogant that not even the Almighty is deemed to be higher than the Pope, but is expected to be submissive to the pontiff!!! The Lord's patience is surely greatly tested! They need to be reminded of Isaiah's 'potter /clay' analogy (3)– ie. It is the Almighty who created man, and not the other way round. Their self-exaltation above our Father, is the very same reason why Satan got himself kicked out of heaven in the first place (3). Cast down to earth he angrily roams 'devouring' whomever he can (4)- destroying mankind until it is annihilated, if he had his own way! But this is not the conclusion prophesied by the prophets, or prophet Daniel or Apostle John, thanks be to the One who created us!!!

Satan has used Christianity as a front or mask to pursue his cause – his destructive agenda. By distorting and corrupting its belief system, he has sullied the name of Christ, and imploded it upon itself. Instead of Christianity being synonymous with Jesus Christ' messages of Good News – hope, salvation, love, kindness, peace and joy-, because of the antics of deceptive Satan, it has become associated with terror, fear, pain and suffering, cruelty and torture, wicked and evilous deeds leading to death. All being perpetrated by people who purport to be Christian, and doing 'God's works. Yes indeed they do claim this. But it is not our Creator's Will for His beloved people to be tortured, abused, sodomised, maimed and murdered. Even newborn babies, just minutes old were not spared, (5). Our Father loves life, which is why He gave it as a free gift to us, at the beginning of Creation. However because of the introduction of sin, this life – Eternal Life – has had to be bought at a very high price. That price was the life –blood of Jesus Christ, His son, who paid with his life, once and for all of us, for all time, to have victory over that curse of death, and to cancel out its destructive effect of eternal damnation and obliteration to nothingness for those of mankind who willingly follow our Lord.

Because Christ conquered death by his resurrection into this life to prove to mankind that there can be life after death if people choose to believe in Christ and are prepared to endure suffering even unto death, as he did, for his name sake, for the love of the Almighty, and to prove the test of their faith, they too can achieve/have LIFE and have it abundantly and forever. This is what many martyrs chose to do, some even singing under deathly endurance before dying. They had the privilege of seeing our Lord Jesus before their eyes as death approached them, hence their bursts of joyful songs!

Unfortunately, many people who are killed or persecuted are not Christian, and hold other beliefs. Satan will infiltrate any belief system in order to realise his power and influence over the people and to try to overtake the world. Whatever it be – religion, politics, education, philosophies, scientific theories, atheism, anything that man chooses to believe in that helps him to negotiate his way through this harsh, non-Eden, life – Satan through religious and political leaders, entices, bribes, compels, tricks, them into carrying out these huge atrocities, the worst being perpetrated by the Roman Catholic Church, under the banner of Christianity. They use Christ' name to conduct Satan's evilous plans. Jehovah admonishes and warns us to 'NOT take His name in vain' in the 3rd commandment (6). The final insult to our Creator is the use of the name of the very servant/instrument of peace and life – His son Jesus, to effect the opposite, ie. War and death. Can Satan and his agents really escape punishment and the wrath of our Creator? We are told and reassured that the victims, martyrs and the faithful pray that the day of Christ' return cannot come quickly enough so He can vindicate those who have been tested through the fiery furnace for His name sake, and for love of our Father, the Almighty Creator. May He come quickly!

Mankind is being desensitised, led into decadence, debased, denigraded, dehumanised, and destroyed....

Most of the music videos of today, and the rise in the development and popularity of video games that glorify war and violence - from its original 'pac man', to 'pokemon' in the '90s to 'tomb raider', 'grand theft auto', to ultimate warfare in 'assassins' and the current one 'Call of Duty' simulating warfare in e.g. Afghanistan/Iraq etc. – are designed to control your mind and therefore your actions, so that you become desensitised to the harsh realities of destructive behaviours. If you are constantly bombarded with degenerative sexual and violent behaviour in all genres – from soap operas, dramas, films, music videos, porn, reality shows, news and even documentaries, and printed materials e.g. magazines, posters, adverts, - you are being exposed to sordid, immoral and amoral, debasing attitudes and behaviour.

You are gradually, and sometimes instantly and dramatically, being removed from observing the strict moral codes that were, and still are portrayed in religious doctrine, but which have declined in influence over the populace. Moral codes that were the fabric of society, which was presented in the Hebrew Moses 10 commandments, as given to him by the finger of the great I AM, our Creator, on the 2 stone tablets, for our moral guidance and spiritual upliftment, and ultimately to enable us to live with one another safely and happily.

Being exposed to immoral and amoral behaviour, you become desensitised to it. You are no longer shocked, even if initially so, but familiarity means you become so accustomed to it, you begin to think it is usual and therefore normal, 'cos everyone seems to be doing it', so it must be okay to do the same yourself, or even for your youth or child to do. This is highly dangerous and is the slippery slope to moral decline, decadence and destruction of societies and eventually the humanity of mankind. This was the state of affairs in the evil and depraved Antediluvian world, practising perversions and abominations, like homosexuality and bestiality, in Noah's time before the Flood. They did not heed Noah's warnings, to their peril!

When a soap opera first showed two gay characters kissing on the TV (I think they were young women), in the 1990s, and then much later on gay men appeared more commonly on another show, I remember my young nephew, then a child, shouting out 'No, no no!' as he recoiled in disbelief. We have seen much more explicit homosexual activity since then in the various genres, as we are now in the second decade of the 2nd millennia (2011), but the public outrage, has turned to acceptance as normality in the promotion of diversity, as the gays have aggressively promoted their lifestyle even amongst children in the schools.

Homosexuality is no longer deemed to be a mental illness or abnormality, and the very public, now worldwide gay pride movement, displayed in annual celebrations, which has overshadowed the Black (Pride) History month of October, with which it allied itself to via diversity strands, has further decreased abhorrence to homosexuality.

It is now considered as politically incorrect (pc) to openly disapprove or discriminate against homosexuality in the West. Just yesterday (18th Jan '11) a judge ruled against hoteliers, who in 2008 refused to allow a homosexual couple to share a bed(room) as it was against their Christian beliefs. The husband and wife said their rule would apply to heterosexual couples who were unmarried also. It transpired that the gay couple

in question had had a civil 'marriage', but this made no difference. So the hoteliers were fined £3,600 for discrimination, or
inequality, which was awarded to the gay couple in damages.
Other outraged Christians have demanded a change in the law,
to allow hoteliers to decide who they will admit or not on their
premises, as is currently the case for other public establishments e.g. night clubs that have age limits for those they will
give access. Additionally the gay couple have been invited to be
interviewed on a popular TV programme 'Good Morning' tomorrow, and so the issue of homosexuality will be given even more
and higher profile.

Furthermore, several months later, 19 June 2011, the news
broke that a homosexual priest of a civil partnership, would be
ordained Bishop of the Anglican church in Reading, England,
and will be allowed to operate in his official post as long he does
not have sex with his partner. How likely is that to not happen
so that he keeps his position? He did not take up that position
due to pressure from public disapproval, halleluiah! However,
he Jeffrey John , did become Dean of St. Albans in May 2004.
Since the 1990s the Anglican communion has struggled with
the issue of homosexuality in the church. In 1998 Lambeth
Conference said 'it was incompatible with Scripture'. In 2002 an
Anglican church in Canada permitted the blessing of same sex
unions. In 2003 two openly gay men in UK an in USA became
candidates for bishop. Whereas in the UK the candidate with-
drew, in the USA Gene Robinson was elected in Episcopal
church as Bishop of New Hampshiore. In 2004 Jeffrey John
was installed as Dean of St. Albans.

Nov 9th, 2012, a new Archbishop of Canterbury England was to
be announced, who was pro-women priests , but against same
sex 'marriages'. Lord be praised!. But controversy still rages,
as the council voted in Dec '12 against women priests becoming ordained; and is still 'uming' and 'ahing' about gay priests,
- still undecided! (source: the Telegraph newspaper, 19/6/11,
Jonathan Wyme-Jones, religious correspondent) In 2012

President Obama came out and openly supported gay unions; and 7ᵗʰ Dec '12, Prime Minister David Cameron said he would 'allow gay 'marriages' to take place in churches, mosques and synagogues! (It is already permitted in secular settings). Now apparently man says it can be permitted in religious holy places of worship. Really?

Daniel 11 v 31 comes to mind, as prophecy fulfilled. NB see following pages for Matt 24 v 15-20, where Jesus said 'when you see the abomination in the desolation of the Holy Places, that Daniel 11 v 31 talks about' watch out, for Christ is coming soon to deal out defeats and punishments! Whilst the churches and state deliberate and are indecisive about what should be going on in the Lord's holy places, be certain that He is decided, and always has been – He is dead set against homosexuality of any kind and in any place, but especially not to be defiling His holy and sacred and sanctified places of worship! He is not pleased with proceedings in the church at present at all!!!!

However not all countries have been convinced of its 'normality'. Some Eastern countries in Europe, and other countries and cultures and religions, Eastern, African, some Christian religions, Islam and others consider it to be an abomination as described in the Holy Scriptures by the Almighty Creator, by whichever name He is known, Our Father in heaven, Allah, YHWH(Yahweh).

Even if you do not agree with these doctrines, let us take homosexuality and all its forms, to the logical conclusion. What is the likely outcome for mankind? Whether it is self-love through masturbation, or gay and lesbian, or gender-bending transsexuals, transgender, or asexual (no sexuality at all, as different to 'eunachs' or celibacy), androgeny and whatever else they come up with, all these are non-productive. They are contrary to our Creator's decree or instruction to Adam and Eve, man and woman, to 'be fruitful and multiply' ie. be productive and populate the world. Had he created Adam and Steve, or Marion and

Eve, or any other androgenous combination, we would not all be here now, generations later from the first man and woman, biological ancestors, the original parents. If we did not procreate and populate the world, mankind would have died out eons ago, and either Our Creator would have had to keep creating/making humans, or He would have just stopped at Adam and Eve. In either scenario, this was not His original plan A.

Mankind was meant to live forever, be immortal, and would have been so, had Satan not tempted Adam and Eve into disobedience, and brought about original sin and hence, death. Death was Our Creator's punishment for the disobedience, which Satan, and then Adam and Eve actively decided to do, contrary to His instructions. The introduction of sin and death was therefore Satan's fault, and these are what he continues to impose on mankind, through his various puppets and means of mind control.

Satan's agenda is therefore the destruction of mankind. When Aids and HIV epidemic broke out in the 1980's it was hailed as a punishment for homosexuals, as proof of our Creator's disapproval for this abomination, a modern day form of what happened to the evil perpetrators in Sodom and Gomorrah who were destroyed and consumed in the fires from His wrath. However further examination about the origins of the disease, which is still incurable, although more containable, shows that man, motivated by devilish agendas of genocide and population control, was more likely the creator of this fatal disease.

One preposterous rumour that was spread inter-nationally, was that it came from an African man who'd been bitten by a *green* monkey in Africa! Another rumour said it was God's punishment for homosexuals' then, unacceptable, conduct. However, not long after, a counter-claim emerged stating that Aids originated in a laboratory in France. It was discovered by chance, as a virus that mutated, with effects that we now know of; and it was exported to and injected into male American inmates, (disproportionately African American) as an experiment. Subsequently on contact with their wives, and spouses the disease spread amongst the general heterosexual population. Since then another claim for the origins of Aids said that it was deliberately introduced into the hepatitis D vaccine, which was used to treat those with severe liver deterioration. Hepatitis is a viral disease that is a self-cleansing substance that reverses the toxic conditions in livers that are about to stop working. The powers that be discovered that 90% of the people being treated for hepatitis were homosexuals, and they decided to target these 'undesirables' in society to give them the hepatitis vaccine they had now contaminated with the Aids virus, and thus we had the most explosive and widespread epidemic seen(7).

Other disease pandemics like small pox in African children (whose life-saving vaccine, it is claimed was deliberately contaminated with the aids virus, for economic reasons); Bird flu, Asian flu, Swine flu and Mexican flu – are all it is claimed have been deliberately cultured and manufactured and used as contaminations in other vaccines, as part of a population control agenda, by certain very powerful world governments (8). A Black South African woman recently (2011) relayed to me of when she lived in South Africa, a few decades ago, children were vaccinated by teams of doctors under the auspices of WHO, who afterwards suddenly had boils and sores break out on their skin all over their bodies. The children suffered and there was panic in the communities. Vaccinations are meant to prevent disease, not cause it!

Concern for the over-population of the world and fears that there will not be sufficient food and resources for everyone has been an idea that has been circulated for years. There is an argument that suggests that if numbers of people are reduced, through natural causes, diseases and wars, then there would be enough food and resources for those who remain. This is why propaganda is spread to gain popular consensus for governments' population control schemes. Unfortunately the means by which they intend to achieve this control have been revealed (at great personal life risk to those who are courageous enough to expose and challenge the people, corporations, scientists and governments involved) (9). As stated above the deliberate contamination of proclaimed 'health promotion' and 'life-saving' programmes are to: firstly *de-populate* the world under these guises; and secondly to *profit* economically, and gain resources and territories by stealth, even using 'trojan horse' deceptive tactics(10). These are modern day genocidal schemes perpetrated by the powers that be, motivated by greed for money, resources, power, control but are actually working hand in hand with the devil's agenda for destruction of not some of mankind, but all of it!

The disastrous results for mankind of biological germ-warfare and de-population by Aids and other viruses can be seen for generations afterwards. The deliberate attempts to 'wipe-out' their enemies by the soldiers infected with Aids disease already, by raping the women of their 'blood- relatives' now turned enemies (Hutus and Tutsis in Rwanda, 1994); the rapid and escalating spread of Aids amongst the women in America,(51% of those who contracted HIV in 2010 were women)(12), and the consequential effect on their children, through pregnancies, or other ways of contracting the disease – mean depopulation and EXTINCTION in the long run!

But the programmes shown above, are just the latest in long line of population elimination schemes. In past decades there were systematic sterilisations carried out on poorer Black and Hispanic women in prisons and in hospitals in USA, even in the UK, without their consent and often without even their knowledge, 'til discovered later. In the 1980s the population in certain poor areas in Africa were severely decreased by the promotion of formula (powdered and tinned) milk for babies, with no means to sterilise the bottles, the children contracted illnesses and died. For some inexplicable reason the World Health Organisation (WHO) gave its blessing to this programme, rather than encourage the mothers to breast-feed, as they had been doing since time immemorial! You would expect the WHO to encourage natural practices that had been perfectly good, beneficial and LIFE-GIVING healthy breast milk from breast feeding. Yet that was not the case. Instead, 'first world' governments and organisations sell out-of- date or discontinued products and medicines to the poorer countries in the 'third world'. If they are not considered good enough or safe enough for first world peoples, why would they be then sold on to poorer countries, unless there were genocidal and profit-mongering motives?

And even today obscene numbers of children die in other parts of the world of diseases that are no longer existent in the 'first' or 'progressive' worlds. They are dying of diseases that could be prevented; we have the science and technology to do this. It remains for humanitarian champions and human rights activists to enlighten and galvanise support from the general public, which we can only hope will prick the consciences of those in power, to change their current tactics and *actually* save lives instead of destroying them! Unfortunately racism underlies much of first world agenda for poorer countries. This is evident when for instance, during the 1980 -90s, Western governments preferred to give butter and wheat from their gross food mountains stored for years, to their (former) Cold War enemy, Soviet Russia, which is mainly white Eastern European, than to allies and former colonies, Africans and Asians who are in dire poverty. Their humanitarian gestures are somewhat biased.

In recent days (Feb '11) the UK govt has announced its plans to inject money into Mental Health programmes for school children, this whilst at the same time slashing funds from every other health and welfare programme nationally! Puzzled? You should be alarmed! This is just another of the schemes targeting our youth, some not even of school age yet, to get them 'hooked' into the psychiatric drugs industry, as they currently do especially in USA. For last 10 years or so certain politicians have made noises about early intervention in MH drug(cannabis) psychosis to detect potential mental illness amongst school children. It seems like they have managed to persuade the government to go along with this 'good' idea.

But like the psychiatric drugs that are given out so readily to young children, especially Black ones, for ADHD (attention deficit hyperactive disorder), ie the kids can't keep still – which is understandable if you give them a regular diet of coca cola and chocolate and crisps and other inadequate drinks and foods , will get them prancing around like 'they're on rocket fuel' and other health disorders and allergies – this new planned intervention is none other than a racist attempt to get even more Black people secreted under the mental health system, even if it means targeting their children. Many of these children who currently take the drugs for ADHD suffer terrible side effects (13a 'Psychiatry – Industry of death'), ranging from suppressed and 'unnatural' behaviour for children, because they are prevented from being their natural state (which is boisterous, energetic and inquisitive children), to irritating skin sensations, to depression and even suicidal thoughts – in children! Is this helping them? Are suicide and depression and passive aggression and inactivity normal behaviour for innocent children? Is the introduction of such psychiatric 'treatments' progressive or regressive and harmful? I suggest rather it less about 'treatment' and 'cure', but more about making more financial profits for the pharmaceutical companies and the government and associated bodies, off the 'perceived' illnesses of people, especially of children. This is shocking and disgraceful!

Not Altruism but greed: Selfishness and greed motivate the chemical experimentations with drugs and treatments. For instance, medics and psychiatrists promote the idea that 'medication' or psychiatric drugs are 'good' for service users/patients, and that it is not a good idea for them to come off them. They insist that for many people they need to take the 'medications' 'for life', often arguing that it is not in the best interests of the patient to cease taking them, even that it is 'dangerous' to encourage them to stop! Does this mean they should be on meds forever? Will they never be cured? Or are they simply to be maintained and kept on these toxic drugs until they die? Service users who want to come off their medication are aggressively discouraged, and are virtually told to 'put up and shut up'! How is this encouraging self –determination in personal healthcare? How are healthy lives to be achieved with drug dependency?

Psychiatry has been challenged over the years for its sometimes inhumane, invasive and often debilitating 'treatments'. From psychosurgery, lobotomies, Electro-Convulsive therapy (ECT), heavy sedatives and tranquilisers, some of which have left permanent and crippling side effects on users – from gross obesity and attentive secondary illnesses e.g. heart disease, diabetes, etc., to physical deformities and involuntary reactions such as lock jaw, and repetitive involuntary facial movements or spasms in body parts. Never mind the oppressive and abusive regimens and procedures, such as restraint and control, that have left more than a few patients in coma or dead! (13b) Rather than being good for service users these have been disastrous.

Even psychology's own research has proved this! In autumn 2011, the Biomedical Research Centre, based at south London's Maudsley psychiatric hospital, along with the Dept of Health's huge funding (£48 million over the next 5 years), announced that 'serious mental illness shortens lives'. But what transpires from the article is that people suffering serious mental illness can expect to live up to 18 years less than the national average (women with schizoaffective disorder, 17.5 years, and men with schizophrenia, 14.6 years, less). They give reasons for this as a combination of factors including: social disadvantage, long-term antipsychotic drug use and higher risk-lifestyles. (source SLaM news, summer edition 2011, p12-13). They even try to shift the focus from the drug use 'medications' to blame the 'patients' themselves for not making better life-style changes, eg stop smoking, better diet and exercise regimes and so forth. Really? I for one, know this to be a lie, having made over and above life-style modifications for years, and seen the positive effects of withdrawal from these drugs including clarity of vision and mind, (perhaps too quick and perceptive for some!), and great weight loss, with commensurate improved blood pressure and diabetes prognosis!

Psychiatry and pharmaceutical companies have their own agendas for 'pushing drugs' or 'medication' onto people. It provides careers and job security for staff, as well as financial rewards – the huge profits generated are spurred on by the SIN of GREED. They ply the drugs under the rouse of promoting 'good health' and 'staying healthy'. But the reality is the complete opposite to that ethos. Being kept on legal or medical drugs creates as much drug dependency and damage to health, as does illicit drugs and alcohol misuse. Addicts are prescribed methadone drug substitute to in theory 'wean them off' drugs. But they are merely replacing one drug with another. So many thousands of addicts are on this methadone programme in the UK at present, costing the NHS millions of pounds sterling (2011). It would be far better and achieve greater success of quitting addictions if they are allowed to go 'cold turkey' for a short time in rehabilitation centres, and this would promote better health life-styles and independence, reducing the likelihood of returning to bad habits, and would be less drain on the country's resources.

Unfortunately this is not popular with the 'powers that be' and those who depend on the megabucks raked in from drugs, and secondary drugs that are needed to counteract the side effects of primary ones. According to Readers Digest Magazine, (Aug 2011, p53-58), in an article called 'Drugged – Up Britain', -'How did we get to the point where £22m is spent on prescribing drugs – *every day?* In Jerome Burne's 4-part special to launch our campaign to tackle drugged –up Britain. It even gives useful advice in the 'what can you do?' section –where for instance, it informs us that 'statins lower levels of a very important antioxidant called coQ10, and that the diabetes drug Metaformin, may block the absorption of vitamin B12', essential for healthy muscles and bones. He also reminds us that '2 NON-drug treatments are supported with mountains of evidence – a healthy diet and exercise... Every doctor recommends them... The results can be remarkable – and long-lasting'!!! But this is not what the drug pushing pharmaceuticals want. For not only that, they create a drug dependency culture, which again means more financial gain, and also control over the minds and bodies of people by Satan and his accomplices. For, if we are pre-occupied with our body's mental and physical health and looks, we will have no time to reflect on and have a relationship with our Father and Creator. Our spiritual health will be neglected, and so our moral upliftment and development in our humanity will be diminished.

By giving us various medical 'treatments' (few of which are 'cures') e.g. drugs for mental illness, whether it's schizophrenia, bi-polar, depression in adults to ADHD for kids, to drugs for blood pressure, diabetes type II and cholesterol, and obesity and smoking habits and various other ailments, we are being controlled and constrained to the pharmaceutical companies, who give incentives (usually perks or financial) to the medics so that they prescribe them to the trusting and unsuspecting patients. Are these drugs really necessary for good health and cures?

It is has been proven that good health management and maintenance, even cures, can be obtained by making lifestyle changes in diet and exercise activities and fostering good habits. Certainly diabetes type II can be reversed and cured by making these changes, but this is not promoted by either the medics or the pharmaceuticals, because that would be bad for their business. Rather, opposed even to natural holistic remedies, people are told they will often need these drugs 'for the rest of their lives' thus creating drug dependency culture. The side effects of these drugs are often cause for more damaging and even debilitating effects on health, sometimes worse than the original complaint. In effect one condition is being 'swapped' for another, both of which now require 'life-saving', (more like life-threatening) 'medication' /drug 'treatments'. It is ludicrous, and very sad and worrying, because the people naively 'trust' these people to take care of their health. And to make matters worse, sudden cessation from taking these drugs may cause unpleasant withdrawal symptoms that 'mimic' symptoms of the original presented symptoms or of another condition. Sometimes more damaging and permanent irreversible conditions occur from the medication than the original presenting ailments.

Drug dependency – through legal drugs i.e. medication – is just another form of mind control and slavery that is to our detriment rather than for our physical and mental well-being. We become slaves to our bodies- what we look like, how we feel/emotions (anger, envy, jealousy, pride) – and slaves to 'medications' all of which are preoccupations that take us away from focusing on the one being who is the source of our happiness and is the greatest physician – the one and only Lord, our Creator! And all He wants from us is that we remember to acknowledge, thank, love, praise and worship Him. For this is the sole purpose for why we, like the angels, were created. We were all meant to worship and adore Him. For, really He is *the* Magnificent One, who gives us all His love, nothing spared, even if it means that it is unrequited by those who reject Him. How unreal is this? Awesome!

However Satan is still at his destructive worst. We already know how European pioneers used blankets infected with small pox, to kill off many of the American Indians they discovered living there, so they could take over the land. As stated earlier the motivation for such behaviours is GREED in the pursuit of capturing as much resources -natural and human, land, food and money and ultimately control and power for the selfish few at the expense of the majority of others. Throughout history selfish people have exploited, conquered, ruled and killed their fellow man to achieve their desires. But they can't always continue, as there are those who will challenge and oppose them successfully. Other huge world atrocities, Jewish Holocaust, African slavery and Apartheid, despotic rulers, all have been overthrown or forced to end, under economic pressure as well as by humanitarian liberators and supporters, human rights and emancipation activists. The counter desire, and concern for the continuance and sustenance of life, that is so precious, can be a powerful force to save humanity, and resist Satan's plan for the extinction of mankind.

Unfortunately man's capacity for killing and destruction is not new, since Cain, of similar inclination to Satan, killed his brother Abel, it has recurred throughout the ages, from individual murder to mass killings/murders and from enslaved deaths to war crimes of the modern century. After being cast out of the Garden of Eden, and denied access to the Tree of Life, man grew to rely more on the other still beautiful and abundant and wholesome fruits and vegetation on the earth. But after the first killing, the shedding of blood brought with it, increasingly widespread disregard for, and devaluing of life, be it animal and worse still, of human life. For as blood was spilt to use animals as food, meat eating thereby encouraged bloodshed,(14) and led to prolific warfare. Death and bloodshed are all contrary to Our Creator's plan A, and these were the reasons He established the law 'thou shalt not kill' in the 10 Commandments. He could foresee these monumental man-made genocidal disasters that have arisen through time. He could see years into the future, where this was heading – population control by depopulation and deliberate killing tactics!

TOTAL WIPE OUT! This is Satan's hidden and not-so-secret agenda for mankind. By destroying mankind, the pride and joy of our Creator, Satan hopes perhaps to ruin Our Father's credibility amongst the people, who blame Him for all the disasters and deaths in the world, believing the claims of the various religious leaders that He is angry with them, that He is ever wrathful and punitive and cannot easily be appeased! This is due to the circulation of the devil's half-truths and lies, to prevent the people turning to our Creator for help, and thereby benefit from His benevolent forgiveness and mercy. Satan also wants to hurt Our Father, through his spite, in the ruination of people, and so diminish His sphere of influence and power, so that he, Satan, could take over and become God in His place.

How deluded is he? This is not how Our Father works. Having power and adulation is not all that He is about, and this certainly is not what is the most important thing that matters to Him. We, mankind, His creation, matter most to Him, because He loves LIFE. He creates life out of Love. He IS Love and Life itself. For He is the Alpha and Omega, the Beginning and the End, who was, is and is to come (15). He lives for all eternity. Death is temporary and will be abolished, as will the evil doers who follow Satan unto their own destruction in hell- fire. At the end of Time when Our Father's revised plan Z, which he foreknew from the beginning as described in the Bible's book of Revelations, comes into existence, then there will be no more death, disease or EVIL. And there will be LIFE and LOVE and JOY forever and ever. LOVE that is UNCONDITIONAL and permanent, which we will live in perfect(ed) circles. Selah.

Debasing...

However, we have not reached that point of blissful existence yet. Satan still reigns over this present world and is as destructive and enraged as ever. He is very pervasive, infiltrating many areas of our lives, so much so that we are impervious to it. We don't even notice or realise how much we are being controlled by him. ('God is in control.') He affects and infects us mentally and physically, from what we eat and drink to how we think and behave.

Amongst ourselves we differ and argue about our religious practices, from not eating unclean things e.g pork, fish without scales, scavenging creatures, to those animals and insects that are considered as delicacies in many countries – from monkey brains, locusts, snakes, dogs, oysters, squid and even rats! Pork for instance, is so prevalent it is used in many formats, even those we don't suspect. It is hard to avoid, unless you have a strict 'kosher' diet, like the Jews.

Pork is unclean and forbidden (Is 65 v4), not only because the pig/ swine eats/ scavenges anything, even other pigs flesh as pork, (sausages and ham also), but because it has cloved hooves, but does NOT chew the cud (grass/hay), Levit 11 v 7. And the carcasses of fish WITHOUT fins and/or scales are to be regarded as abominable, Levit11 v 9-12, whether they come from the sea, rivers or other waters, (so no mussel, squid, prawns, lobsters, eel, oysters, and so forth). And a definite no-no is the eating of blood, for therein lies the life of the creature, -so no 'black pudding' sausage, nor steak 'tartare'/ rare, or such like. These are abominations to the Lord YHWH, who created animals and humans and angels, and all living things, and is to be respected and obeyed!

Unfortunately some religions are so focused on strict religious observance to rules, like not eating pork, or just keeping a strict vegetarian diet, that many ordinary folk are confused. However, Jesus, back in the day, rebuked the religious leaders – the Scribes and Pharisees – for being too concerned with such things. He said it is not what we put into our mouth, that is important, but what comes out of it, meaning what we speak. For what we say reflects what we think and what we feel in our hearts, and in their case, it was evil or full of bad intentions(16). They focused on minor things, like appearing to be righteous and holy, when their practices showed that they were not genuine, as they didn't do good works, or help the needy in their communities (17).

We watch debasing shows put on for our 'entertainment' where contestants eat and do things, usually disgusting, that regular people would not. Popular shows like Japanese 'torture' game

shows to UK 'I'm a celebrity – get me out of here!', are insidiously infecting our normal sensibilities and degrading both the
participants and the viewers, taking us down the slippery slope
towards the destruction of our humanity. We are unwittingly
being led, like Jesus was, like lambs to our slaughter, to the
death of our souls.

For at the same time in our daily life we are being enticed
into getting our foods and drinks in bulk, and cheaper. We
are being fed the line that this is what the consumer wants,
and it makes sense for us economically and is good for the
country. But what is happening is that the big conglomer-
ates – the supermarkets, who increasingly dictate what and
how much the food producers can bring to the market for the
consumer, are actually the ones who benefit financially (18).
Worryingly, food production on a huge scale has meant the
'battery farming' of chickens, pigs and now cows, in USA and
UK, and have forced the animals into unnatural and cruel living conditions so that they can be 'better' harvested to give
bigger yields of meat and milk. Even our fruit and vegetables
are subjected to the scrutiny of the supermarkets 'buyers'
who dictate the size, looks and proportions of the product,
and thus place restrictive and unfair pressures on the food
producers.

Not surprisingly many businesses have been forced to close,
whether they are the food producers or the smaller food shops,
who cannot meet or compete with the demands of the huge
supermarket chains. And do *we* benefit? Is it good for *us*? The
quality of the food products are becoming inferior, and their
nutritional value diminished with increased risk to our health;
and resultant sickness requires more medical treatments, thus
fuelling the pockets of the pharmaceutical companies. Once
again, they claim it is for our good, but the real beneficiaries are
the greedy power magnates. We are being sold lies and being
destroyed, for their financial profit.

Dehumanising...

Not only are we being maimed, poisoned and killed for profit, but for sick 'pleasures'. The 'thrill of the hunt' which is now reserved for fox hunting and rabbit stalking and other animals, was applied to Black slaves in America, formulated under Ku Klux Klan (KKK) terrorism and lynching post-slavery. But even as recently as 1990, I read an article in an American magazine that decried the scandalous activities being perpetrated in Brazil. It described an advert inviting anyone to come on a night hunt of pest control. They would be able to shoot vermin for pleasure. The only problem was that the 'vermin' were not animals but CHILDREN! They were little infant 2 and 3 year olds, orphaned, unsuspecting, sleeping rough on the streets for lack of anywhere else to go, and being looked after by slightly older children, also helpless. These were the 'vermin'! Can you believe it? No wonder I began to lose my mind back then.

And again, not only are children victims of crime, but are forced to become perpetrators of it too. It is this greed for power, land and resources that has seen one of the most serious crimes of this century – forcing children to become soldiers in the most brutal wars, notably the Congo in Africa. Young boys and girls, as young 8 years old, are kidnapped from their villages, torn from their families, beaten into submission and compelled to perform sub-human acts upon other human beings that even most adults would refuse to do. Their military training involves raping even their own female soldiers, as well as the enemies', torturing, maiming and killing their enemies. And even more horrific, they are made to drink the blood of their enemies, which they are told, will make them stronger than them, and make them invincible (19).

Drinking or eating any blood, of an animal, but especially that of a fellow human being is detestable and forbidden by our Lord Creator (20) for 'the life' of the creature is in it. Not even meat with blood still in it, whether for sacrifice or secular consumption, should be eaten, as it is the blood that 'is to be offered as atonement for one's life'. This is why Christ's sacrificial blood is so important to save mankind. His life was in the blood, and this was offered as atonement for the sins of all mankind, by which their sins could be cleansed and eradicated. By this means, the way would be cleared for mankind to have a bridge or ladder back into the good books of our loving Creator. The drinking of blood, especially of humans, is akin to cannibalism and is demonic and in line with the evil practices of Satan, who hates mankind.

It is Satan who plants the idea of invincibility into the minds of men to encourage them into doing his demonic practices. He thinks that he is invincible, because he has existed since before creation and time began, and has not yet been defeated by our Creator. However it is not because he is invincible that he has lasted this long.

It is because our heavenly Father is patiently exercising His plan Z – waiting for the very last of the 'elect' namely, those who have yet to be born, who will give their lives to the Lord Jesus, in allegiance and love of the Father. When that number has been complete, Our Father, at a time and date known only to Himself, will allow Jesus to return to claim His elect, and then Satan will be dealt with. He is not invincible. He *will* be defeated and destroyed, but not in his time, but in that of our Father *the* invincible Creator.

So the claim of invincibility is another lie, because the blood-drinking did not make the child soldiers invincible. They could see their fellow comrades being killed in front of their very eyes! The practice did not make them invincible. It made them barbaric monsters, who were less than humans or even bestial! They were dehumanised and debased into beings that are far-removed from, and unrecognisable as, their former innocent child-status; and who if they escape, or are ransomed back from the militia – are then greatly feared and usually rejected by their families. The atrocities they have been forced to commit, and witnessed being committed against other human beings, in turn bring anger, shame and self-hatred on young shoulders, who require a period of re-adjustment, counselling, support and kindness before they are considered to be 'safe' enough to reintroduce into civilisation. Even then there is still a risk that their learnt violent behaviour may erupt unexpectedly. They have been damaged psychologically, emotionally and spiritually, from which it is hard to recover. This is just what the devil wants to happen to mankind, whether they be man, woman or child – devastation and destruction.

Parallels to child soldiers can be seen in other societies. The constant portrayal of warfare –from cowboys and Indians, world wars and currently those in Iraq and Afghanistan - in news, documentaries, films and even music videos - glorifies war, and incites similar situations on home territories. For instance, in USA and UK, the gang warfare that has been played out on civilised streets has erupted in recent decades. Black – on-Black violence, turf wars and post code wars, devolved from Mafia and mobster gangland wars, are now destroying younger and younger lives, bringing fear and destabilisation to the cities. At the root of it is selfishness and greed and man's inability or unwillingness to share resources and live alongside each other. Killings and prostitution and other degenerative behaviour are often instigated by the huge financial rewards that can be gained from the selling of illicit drugs, alcohol and other substances that appear to induce 'emotional highs' in the substance users, but which ultimately produce their ruin through addiction and even death. Death - the opposite of LIFE. Life, which is the manifestation of the gift of LOVE from our Father - the One who created us all - in His original plan A.

Other atrocities that children are perpetrating against others, even against the young, children like themselves because they have been exposed to the darker side of humanity that they should never experience. Whether it be as extreme as being forced or drugged to perform in Satanic rituals, of drinking blood and urine or eating faeces and other sub-human and perverted sexual and violent acts, to being exposed to an ever increasing and pervasive diet of pornography, violence, profanity, immorality and amorality on our TV screens, films, magazines, internet, music and other media. One if the most extreme examples of a child's inhumanity to another child of the century, was the deviant young offenders who perpetrated the torture and murder of a 2 year old toddler, Jamie Bulger in England in Feb 1993 (46). The offenders, Robert Thompson and Jon Venables, were only 10 years old when they carried out a horrific attack on this child that they had abducted, including violent and perverted sexual assault and terrorised the poor innocent child, pouring paint over him, stoning him and abandoning him, dead, by a disused railway track.

There was, and still is, international outcry against these two boys who became the centre of a debate: 'were they sick or evil?' The world could not conceive or contemplate the idea of a child being evil. But we had made them so. They had failed to attend school and spent their time watching porn and violent videos, especially a 'video nasty' called 'Child's Play 3' - 'Chucky' about a boy puppet who could talk and make evil things happen. The devil makes work for idle hands, and this was surely the case for these two boys. Consequently they were imprisoned in secret locations, till they reached maturity of 18 years old, when it is alleged they were given new identities and sent off to Australia.

In 2010 and recently(2011) 2 men have come to light in further crimes of which people suspect they may be those same two boys now grown up and continuing that now ingrained deviant behaviour. One is said to have struck up relationships with women with children, and something happened, undisclosed because protected under human rights legislation, but later reported in a newspaper that Venables was arrested for watching child pornography on the internet, and had boasted about abusing the woman's 8 year old daughter. He was imprisoned again for two years. Earlier this year (2011), there was a news item in Australia about a little girl who was with her dad and brother in a shopping centre, who had gone to the toilet, but after some time was found there, flopped beside the latrine with both her knees broken, dead. She had been raped and the force of the attacker was such that she her knees were broken under the attack! The rumour circulated that the perpetrator was a man with ginger hair using the same surname as one of the Bulger killer's grandfather – too much of a coincidence?

Clearly those perpetrators are so severely damaged they are dangerous and cannot now be expected to live amongst regular human beings in society. They are to blame, and so are we - for not protecting our children from such demonic debasing influences in society. We have a right and a duty to say no! We do not have to let our children do or watch, hear, or play dangerous, perverted, violent things. We can take a stand and say: 'No! I don't want this for my child'. We have been given responsibility from our Maker, not only for our own children, but all children. They are His gifts to us, and He expects us to treasure them and safeguard them, so they do not fall victim to, or become perpetrators of evil. Right about now we are failing so many children. It's time to shape up! *Be* a responsible father or mother, or sister or brother. *Be* a responsible adult. And be someone who gives a damn. *Someone who cares.* For all our sakes take care of them. We *are* accountable, if not now, certainly on Judgement Day, when Christ asks us, 'what have you done with my beautiful flock I gave you?' (47).

But the majority of gross inhumanity is done by adults to children, and notably by those who are supposed to care and love them. The immense cruelty that children suffered during Victorian England is well documented, with life, no, existence and slavery in the workhouses characterising that century. But as long as I have been alive these last 50 years or so, there have been numerous cases of children being neglected, abused, killed by parents, step-parents, associated partners of parents, and all under the supposed watchful eye of the authorities, notably the social services. In 1973,

5 year old Maria Colwell (47a) was kept in an attic, separate from the other siblings, and was starved to death by her step-dad and mother. She was so hungry that they found she had eaten her own hair and faeces, before finally giving up her meagre life.

In 1984, 4 years old Jasmine Beckford (47a), was rushed into a hospital and abandoned there, and was pronounced dead at the scene. It transpired that her mother suffering domestic violence in fear had used the child as a shield to block the blow that was aimed at her, but proved fatal for the little girl. She had been starved and beaten to death. Her step-father's brutal blow dislodged her brain! Also in 1984, 21 month old Tyra Henry (47a) died after being battered and bitten by her father, while she was under local authority care. The social worker sent to her care became too familiar and trusting of the family to spot warning signs. In 1992, 3 year old Leanne White (47a) was beaten to death by her step-father, and social services had not heeded the reports from her grandmother and neighbours that she was at risk.

In 2000, 8 year old Victoria Climbie (47a) suffered terrible physical and mental abuse from a so-called aunty who had taken her from her parents in Africa to give her a better life in England. The aunty and her boyfriend subjected the poor child to what I would describe as demonic attacks, shaving and cutting her scalp with a razor then hiding it under a misshapen and ill fitting wig. Beating her and terrorising her, and then had the gall to take her to church to get the demons that were allegedly in her exorcised! Rather it was the aunty and the man who perpetrated demonic acts upon her. The poor child was resigned to her plight, saying to a church member that no-one could help her. She felt hopeless and helpless. Imagine! She died of hypothermia, having been made to sleep in a cold bath at nights. Her death inspired the government's 'Every child matters' legislation and policies to protect children at risk of harm in the future.

However, unbelievably it failed. In 2002, 2 year old Ainlee Labonte (47a) was starved and tortured to death by her vicious parents, who deliberately punched, scalded and burned the toddler. She had 64 scars and bruises on her body at death, weighing only 9.5kg (21ibs)- half the weight of a normal child her age. It transpired that the social workers failed to protect her because they were paralysed with fear of her parents! If they were frightened, imagine how terrified the little 2 year old child was, that they as adults, were paid to protect!!!

Yet again in 2007, a child died, who was known to social services and the police and doctors and hospitals. Yet they all failed to save the child from such immense cruelty and sadistic torture from his step-father, who in addition to cutting off the ends of some of his fingers so that it was easier for him to pull out the child's finger nails, so badly beat and abused him/ He punched and bit him, and even egged on their three 'pet' dogs, vicious breeds, to also bite him, and these bite marks were observed on his head. Finally the Nazi – inspired, drug and alcohol taking abuser, put the child across his knee, and whilst watching popular TV programme, 'the Jeremy Kyle Show' about live disputes between dysfunctional families, forcefully broke the child's back with his own hands!!!! Can you imagine the child's screams and pain and terrors. Even his grandmother reported the child previously running away to hide in terror from this evil creature, yet felt powerless, or even afraid to intervene and save the babe.

Not content with breaking the child's spine, the perpetrator took the child to 'walk' in the nearby forest, which obviously the child couldn't as he kept falling down as his spine was broken. Can you comprehend the immense pain and suffering this child endured. Yet he still managed to smile at the visiting social worker a few days later, no doubt the child realised his end of suffering was near, maybe Jesus showed him the gates of heaven, who knows why the child could smile so sweetly. His mother had propped him up in his buggy to hide the fact that his back was broken, and had smeared melted chocolate on his cheeks to hide the bruises. But the boy was dying, slowly and

In agony, and eventually became senseless to even the blows the abuser dealt him across his face, that he didn't even wince.

Finally the day that the child could find no relief, and was scream-ing and crying endlessly, his attacker brought his cries to an end with a final fatal blow whilst in his cot. Yet even then it took his mother a further 2 hours after discovering him dead, to call an ambulance, who rushed him to hospital and pronounced him dead. They found one of his teeth in his stomach that had been knocked out from the force of one of the blows to his mouth from his evil step-dad. Incredibly the mother had just the day before been cleared of charges of abuse against him, yet he died whilst in her care. The cowardly bullying step-father and his equally abusive brother fled the 'house of horror' to avoid detection. They and the mother were arrested and imprisoned, for not long enough a sentence, as outraged and shocked pro-testers agreed.

Who was this child and how old was he? The social services, protecting his identity, called him 'Baby P', but the justices and reporters discovered that his full identity was Peter Connelly (47a). He was just 17 months old when he died. He had suf-fered neglect and abuse from birth, and cruel sadistic onslaught from the moment his step-father walked into his life. He had endured about 12 months of torture, and no-one saved him. His only reprieve was the few weeks he spent in the care of a child-minder when the social services removed him from the family home amid concerns for his care and safety.

Baby Peter was seen by the authorities over 60 times in his short 17 month life by a string of professionals. And even when he was brought to hospital obviously suffering and DYING from his broken spine, amazingly the paediatrician, a specialist in child health, failed to assess him properly saying that he was too 'cranky'. Yes she would be too if she had a broken spine and multiple injuries!!! Needless to say she was struck off. Social services were concerned to protect his identity, but failed to protect his life, which was surely more valuable and precious to him.

I am still shaking with the enormity of how much this poor toddler must have suffered innocently. He was not even able to speak properly yet, but yet he was beaten as if he were a fully grown boxer or adversary in a ring. Spun round on a chair till dizzy he flew off onto his head on the floor. Time and again he was dropped from the height of his step-dad onto his head onto the floor. How much more untold horrors we do not know, but enough is documented in social services and courts records and books about his 'case', - his oh too short and painful life (47a).

These children died needlessly. Little innocents, suffering and dying at the hands of those who were supposed to love and care for them, and protect them. Where was the support for obviously troubled and dysfunctional parents and guardians? Why were they not given parenting classes, and support in how to bring up children properly and well? Why were the children left in their overly far from adequate care? Where was the rescue plan for these 'safe-guarded' children? Children who were not far from being born, and who certainly did not make it to teenage years? This is supposed to be a modern society, technologically advanced, supposed to have human rights and where children have their basic needs met. Where was the humanity and compassion for these children? In this 21st century why is this abuse and murder still happening, and not being addressed till it is far too late??? And what about those who are still suffering today in our midst, whose plight are not being heard, or are ignored, and are not publicised? Rest assured Jesus hears their suffering, and is suffering alongside them, excruciatingly. He feels their pain.

He is also enduring the pain and suffering of children the world over, who are undergoing abuse, neglect, bullying, starvation, danger, sickness and disease, lack of appropriate care, clothing or shelter and protection, lack of education and means for economic security, exploitation – work, sexual, violent, wars; domestic violence, seclusion and loneliness, gang cultures, subjected to drug and alcohol abuse, sodomy and other sexual perversions. Whatever it is that innocent children are being subjected to needlessly, cruelly, fatally, because of the inhumanity of others, at the behest of the devil, evil Satan, and his legion of agents –demons and humans, know that Christ too, Himself innocent, is also suffering and agonising. He is enduring the cross daily as He watches the children being victimised and ruined and corrupted and made to endure what most grown-ups would be unable to take. He watches and waits until they can be given hope of release, and relief from cold and heartless, murderous, remorseless perpetrators of evil. He waits patiently until the day when His father, Yahweh says he can return to earth to claim his own, and take the little children into his bosom and fold them safely and securely and lovingly in his arms, always welcoming them home, surrounded by little cherubs and cherubims. Jesus will give them sanctuary and solace in his safe haven, his ark, that is the holy city of the New Jerusalem, that sacred, life-giving city, for the rest of Eternity. Selah.

Jesus said 'Suffer the little children to come unto me' (47b), for they are innocent and precious in his sight. And woe betide those who would do them harm in this life and also prevent them attaining life in Eternity, through wrong teachings. He 'will repay', for 'Vengeance is mine' (47c) says the Lord, and he will do it. And although no justice on earth seems comparable enough to the lives taken so cruelly, rest assured, they will be held accountable and given just judgement on that all important day when books are opened in heaven, after Christ has returned in glory.

Thankfully, in recent months (early 2012), the UK public have begun to wake up and take responsibility for some abused children, as more cases were reported than the previous year, and thus more children have been rescued and taken into care, (such as it is). BUT unfortunately, much to our shame and dis-grace, many children are still living hell on earth. But know who is responsible. Make no mistake, the devil cares not for children or even babies. Since the time he was cast down to earth from heaven (44), he has been to-ing and fro-ing about the earth (44a) seeking whom he can devour. The book of Revelation tells us more about his purposes in regards to mankind.

Rev 4 states that the dragon waited for the sacred woman in labour to give birth so that he might devour the child. As well as being taken literally, as Satan wanting to kill Virgin Mary's child – Jesus Christ- this is also symbolic. It pertains to the state of persecution that the people who choose to follow Christ and who obey our heavenly Father, Yahweh, are to endure under the Anti-Christ and his agents. The image of a woman in the Bible is often used symbolically to represent the church, or the people of 'God'. The dragon is that serpent of old, Satan or the devil (44) and the child is our Lord Jesus Christ.

The woman escaped being the chase of the dragon, and was given wings to fly into the wilderness where she was given suc-cour, fed and nourished by the Father's helpers (angels?) (44). She was protected for a time, times and a half, namely 1260 days or prophetic years. But we know from history that the woman ie church or Yahweh's people, were persecuted for 1260 years during the Apostasy or Dark/Middle Ages of 538AD to 1798. This was a time of great persecution by the pagan influenced Roman Catholic Church during Crusades and Inquisitions. The believers were branded heretics and were terrorised, tortured and martyred by the RC Church in their fanatical zeal to excom-municate and exterminate those they considered to be Anti-Christs. Yet in this very extermination they were perpetrating one of the deadly sins going against the 6th commandment 'thou shalt not kill'.

Because Satan could not get the woman (44) incensed, he went after the rest of her offspring, namely those who keep the commandments and have the testimony of the Lamb (Jesus Christ) in how they live their lives. These commandments are the ones given to Moses by I AM that I AM (Yahweh), and not the corrupted version that the Roman Catholic Church has deceived its laity with (see earlier chapter 8 for evidence). These offspring testify to Jesus influencing their lives, for whom they are willing to endure persecutions, and they loved not their lives, even unto death, because they love Him so. They believe His promises, and have the hope of salvation when He returns in His second Advent, to claim them as His faithful servants.

Rev 12 v 17 refers not only to the persecutions of the Christians during the Middle/Dark Ages, by the pagan-influenced Roman Catholic Church. It also points to these latter days before Christ returns, when there is more persecution for Christ's followers worldwide, across the continents of Africa, India, China and Russia and elsewhere. Saints and martyrs are being tortured and killed today in these current times. And the persecution will come again to Europe and the Americas, where it will not be for only being a Christian. This time it will be for keeping the commandments of the Lord, especially the 4th commandment – keeping Yahweh's Sabbath (on a Saturday) holy and reverent. Which Christian church keeps this Sabbath holy and marks it as different for reverence and celebration for Yahweh, our heavenly Father and Creator? It is the 7th Day Adventist church.

Just as in early Christendom, the R C church outlawed Judaizing (ie keeping the Sabbath as the Jews still do) for Christian followers keeping the Saturday as Sabbath, (see chp 8). Already in the last few years, the Church has spearheaded a movement to make only Sunday worship lawful. This is being pushed forward currently, and as such, Adventists will be under pressure to comply to the man-made law, or stay faithful to Moses 10 commandments which are those laws written by the fiery finger of Yahweh Himself. Therein lies the stuff of persecution once again.

However these self-proclaimed 'Gods' are at variance with what is happening In the secular world. For several decades now, there has been a decline in the number of traditional church goers, replacing reverence for God, with obsessions and leisure activities and business. This is so prevalent that their precious Sunday observance, is now filled with monetary pursuits and ordinary daily activities. Alarmed at this degeneration there is a current movement in the USA to insist that no-one does any commercial activities on their precious Lord's day, ie the Sunday. I already established in chp 8 that this Lord's day was the day that the emperor collected his treasury from his subjects. Ironically *his* Lord's day was one of commerce and not of reverence and holiness!

The Adventist church stands firm on Sabbath keeping, but is mocked and reviled as a cult by the Papal Roman Catholic church. This is especially because the Adventist church holds fast to the Truths revealed in the Bible, and holds fast and firmly to the spirit of Prophecy that is pouring out on the churches in these last days before Christ's second Advent. Lay people (ordinary people) in the church – from babies to old men – will prophesy (48). They will speak prophecies and they will dream visions pertaining to these last days. And in Truth, many prophets from all walks of life and unexpected quarters, - from spirit-filled, gifted evangelists, pastors, to mental health sufferers, single mothers, to young children, elderly men and women - are uttering and writing and singing prophecies, in this present time and in our midst. Praise the Lord Jesus!!!

Christ told us that when these things are occurring, be wise and know that these are indications that He is already on His way back to us. His second coming is not that far off now.

Various forms of depravity, dehumanisation and horrific examples of 'man's inhumanity to man', some carried out even in the name of religion, even for Christ's name sake, are actually the depths of degradation, and result in the death and destruction of souls. Whether it be - the 'hung, drawn and quartering' of Protestants who refuse to comply with the then too-strict Roman Catholic doctrines that had been infiltrated by pagan (Satanic) influences; or Christian crusades against heathens to convert them to Christendom; or Moslem Jihads to convert others to Islam; or Communist vs Capitalist world and Cold wars in their various guises still today, the recent atrocities in African Rwanda, and Eastern European dissolution of Czech republic and Yugoslavia into Croatia, Serbia, Bosnia and other smaller states/principalities (152) – wars fuelled by racism; the Jewish, Christian and Moslem religious wars in the Middle East (Kuwait, Iraq, Afghanistan, Israel and Palestine, Syria and other countries internal civil warfare) - which are really about territorial control and of oil resources. In addition they are accompanied by all the concomitant activities associated with war – spying and covert operations, intelligence gathering of FBI, CIA, MI5 and MI6 and various other agencies. ALL of these and more, are merely the manifestations and puppets and agents of Satan, who is out to destroy mankind.

His quest is to ruin and desecrate our bodies, the blessed human temples that our Creator has lovingly given LIFE to. He entices, tempts and forces us to defile these body/temples that our Lord so beautifully made back in the garden of Eden. According to Ellen G White, 'man was made a little lower than the angels. Yet when he shall be purified and translated to the heavenly courts, he will be even more privileged than the angels' (45). We are a far cry away from that once perfect state of being, now so far removed from His perfection, that we have degenerated into the dark and ugly state that Satan brought himself into. Although our outward appearance still looks human, like Dorian Gray (21), our humanity has disappeared in such sinful evil ways, that inwardly we are swirling around in murky, black mire, in utter degradation and disgrace. We are almost unrecognisable as gracious, humane human beings, but have become bestial, lower in status than the animals our Father gave us dominion over. Like Lucifer, who was created *the* most beautiful and graceful angel, whose sin got him kicked out of heaven, who so disgraced himself and is since angry, jealous, spiteful and malevolent, and is now *the* ugliest and most frightful of all beasts, we, too, have so debased ourselves that we are not much better than him.

Satan has succeeded in his plans thus far, to turn man against his fellow human beings. We so don't consider ourselves as specially created beings that we deny the existence of the author of our very lives. Slogans like: 'there is no God!'; 'God does not exist'; and confusingly 'God is in control', show the depths to which we have sunk that we don't even consider that we are of divine invention. Such slogans confuse and encourage people to descend into decadence and lawlessness, so that they do not adhere to the laws our Creator gave us for right living standards. These laws that He designed to preserve the lives of His beloved people. Impudent and malicious Satan, gleefully upsets our Father, mocks Him and affronts Him. He challenges Him and denies His sovereignty as Lord of all. Can you credit it? Unbelievably, Satan sets himself up, not only as the enemy of mankind, but more incredulously, as the enemy of our Creator Himself, and all that He stands for – LOVE & LIFE!

He's achieved his destruction through manipulation and mind control. One of his most successful tools has been the focus on the idea of difference. He instils the idea that 'as I am perfect, I must therefore be better than, and superior to, others'(22). He knows our Creator and Father is far, far superior and greater than he is, but he is *so* craven and covetous and envious of Him, that he wants this for himself. He wants what our Creator has, and wants to be the superior one, and this is the very sin that got him kicked out of heaven. So he insidiously instils the same sinful streak into man's psyche – so that we have the various forms of inequality that have led to wars, genocide, atrocities and segregation. *He* is separated from our Father, so in his eyes, we, mankind, should be too. If he can't be close to our Father who created him and gave him love, but had to reject his hatred and evil condition, then he doesn't want us to be close to Him, or to have our Father's love either. He is spiteful and jealous, 'bad-minded' and destructive. He would rather destroy all mankind and be damned himself, than let us live and bask in the glory and love of our Lord. But we don't have 'to go there'. We don't have to share his destructive fate...

There *is* hope for us! Our Creator and Father loves us even still, with all our faults, and as imperfect as we have become. And because He loves LIFE and wants to enjoy the company of His creatures, He has given us a way back into His grace and favour. He loves us so much that He has given us His only begotten son, Jesus Christ, to live and die for us, and to rise and live again, so that all of us who believe on Him, shall have a chance to gain eternal LIFE (23) - that same immortality that Adam and Eve, had they not been disobedient, would have enjoyed even up to the present time. 'For none but the son of God could accomplish our redemption...Nothing less than the infinite sacrifice made by Christ on behalf of fallen man could express the Father's love to lost humanity' (45). The sole purpose for Jesus coming down from heaven to earth was to SAVE lives, which is the ultimate desire and love of our Creator. Anyone thinking and/or doing differently is against Him, and is pro- death and therefore in allegiance with Satan, who is the Anti-Christ.

Unfortunately, in our modern times, many of us, including the most devoted and righteous Christian, is so bedazzled and hoodwinked by Satan's deception, we are content 'to just go with the flow'. No-one wants to draw attention to himself and stand up against wrong-doing. No-one wants to stand out and stand up for Christ, as His champion against sin and evil. It's not 'p c' (politically correct), and is unfashionable to do so. People are complacent. Even the majority of the churches are content to just 'let things slide', and 'not make a fuss'. Is this 'what Jesus would do'? Did He not berate the scribes and Pharisees as hypocritical who led the unsuspecting people down the slippery slopes to destruction? Did He not throw the money-lenders and traders who were defiling His Father's house, out of the syna-gogue? Did He not lay down His life for us? So why is it so hard to do the same for Him, and stand up against injustice and evil?

'Christ ..identified Himself with the interests and needs of humanity. He who was one with God has linked Himself with the children of men, by ties that are never to be broken...Jesus is "not ashamed to call them brethren". He is our Sacrifice, our Advocate, our Brother....' (45). Are we ashamed to be called Christians, because it is not 'cool' or acceptable in this modern day? Rest assured Jesus said those who are ashamed to be associated with Him, and His name, He will denounce in front of His Father on that critical day of Judgement, and they will surely be cast down to hell with Satan! (24).

We are the 'modern day Laodiceans' (25) as we have become lukewarm in our affections towards Him and each other. The Laodiceans that apostle John discusses in the book of Revelation (26). Described as 'the salt of the earth' they were 'proud of their personal virtue' and self-sufficiency because 'they felt they could solve any problem through industry and through their wealth' (27). They were not 'hot' towards our Lord, nor were they 'cold' in their spiritual inclinations. They were lukewarm, and complacent. Like those who carried out gross atrocities and cruel experimentations in the genocidal Jewish Holocaust, who tried to portray themselves as blameless and so escape due punishment for their evil deeds, by saying in their defence that they were 'just following orders'. 'Hush, keep your head down' is a familiar attitude, even in the modern work-place where wrong-doings are seen, but people fearing for their own skins, and wanting to avoid trouble, keep their mouths tight shut . What is it that makes us fearful? Our own vulnerability, or possibility of suffering as a result of speaking out about wrong doings? Do we fear something bad will happen to us or loved ones if we stand up for justice? Do we think we will make mat-ters worse for the person we are championing or protecting?

Wake up! Bad things are already happening - to the victim *and* to you too in the future!

For Jesus says because you are lukewarm He will 'vomit'/ 'spew' /'spit' you out of His mouth' (28) and into hell fire. He says it is better to stand up and be counted on His side, and choose to be like Him- a defender of the weak and needy, protector of the widow and orphan, champion and advocate for Christ. He advises us to 'buy from (Him) gold refined in the fire, so (we) can become rich; with white clothes to wear...to cover (our) shameful nakedness, and salve to put on (our) eyes so (we) can see too' (29)...our sinful condition, that we are so in need of repairing, and thereby humbly accept that we *do* need His help. We are nothing without Him. If we do this, He will give to those 'who overcome...the right to sit down with Him on His throne', as He did (30), to share life in His kingdom in the New heaven and earth.

So it's no use 'sitting on the fence' or 'just going through the motions'. This attitude and lack-lustre behaviour will not save you from pain and destruction. We need to wake up! and stand up for Christ. Shake ourselves! out of this sleepy stupor and be decisive and take action. Indeed take up your cross, and valiantly and confidently stride forward to reprove, correct and stop wrong-doers; and to encourage the weak and needy to have hope in a future life of happiness, peace and justice. And don't be a coward and fear reprisals from those you are berating, because Jesus will be your supporter beside you, and He will never leave or abandon you. For he who is not for the Lord is against Him, and He stands by those who are on His side, and pledge allegiance to Him. He is faithful and true, and you *can* count on His word. And His word, Jesus Christ, will win in the end (31). He will have the final victory, and so will you too it you choose His path. So take heart! Be happy! You are onto a winner if you choose Christ!

Mercifully, since I wrote this piece last year (2011), the British public have come up trumps, and have reported record numbers of children to get help from social services. So they have woken up to the cries of distressed children and taken appropriate action. Although it means unfortunately that so many more children have been victims of abuse, it does mean that many of them have been rescued from harm, under the auspices of Christ-led, compassionate and responsible people. Lord be praised, (2012) !!!

So what will happen to the wicked, and is there hope for them and us as well?

Unfortunately many people think they will come to no harm if they continue doing whatever they want. They even think they will avoid, or be saved from punishment or destruction. But those who are puppets/ agents / or complicit in evil ways will not escape punishment. And will they be saved by the one on whose behalf they carry out their wickedness – the devil? No, he is not their saviour. Instead when the 'shit hits the fan' and punishment is about to be administered, where is he? Gone! He turns on his heels and runs away, abandoning his faithful agents, and even worse turns around, from a safe distance, and mocks and laughs at them in the distress he has caused. He laughs and jeers, being very pleased with himself, for achieving some of his aim – that is to 'put a finger up' to our Father, disrespectfully challenging and spiting Him, because he has ruined and destroyed some of His beautiful creatures – mankind.

Another popular belief that is circulating and influencing even the 'elect' Christians is that 'if a person dies who is wicked and evil like, e.g. Hitler, if on his death bed, with his dying breath, he repents and asks 'God' for forgiveness, he will be saved and still go to heaven'. Moslems famously believe this as one of their creeds. But even this idea of repentance is corrupted. For, this would mean that everyone can go on being lewd, debauched, murderous, wicked and evil, as much as they like, and then at the very last minute, repent, and that would be enough to get forgiveness and to save their souls. The logical conclusion would be that since your confession of your sins, is between man and our Father, and He forgives, then no-one else needs to know or hear your repentance. So what is the point of Christ? What did *He* say about repentance? Christ clearly states that 'the wages of sin is death'(32). This does not mean you can continue deliberately sinning and still gain eternal life. This is contradictory to the purpose of repenting.

What did Jesus say to the woman caught in adultery, who was about to be stoned to death by 'righteous' men, whom it turned out were not sinless themselves, and so left her alone? When He had finished writing in the sand, and her accusers had left, He told her that neither did He condemn her, that her sins were forgiven, and she was free to go (live), BUT that she should sin NO MORE'(33). He expressed the same sentiment to the tax collector, whom the Jews despised and considered 'unclean' (34). Jesus however, chose to associate with him, 'defiled' himself according to Jewish laws, by having supper with him at his house. For He came 'not for the righteous' but for the sinners (34) – the 'poor and needy', the 'lost sheep' - to lead them 'to repentance' away from sin and evil ways, and turn them back to our heavenly Father, on the path of humility and right, Christ –like living. The tax collector, Matthew, was so overjoyed that Jesus had come and dined with him, and told him about the chance for salvation by repentance and forgiveness, that he immediately left his tax collecting job and followed Jesus.

For when someone accepts Christ into their lives it is a turning point, and once forgiven, it becomes apparent to everyone that he has made this life-changing decision. For, Christ is the 'light' that has come into this world of darkness and sin(35). He is a beacon showing people how to live better, and achieve the salvation of their souls, and immortality, which was our Creator's original plan A. So when you have a light/lamp you don't hide it under a bush, but you place it somewhere high so that it's light can shine all around for all to see and benefit (36).

The point is, that after repentance, and forgiveness, comes a reaction – such a joyous change of heart and mind, that the person is compelled to change from, and stop their sinful ways. They are to actively show that they have changed, that they are no longer doing the sinful things they used to, and that they were turning their lives around. This means they have to be seen/ observed making the changes. If they have truly repented, the light of Jesus will be seen in them as they make these positive changes. And it is this positive influence that others will see in you, that stands as witness and testimony to the magnanimous forgiving mercy of our Father, that glorifies Him, and that gives hope to, and will encourage others to also repent and change their ways, so they can have eternal life.

So repenting in secret, or just before you die, won't benefit you or anyone else. Jesus requires us to repent and make the positive changes in your life, visibly, before you die, whilst you are still able to demonstrate your love for Him by helping others to also repent and give up evil ways. As Jesus said 'a tree shall be known by its fruit' (37) in other words if you have truly repented, your attitude and behaviour should show a corrected, positive change.

If you forgive, you release the other person from the burden of guilt and sorrow of realising his wrong-doings and hurtful tendencies and actions. We would like to be forgiven for our own hurtful actions likewise (38). Simultaneously, in forgiving we are released from the burden of our grudges and bitterness festering in our minds and hearts when we refuse to soften and forgive. Without forgiving we become like Satan, simmering and brewing the sin of hatred that turns us ugly or unlovable, and is definitely NOT Christ-like. We need to forgive others so that we too might be forgiven.

In fact, forgiveness is the only way to defeat pain, and overcome the hurt that others do to us or cause us. Forgiving others is the only way to defeat the devil, so that he can no longer wound us with his stabbing attacks via painful memories that he reminds us of. I pray that Jesus helps me to forgive others that have and still hurt me, even my deceased mum whose painful memories still surface to hurt and wound me and churn my stomach into painful emotional knots. Lord Jesus, *please* put your healing seal over my hurting - you, my loving, forgiving and merciful Lord!

Some people try to be clever, and openly or publicly, say they repent and ask for forgiveness, but they don't mean it, because they continue to practice sin and wickedness just as before. Or they think that they can avoid censure, criticism or punishment and death in hell, if they beg forgiveness at their death bed. They think they can trick forgiveness out of our Father. But they cannot outsmart Him. For, He is omniscient, i.e. 'all-knowing'. He sees and knows everything, even attempts to 'trick' and deceive Him. He can see whether or not, in your heart, you are genuinely sorry. This is why the criminal who was being crucified beside Jesus, received forgiveness from our Father, because he was genuinely repentant, and he showed by his words that he knew he was guilty and deserved punishment; but also, even whilst dying, was not afraid to declare that he knew Jesus was innocent, and was bold enough to ask for forgiveness. He was rewarded by Jesus saying 'this day you will sit beside me in heaven' (39).

For those who refuse to repent, and continue in their wickedness, 'the wages of sin is death'(40). Don't be fooled by Satan into thinking you can live in whatever way you want, and continue in wickedness. Just look at what happened to the wicked in Sodom and Gomorrah, and disobedient Lot's wife (41); and to the impatient and fickle Israelites who whilst waiting for Moses to return, made themselves a golden calf (graven image) and worshipped it as they danced lewdly and prostituted themselves around it (42). Our Father was so disgusted and angry with them that He destroyed them with fire and brimstone. And where is the destination of the wicked? It is Hell/Hades – the furthest place away from the sight, and blessing and love of our Father in heaven. It is the ultimate state of being UNLOVEABLE and so means DEATH – permanent death. Hell is a place from which there is no return. No second chances. No 'purgatory' or place of remission, as the Roman Catholic doctrines preach. No. Hell is the end of Life and NO immortality. *The* final destination for the wicked.

The purpose of Hell is as a cleansing agent. It is a place of fire, burning and purifying, as when gold is refined and purified in the fiery furnace. So as fire burns there will be pain and suffering for the wicked in Hell. It is for the elimination of sin – the cancellation and negation of evil and wickedness. It is for the eradication of rebellion against our heavenly Father. It gets rid of disobedience, and hatred and pride and anything that is contrary to, or counter- the goodness and wholesomeness of our Creator. This is where Satan, his followers – demons and evil people, are destined to end up, at the end of Time, when the day of Judgement arrives. It will be too late to repent and ask for forgiveness then! And it will be perpetual hell fire burning, or eternal torment and punishment. It will consume itself and be destroyed in the raging fire. It will be consumed so that only ashes will remain as evidence that wickedness existed (43). The wicked will be consigned to oblivion so that no memory of their existence could remain and ever defile or pollute the New heaven and New earth, that will be created for those who have proved themselves faithful and worthy to have eternal life – that life in eternity with our Lord and Saviour, our Creator and His spirits, the Great 'I AM' – the Alpha and Omega, the Beginning and the End, the Author and Finisher of things.

The Bible clearly states what will happen in the latter days and the final battle, Armageddon, and what the outcomes will be for the wicked and for the faithful. Who will be the victor and who will be vanquished? As my nightmare of Jan 31, 2011 revealed Satan is busy amassing his army right now. He is conscripting them from right amongst us, before our very eyes, and they are not strangers to us, but are our family members and friends, and even some of ourselves, for in those days even the elect might be persuaded to stray from the righteous path they have been following (49), as they 'will be joined by many by intrigue' (49). No-one is safe. No-one is immune. It is only those who depend wholly and solely,(soulfully) on the good grace of the Lord Most High, who can be protected and sheltered under his huge shielding wings like a force-field (50). Now is Satan's time of raging and gathering- in. For a thousand years he (the dragon or serpent) was bound and chained by the angel with the keys to the bottomless pit, where he 'could deceive no more'(51). But his imprisonment was temporary.

As for the saints and martyrs, those who were beheaded for their witness in Jesus Christ for the word of the Lord, and 'who have not worshipped the beast nor his image nor have its mark on their foreheads' (52), 'they shall partake in the first resurrection'. This is the resurrection at the time of Christ second coming, when those who have died for Him, and the wicked who pierced His side and accused Him, shall rise first to witness His return and be caught up with him in the clouds, before the faithful who are still alive at that time (53). 'Blessed and holy is he who has a part in the first resurrection, (for) over such the second death has no power, but they shall be priests of 'God' and Christ and reign with Him a thousand years' (54). They shall be truly blessed.

However, after 1000 years Satan will be released from his imprisonment. He is loose now and runs amok 'devouring' whomever he can, and gathering his army from the four corners of the earth. He will go out and deceive the nations, to 'Gog and Magog' ie everywhere, to gather them for battle, and whose number is as the sand and the sea' (55). They will be too numerous to count. Moreover as revealed in my nightmare of 31 Jan 2011, they look like ordinary people. They could be your family members, friends, and even you yourself could be deceived and led into battle, willingly, knowingly, or conscripted forcibly and by trickery, to fight in Satan's army that he is raising against our Lord Jesus and the saints and the elect. As He says don't put your faith in man for they will let you down and deceive you. 'Trust no man. Trust only 'God' (56) the Lord, and His Holy Spirit, the Counsellor, will guide and protect you.

Jesus warned us about these things, in Matt. 24 v 4- 30, and told us to watch for the 'Signs of the Times'. We will hear of wars and rumours of wars, and nation will rise against nation, king-dom against kingdom. There will be famines, pestilences and earthquakes in various places. All these things are the begin-ning of the sorrows. 'Then they will deliver you up to tribula-tion and kill you, and will hate one another. Then many false prophets will rise up and deceive many. And because lawless-ness will abound, the love of many will grow cold. BUT we are encouraged, for v 13: he who endures to the end will be saved. And importantly for this time, v 14: the gospel of the kingdom will be preached in all the world as a witness to all the nations, and then the end will come.

The end is surely nigh, for just this weekend 6th August 2011 for nearly a week long rampage and eruption mainly from the youth on the UK city streets, starting from community outrage at police 'execution – style' fatal shooting of a young black man, followed by the severe beating with batons of a 16 year old girl, who demanded answers for the killing of this man, all perpe-trated by police, who are supposed to protect the citizens. What followed was appalling – arson to shops and premises, looting and opportunist criminality, whilst the police did little and noth-ing to intervene, and did not facilitate the fire fighters to tackle the horrendous blazes, so in effect, 'Babylon a burn' once again amongst their own community. No doubt police will claim this criminal behaviour will justify their demands for more resources, increased rather than reduced police force, and introduction of more sinister and stringent measures, like use of heavy artillery – rubber bullets for (Black) crowd control and stiffer immigration with introduction of ID cards for ALL UK citizens as has been long sought after. It remains to be seen just how far they will go, not content with detaining as many Black people as they can in prisons and secure units in mental hospitals.

Post script: The governments solutions to the riots in following weeks – lock up those perpetrators arrested, even if ludicrous eg. 1 man given 6 months custodial sentence for 'looting' a bottle of water (evidently more thirsty than criminal); the oldest looter, 70 year old man, let off with a caution for his part in looting in Ealing; a mother sent her child to 'loot' a bag of rice to feed her ten children (more need than greed, and signifies the government's failure to address the needs of the poor); 1 person arrested for stealing a packet of chewing gum. It is left to the imagination of what punishment lies in store for those guilty of weightier crimes, like stealing TVs, mobile phones and arson. Some of them will never see the light of day again. Additionally the Prime Minister David Cameron has petitioned the UN to put an end to human rights for the prisoners of the riots. What injustices are and will be perpetrated on the 5,000 arrested, especially the youth, who have no appropriate adults or proper representation whilst they are being holed up in police and prison cells awaiting trial can only be imagined.

More unbelievably, the families of some of them, are now being targeted for eviction from their council homes, as unsociable and undesirables. What has that got to do with the price of milk? What has one got to do with the other? This is really going too far! And they call this a just and fair democracy!!! It's more a case of vindictive and spiteful retribution for those who dare to voice or show their displeasure at the racist and punitive police and government agencies, who have been put in power to represent the common man, and SERVE him. They have forgotten why and for whom they are in office, and this is a reminder of their *humanitarian* duties. Worse still, a year on, and only 1,500 of those 5,000 arrested, have been convicted, despite trawling through hundreds and hundreds of camera footage! But the riot is much televised and dramas and documentaries and research, and calls for more funds and resources for emergency services, all using much needed money for the growing poor and disaffected in our British society. Who is milking it now?

In one moment we have gone back 500 years to slavery and lynching and abuse of Black people with no recourse for redress and justice, not without risking a beating!!! All the civil rights movements in the 1960s and liberation struggles that followed internationally for Black people have been reversed and virtually negated under the present Conservative (Liberal) government, who gave tribute to the Maggie Thatcher with her draconian measures of the 1990s.

Whilst the elite and elected government ministers escape punishment for the 'expenses scandal', the rest of the country is being taken to the cleaners, squeezed too tight to barely get by, if at all, with banks and countries being bailed out, even the great USA this week lost its privileged triple credit status, and caused the lowest stock exchange crash in recorded history. Yet bewilderingly, instead of letting America pay up its debts, especially to China for its consumer goods, the IMF offered to pay Americas debts for her, arguing that the other course of action would be more catastrophic for the world!!! Can you credit it? It beggars belief, it really does. Yet the so-called 3rd world countries, mainly African, are not allowed to have *their* debts written off, though so many more people and children are dying of starvation, disease and wars, and could really benefit from a bail-out too..... Racism, fuelled by Satanic forces surely keeps them downtrodden and puts the boot in...

More signs of the times Jesus warns are to come. 'When you see the 'abomination of the desolation, spoken of by Daniel the prophet, (Dan 11 v 31), standing in the holy place, (whoever reads, let him understand), then He says don't bother to go back and collect your belongings, and pray that you are not a pregnant or nursing mother, or that you are naked, or in the middle of winter, nor celebrating the Sabbath, when the tribulation comes, (57). 'For then there will be great tribulation, such as has not been seen since the beginning of the world until this time, no, nor ever shall be. And unless those days were shortened, no flesh would be saved; but for the ELECTS' sake, those days will be shortened (58)'. Then if anyone tells you Christ is over here or there, do not believe it, (Mark 13 v 32-37; Matt 24 v 23-27).

> 'For as the lightening comes from the east and flashes to the west, so also will the coming of the Son of Man be' (59).

There will be various other signs immediately before Christ returns. Then the sign of the Son of Man will appear in the heaven and all tribes of the earth will mourn, for they know their judgement is nigh, and they will want the mountains and the stones to hide them from the face of the Lord, but to no avail. Luke 23 v 30 says that people will cry out to be crushed so as to avoid the terrible things they will see and endure in the time of great tribulations that is to come. Jesus told the women weeping at his struggle and tortured journey to Calvary not to weep for him, but to weep for themselves and their children for the terrible times ahead. Indeed the 5th trumpet will arouse locusts to torture the wicked for five months with the stings of their tails. In those days people will seek death but will not find it. They will want to die, but death will flee away (Rev 9 v 6). Ultimately there will be no place to hide from the bright glare of the all-seeing and all-knowing mighty Judge, Jesus on that decisive day. 'And I saw the great white throne (of Judgement) and I saw the One who was sitting on it. The earth and the sky fled from His presence, but they found no place to hide' (60) (Is. 2 v 10, & v 19-21; Rev 20 v 11; Rev 6 v 15-17).

The 1960s Black soul singer, Nina Simone depicts what will happen on that day vividly in her song 'Sinner man. Some of her words follow:

'Oh sinner man, where you gonna run to...all on that day?

I ran to the rock, but the rock cried "I can't hide you, I ain't gonna hide you"

I ran to the river, the river was bleeding; I ran to the sea, the sea was bleeding,

I ran to the river, the river was boiling, the sea was boiling, the sea was boiling,

I ran to the Lord, "please hide me Lord! Don't you see I'm praying?"

He said "run to the devil".

The devil was waiting.

I cried: "Power! Power Lord! Send down power, Lord. Bring down power, Lord!"....

Lord said "child where were you when you ought to be praying? Sinner man you ought to be praying, all on that day."

"Power! Power Lord! Pour down power Lord. Bring down power Lord, don't you know I need you Lord? Power Lord!"

("SINNERMAN" ADAPTATION BY NINA SIMONE, (C) 1965 (RENEWED) WB MUSIC CORP. (ASCAP) ALL RIGHTS ADMINISTERED BY WARNER/CHAPPELL NORTH AMERICA LTD).

Listening to her sing, the lyrics sound more like the river and the sea were 'bawling' which better explains how distressing the whole plight of the people and the world will be. Even now, with increasing frequency, tsunamis, earthquakes and hurricanes/ tornadoes show us that even the earth is crying out in distress at the destruction man has caused on it! And global warming, like the frog who has the temperature in the kettle slowly turned up and doesn't notice to get out of the heat, we are sitting ducks on a planet that is getting ready for its final destruction, when our Creator allows it to erupt into the lake of fire and brimstone, that molten lava of volcanoes cannot match!

(NB. EGW, Story of Redemption p428-429:, 'Fire from heaven', ..."upon the wicked He shall rain down of quick burning coals, fire and brimstone, and horrible tempest", Ps 11 v 6. From the earth's bowels and chasm, the day has come that "shall burn as an oven", Mal 4 v 1. "The elements melt with fervent heat, the earth also and the works that are therein are burned up", (2 Peter 3 v 10). The fire of Tophet is prepared for the king, the chief of rebellion; the pile thereof is deep and large, and the breath of the Lord, like a stream of brimstone, doth kindle it", Is. 30v 33. The earth's surface seems one molten mass – a vast seething lake of fire. It is the time of judgement and perdition of ungodly men- "the day of the Lord's vengeance, and the year of recompenses for the controversy o fZion", Is 34 v 8. The wicked receive their recompense in the earth.')

In fact, Rev 20 v 13 says the sea, death, graves, all gave up their dead – so that they could face the judgement of Christ, 'all on that day'. No – one can escape. 'They were all judged according to their deeds. Then (61) Death and Hades were cast into the Lake of fire. This is the second death. And anyone whose name was not found in the Book of Life, was thrown into the lake of fire'. This is the destination of the wicked, whose smoke of their torment will be sent up to heaven, where the martyrs and saints, the elect whom the Lord has avenged (62), will enjoy their rewards and recompense in the presence of the glory of the Lord and angelic hosts. So, as Jesus advised us to repent and be baptized as His followers, I advise us to repent and pray for His mercy and forgiveness all BEFORE that day arrives.

Indeed Jesus warns: 'Behold, I am coming as a thief. Blessed is he who watches, and keeps his garments lest he walk naked and they see his shame' (63). We must be like the 5 wise virgins who brought oil with them whilst they waited to meet the bride-groom (64) we must be prepared for the return of the master, like the good servants who did his bidding till he returned (65). The hour when Jesus Christ will return is unknown, but we must repent and be ready as if he were coming this very day (66). For he said: 'And behold, I am coming quickly, and My reward is with Me, to give to everyone according to his work.' (67).

As for the faithful, when we see these signs, we are not to worry or be dismayed. We are to 'look up and lift our heads, because our redemption is near' (68). At this time Jesus will send His angels with great trumpet sounds, to gather together the elect from the four winds from one end of heaven to the other. (69). The elect or '144,000' will be gathered by the angels as the holy city of the New Jerusalem, who will be protected from the final onslaught from Satan and his army 'that went upon the breadth of the earth and surrounded the beloved city (70).

As the hymn sings 'Redemption Draweth Nigh':

"Years of time have come and gone

Since I first heard it told

How Jesus would come again some day,

If back then it seemed so real

Then I just can't help but feel

How much closer His coming is today.

Chorus:

Ahhh .... Signs of the times are everywhere,

And there's a brand new feeling in the air...

Keep your eyes upon the eastern sky

Lift up your head, Redemption draweth nigh.

Wars and strife on every hand

And violence fills the land,

Still some people doubt He'll come again,

But the word of God is true,

He'll redeem His chosen few,

Don't lose hope, soon Christ Jesus will descend

Chorus...Ahhh.... signs of the times are everywhere.....

Lift your head, redemption draweth nigh.

Lift up your head, lift up your head, lift up your head,

REDEMPTION DRAWETH NIGH!"

("REDEMPTION DRAWETH NIGH" WORDS AND MUSIC BY GORDON JENSEN (C) 1970 (RENEWED) WB MUSIC CORP. (ASCAP) ALL RIGHTS ADMINISTERED BY WARNER/CHAPPELL NORTH AMERICA LTD.) (71).

The elect will be safe, but as for Satan's army 'fire came down from 'God' out of heaven and devoured them, (72).

The outcome for the devil was that he was 'cast alive into the lake of fire and brimstone, where the beast (Satanic) and the false prophet are' (73). They were thrown into this hell where 'their worm does not die' that eats their rotting flesh, and burn in a fire 'that shall never be quenched' (74). This quote is repeated 3 times in the citation as Jesus emphasises the certainty and the severity of the punishments that await those who would defy Him and refuse to repent of their sins and return not to the Lord, their Creator and Redeemer.

So be sure you comprehend and fully understand that He is not joking. Heaven and Hell are real and you will be recompensed or punished depending on your choices in life. So be warned and take heed of the messages brought down to you from the prophets of old and the prophets of the present times. Rebuke Satan, Repent of your sins and Return to the Lord Almighty for your hope of salvation and eternal life spent in communion with Him.

(PS Hell was designed for Satan and his demons, not for humans. The deceased do not go to heaven or hell at death. They return to the dust whence they came, and their spirits, or breath of life, returns to YHWH whence it came. The soul, which is a combination of both body and spirit, also therefore dies when the body does, and cannot exist on its own; neither does the spirit. So no ghosts and ghouls and communicating with the dead. It's all a fallacy. A huge lie. A hoax. See Eccles 9 v 5-6, 'the dead know nothing'; Psm 146 v 4; Eccl 12 v 7; John 11 v 11-14, Lazarus dead as asleep, the sleep of death, psm 13 v 3; John 5 v 28-29 – those in the graves will awaken to 'His (returned Christ's) voice and come forth, - those who have done good, to the resurrection of life, and those who have done evil, to the resurrection of condemnation', Jesus said).

Again the punishments are spelt out clearly for us: the rest of the wicked who had joined Satan to attack the elect at Armageddon 'shall be killed by the sword which proceeded out of the mouth of Him (avenging Jesus) who sat on the horse. And all the birds were filled with their flesh' (75). And the 3, namely the devil (Satan), the beast and the false prophet, shall remain tormented in the fire and brimstone in the presence of the holy angels and in the presence of the Lamb (Jesus Christ) (76), where they will be tormented day and night, until suffered their due, they perish. Satan 'is made to suffer, not only for his own rebellion, but for all the sins which he has caused 'God's' people to commit. His punishment is to be far greater than that of those whom he has deceived... In the cleansing flames the wicked are at last destroyed, root and branch – Satan the root, and his followers the branches. The justice of 'God' is satisfied, and the saints and all the angelic host say with a loud voice, "Amen", '(EGW 'Story of Redemption', chp 66 – the second death, p 429).

There is waiting for the wicked certain tormented damnation, 'where there shall be weeping and gnashing of teeth (77). Those who join forces with Satan, whether before Armageddon or at that time, will be tormented and 'the smoke of their torment ascends forever and ever, and they have no rest day or night, (78). Again, those who are party to Babylon, the great harlot, shall not escape punishment when Jesus 'avenges on her, the blood of His servants shed by her... and her smoke rises up forever and ever! (79). However when Babylon falls, heaven and the holy apostles and prophets are to rejoice over her burning downfall, for Yahweh has avenged them on her (80).

But don't get it twisted. Lest you forget and carry on sinning. Judgement day assuredly awaits all of us and will occur as foretold in Rev 20 v 11 -15:

> 'Then I saw a great white throne and Him who sat on it (Yahweh) ,from whose face the earth and the heaven fled away. And there was found no place for them' (i.e.

the first heaven and earth – our current earth – had disappeared and no longer existed).

'Then the dead – small and great were standing before 'God' and books were opened. And another' book detailing the deeds of the people, especially the wicked. And the Book was opened – The Book of Life.

'And the dead were judged according to what was written in the books – their deeds. The sea, Hades and Death gave up the dead that were in them so all could be judged according to his or her works.

'Then Death and Hades were cast into the Lake of fire, along with anyone not found written in the Book of Life. This is the 2nd and FINAL death.

NB Some people will be alive when Christ returns, just as a few of the prophets and patriarchs were translated into heaven, and did not die, or see their bodies corrupted in death. But all shall be judged, the living and the dead, on the Final day of Judgement. And each will receive his or her own punishment or reward accordingly.

The old heaven and earth will have passed away, and there will be a New heaven and a New earth, of the kingdom of Jesus Christ, with the holy city of the New Jerusalem. This city will be bejewelled (Rev 21) with gems, which are all the souls of the saints and martyrs, those elect that have been tried and tested through the fiery furnace of life's afflictions from Satan, and have overcome and been victorious through the intercession of our living Saviour and Redeemer, Christ Jesus our Lord.

As our reward for overcoming and doing His will and kept His commands to the end, Jesus will gives us authority to rule over the nations, with an iron rod of justice, and He will also give us 'the morning star', who is Lucifer aka Satan (Isaiah 14 v 12), and his followers, to make them come and fall down at our feet, and acknowledge that Jesus has loved us. And He will give us a permanent welcomed place as pillars in His temple, as shining examples of dedication and having pleased Him and His Father. He tells us to 'hold fast to what (we) have, so that no-one will take (our) crown(s)', (Rev 2 v 26-28 & Rev 3 v 9-11).

Thank you Jesus for not abandoning us and saving us and for your love!!! Christ has revealed that the final victory is His, at the end, and He has chosen some of us to share in His victory and to spend Eternity in communion with Him, and the Counsellor and our Father, Yahweh, who is 7 spirits of goodness and love, and with the faithful angelic hosts and the fellow saved human beings, the remnant few, the elect, the '144,000' to live in peace and happiness and harmony and unity and righteous law abiding existence forever and ever, Amen. Halleluiah and praises and exaltations to Him!!!

Take heart and be encouraged, for what was prophesied has already come to pass, and what is promised will surely come true. Our Lord will avenge the blood of the souls who were killed by the wicked for His name sake. And the saints and the martyrs who were persecuted and killed during 1260 years of Apostasy (538 AD to 1798 AD) will have their reward in the first resurrection when Jesus returns. But additionally, Daniel 12 v 12 says: 'Blessed is he who waits and comes to 1335 days (years)' for I am sure they will not be disappointed in the rewards for their sacrifices.

I also note that Dan. 12 v 11 says: 'And from the time that the daily sacrifice is taken away unto when the abomination of the desolation in the holy places is set up, there shall be 1290 days (years)'. 1260 years brings us to 1798 AD, and 1290 also refers to 1798AD, having begun 30 years earlier.

It began in 503-508AD under Clovis I, king of the Franks (France), who led a violent campaign to subdue the kingdoms that were hostile to the Papacy. In 503AD, Rome's ecclesiastical council decreed that the Pope was judge as God's vicar, and could himself be judged by no-one. The Bishop of Rome exalted himself to Prince of hosts, 'lifting off Christ's daily, (Daniel 8 v 11), and setting up the abominations, with the Pope as Peter's representative in the church. This is impudence, when Christ Himself, is the 'rock' and cornerstone of YHWH's church. The Pope usurped Christ's ministerial position.

Then 508AD is another significant year, as it marks a new era in the course of world history; and the establishment of the first Catholic kingdom in the West, under the French king Clovis. It also marks the union of the church power – the ecclesiastical power with the winning political power, that was to dominate European history for centuries to come.

'They took away the daily' refers to Roman Catholic church setting up saints as mediators for the people, instead of Christ, who mediates in the heavenly sanctuary. So we have the icons and so forth, like the St Christopher's for the travellers, St Anthony who took care of pigs, and so forth – Remember idolatry, and worship of graven images or of persons and things other than our most gracious Lord and Saviour, is forbidden by YHWH in His commandments!

Finally, 1335, brings us to 1843 AD, as the Adventist Movement began in religious revival, and is the year that the '1st and 2nd angels messages swelled into a loud cry' (Rev 14 v 6-9). They proclaimed 'the hour of His judgement has come', and 'come out of her (symbolic Babylon) my people'. In 1844 there was the Great Disappointment, when the calculated and predicted return of Christ did not happen, but out of which came 17yr old prophetess Ellen G White, who founded the Seventh Day Adventist Movement, which has since grown worldwide down to the present day

How can we as sinners be saved from Hell and this permanent frightful end?

We can be saved by following the lifestyle that our Father instructed to in His Commandments, by following it as reaffirmed and demonstrated by Jesus Christ, and by resisting Satan's temptations and rejecting and refraining from wicked and sinful thoughts and behaviour. Doing this is hard enough for most of us, but in addition we must go 'the extra mile' and do the extraordinary.

Our Father, ever-loving and ever-merciful, wants to receive and welcome us back to Himself, like the father in the story of the prodigal son, (81), so that we might gain and enjoy the blessings of His gifts – Love and eternal Life. He wants the best for us, which is a life free from strife, shared with Him in Eternity. But we must do our part too. We must take the necessary steps to make this happen. He wants us to be perfect as He is, and He is perfection – Love itself, and moreover – is UNCONDITIONAL Love. Jesus Christ said we must 'love, forgive and...pray for those who' hurt and persecute us...our enemies,' if we are to 'be perfect as our heavenly Father is perfect' (82).

This kind of love is not that which is called 'Stockholm Syndrome'(83). This is the warped kind of love that a victim may start to feel towards her kidnapper, or an abused child towards his/her abuser, or a person towards the perpetrator who is domestically violent/abusive to him/her. Their 'love' is a confused emotive state of love (dependency) and fear (hatred) of their abuser. It is not healthy, and victims require emotional support, and sometimes counselling to help them recover from these traumatic experiences.

Nor are we to show *gratitude* to our abusers and tormenters, as is the current idea being circulated, because 'if it wasn't for them, we would not be who we are today'. In other words we are to thank them for 'moulding' our stalwart and hardy characters by their abusive and violent behaviour towards us. How ludicrous is this? What madness! This is like saying to the surviving Jews who've managed to forgive the Hitler and his agents for the atrocities they perpetrated against them, that they should *thank* them for torturing and nearly exterminating them! No, no, no. Please don't get it twisted. We should not be thanking our abusers. We should be thanking and praising Jesus Christ, who endured torment and death from His accusers and Satan, and who carries us even now, through our sufferings and torments so that we can survive them, and be freed to have life that is bearable again.

Loving your enemies is another dimension of unconditional love. This is the unique, unbelievable, incomprehensible, seemingly impossible, ability that we are to have in order to be considered 'perfect as our heavenly Father is...' Such love requires us to forgive those, who have hurt, abused, tormented us physically, sexually, emotionally and psychologically; those who have ruined our relationships, or who have destroyed our securities in our home, work and finances, who make us feel anguished, terrified, angry, bitter, twisted, hurt, worthless and virtually hopeless. Forgive those who, egged by Satan's influence, have made our lives a living hell on earth. Love them. Forgive them. Pray for them. Like Jesus did. We must do the same if we are to prove our love for Him and for our Father in heaven.

Jesus encourages us to 'bless those who curse' us and pray for those who ill-treat us...even turn the other cheek if someone strikes us....' We must 'do good to our enemies... expecting nothing back from them...' and our reward will be great. For we will be called 'sons of the Most High' our Father, 'because He is kind to the 'ungrateful and the wicked'. We are to be 'merciful as our Father is merciful' (84). If we forgive, we will be also be forgiven by our Father, who will reward us greatly with 'a good measure, pressed down, shaken together and running over....' (85). This all-encompassing quality of love and forgiveness is only possible with the help of the Holy Spirit, once we decide to live according to the Lord's principles for 'clean living'.

This unconditional love is not to be confused with the emotion-ally charged sexual love, in whatever various forms it is demon-strated from heterosexual to homosexual or even asexual. No. It is just love, of the purest kind. Love is the opposite of hate, and hate can be devastating. And our Creator hates disobedi-ence, lies and deception, because it leads to pain and suffer-ing. It hurts Him to see so many of His created people suffering because of sin. Jesus said woe unto those whose 'hand'/behav-iour cause children and those who are humble like children to sin (86). He is angry and upset at those who cause sin in this world, ie Satan and his like-minded followers, whose deception brought curses and death upon mankind (87).

But don't be alarmed. Our Father hates sin, but not the sin-ner. The sinners Jesus forgave are proof of that, including the criminal crucified alongside him (88). Because He loves us so much, He gives us many chances to use our emotions wisely. It is good to hate sin, but not the sinner. For, as Jesus told the hypocritical and scornful religious leaders, 'the well (healthy) have no need of a physician' so they were not His priority. But He came to heal the sick (89), and to call 'sinners to repen-tance'(89), so that they might be saved from damnation in Hell. This helps us to understand how it becomes possible for us to love and forgive those who have hurt us, and even pray for them. It is good to despise wrong-doing, but exceptionally, our duty is to help others by - pointing out their wrongs, and show-ing them how they can positively change their minds and hearts to live more in accordance with Our Father's wishes. He still loves us, and encourages us to 'come, just as we are' (90), and not wait till we achieve what we think is perfection, before we approach Him, otherwise it might be too late and we'll miss our chance for forgiveness and salvation.

The love of our Creator surpasses all understanding. It is abun-dant and without measure. Such is the extent of His love for us that 'He gave us His only begotten son, Jesus Christ (John 3 v 16) – who is the embodiment of Love. He is Love personified.

And He is the route to our ultimate satisfaction. (Unlike Satan who is the root of all evil). If we do what is required of us, Our Father will give us 'the desires of our heart' (91). He has already given us Jesus, who is the 'joy of man's desiring' (Bach's Cantata BWV 147, choral). He has given us 'sacrificial love', unconditional love, -perfection Himself. Our Father gives us priceless gifts of Love and Life. So, as Jesus said, it's no use 'storing up' for ourselves earthly 'treasures that are perishable'(92), but rather we should collect treasures that are valuable, priceless, and long-lasting, in heaven, - like joy, peace, and love(93) - that bring Life and the fullness thereof, for all Eternity.

In order to attain these goals, we must be willing to reject evil and wickedness; to make our own personal sacrifices – not pursuing worldly 'lusts', treasures and pride-inducing accolades (94); endure and overcome afflictions, and most importantly, LOVE unconditionally, by even forgiving and praying for our enemies. This is so that we can be 'perfect as our heavenly Father is perfect' and be remade into His image, that He intended in the garden of Eden, at the start of Creation. This is how much He loves us. Do we love Him as much to do as He asks?

Yes, there will be hard times ahead, trials and tribulations. We will be tested in the fiery furnace and the flood will come again – the ensuing flood that our loving Father is sending again. You may counter argue that He promised not to flood the earth again. But the flood that is coming our way is that of terrible afflictions and destruction in punishment that our Father will allow the avenging angels of death to inflict on the wicked at the End of Time (book of Revelation), when Christ has returned. For indeed Christ IS the flood that is to come soon and very soon from now.

So don't be envious of the wicked (95) - of their evil ingenuity, fame, riches, 'cribs' or wealthy life-styles. For, their end is destruction and their destination is Hell.

Instead take heed of the Lord's words as He instructs us on the path to righteousness and safety, through the tests and refinement in the fiery furnace, back into His loving arms, that is our refuge (96) into Life of Eternity –reconciled in perfect communion with Him.

For the Lord does not abandon us. He loves us still and will claim us back from Satan, and take us under His protective wings (96) into life with Him and the angels in the New heaven and New earth, that will be everlasting, for all Eternity.

BEWARE AND BE A WINNER – WHO IS GOD, REALLY?

Before we go any further I must fulfil my duty and reveal to you, as was painfully and excruciatingly, through frightening sweats and shakes and my nerve wracking reluctance to accept what was being revealed to me during the whole night of Christmas Eve 2010, - just who God really is ... He is not whom we have been led to believe he is.

Some years before, when I was going through another vulnerable emotionally distressing time, just before my second severe nervous breakdown in 1994, my sister, Betty, told me that I should not use the name God, but Father, when I was referring to the Almighty. For, she asked me what does God spell backwards? Flabber-ghasted and alarmed I told her not to blaspheme in my house.

And it never resurfaced again till last year Christmas, when I was being informed about the Illuminati in the music industry, as I was having reactions from a reduction in psychotic medication (symptoms of illusion and paranoia that were temporary as my mind and body experienced withdrawal symptoms from 20 years of psychotic drugs, until I adjusted to the reduction a few months later). I was being haunted and tormented by the devil in my waking and sleeping, as even close family members and friends and church family members appeared to be demon-possessed to me, and I began to trust no-one. I was writing chap 8 about the pagan influences in Christianity and of Saturnalia and Christmas.

As I was dosing off to sleep in my night bath I heard a loud and sinister whisper in my ear that jolted me in fright to awaken: 'Thank you Satan!!!' I was alarmed as I'd learned from Prof Griff's You tube expose (97) that President Obama's campaign and winning election slogan: 'Yes we can' heard backwards was those very words – 'thank you Satan'. You can imagine how terrified I was. That same night became one of mental and spiritual torment as I got no sleep. On the wall adjacent to my bed I had a poster that had been given to me years earlier, again in 1994, that proclaimed that God is the great and mighty king of all the earth, in big writing over the globe. For days before this Christmas I had started to feel uneasy about it hanging there as if tormenting me, as I began to remember what my sister had told me about God/dog 17 years before, and now discovering the devil amongst the Illuminati, the Free Masonry/Lodge, and seeping through so many areas of our lives that it is imperceptible to us, as if normal. I tore down that poster and destroyed it.

This Christmas Eve night 2010, I dreaded falling asleep as I did not know what the devil would put in my mind, and every time I started to drop off I would awake abruptly sweating and trembling in fear. Eventually I gave in and the Holy Spirit revealed to me that indeed God was not the being I had been worshipping all my life! God was Satan's name!!! He was the USURPER of our holy and heavenly Father Yahweh's rightful place for adoration and worship. God was indeed dog! The ancient Egyptian dog-headed god, Anubis – animalistic, bestial and pagan, as you would expect from the fallen conceited angel Lucifer now called Satan. I am sorry if you are shocked and devastated, but hear me out.

For since I wrote this piece last year (2011), I have had even more definite and serious confirmation from the **Lord YHWH'**

Holy Spirit of Truth and Prophecy, Christ – THE Word of Truth Himself, that Satan has been deceiving and tricking the WHOLE world into worshipping him as God (Rev 12 v 9), instead of our Rightful Ruler Christ /YHWH (Yahweh)! This confirmation came in revelation and discovery on the very significant date of **25th June 2012!**

As explained in revelation about the Flood being Christ Jesus in this 2012 elsewhere in this chap 9, Rev 10 v 7 marks the 'days when the mystery of God is finished' as it is about to be sounded/announced by the 7th angel, when the secret ID of God is about to be made public to the world, and thus undermine and destroy his power and influence over the mankind, as he has gleefully been deceiving the whole world with this identity for thousands of years, the significance of YHWH choosing this date as the unveiling is very telling and powerful.

June is the month halfway through the Julian (Roman pagan calendar). The 21st June is the summer solstice, and is deemed the longest day of the year, having more hours of sunlight/daylight than any other in accordance with British Greenwich meantime, the source point from which time all other time zones are set. However, June being the height of summer is the opposite/antithesis of the darkest and coldest month in winter, December. The 21st December is the shortest day of the year and is in the winter solstice.

Not only this, but the date of 25th of June is in direct contradiction and contra-distinction to 25th December, that Roman Catholic Church has taught most of the Christian world to worship and celebrate as Jesus Christ's birth date, aka Christmas. However as I have discussed in chapter 8, the 25th December was chosen in AD 354, by the R C Bishop of Rome, Liberius, to coincide with the pagan worship of 'dies natalis solis invicti (birth of the invincible sun-god., the same date as birthday of Mithra, the Iranian 'god of light'. It is also celebrated as the birthday of the sun in some religions/mythologies. The Roman Catholics in their attempts to popularise Christianity and attract more follow-ers, adopted some pagan gods, traditions and practices, thus corrupting the sacredness of our Creator's Truths and Laws and Covenants! And this they have continued to do intensely for centuries since Christ became incarnate as a human being in infant Jesus grown into a man of prophecy and Truth 2,000 years ago!

The actual date of Christ' birth is not known, although one of my secondary school teachers, a convent nun, told us that his birth was probably around September, more than December; and elsewhere other Christians take 6th January as a more likely date, having traced back lunar times. Regardless of mere spec-ulation, for that is all it is, the actual date is unknown, because the birth date of the Living Word Jesus Christ, is not recorded anywhere in the written word, the Bible. YHWH is smart, for He knew what Satan's champions would claim, so He outfoxed them and Satan!!!

Indeed YHWH chose 25th June in this Revelatory year of 2012, - 6 months before their pagan celebration of Saturnalia (see Chap 8), their pretend celebration of Christ's birth – Christmas, - to ful-fil His prophecy of Revelation 10 v 7, about the 7th angel being about to sound the mystery of God would be finished. Namely God's secret ID being the devil himself, aka Satan, that serpent of old (Gen 3) , or dragon that causes wars and persecutes the innocent (Rev 12), and speaks lies and deceives the whole world, along with the beast and the false prophet, causing the whole world to worship him (Rev 13) and (Rev 20 v 1-3, v 7-10 – note the Deceiver's end is the lake of fire & brimstone - the 2nd and final death of everlasting torment!!! Selah.)

So Satan has gleefully been getting the world to celebrate his ever increasingly commercialised and money-grabbing Christmas festivities, that barely mention Jesus Christ, but divert everyone, especially the younger generation, - the chil-dren-, away from Christ. They are led to focus instead on Santa

Claus, St, Nicolas (St Nick), aka Bishop of Myra in Lycia AD300; and his present – giving practice, after the precedent of Norse pagan goddess Hertha entering the house through the chimney bringing 'good luck'.

Worse still, the powers that control the media and the entertainment industry have been aiding this deception of the devil, with cartoons such as Tom and Jerry and Mickey Mouse and more recently the Simpson's irreverent and disrespectful boy character, Bart Simpson. He not only pulls down his shorts to expose his bottom irreverently (and more sinisterly inviting paedophilic abusers to prey even more on innocent children!!!), but his dog that he call's Santa's little helper, has had his secret identity revealed to me too. The anacronym for Santa is Satan, and Santa /Satan's little helper is dog –aka God. And as I've established earlier this is none other than the ancient Egyptian's dog-god, Anubis!

Now ancient Egyptian goddess Isis of whom Queen Cleopatra claimed to be the goddess reincarnated, has according to ancient Greek writer Proclus, a statue bearing the inscription: I am that which is, has been, and shall be. My veil no-one has lifted. The fruit I bear is the sun', (Encyclopaedia of Literature, p 506, book I read in 1990). In other words her veil shall never be lifted to reveal the mystery contained underneath it, or within its covers. To lift the veil of Isis is to pierce the heart of the great mystery. On 25th June 2012, that veil was lifted, and would have been uncovered sooner, in August 1990, had the devil not slapped the maddening mental illness of schizophrenia, his affliction, upon me, like he did upon Biblical Job, to try and prevent this discovery and his secret ID being exposed. Well he succeeded in delaying the time, but YHWH's and Christ's Truth will be revealed, at His given time, no matter what or how Satan tries to prevent it.

So there it is. God is Anubis. And he started life as a jackal that scavenged and dug up and ate the rotting flesh of buried dead people.

So he was a very unwelcome guest. The ancient Egyptians show him as a jackal –headed god associated with mummification in their religion. In mythology he was the son of Nephthys and Set. The oldest known mention of him is in the Old kingdom pyramid texts, where he is associated with the burial of the pharaoh. At this time Anubis was **the** most important god of the dead, but he was replaced/ usurped by Osiris in the middle kingdom. Anubis name connection is as: he who is upon his mountain as the protector of the deceased and their tombs; and he who is in the place of their embalming or mummification. YHWH was angry, (Ezekiel 8, and 9 v 1-11), at the Israelites priests and princes secretly worshipping pagan idols that made Him angry, and who had adopted idolatrous practices of ancient Egyptians.

(Hence YHWH's anger shown by Ezekiel 8, v 5- pagan Egyptian influences, by using His incense, that they pretended was intended to worship Him, but really was used for devil worship – gods/aka Anubis/ aka Satan. For as Jeremiah 2, especially v 5, explained: Israelite's ancestors terrible and wilful sin, was that 'they worshipped foolish idols, only to become foolish themselves'.....v 11-13 'Yet My people have exchanged their glorious YHWH {God} for worthless idols! The heavens are shocked at such a thing and shrink back in horror and dismay, says the Lord. For My people have done two evil things: They have forsaken Me – the fountain of living water. And they have dug for themselves cracked cisterns that can hold no water at all!' They 'have entered into a covenant with death, with the grave (they) have made an agreement' trusting in the 'lie (as) refuge, and falsehood (as) hiding –place from the overwhelming scourge'. So our 'Sovereign Lord....will make justice the measuring line, and righteousness the plumb-line; hail...and water will sweep away your refuge, the lie,.. and your ..hiding- place. ..Your covenant with death will be annulled; your agreement with the grave will not stand, when the overwhelming scourge sweeps by... and beat(s) you down by it... The understanding of this message will bring sheer terror', (Isaiah 28 v 14-19), saith the Lord Almighty!!!

This idolatry was the mistake that the early ancient Egyptians made, when their 'princes of Norph and of Zoan' listened to their 'wisemen'/ 'officials', who in fact led them astray and made them worship idols, (Isaiah 19 v 11 -17) instead of their first love YHWH, and because they have followed deluded counsel, YHWH confused, confounded and punished them severely.

As prophesied, history has shown the increasing drying up of the river Nile, and expansion of ever increasing desert ; the destruction and obliteration of their cities and most of their vast number of pyramids and temples hidden under deep sand (in May 2011 Dr Sarah Parcak, an American archaeologist and Egyptologist, through work pioneered at University of Alabama at Birmingham, USA, discovered evidence of 17 pyramids, and 1,000 tombs and 3,000 ancient settlements in city construc-tions buried deep beneath sand in Egypt, notably Saqqara and ancient capitol city Tanis, near modern-day San El Hagar, north of Cairo. They used the latest infra red image detection in satel-lite technology, sources various on net including: 'Mail on-line, Egypt's lost pyramids:Spied from space by satellite,17 tombs buried by sands of time, 26 May 2011, by Fiona Macrae.'). Most controversially and sadly has been the traumatic enslavement of her peoples – East and West slave trades of African peoples for over 400 years in recent times. This will continue until such times as a remnant, that have been tried and disciplined, return to offer him worship and sacrifices at His altar, together with Assyria and Israel (Is. 19 v 23-25), most likely in the last days before Christ returns, like some of us Black descendants of the ancient Egyptians do now).

Back to Anubis, who assumed different roles, according to dif-ferent contexts. He is seen attending the weighing scale in the Afterlife, during the weighing of the heart (to assess the truth or not of the person's life been good or bad). This parallels as counterfeit to YHWH's weighing scales, where for instance Babylonian king Belshazzar, son of Nebuchadnezzar, was found 'wanting'/ lacking, and not in balance: 'MENE, MENE TEKEL

UPHARSIN', and earned His condemnation, -punishment of death. For he had defiled Israel's YHWH's sacred gold vessels fro carousing and getting drunk with his wives, concubines and courtiers at a feast, when a finger appeared writing on the wall. Fearing foreboding, a bad omen, he called prophet Daniel to interpret the message. Daniel said that 'Mene, mene' meant 'God' had numbered his kingdom and finished it. Tekel, that the king had been weighed in the balance and found wanting. And Peres, that his kingdom would be divided between Medes and Persia. That very night the king was slain, and his kingdom was received by Darius the Mede. (Daniel 5). Prophecy came true.

Anubis wife was goddess Anput,. Their daughter is goddess Kebechet. As scavenger jackal, the black colour assigned to Anubis is the colour of the rotting flesh; and the black fertile soil of the Nile valley, symbolising rebirth. The embalming priests wore a jackal headed costume to perform their funeral rites, as are depicted on the Egyptian tombs and in their book of the Dead. Anubis was therefore Lord of the Underworld, the Afterlife, the Ruler of the Dead. He paled into insignificance, as usurper Osiris became more prominent, along with Isis, Set and Ra. There is some confusion about who his parents were, and later myths stated he was the son of Osiris and Nephthy, and in this role helped Isis to mummify his dead father. Indeed when the myth of Osiris and Isis emerged (mother/husband/ son –incestuous; of later 20th century psychotherapist Sigmund Freud's Oedipus Complex), it was said that Osiris had been killed by Set, and his organs had been given to Anubis as a gift!

How jackal became dog, and then god, God, were due to perceptions outside Egypt. In later times, during the Ptolemaic period, Anubis was merged with the Greek god Hermes (becoming Heranubis). The centre of this cult was in Cynopolis, whose Greek name means 'city of dogs'. In book XI of 'The Golden Ass' by Apuleius, is evidence that worship of this god was maintained in Rome, at least up until the 2nd century. Indeed Hermanubis also appeared in the alchemical and hermetical literature of the

Middle Ages (also known as the Dark Ages, of Apostasy),and the Renaissance, (approx. 11th century to 15th century).

Anubis was called mockingly 'the barker' by the Greeks, and is sometimes associated with Sirius dog-star in the heavens (Harry Potter's Sirius); and with Cerberus in Hades. Plato and Socrates (eg Republic 399a, 592a) have also referred to him in their writings as 'by the dog', 'by the dog of Egypt', 'by the dog, the god of the Egyptians' (Georgias 482b). He was also known as the god of mummification and death. (source internet Wikipedia – Anubis).

So don't get it twisted. Be bright and get it Right! God and YHWH, God and Christ Jesus, and God and the Holy Spirit are not one and the same! They are NOT co-terminus. They are NOT synonymous. God, as Satan, is very far removed from YHWH's Light, Love and Life. God is Satan and is evil, and bad, wicked and sick, in the true meaning of the words; and not as currently reigns the distorted meanings attaching goodness to them, as Michael Jackson and others have done in recent decades!

So the Roman Catholic's doctrine teaching of the Holy Trinity as the God-head 3 ie.: God the Father, God the Son and God the Holy Ghost or Holy Spirit, is a TRAVERSTY!!! It is wrong and disrespectful to the TRUTH that is our Holy and Most Gracious Father YHWH, and Christ Jesus, and His 7 Holy Spirits, who far exceed that dog in supreme superiority and power and authority!

The Godhead 3 is wrong, and henceforth is to be revoked, and the usurpation by Satan as God needs to be removed/ unseated/dethroned. The TRUE and RIGHTFUL and JUST RULERS, YHWH, CHRIST and HOLY SPIRITS must be rein-stated!!! Selah.

Unfortunately the word God is so intrinsic in our everyday lan-guage: 'God is love', 'Godsend', 'God bless', 'OMG!', 'Oh my

God!', etc. But when you use the wrong name for our Creator, you are bringing curses upon yourself, instead of blessings, for YHWH is incensed with the offence, and Satan jumps up and down gleefully. And when you cry 'oh my God, I don' wanna die, help me!', or when you call on Christ to save you from death, know the real reason why you seek help. Is it because you are afraid of pain and suffering, or 'cos you want to save your own skin, or of the unknown aspects of death, or because you truly love Jesus with all your heart, mind, body and soul (Matt 22 v 37-39)?

When you know that you have rebuked Satan, repented, and chosen to follow Christ in your daily life, you will be assured of His promised salvation from the terrible tribulations to come, and of your place beside Him in His eternal kingdom, in the New earth that will be wholly complete like the garden of Eden was, and in the bejewelled new Jerusalem – the crowning glory of the new earth. How wonderful to contemplate, and hopefully, one day behold and enjoy!

So when you pray, or call upon the Lord, to whom are you speaking? Who are you worshipping? Are you 'down with the God Squad'? Or are you now having a reality check, and using the Lord our heavenly Father's Rightful names? Any of the Hebrew Jewish names will do – from YHWH (Yahweh), Jehovah, Eloihim, El- Shedai, to even the name Allah, that the descendants of their half brother Ishmael, first son of patriarch Abraham, have called YHWH.

But not god, goddess, or deities, idols or even God. Old habits die hard, and often slip ups will be made, but now you know that God is Satan's secret identity, please try your best not to refer to God when you really mean our heavenly Father. Remember the Lord's prayer that His son Jesus taught His disciples to pray, He said: 'Our Father, who art in heaven, hallowed be thy Name,...'. He did not say 'our God'; and He never called Himself 'son of God', but rather 'son of Man'.

For, He had to save mankind, human beings, not the devil and his demons. As Ellen G White wondered, oh man, who are you, made from dust, yet once you have overcome evil, you are more precious to the Lord, than the angels? Even Lucifer in his most beautiful and talented state, before he fell, pales in comparison to the pleasure we give our Father in heaven, sat upon His throne. He is 'well pleased' with those of us who have chosen to love the Lord, rather than succumb to the devil, or even our 'own way'/ wilfulness. Surely this proves we are worth the sacrifice that

Jesus Christ made for us on the cross at Calvary, and deserve to be resurrected (once dead), or be taken alive to live with Him in communion of Perfect Circles!

Unbelievably, ancient Egyptian Anubis and Isis influenced Greeks, Romans, and by the paganised Roman Catholic church, spread into the modern day, and now disguised as God, the usurper Satan, has taken credit and honour that rightfully belongs to YHWH and His son Jesus Christ.

This is why the version of 'Agnus Dei', written by Michael Smith, and performed so superbly and beautifully by young Brazilian lad, Jotta A, winner of Kids Got talent 2011, and elsewhere by Michael W Smith, and others, was so poignant to me during this 6 weeks of May and June, under inspiration of the Holy Spirit, and during my incarceration in hospital. For really who is God really? As the song lyrics go:

'Holy, Holy, Are you Lord God Almighty?

Worthy is the Lamb, Worthy is the Lamb, Amen'

And I would never disrespect the song writers who did not know all of this about God, and truly I do believe worship Christ and His Father YHWH. But I ask the question of 'God': Are you Lord Almighty?' And as he is Satan and definitely NOT YHWH or Christ, 'though a lord, he certainly **cannot** be Almighty nor OMNIPOTENT, OMNISCIENT, OMNIPRESENT NOR OMNIBENEVOLENT. And he cannot CREATE. All of these characteristics belong **only t**o YHWH in His various KINGLY Persons, of Jesus the Christ and His 7 Holy Spirits. Only to Him should our credit and worship be directed and to none other, and certainly to no idols or Satan and his various aliases.

Be warned and be wise, lest you lose your reward and inheritance in Christ's eternal kingdom soon to come!!!

Satan who had envied and coveted our Father Yahweh's praises and adoration and worship that the angels gave Him, and he so conceited in his own beauty and talents, craved the same for himself. He wanted to be worshipped and adored and have accolades directed at him too. In fact he wanted more than the same as Yahweh, he wanted to USURP Him and take over his highly esteemed place and subjugate Yahweh, his and our Creator, beneath him!!! How impudent and preposterous and outrageous!

This is why he deceived the whole wide world for centuries, from the beginning of the Fall, to worshipping gods and God, which are himself, rather than the One who created all of us, our true Creator, heavenly Father Yahweh. In so doing he feels he can become adored as equal to, or greater than Yahweh. Not only that, he also feels so rejected and 'alone' and miserable and angry, SEPARATED from the light and glow and warmth of the love of Yahweh, out of the spot light, demoted from his once highly esteemed and privileged position as 'covering guardian angel of the Lord' (98), that he wants so very badly to get back into that hallowed place of heaven.

It was he who was behind the people building the Tower of Babel. It was he who instilled the desire to build the monolithic pyramids and other tall obelisks, structures reaching to the skies. It was he who instigated man's desires to build aeroplanes and rockets to fly, and especially into outer space at obscene astronomical costs, in attempts to find heaven, not merely other habitable planets as it is cloaked under. Satan wants so badly to get back into heaven to take over the rightful place of our Father Yahweh, and be 'in charge', so that he can have all the power, and be worshipped and adored infinitely.

And to this end he already deceived and took with him nearly half (98a) of the angels after the controversial war with Michael(Jesus) in heaven at the beginning of Time, and then jealously deceived Adam and Eve to upset Yahweh further. And ever since he has been deceiving mankind into worshipping himself and doing all manner of evil, and warring and galvanising his army of demons and evil and otherwise misguided and selfish humans to fight against Jesus/ Michael, and ultimately at Armageddon against Yahweh Himself, in attempts to defeat Him and take over and be the Ultimate Ruler to be worshipped and adored forever!!! Can you believe it! Can you really Adam and Eve it??? Can you imagine what Eternity with Satan as Ruler would be like, given what the devastating destruction he has done on this planet earth, and the disruption he caused in heaven? Would any of us survive? Most likely not! There would be nothing but death and desolation.

Knowing this would you still want to worship this Usurper who calls himself God, who is evil personified? Would you want to be identified as being one of his footmen? Would you even want to associate with him, or want anything to do with him? Would you be foolish, or even wicked enough to give your allegiance to him, over and above the True Ruler, Jesus Christ?

When Jesus Christ was crucified and buried 3 days in a tomb, He visited Hell and Hades to give comfort to those true to Him and His Father YHWH, who had died before, that their resurrection and salvation would soon come. The Roman Catholics commemorate His death on Good Friday, and resurrection on the alleged 3rd day – Easter Sunday, which I've pointed out in chapter 8, is their pagan sun-worship day, and that the 3rd day was really the Monday. But what really we all should celebrate and be thankful/grateful for is the fact that His Father YHWH resurrected Christ from the dead underworld of Anubis, and thereby annihilated Satan's power of death over mankind!!!

YHWH brought His son Jesus out of the darkened world, back to Light and Life, for Love of Him and of us, humankind, His beloved creatures!!! How amazing is that! Yet we are so far removed from His sight, and deep in sin, that few of us appreciate or comprehend/understand the immensity and magnitude of this gesture of LOVE. Do note that it is only the Creator, YHWH of Life, who is able to bring people back to life, as Jesus showed when He prayed to Him to raise Lazarus from the dead, and other examples of miracles done by Him and others since. And it is He who is the ultimate Judge, accompanied by Jesus Christ - who will defend His won-over, prized overcomers, the redeemed 'elect' '144,000', and YHWH who will authorise the immortality of those men, women and children who have been found 'faithful and blameless'. He alone, will give permission for those blessed redeemed, countless millions of people, 'multitudes of nations and tongues' to live forever in the new heaven and new earth, with the true and loyal angels, and other beings that exist in the universe that have remained faithful and not contravened His laws and authority.

Satan, as God, has been blocking mankind's access to our Father YHWH, and has done his level worst to prevent people accepting Christ's invitation to come back to our Father through Him, His son. Christ gave His life's blood on that cross at Calvary. He lay down His life willingly, of His own accord. No-one took it from Him. As He said 'I have authority to lay it down...and to take it up again. This command I received from

My Father' (John 10 v 18). He OBEYED Yahweh's command. This Lucifer/ Satan refused to do. But Jesus did not do so in vain. It was not for nothing that He endured persecution, torture, torment, mental and physical, and emotional.

His spirit was uncowed, and triumphantly *He* overcame Satan's temptations and trials and tribulations, showing us that we as mere humans, can do likewise if we choose to believe on Him, and follow His teachings and example. By power of YHWH's Holy Spirits we can overcome and be victorious and share in the rewards due to Christ's flock., the mansions in YHWH's house, and to be seated as a bride at the bridegroom/Lamb/ Jesus Christ's marriage feast, more than just an invited guest!!! Imagine!

We can be true and real 'brides of Christ' the Lamb Jesus, - who is worthy and sits beside His Father at His RIGHT side (Right hand man). Together they are RIGHT, RIGHTEOUS IN TRUTH, RIGHTFUL, LAWFUL, and Jesus has EARNT His legally binding place of HONOUR, crowned with many crowns, on His right royal throne!!! So He, Jesus the Christ, the sacrificed Lamb, is worthy to be praised. And for how long? Forever, and ever and ever ad infinitum. And by whom? By everyone and everything that exists –whether animate or not, forces of nature, or spirit, or human and all other creatures that have breath, ALL in Creation, in heaven and earth and other planets are to bow down and worship Him. He truly deserves it. Let no- one fool you. No-one else has sacrificed so much for ALL of mankind, past, present and remaining future. Dutifully and happily rejoice, for He is GREAT!!! This is the Word and Spirit of Truth and prophecy as revealed and confirmed to me on 25th June 2012, which I faithfully and dutifully record here, this day 20th August 2012. Lord be praised! Halleluhiah! I've made it through Satanic afflictions and obstructions.

When Jesus taught his disciples 'the Lord's Prayer' (99), he did not say 'our God who art in heaven'. Rather he said say 'our

FATHER who art in heaven, hallowed be thy name...' The name Father is hallowed. It is holy. It is not to be taken in vain (the 3rd commandment, after the 2nd to not make any graven image or worship any other gods). These are grave and serious issues. They are not to be taken lightly or in jest.

You may ask: 'what's in a name'? What difference does it make? Surely our Father knows that we mean Him when we worship Him, even when we call Him 'God' as we have been taught to do for centuries?' Yes, our Father is omniscient and all-knowing. He knows whether you are referring to Himself or to the devil, as He knows what is in your heart and mind. He knows this. But that does not mean He likes being disrespected, or being called by a name that is the antithesis to who He is, ie, the name of the devil, Shaol, Baal, Satan!!!

Would you like to be called the name of one of the evil monsters of this world like Hitler, Mussolini, Saddam Hussein, Gadaffi? No, you would be very upset and highly offended. Would you call a rose shit? Shakespeare wrote 'a rose by any other name would smell as sweet'. But if you called it shit –foul smelling faeces, dog excrement, would you imagine it to still smell as sweet as a fragrant flower? I think not. Just by association the flower loses its appeal and becomes defiled. Similarly, and greatly more importantly, our Father Yahweh does not want to be associated with the evil Usurper Satan. He does not want His good and sacred name defiled. And why should He? He is the Almighty, Creator of heaven and earth. Why should he be so debased to disgusting filth, filthy menstrual rags, dog excre-ment? He, who is so pure and high and mighty and holy and to be revered? He, whose name is to be blessed by sun, moon, stars, weathers, creatures, trees, and angels, and yes us too, us humans (see ref 40 -4, chp 8, Extract from R C Bible, verses 1-68, between Dan 3 v23 to 24).

We should be blessing, and not cursing His holy name, that of Father, as He has commanded us to. Are you going to be obedient and call Him by His rightful, holy, sanctified, redeemed, blessed name, and so be mindful of, and respectful to Him? Now that you know that 'God' is NOT our heavenly Father, are you going to be right- living with Yahweh? Is your desire to live right with Him, become righteous according to Jesus' ways, and so become acceptable through loving, obedient faith, and be pleasing to our most high Lord and Saviour, our heavenly Father, Yahweh? If so ask the Holy Spirit to guide and protect you as you go forward in life, wiser and more spiritually assured in Christ, in honour and adoration and worship of the One and Only True Ruler, our heavenly Father, Yahweh. May He bless and keep and sustain and protect you against Satanic attack and deception and oppression. This I hope and pray in Jesus name. Amen.

The Lord's Prayer that Jesus taught us to pray:

The Our Father

Our Father

Who is in Heaven,

Holy is your Name.

Your kingdom come,

Your Will be done,

On Earth as it is in Heaven.

Give us this day

Our daily bread,

And forgive us our wrong doings

As we forgive those who hurt us.

And lead us not into temptation,

But save us from evil,

For Yours is the kingdom,

The Power and the Glory,

Forever and ever,

Amen.

(ref 99, Matt 6 v 9-13; Luke 11 v 2-4).

Rebuke Satan and all his evil!!!

Stop your wickedness and

Seek your blessed inheritance,

That was so painfully and preciously won

By Jesus Christ, our Saviour.

Oh my fear and desire is in the Lord Most High,

Whom I love immensely!!!

Thank you Jesus,

You are truly magnificent

In your splendour and glory!

Congratulations on your hard-fought victory!

You are Almighty!

The Great I Am!

The Alpha and Omega,

The Beginning and the End,

The Author and Finisher of things,

The Awesome and most Holy Creator!

All laud and honour and praises are due you,

Bless your Holy Name!

Amen.

(Is. 33 v 6 – 'the fear of the Lord is a righteous mans' treasure'; Jerem 9 v 24, "let me boast in this alone, that I truly know the Lord, who is just and righteous, whose love is unfading and delights in these things");

{also refer to EGW's The Story of Redemption, (1947) 1980, p273, for Jesus as 'the *author* and foundation of the religion of 'God's people from the days of Adam, and the *finisher* of the faith now so clear to his (Saul/ Paul) enlightened vision; the vindicator of the truth, and the fulfiller of the prophecies'. Although I wrote this poem in Jan 2011, I had never come across **author and finisher** for Jesus or YHWH before in text, as describe by

Ellen White, or any other until June 2012. How the Holy Spirit moves without contradiction, amongst His people! Awesome!}

Thank you Lord Almighty, thank you Jesus Christ, and thank you Holy Spirit for guiding me to your other prophets in the Bible besides Isaiah – chps 18-20 on the prophecies of Egypt, Assyria and Israel; but also chp 14 on Assyria and chp 17 on Israel and chp 22 on Jerusalem, & Jerem 25 & 46, – to prophet Hosea on Israel, and prophet Ezekiel chps 29-32 on Egypt, and especially chp 33 on the commission and duty and responsibility of a prophet, and chp 34 on the difference between a false and a good shepherd.

The Good Shepherd is You, the Lord Most High, who later chose David to be prince of Israel, whose royal line of Jesse Jesus descended from - Jesus who is Lord, the Creator Most High. Awesome!

These prophecies were written time immemorial ago, before Jesus was born, possibly as early as around Ancient Egypt's and Babylon's zenith (hay day) – Hosea's ministry from 755 -710BC, Isaiah's ministry from 740 -680BC, Ezekiel prophesied from 592 -570BC (The Open Bible NLT, Thomas Nelson,1998/1966). Yet written then, we have since seen the evidence of what was to become of her. All that was prophesied for Egypt, Cush, Ethiopia, Assyria, and Israel have come to pass in history up to the present time. This is a very sobering lesson to take note of: that the Lord's prophecies DO come true. He does not tell lies or deceive. He is faithful and true. And, if He says something will happen, rest assured it will. In the beginning He spoke and creation came into being. So if He says the wicked will perish they will and so will Hell. If He says you will have your reward – good or bad- rest assured that you will be judged and treated accordingly. So if you remain wicked, punishment, death and Hell is certainly yours. If however, you repent and turn to righteousness, are faithful to the Lord, you will be handsomely rewarded with abundant love, joy, happiness, peace and long, eternal

Life. 'He is able' to reward you 'exceeding and abundantly' so (100). Believe this. For He has said it, and it will be just so.

But wait! Don't be deceived by Satan. Our Father and Sovereign Lord is not vindictive. He hates death. He loves Life. For, He 'take(s) no pleasure in the death of wicked people. (He) only want(s) them to turn from their wicked ways so that they can live. Turn! Turn from your wickedness people of Israel. Why should you die?' (101). When the Israelites refused the gift of Himself, Jesus Christ, the Lord turned His back on them, and opened up His arms to give this window of opportunity to the rest of the world, so that all of us, 'though not beloved, can be blessed. We can be blessed via the stone that the builder rejected, the rock and cornerstone of our blessed hope, namely Jesus, who is *the* gateway to heaven and reconciliation of man to our Sovereign Lord, our Father and Creator. History has shown what has happened to the original Black Egyptians, Assyrians, the Israelites and Jerusalem. Egypt has over the centuries, become drier, more desolate and robbed of her treasures. Her people have been enslaved by Eastern, Arab, Moslem, and

Western, European, Christian countries, with racism fuelling slavery, colonialism, exploitation to modern day mental slavery. But as Isaiah 19 v 18-22, prophesied the Egyptians will come to bring offerings and worship at the altar to the Lord. In recent decades we have seen the rise of Black churches in USA and UK, as their descendants come to Christ, redirected and returning to Him, hoping in, inspired by, and carried through by His delivering us from slavery, emancipation, liberation struggles, civil rights movements, and from mental psychiatric imprisonment, to give Him thanks and praises at the altar of the Lord. Isaiah 19 v 25 has already begun to happen and become reality before our very eyes. For, the Lord says Egypt, Assyria and Israel will be allies, and Israel will be a blessing to them. The Lord Almighty will say: 'Blessed be Egypt, my people. Blessed be Assyria, the land I have made (the work of my hands). Blessed be Israel, my special possession (my inheritance).' (Isaiah 19 v

23-25). Israel is still beloved (Is. 43 v 1-7), and a 'remnant' will come to Jesus Christ and be saved, Halleluiah!!!

We have seen the Israelites scattered and almost wiped out in the genocidal Jewish Holocaust, which was also prophesied by Hosea. And as prophesied in Isaiah 10 v 5-19 and Is. 14 v 24-27, Assyria will be destroyed for what it did to Israel, namely over-powering and dominating them (even though our Creator used the Assyrians to discipline the Israelites so that they would return to Him). But still the Assyrians will be punished for being pompous about attacking the Lord's beloved Israelites. So as Isaiah says the Assyrians will incur the Lord's wrath and destruction will follow.

Prophecies do come true, and they are being fulfilled even as we speak today. Prophecies over the ancient Egyptians have come true, and also of the great Romans and ancient Greeks. All their countries and economies have declined over time, with their currencies at rock bottom and requesting bail-outs at this present time, summer and autumn 2011. The ancient Egyptians were punished by Yahweh, with Moses as His instrument of destruction, for turning their worship from Him towards Satan in their devil worship of their gods. Similarly the Romans and Greeks have been punished for their paganism. Egyptian devil-worshipping mythology influenced the Romans and Greeks, and is still very much present in modern day religions, even the so-called Christian, Roman Catholic religion, as well as in other spheres like the Secret societies of Freemasonry, the Lodge and the Illuminati, pervading many sectors of societies worldwide.

Those nations that were once so great in the West, Great Britain, United States of America, are not so confident in their greatness, rocked to their foundations by uprisings, revolutions, countries becoming independent of them, and even terrorising them in 9/11 and 7/7 Muslim attacks, in retaliation for their aggressive international policies and warfare. A few weeks ago USA experienced the worst stock market crash since the markets began a century ago, worrying its biggest creditor, China, and the worried IMF offered to bail them out. Today the rest of the world waits nervously to see if recession will give a reprieve, or if it will sink us deeper into the mire. Greece, Ireland, Italy, all face deep economic financial crises, as their money is not worth the paper it's written on. A few years ago the financial market was shaken by the devastating fall in the housing price markets in USA and UK and Ireland.. The governments opted to bail the banks out, arguing that the situation would be untenable without it. I ask you, are banks living, breathing entities of their own, that they must require more consideration and aid than the rest of living, breathing humanity??? Now thriving, the banks have the world so hooked into its slavery in the credit system that they even own countries! Imagine that! People, we, are being owned by banks. You wouldn't credit it, would you?

Worse is yet to come. Be warned, and watch out. Isaiah's prophecy for Assyria is coming true. The Lord *will* repay! First world countries are, as we witness in front of our very eyes, these countries are NOT immune to collapse and destruction. Watch out! The proclamation 'Babylon is falling!' is very apt. PROPHECY SHALL BE FULFILLED! The Words of the Almighty are TRUE. So don't believe the hype. Don't be deceived by Satan's dazzling, masking lies.

The only kingdom that *will* stand, is the one built on the firm and solid foundation - the rock that is Jesus Christ, our Lord and Saviour. Will you follow Him? Who do you believe, the devil, or the Lord Almighty whose Word stands true for all time?

Today 'Babylon is fallen, is fallen' (102) becomes apt! 'Babylon' has surely fallen. This last week, week ending Sabbath 9th July 2011 has seen the end of 3 major phenomena of the 21st century. We have witnessed the end of one of the great sleaze-bucket newspapers – the News of the World – due to the 'phone – hacking' scandal, of a victim of crime and public figures and celebrities. Invasion of privacy and bribery and corruption of policemen by unscrupulous journalists anxious to get a 'scoop' at whatever cost (monetary gain for them, or soul-destroying for the victims). Thank you Jesus for justice, and for the clean –up campaign spurred on by the middle class women in their 'twitter' – internet campaigns.

Then virtually the same day (Fri 8th July '11) we had the last ever USA space shuttle launched, under President Obama. At last, after first berated in this book 21 years ago (chp 3 ref 23), for the obscene expenditure on space exploration when so many people are starving in this world, now for whatever reasons, such extravagance and search for another home, has proved wasteful and futile and amoral. Thank you Lord for bringing it to an end!

Finally the last of the Harry Potter film series premiered Thursday of this same week. It was aired world-wide and on-line and went on for hours! 3000 people camped outside in Trafalgar Square for up to a week in the torrential rain just to be there, and not even watch the film itself! Praise and accolades were given, tears were shed. But the greatest thanks came from me for the end of demonic persuasions and brain-washing and influencing the populace – generations of people, especially the young children who were transfixed and 'hooked' on these occult books turned into films series, by author turned producer, J K Rawling, and 3 young actors/actresses. A decade of books and films (8 films of 7 books) that began from an idea she had on a train journey in Scotland, whilst she was a penny-less single mother. Today she is a billionaire, of world renown, yet she still does not look happy, and how many souls has she saved? None. Rather she has led many astray, and even poisoned their minds and led them to demonic lives and hell!!! End of an era? It was hailed as 'bizarre', 'a phenomenon'. I say a freak episode in the world of 'entertainment. Yes it is the end of the reign of the occult influence, of Satanic rule. He himself is soon to fall down, soon very soon, when Christ returns to wreak vengeance on him and his agents, and to claim back His saints who were ransomed by His saving, life-giving blood. May that day hasten quickly! Thanks be to Jesus and our heavenly Father, Yahweh!

This morning, 5th Aug 2011, I awoke with the gospel song 'I am a friend of 'God' ... He calls me friend' singing in my head and this admonition that follows, dreamt 2 days before the riots erupted in London and rest of UK. Riots sparked by the racist conduct of the police who are paid to serve and protect citizens, but who fatally shot a Black man in an execution- style manner a few days earlier, and then on the evening of a peaceful pro-test, the 7th Aug '11, brutally beat with their batons, a 16 year old girl who was demanding answers and human rights justice for that same killing. Following the biased racist media reporting of 'Black youths' being blamed for the ensuing criminality of arson and looting and violence, the Prime Minister is now this week calling for the end of human rights!!! Can you Adam and Eve it!!! Yes I can for this is Revelation Times and Satan runs amok creating havoc as his time is short for his due punishment in hell along with all who pledge allegiance to him.

But remember the following: Christ' universal appeal -

Christ was not a racist!

You cannot be Christ – like and racist!

When he visited the region of Tyre and Sidon, he spoke with a Canaanite (103)/ Greek, a Syro-Phoenician (104) woman who begged him to heal her daughter who was severely demon-possessed. But when Jesus replied that he was sent only for the house of Israel, she worshipped him and begged his help. On his reply that 'it is not good to take the children's bread and throw it to the dogs' the woman then argued 'yet even the little dogs eat the crumbs which fall from their master's table'. She was referring to the crumbs of blessings even that he gave to the chosen people, the Jews. This woman's faith so moved Jesus that he answered her request for help.

Jesus narrated the parable of the good Samaritan, who 'though despised and considered an outcast or pariah of Jewish society, was the only passer-by to stop and help the Jewish fellow who had been mugged and beaten and left by the road side. The so-called 'righteous' and 'good' Jewish passersby failed to stop and help the distressed man, their fellow brethren (105). Jesus showed no partiality, anyone could be helped. Of the ten lepers whom he healed, only one returned to thank Him, and he was a 'foreigner', a 'Samaritan' (105a). Presumably the others may have been Jews, but only the despised foreigner could be bothered to show his gratitude.

Not only did Jesus relate stories but he practiced what he preached. There is another instance where he talks to a Samaritan woman, passing by the well of Jacob, and asks her to get him a drink of water. The woman knew that Jews despised the Samaritans, and was reluctant to help him, but then they talked about more than the physical drink of water. Jesus revealed to her who she was, (a woman who had had several husbands and was associating with someone else's husband). And that the Messiah she and her people, descended from Abraham, like the Jews, was awaiting, was himself. Jesus was that Messiah, who is the living water, of whose drink you will never thirst again (106).

Similarly apostle Paul's vision about 'eating unclean animals' was a divine message to say that those considered 'unclean' or 'defiled' namely the Roman Gentiles, or heathens, were now to be offered the hope of salvation and blessings that were once only meant for the beloved Jews who had failed to accept Jesus Christ as the Messiah (107). The Jews search the scriptures that themselves testify about Jesus Christ being the Messiah and son of the Father. Yet these Jews refuse to believe or accept him (ibid v 43), for they do not have his word dwelling in their hearts (ibid v 38). They so totally rejected him that they demanded that Pilate change the inscription on the plaque nailed above Jesus' cross to 'he *said*, he was king of the Jews', but Pilate refused (108). Instead, along with one of the others being crucified beside Christ, they mocked and jeered at him for claiming he was the son of God and yet not being able to save himself. They failed to understand the purposes of Christ, the Messiah's need to be sacrificed. Rather, it was these now acceptable Gentiles in our Father's eyes, who became followers of Christ, and therefore Christian, after the first Jewish converts in Jesus' time.

There are many instances in the Bible, both in Old and New Testaments, that clearly show that Jesus' Good News of hope and salvation was to be spread throughout the world from time, to all the nations, no matter the colour, race nor creed. It was no longer exclusive to the Jews/Israelites. All the peoples in the world could have the chance to reconcile with our Creator. Yahweh's promise to Abraham that his descendants would be as numerous as grains of sand on a sea shore, or as the stars in the sky, was not limited to his blood line. It extended to all peoples – all the people who were of the promise spiritually. In other words, all those who took on Christ's mantle and thereby identified themselves with our Father's promise to Abraham, by walking in the faith of Jesus.

Christ appeals to everyone of all races, nations and 'tongues' (languages). He appeals worldwide and universally to anyone who would follow his teachings and lived examples, and who refuses to be associated with Satan. This Anti-Christ is racist and revels in division warring factions. But those who repent of their evil ways and look towards the Lord Almighty for mercy, forgiveness and deliverance from the Evil One, and seek sanctuary in our Beloved Saviour's arms, will rejoice with Him in that day of victory when He returns to claim the faithful - tried and refined in the fiery furnace of trials and afflictions that are imposed on them from the devil and his agents.

Christ appeals worldwide. He is universal. And anyone who wants to be called a friend of the Lord, who would be His friend, must not be racist. As his disciples, we must tell all nations about Jesus. His Good News is for all. It is impartial and is on offer to everyone, for Christ died as atonement for everyone's sins. His love is universal, unifying and harmonious. His love conquers all division. But we must do our part. The 3 Rs: Rebuke, Repent and Return, is all that is required of us. And we must love every-one, even our enemies and forgive them in our unconditional love.

Further proof that Christ does not approve of racism occurred on the 3rd Jan 2012 as a momentous verdict was finally passed on two of the racist murderers of teenager Stephen Lawrence, killed April 1993. His parents, Doreen and Neville Lawrence, lived to see that justice was served on the perpetrators of rac-ism, after campaigning and challenging the Metropolitan Police System for 18 long years. Notwithstanding the judgement, the Lawrences' endeavours forced changes in the law and police policies on conduct as established from the McPherson Inquiry and Report in 1998. These sometimes lone campaigners, were modern - day Davids, who fearlessly and doggedly challenged the Goliath police force, which was permeated with 'institutional racism'.

So many supporters including President Nelson Mandela, forced the hand of the police to conduct more thorough and open investigations, which transparently revealed the racist undertones that had underscored their unwillingness to arrest and charge the perpetrators, despite overwhelming evidence and callers naming the 5 or 6 perpetrators of the fatal knife attack. These have walked free for 18 years, whilst they cut Stephen's life short, a promising architect, in whose honour his parents have established a foundation for budding architects.

However, this is Revelation Times, and modern day techniques like DNA of microscopic damning evidence can no longer be disputed. Two men, Dobson and Norris, have been convicted, and no doubt soon the other culprits will be brought to justice too. Unfortunately, ironically, due to quirks in the law, these, though now in their 30s, will be sentenced as if they were teen-agers, the age at which they committed the crime! So instead of a 30 year plus sentence, they may only receive half of that; unless by divine intervention the law is changed once again to fully mete out justice. We can only hope and pray. The blood of Stephen Lawrence cried out for justice, for 'vengeance Is mine, saith the Lord', and finally his parents can sleep better at night and he can rest in peace.

But racism still abounds and just a few weeks ago, before Christmas 2011, a young PhD student, who had recently come from India to study, was murdered in another unprovoked attack, on a Salford Street, Midlands, whilst he and friends queued in the early hours for the shops' December sales. The police were quick this time to brand it a 'hate crime', ie rac-ist, and I just hope that he does not have to wait 18 years for his justice to be realised. The Asian student's parents had to make a brief visit to collect their son's body to return with him for burial in India. They did not express anger, but just disap-pointment for their great hopes for their son on British soil, and hoped that the perpetrator would be caught and punished. A young white man has been arrested. We watch with interest the outcome of this case.

NEWS UPDATES IN BRIEF 2012:-

Weds 8th Aug 2012, on the anniversary week of last year's (2011) 4 day London riots spread UK wide, although the police and authorities were alarmed at the alacrity and speed of how dangerous criminal activity spread, facilitated by the ease and availability of social networking via the internet, especially on mobile phones the Blackberry, enabling them to outrun and outsmart the police. One year on the slowness and ineffective-ness of the authorities is highlighted by the fact that they are still trawling through countless CCTV camera footage to try and catch perpetrators.

And the fact that of the 5,000 plus who were arrested in that period, only 1,500 have been tried and convicted for their crimes.

However, since last year's riots, there was a brief news bulletin stating that it is unlikely that the police, who perpetrated the original crime that sparked and ignited the outrage and lawlessness of the rioters and looters and arsonists (and unfortunately opportunist killers), namely, the execution-style cold-blooded murder of a defenceless young Black man in North London, whose anniversary memorial was earlier this week, 'it is unlikely that there will ever be an inquiry into the police conduct in this matter', nor therefore will the offending police officers be brought to trial and justice meted out, with *their* imprisonment for a very long time!!!! Remember Jesus Christ was not a racist, and neither was He a murderer, but fair and just and righteous!

As the whole country of Britain and worldwide are gripped in London 2012 Olympic Games fever, (of pagan ancient Greek origin), following close on from the national and Commonwealth celebrations of Queen Elizabeth II, 60 years on the throne – Diamond Jubilee- viewed worldwide in June this year, people have been distracted from the more sinister and insidious and more dangerous furtive evil aspects of the internet and its social networking capabilities.

In the 9 days from 30 July to 8 Aug, a Channel 4 documentary has been aired 4 or 5 times. What is this programme? It is the promotion of a book that has had meteoric rise and phenomenal success, from its beginnings in internet social networking fan-based blogs, in particular for the film and TV hit series 'Twilight' about a love affair between teenage vampire and girl, and a werewolf. The book is bound in a non-descript grey cover with a dagger suggesting a murder mystery, nothing remarkable about that. It is called '50 shades of grey'. However within its covers is salacious and dangerous seduction of women, being enticed into becoming submissive, as mere nothings and nobodies, to domineering men, who they allow to assault them violently,

under the guise of heightened sexual arousal and sensual pleasures – D S and M (Dominatrix and Sado-Masochism, derived
from the infamous Marquis de Sade of a mediaeval century).

Apparently it has millions of readers, especially middle aged
women/middle class women, who apparently don't have enough
housework, fitness regimes, or husband/ lover relationships, or
families or work, to engage, enthral or stimulate them and use
their time and energy constructively! I am appalled, as if we
don't have enough women suffering and enduring domestic violence –mental, physical, emotional, psychological, financial bullying and control by partners already in the world!!! 1 in 5 deaths
of women in London alone are by men they are in relationships
with –husbands/boyfriends, or even fathers in honour killings
(the latest scandal).

So this book lures women into false sense of sensual happiness, when they are made more vulnerable to sexual and domineering abuse by men, who regard them as mere objects or
non-persons, which they don't mind as long as they can be
teased and delighted in their carnal lusts. There is no mention
of the victims/ sorry women or girls, being wanted, needed, or
Lord forbid! Loved, respected, cherished or adored and cared
for, no!!! Sex, is utterly and abhorrently disguised as something
to be longed for, desired, when in fact it is giving men total permission to abuse, destroy, annihilate a woman's worth and self-
esteem, denying her very existence as a valued and valuable
human being – a creature, beautifully designed and created
in love by YHWH and Jesus Christ from the foundation of the
world!!!!

Not only has this documentary been repeatedly shown on TV,
but there is talk of it being made into a film, and discussion
revolved around which famous actor should play the male lead,
but no such discussion or importance attached to the possible
female lead, compounding the idea that the woman herself does
not matter, just as long as she is the object of the man's actions.

Really! Is this what the world has come to after the Suffragettes in Victorian England endured gross inhumanities to gain women's vote and rights, and after women campaigner in the last few decades have fought for women's rights against domestic violence, and equal opportunities in employment and earnings? Feminists would be turning in their graves if they could.

Not to mention the impact such SDM thinking will have on impressionable young minds, teenage girls and younger children, as they are being acculturised / socialised/ groomed/ made accustomed to expect physical and sexual abuse as the norm, living as we do on a diet of sex, violence and perversion and degradation on TVs all over our homes, and more secretively on TVs and computers in privacy of supposedly safe bedrooms, of our precious children who are vulnerable to having their innocence stripped away through exposure to porn, and sexual dating on social networking sites, even very young children, to virtual reality rooms, where predators and paedophiles lurk in disguise. Lord help our children and women, before more fall victim to Satan and his cronies!

Also in this summer period, another documentary was aired on TV called 'The girl who was 3 boys', about a teenage girl, who disguised herself as 3 different boys, and simultaneously had relationships with two impressionable and naive teenage girls, who were also friends, but who were unaware of love quadrangle they were in. Sounds unbelievable? Unfortunately it is true, and the case went to trial last year (2011) highlighting the paedophilic deception of a controlling teenage girl, who wanted to be the centre of attention, whose parents feared to displease, buying her a brand new car when she said she wouldn't commit suicide if they bought it!!! Her deception was made possible again through the internet, on computers in the girl's bedrooms, and via 'speech' by texting on mobile phones, as the 'boy' in his/ her aliases, said 'he' had a speech impediment and was shy, so 'he' could not speak (knowing that her voice would identify her to her friends).

The culprit predator was charged with deception, fraud (because she put in a false insurance claim for an alleged accident to one of the 'boys'), and for sexual assault on the girls, and jailed. I would have added rape, for she used a sex toy to rob the girls of their virginity, which they naively thought was 'himself', never having had sex before. One girl, though she disclosed some thoughts on the whole appalling affair on the film, was too embarrassed to show her face, whereas the other bravely and openly discussed it, admitting she was naive, not 'thick or stupid', but too trusting and gullible. She now has a real life, not virtual or pretend gender, boyfriend and is recovering from her ordeal. This is the very real sinister and frightening and alarming side to the social networking capabilities of the internet. Parents be vigilant

Also during this summer of 2012, whilst the whole British nation and the world have been captivated and entertained, partying and celebrating Queen Elizabeth II Diamond Jubilee (60 years on throne), for 4 days at the beginning of June; followed by 2 weeks of London 2012 Olympics in July; and now ParaOlympics at the end of August to first week of September; not to mention the other sporting highlights – Wimbledon, Golf Open, Cricket and Football Eurovision 2012 – other more important real life events that affect peoples' lives crucially, have occurred. From May to August notable events have been:-

28/5/12 'Cyberattacks' – other aspects of the internet capabilities shown up this day, when police complained about the possible terrorist activity on UK banks, saying that customers are having their accounts robbed (through on-line banking, and hoax money 'begging in distress' letters from 'friends' – people's contacts in their email lists/ addresses). Police are alarmed at the potential for UK born citizens, becoming 'home grown' terrorists from the increased numbers of vacations/ holidays to countries like Turkey and Arabia!!!

26/6/12 The Telegraph newspaper, alerts us to 'Arab Spring provided new breeding ground for British terrorists' in propaganda scaremongering. They state that 'the Arab Spring has spawned a new generation of British-born terrorists after al-Qaeda lured dozens of would-be-bombers abroad to train for possible attacks on the UK, the head of MI5 warned'. All this sparked the flurry over security for the Olympic venues, and surrounding areas, including a war of words from residents who had machine guns and missiles from MOD placed on their block of flats roof tops in east London, with MOD remaining put. News flashed on same day on MSN 'cyber attacks' and 'cyber –bullying', about the ability of terrorists from Nigeria, Arabia etc., to infiltrate UK. According to an MI5 official 'terrorist tactics and plots are being discussed everyday, in cars, homes and on the streets'. I would question how he knows, is this what the hidden capability of CCTV cameras, mobile phones and computers enables, 'Big Brother watching' our every move, and listening in on every conversation? Is this what paranoia is about?

However it revealed more cyberactivity by them than terrorists. For, all the gathering of data/ information on customers, that companies, and even big shops like Tesco's do to better know how to target your favourite or more likely shopping of products, significantly goods promotions and sales potentials, actually help government and MI5/CIA intelligence gathering about people, and potential terror suspects. All the governments and businesses hard promotion of internet capable devices and equipment, from computers to laptops, mobile phones, ipods/ ipads, DAB radio communication, whether within country – as in USA government drive to ensure every home or every community has access to a computer; or internationally export to poorer countries like in Africa of second – hand computers, etc;- have dual purpose. Overtly they are to enable everyone to have access to information readily, but covertly it will more easily facilitate undercover intelligence gathering operations *and* enable mind control of the masses, by pervasively influencing the trusting and unsuspecting populace.

However, note the government's and banks frustration and embarrassment at being made to look foolish, and laughing stocks to the world by the One who can, and the One who matters, Yahweh. Like the proud arrogance they showed over 'Rule Britannia' and the 'unsinkable' Titanic, and the Hindenberg (Nazi German), and the British/ French Concordes, they were 'shook' when their 'secure and invincible' fortresses came crashing down to the depths. After all the disgusting bail outs of the banks, *and* countries, and the expose of politicians scandalous thieving 'expenses claims'; and businesses, and pharmaceuticals like GlaxoSmithKline, celebrities (and politicians and their dads'), (with some celebrities being publicly humiliated and penalised – comedian Jimmy Carr; whilst apparently others, having royal seal of approval, knighthood bestowed on them, apparently haven't – now Sir Gary Barlow for his orchestrating the Queen's Hyde Park concert and specially collaborated commemorative song), and now banks, ALL for tax avoidance/ evasion/ schemes –theft-, all robbing the ordinary folk, hard working tax payers, the rich are still stealing from the poor again!!!

As Christ said: 'the rich will get richer, and little that the poor man has will be taken away'! How true has that been with this recent government, and its predecessors of similar ilk. With all the banks scandals being exposed and their walls of insured stability came plummeting down around them in June, I'm sure neither they, nor the public were LOLing (laughing out loud) anymore! (Watch out pensioners! As the income bracket with the most disposable income, according to latest figures, you are sure to be targeted by the unscrupulous businesses, banks and government for your hard earned and saved nest eggs. My warning June 2012, became reality on Mond 24th Sept '12, when co-PM, Lib Dem leader, Nick Clegg, told young people seeking to buy homes, to raid their grand-parents pensions! Unbelievable! So what are the pensioners supposed to live on? And isn't parents' or grandparents' assets supposed to be left to be inherited, AFTER they have died???)

-News update Dec 6th 2012, International multinational giants Amazon, Google and coffee shop Starbucks, all been exposed for their tax avoidance in UK. Starbucks only paid 3 years tax, 'though been operating in UK for 10years. The outraged British public voted with their feet taking their custom elsewhere in the 6 weeks from October , so that Starbucks feeling the pinch now offered to pay £20million in next 2 years! Since when do people get the chance to offer to pay whatever amount of tax they feel like? Most of us get it calculated and deducted from us, - no choice. I agree with panellists and audience members on the TV programme 'Question Time', same week in Dec, for the government to get rid of loopholes, and set up a fair system for *everyone* to pay fair taxes, and no more tax evasion/avoidance!

As for the rest of us, with unemployment so high, and recession deepening in 'double-dip', and students facing university fees tripled to £9,000 annually, and EMA instituted by Labour government to encourage young people to stay on at school and keep out of trouble on the streets (all went to pot in protests last year 2011) being phased out by Conservative/Lib-Dem government, and other cuts and squeezes in welfare benefits and spending, in severe austerity measures for the poor (but not for the top income bracket the super rich!!!), and the unemployed threatened with benefits stopped if they refuse to work for their benefits, - roll back the years, and what do we have POOR WORK HOUSES and SLAVERY being reinstated by the back door!!!! This last weekend of August, has seen protests by disabled groups against the cut backs in their benefits, and having their disability higher rate premiums stopped altogether by the government, creating even more hardship, under the guise of stopping the dependency culture, and forcing people into work. 2012 is bringing a very stark reality check for the majority of us. Prophecies are not said for nothing. They are spoken to warn us and prepare us. So take heed! Christ 'soon come'.

26/6/12 'Many struggling to afford childcare' – 'more than a third of parents have considered quitting work because of the struggle to meet childcare costs, a survey found'...around 1 in 8 (12%) actually left a job, whilst 1 in 5 have turned a job down for same reason,' (MSN News). It came just days after PM David Cameron launched a commission on childcare to examine how to reduce the cost of childcare and increase the supply of places. Reality check, some parents are even resorting to borrowing in order to send their child to nursery or childminder, with 14% taking money from friends, or family, or paying on a credit card. Survey of 1,000 parents showed that 1 in 5 (20%) had childcare costs that were more than their family's rent or mortgage! Ironically, as a nation we spend more on childcare than most others in Western Europe, yet lots of parents are unable to work because childcare costs make it uneconomic. Childcare is one of the top cost-of-living burdens on families, with average annual cost of part-time care for an under – two now tops £5,000 – with prices up to 3 times that level in London. So much for government encouraging mothers back to work and reducing unemployment. The realities make it almost impossible!

Also todays' news item 'Families pushed to breaking point', because of the state of their finances according to report from the Scottish Widows think-tank, the Centre for the Modern Family. Research among 1,500 audits revealed 'increasingly desperate' measures are being taken to cope with the impact of recession. 1 in 5 struggling to cope financially, while a further 2 in 5 were 'just getting by'. All this is due to increased living cost and falling wages, coupled with rising costs of childcare, and the ongoing economic climate, were creating a nation of 'on –the – brink Britons'. 18 to 34 year olds were more likely to selling items on-line in the past year to make ends meet, and were twice as likely as other adults to have taken out a payday loan to tide them over. (And the unprecedented rise in pawn-brokers on high streets, coupled with also increase in gambling both in bookies and bingo halls, but also lotteries, and TV and on-line gambling, as people hope for that 'big win' to take care of all their troubles). Report stated that 1 in 5 young people have been left unable to pay household bills, and 1 in 8 have skipped meals to ensure their family eats well.

The poor and vulnerable adults – the mentally ill or incapacitated and the elderly, and those living at or below the bread line are being driven to rely on lenders, especially door-step loans from companies like the Provident HQ in the Midlands, as an income stream, rather than a credit stream. With loans offered to them so readily, credit is becoming a way of life, or life line, because no other earned income is available in this dire economic climate and rising unemployment. Did not the Lord speak out against 'usury' /charging interest, especially exorbitantly or charged upon the vulnerable in society? See His condemnation of the scribes and Pharisees whom He called 'blind guides...full of extortion and self-indulgence, (Matt 23 v 25, Luke 11 v 39-42), who 'devour the houses of widows' impoverishing them (Matt 23 v 14), and binding heavy burdens upon people which they themselves will not lift a finger to help them, or bear themselves, (Matt 23 v 4). Are they really going to pull blood out of stone, these greedy avaricious blood suckers?

The grim reality of governments austere measures to reduce borrowing, according to their election pledge 2 years ago (2010). However, rising unemployment, deepening economic recession, and reduced welfare benefits, are pushing more and more people, especially families into real living poverty, (not virtual or statistical, but real felt and experienced hard times!). Meanwhile, contrary to election pledges, again news today 26/6/12, (1 day after the secret ID of God was revealed to me), EUROZONE CRISIS: public sector borrowing (excluding financial interventions) ROSE to **£17.9billion** in May 2012, **up** from £15.2billion the year before per annum!! Then announced that the cost of BAILING OUT Cyprus (yet another country) may be E10 billion (euros), representing HALF of its economy! (Reuters

26/6/12). No wonder people in UK don't want to be part of European union (EU).

Average UK household disposable income fell in 2010/2011 according to statistics ON5, by approx £200 p.a. in real terms. The biggest drop was middle fifth income bracket, by 4.3%, £25,500 down to £24.400 p.a. I would not be surprised to see middle income families reduced to plight of those in USA last Christmas, in cardboard cities and families having lost their homes, now living in cars, until these to are removed by police, so families split up or worse catastrophes. How frequently now are we hearing in UK news of parents murdering their families and committing suicide unable to cope? Desperate and dire times are felt for more and more people.

Whilst simultaneously and scandalously the rich are getting richer. Even our right royal family have been faring better in these austere times. Not only with the Diamond Jubilee and Olympics celebrations, but personally, for in briefly mentioned news item the Prince of Wales, Charles, published his financial accounts for last financial year (2011-2012). It reveals that the Prince's funding from the taxpayer for his Duchy of Cornwall – the landed estate given to the heir of the throne – increased by nearly 18%!!! Charles income from grants-in-aid and govern-ment departments rose from 17.9% £1,664,000 to £1,962,000 during 2010-11. He also saw his private funding from the Duchy of Cornwall go up by nearly 4% to £17,796,000 in that period. The Prince's tax bill soared by more than £900,000, rising 26.2% to $,398,000. The cost of his travel by air and rail were to be announced later, and are paid for by the taxpayer through grants-in-aid. During this same financial period, the Prince and the Duchess of Cornwall, Camilla, toured, Norway, Sweden and Denmark in March this year, and last autumn visited South Africa and Tanzania, while Charles also visited Kuwait and Qatar.

This last weekend at the end of August 212, with the para-olym-pics happening in full view of the world, disabled people were protesting in London, about government cuts in their Disability Living Allowance (DLA) entitlements. These cuts were causing dire straits for many of them. Pensioners are already being targeted by the government and unscrupulous businesses, because they were disclosed this year as the income bracket with the most disposable income. However, many other pensioners face, yet again, a Thatcherite/SCameron Tory government type winter – having to choose between heating or eating this winter, as the country is held to ransome in very austere retrenchment measures by this Conservative/Lib/Dem coalition government. Meanwhile Lib/Dem leader Nick Clegg, calls for those higher income brackets to pay more taxes, but he has been disregarded by the belligerent Tory MPs. (Rich get richer and the poor have their assets stripped!).

October 2012 newsflash- enforced pensions (to replenish depleted treasury of mishandled tax payers money???). UK Conservative government is forcing all workers to join work based pensions (private pensions). I soberly, (not as drunken MPs debate/brawl in parliament) recall the time when people lost up to half their pension fund due to private pensions scheme investments collapsing. That was not so long ago, but a few years. Watch out workers for where your money is invested! It seems choice has been taken away (and union power is being stripped), as present government tactics become less democratic and more of a totalitarian state!!

Also it is worth noting that the practice of USURY is not to be done without conscience or responsibility and care for others. Justification for charging interest on loans often quotes Jesus' parable of the lender(Matt 25 v 27; Luke 19 v 22-23), where the servant who buried the coin rather than invest it is rebuked, and has his coin given to the servant who invested and brought the most profit for his master. But this parable can be seen in conjunction with the one about the sower planting his seeds on good soil, that produced abundant crop, (Matt 13 v 3-23)..Here Jesus was referring to spiritual seeds – good words, teachings and practices that are planted/ taught to people so that they repent of their sins/ wrong-doings, and give their lives and souls to Christ and our heavenly Father. When this happens all heaven rejoices and celebrates, even if for only one sinner that repents and is saved! (Luke 15, Matt 17 v 12-13).

Also please refer back to the Old Testament teachings upon which Jesus founded the New Testament, reaffirming Yahweh's laws. See Exodus 22 v 25; Levit 25 v 36-37; Deut 23 v 19-20, where the Lord says it is not lawful to take usury from your brother, but only from a stranger. But note Ps 15 v 5, and Ezek 18 v 17, where it is commendable to 'not put out' your 'money to usury, nor take reward against the amount' lent; and 'he withholds his hand from sin and takes no usury or excessive interest'. For the Lord knows this can end up in debt-slavery or bond-slavery/ bondage, that can be inherited for generations afterwards in families, and is never-ending debt. Today in these austere and credit-driven, impoverished times, this is becoming more evident. As Jesus prophesied ' the rich will get richer, and the little that the poor man has shall be taken away' is becoming more real daily for many people, as wicked extortionate lending practices increase. But they will not go unpunished, for the wicked end up perishing in hell fire, as parable of the wheat and tares/ weeds shows (Matt 13 v 24-43).

Rather than usury, Christ encouraged his followers to extend brotherly love and consideration and compassion to each other, and especially to the poor and needy, vulnerable, in society, (Mark 12 v 29-31; John 13 v 34-35). For, when we give charitably (not as corporate greedy exploiters), but genuine alms giving, and good deeds, it as though we are do so to Jesus Himself, (Matt 25 v 31-46), by blessing others we are blessing Him and giving glory to His name; and for such we will be rewarded abundantly by Him and Yahweh, especially in the new heaven and new earth, where we will be given crowns to wear (EGW Story of Redemption chp 62, p413-414), and mansions to live in, in His 'Father's house' (John 14 v 2-3).

28/6/12 – FINANCE SCANDAL: 'BABYLON 'A FALL!'

More embarrassment for the government and nation's rulers as scandal of bank swindling the public is exposed, and unfurls over several days, and still has not dissapated over the summer, starting with Barclays bank. Chancellor George Osborne, (who chose to launch the National Loan Guarantee Scheme, with Barclays in March this year), is blasted as it is announced that Barclays has been given a £290 million fine for its manipulation of interest rates, to give itself a favourable appearance to potential borrowers and investors, over and above the reality. In March Labour's Ed Milliband called for tougher regulation of banks and financial bodies, FSA and LIBOR, but the Conservative govt was complacent. Barclays bank's CEO Bob Diamond, was unavailable for comment, nor, when found days later, was he able to give plausible excuse, for none could be given, for the outright theft of again, public money! Then he retaliated that he could not be held to alone, account for the misrepresentations of the bank, as it transpired that several other banks in the UK, like NatWest and RBS(of bail out Ireland and housing and banks scandal), but also USA had done the same practices!!!

So the public, having been given Hobson's choice (no choice) by governments but to bail out these failing banks, (whose CEOs still received exorbitant bonuses despite appalling performances), have been paying more costs than they bargained for. Already opportunist companies are trying to cash in on monies that banks owe customers for mis-sold PPIs (Payment Protection Insurance on loan and mortgage repayments), by offering No win, no fee (taking up to 50% of winnings on successful claims). Now this scandal emerged, of banks robbing us again; and later in the summer (25/8/12) banks were exposed for stealthily deceiving customers in 'free' banking that was not, but actually held hidden charges in other services. Not only robbing the cradle (food from families mouths) but all the way through to old age, with pensioners the targets again for money-grabbing businesses! As the very many outrage and scandalised internet bloggers said, 'anyone else would be arrested, tried and keys thrown away' , hung, drawn and quartered if possible, but not these senior officials, no they get a slap on the wrist for their FRAUD and THEFT and DAYLIGHT ROBBERY!!! As yet no-one responsible has lost their jobs over it, or been arrested, at most they may lose this year's annual bonus, whilst being allowed to continue in their posts where they've been shown to be less than competent, but actual thieves! As one blogger wrote to them 'DO NOT PASS GO, (for £200 monopoly game reward), GO DIRECTLY TO JAIL!!!'. My sentiments exactly.

Then even worse, Daily Mail newspaper headline of 7 /8/12 'British Banks links to global terror!' US accuses British bank, Standard Chartered, of hiding billions for Iran and Hezbollah. Although the bank does not have branches in the UK, it is British, and has 1,700 branches in more than 70 countries. This bank hid £160billion of transfers that helped finance terror groups, and Iran's nuclear weapons programme, it was claimed. 'In another devastating blow to the City of London's reputation, Standard Chartered is accused of conspiring with Tehran for almost 10 years. Regulators in New York said it was a 'rogue institution' that broke sanctions imposed on Iran, and put prof-its ahead of global security and the law'. 'The New York State Department of Financial Services accused Standard Chartered of doing business with Burma, Libya and Sudan which are also under sanctions', for human rights issues and atrocities.

But wait, did not this summer 16/6/12, the British government, and the Queen *and* American head of state, Obama stand beside and publicly approve of the newly instated Opposition MP of Burma, Dr Aung San Suu Kyi, at her acceptance of the Nobel Peace Prize awarded her in 1991, but could not accept until released from house arrest as a dissident in November 2010, in great public coverage, in Oslo, Norway? She was hon-oured ostensibly for her standing and decades of campaigning for human rights against terrible abuses by Burma's military regime, that had held sway for half a century. Suu Kyi was on a 17 day tour of 5 countries, including the Uk and Ireland, beginning in Geneva, Switzerland, June 13th 2012.

Earlier this year January 5th '12, Foreign Secretary, William Hague, became the first British politician to visit the former British colony Burma in 56 years, now renamed Myanmar. Hague announced 'We are ready to respond positively', as he made the historic visit, in a two day 'aid – for –reforms' talks (trade negotiations). He told their equivalent minister, Wunna Maung Lwin, that he 'emphasised the importance the British Government attaches to the reforms that the Burmese Government has undertaken in the last six months' (prior to Jan 2012), and 'made it clear that the British Govt expects to see the release of all political prisoners (some 600 of 900 remain detained), credible by-elections in April (since happened with steps towards democracy), and a genuine alleviation of the suffering in ethnic areas, including humanitarian access and peace talks'. Whilst Suu Kyi was honoured to worldwide acclaim, it was also let known that Cameron's ministers were in business negotiations with her for trade.

Then on 19 July '12, it is announced (World, Zeenews.com) that Aung San Suu Kyi is to receive highest US award, the Congressional Gold Medal, when she visits USA later this year (expected September). US Secretary of State Hillary Clinton, in the Obama administration, had invited Suu Kyi to Washington, when she had visited Burma in previous December (2011). In May 17th, '12, Obama appointed Derek Mitchell as the first US ambassador to Burma, (since he had been instrumental in discussions peace talks between US and Burma). This appointment and the easing of trade restrictions signals a 'warming of diplomatic relations between USA and Burma'. According to the news bulletin, diplomatic ties will be strengthened, and US companies will gain new access to markets in 'Obama's "new chapter" in relations between the two countries.

Now US companies will be allowed to export financial services (banking and insurances no doubt), and make new investments in the country. (EXPLOITRADE!!!) Although restrictions on doing business with companies tied to Burma's military regime, long vilified for human rights abuses, will remain in place. (So so can't do business with Burmese companies that supported the military regime prior to all this, but since elections can do business with the same military regime, just because it seems to be making the right moves towards democracy, and singing to the West's tune???) It is 'unclear' whether US businesses would be allowed to work with the country's national energy companies Myanmar Oil and Gas Enterprises. US – owned companies like Chevron, have sought contracts on oil and natural gas reserves in Burma and offshore. (Zeenews). Now remind me was there not a Tsunami in 2004 in Thailand's waters, which suspiciously had connections with gas explosions and oil explorations in the offshore areas? Coincidence or design, that now US companies want to negotiate access to Burma's oil sources of supply??? (Exploitrade) for, these suddenly acute interests appear to be OIL driven, and motivated by GREED, POWER, CONTROL and MONEY – PROFIT = MAMMON!!!

The change in US and UK and following close on their heels will be Europe's interests (according to William Hague), in their policies towards sanctioned Burma, comes after a series of moves indicating a thaw in US – Burmese relations. Hague stressed that 'if the pledge for reforms, which began last year with the handing over of power to a civilian government, continued, then it would lead Burma to have deeper economic and political ties with the West. A disputed but unusually open election in 2010, was followed by the release of political dissident Aung San Suu Kyi from 24 years of house arrest, (July 1989 to Nov. 2010); followed swiftly on in Dec 2011, by a visit to Burma by Hillary Clinton, the first US Secretary of State to do so in half a century.

One wonders if secret talks and negotiations between the countries had not been going on much before sudden turn-around of Burmese military government in 2010? For, 'in Nov. 2010, three years after a new wave of bloodily repressed protests dubbed 'the saffron revolution', and to the surprise of virtually all observers, Suu Kyi was released. The regime appeared to have decided that, to preserve any power and wealth, they needed Burma to partake in the rapid local economic growth. This, the argument went, was impossible while under sanctions and without an element of political reform'. Is there more to sudden changes and 'warming' of economic and political relations than is apparent to you and I? Most poignant and salutary comment from the Peace Laureate herself, Suu Kyi, 'It is not power that corrupts, but fear. Fear of losing power corrupts those who wield it and fear of the scourge of power corrupts those who are subject to it'.

Money, power, territory, control, corruption, terrorism are all linked, and not very democratic or pro-human rights at all!

And then on 13/8/12 the extended news programme on Channel 4 TV reminded us about the scandal that the US have been stalling from erupting over the 'water- boarding torture' interrogation techniques of suspected al-Qaeda terrorists at Guantanemo Bay penitentiary, (which incidentallly Obama pledged during his election campaign to 2008, that he would shut and has not yet done so, 4 years on!). A top US official, Jose Rodriguez Jr., directorate of Operations to CIA, form 2004-2007, admitted destroying filmed footage of the suspect vomiting, and screaming in agony from repeated water-boarding, by various interrogators, why? Because he feared it would be damaging to US confidence and morale. What they showed was so horrific they would be 'devastating to the CIA', and that 'the heat from destroying is nothing compared to what ti would be if the tapes were to come into the public domain'!!! And The New York Times reported that according to 'some insiders' an inquiry into the CIA's secret detention program which analysed these techniques, 'might end with criminal charges for abusive interrogations'. Rodriguez wrote a book, under a pen name, bragging about how they used interrogation measures and 'effective'? deterrents to terrorists. Really? Is the pot calling the kettle black (meaning both are exactly the same, and as bad as each other)?

Actually who is fooling whom? In this propaganda game, and war with words, are we being hoodwinked as to the real issues here, when really ALL the governments and financial institutions are corrupt and amoral, and put profit – power – money-MAMMON before human rights and treating the people fairly, and executing justice where it is rightly and squarely due - on the corporate and political thieves???

Further news on this topic – Nov 5th, (UK Guy Fawkes bonfire night), as Obama and Romney fought US presidential elections (which Obama won), UK PM Cameron was in Saudi Arabia trying to sell £billions of UK manufactured arms and fighter planes to highly suspect, and undemocratic terrorist governments. Excuse given is someone else would sell to them, so may as well be UK as 'saving and creating jobs'. But the weapons industry is highly subsidised. Instead we see more capitalist greed, and highly suspect, amoral policies, that are aiding and abetting, 'fuelling' terrorism. Have we not learnt from Bin Laden US - trained, insider tactics in 9/11 and 7/7 terror attacks?

And also at the beginning of this November '12, quick news item – 'recession is declining'. Apparently Britain is coming out of its 'double dip' recession, (manipulated employment, and sales figures since Jubilee and Olympics – unusual events so skewed figures), have been favourable. But looking around at very real lives, where more children are turning up at school hungry, as parents struggle to feed them and manage spiralling bills, and bless compassionate teachers for feeding them out of their diminishing income, thank you teachers! I am reminded of Jeremiah 5 v 12-18, and 1 Thessalonians 5 v 3 – when the prophets were crying 'Peace, peace!', YHWH was already sending warring nations to crush Israel and Judah,- Jerusalem was doomed! So when our politicians say 'peace and goodwill', when disaster is all around, be sure to run to the hills, for calamity is sure to follow, if YHWH says so! Don't believe the hype. Wise up and take heed of the warning signs.

Other News In Brief:-

26/6/12 (it's all happening on the same day after 25th June '12, revelations of secret ID of God), - explosive controversy over internet, as 'Facebook email switch sparks anger' (MSN news). The government backed £billion private company is seen extending its 'Big Brother' arm and allowing anyone access to people's email addresses without their permission, or even their knowledge. (And the police claim that we, the public, are the secret terrorists, 'the hidden dog that turns around and bites your behind'!) Some Facebook users reacted angrily after the company changed how it displays user's contact information to make it look like they had a Facebook email address. The new facebook.com email accounts allow users to communicate with outside email addresses via Facebook. In defence Facebook spokeswoman Jillian Stefanki said the site is rolling out a setting that allows people to decide which email addresses to show on their pages. In April the company said it was 'updating addresses on Facebook to make them consistent across our site'.

Unfortunately this switching spark followed close on the heels of another upset for internet users with mobile phone company O2s reception abilities seriously disrupted the previous weeks, causing havoc for its millions of customers. What has been going on with these new technologies recently? Gremlins, or higher unseen powers?

28/6/12 Still the scandal of 'phone hacking' that led to the downfall of the News of the World newspaper earlier this year, and the Leveson Inquiry into corruption in the press and police and dent in public vote of confidence in this Conservative led/ Lib-Dem government. I now understand why there has been such a public outcry, and what the true significance of the phone- hacking is. It transpired that Craig Denholm, deputy police chief constable of Surrey police, is being investigated over claims that he failed to act over the 'hacking' of murdered school girl, Milly Dowler's mobile phone by journalist from News of the World newspaper, back in 2002. The IPCC (Independent Police Complaints Commission), is focusing on the senior officer's alleged knowledge that Milly's phone was hacked, and what, if any, actions were taken. Though, they acknowledge that since some 10 years have elapsed since 'Operation Ruby' first investigated her murder, that some individuals can no longer be investigated. To date this officer remains on duty.

The controversy began when it emerged that a journalist, defendant from the News of the World, admitted hacking into the 13 year old's mobile phone, but it remains unknown what the 2 messages were, that were *deleted* (deliberately), as previously suggested, or were removed from the messenger automatically – (why would it, no-one else's does?) The Leveson Inquiry into press standards has pointed to Milly's mothers anticipated call from her daughter after her disappearance March 2002. Whilst waiting at her home in Walton-on-Thames Surrey, the teenager's voicemail generated an automatic response when her message box was full; but when the message had been *deleted* the greeting reverted to her personal greeting.

The Dowlers told the Inquiry they were given 'false hope' after hearing the change of greeting, - thinking that their daughter might still be alive and had wiped a message. But *SHE HAD NOT,* as she was dead!!! So this meant that someone else had wiped it, and therefore hacked into the phone, and now their seruptious intrusion and deception had been exposed, in this long ranging scandal since last summer (2011). Who even knows if it was not related to such scandalous police corruption and cover-ups that Black man was executed last year sparking the London riots???

- News update – 29th Nov 2012, the Leveson Report was concluded, and called for a law and an independent body to regulate the press. Victims welcomed the outcome, but the press and PM Cameron said an outright NO! to regulation. It seems the report was not supposed to have had teeth, but that the press were supposed to be able 'to wreak havoc in people's lives'. So apparently 'freedom of the press' means freedom to abuse. Really. A higher authority begs to differ. We eagerly watch this space to see if justice will be done. A week later, Dec 6th, the press agreed to having an independent body with the ability to fine up to £1million, but still no restrictive law. Dec 17th '12, Leveson found that there should be legislation to underpin any self-regulatory body, ie. Have some teeth and recourse to law and statute. Press editors and PM have yet to implement such a step. And there should be compensatory redress for victims of press intrusion and abuse, for example for the McCanns and Dowlers.

Meanwhile as God in his element of disguise and deception still reigns, and his secret ID is about to be uncovered and 'sounded by the 7th angel' (Rev 10 v 7), more madness abounds — 26/June/12, MSN News: 'Uggie in Hollywood paw print honour'!!! as a canine star of the film the 'Artist' was honoured by becoming the first dog to put its paw prints in cement outside Grauman's Chinese Theatre in Hollywood, California USA. 'The rambunctious Jack Russell terrier was celebrated at a treat-laden ceremony outside the landmark as councilman T. LaBonge declared it "Uggie Day" in Los Angeles'. They must be barking mad for sure!!! Really? A dog gets celebrity status, after in UK this summer a dog wins the Britain's Got Talent TV show, overshadowing his teenage girl trainer, and a favourite backed by the show's megabucks owner, Simon Cowell, of X Factor TV series fame. I think some people need their heads examined!

Then in true explosive style a real catastrophe occurs in Colorado at the midnight premiere of the Batman film 'the

Dark Knight', as a gunman opens fire on in a cinema theatre in Aurora. One headline reads 'Aurora shooting: the more we watch, the less we know', as the whole country, watched world-wide, reacts in outrage, and sympathy for the victims (12 killed and 58 wounded) and their families. The perpertrator is a non-descript university student, who may have been disgruntled, or may have been a loose cannon or volcano waiting to erupt, or just a cold-blooded killer seeking infamy and notoriety, or is it a case of 'monkey see, monkey do', life imitating fiction in the violent films we watch? Whatever the reason he has the nation baffled, and erupted the debate about access to guns and gun laws in USA again. The storm rages.

> - News update – 14th Dec '12, "26 dead in Connecticut school2, as gun man massacred mostly children and teachers shielding children, before shooting himself. His mother, who was pro-gun law, worked in the school, but apparently they had argued at home before hand. In the public outrage that followed, a tearful Obama asks : 'do we want a situation when such occurrences become the norm, and we remain powerless to do anything about it?' I ask: how many more deaths before gun laws are repealed and remove the 'rights' of American citizens to own guns? Are we at war in our cities and villages and countrysides, that we need to defend ourselves with guns, but where innocent children are shot at will by any-one who feels like it?

And then out of the blue, 17 August '12, MSN news 'Police probe "Moors murder letter" ', as a mental health advocate for Moors murderer Ian Brady, Jackie Powell, appointed in 1999, was detained in south Wales on suspicion of preventing the burial of a body without lawful exercise. She had told a Channel 4 documentary that Brady had given her a sealed envelope to pass to Winnie Johnson, the mother of his 12 year old victim Keith Bennett, in the event of his death. Brady and his partner Myra Hindley, who died in jail in 2002 aged 60, sexually tortured and horrifically murdered 5 children over 50 years ago (from 1963-1965).

The boy's mother has been tormented and grieving over the where-abouts of her murdered son's body, and is ill with cancer, and has recently appealed to Brady to break his silence, and end her suf-fering, but so far to no avail. Is the letter a hoax, the investigating police officers enquire, a sick twisted prank by Brady, or are there hidden clues in it , as so far there have been no further leads? This is 2012, the year of Prophecy and Truth, and the truth will out, sooner rather than later. You can depend on YHWH for that!

-Newsflash, Nov 8th '12 – police turn thieves, as two UK police-men are jailed, caught on camera stealing cash from a house during a raid. Stung after complaints of valuables going missing after previous police raids. Police strapped for cash???

These events and more illustrate the 'Signs of the Times' that Jesus talked about in Matt. 24, and indicate as Prophecy and Truth unfold in these present days, that His return will be very soon. Other proph-ecies as elucidated in Daniel and Revelation books also become clearer as modern history unfurls before our very eyes.

Yes some say history is repeating itself, but it is moving inexo-rably forward so that Prophecy may be fulfilled. As governments scream about insisting we the populace endure their extreme measures of enforced austerity, whilst they themselves lavishly tour the globe and have a very nice time at our expense, other events have and are taking place as prophesied in the myster-ies of Revelation, especially books 10 -14:- from the sounding of the 7th angel in Rev 10 v 7, to the 3 angels message in Rev 14 v 6-9 'Fear God, for the hour of His judgement is here, to Babylon is fallen, is fallen, and Come out of her my people, lest you share in her doomed fate'.

Revelation 13 talking about the beast and his image come to life and relevance for today, as it did in the 4th century, when the state and church united to change and enforce their laws and doctrines that were contrary to the righteous commandments of Yahweh as He gave to Moses on Mount Sinai, so many millennia ago. As I explained in previous chapter 8 the changes that the Roman Catholic made, as they adopted parts of pagan religions into the once pure Christianity of the earlier followers of Christ. Then they persecuted heathen Moslems in various Crusades (Holy wars), and so-called 'heretics' of Protestant Christians who broke away from the Catholic constraints and freed up the Bible into layman's languages so the ordinary folk may have real access to Christ and salvation, and not be prevented by the Latin (and Greek) of the Roman Catholic church.

In these modern days we again have a uniting of state and church to enforce laws that are contrary to Moses laws as given by Yahweh. In June 2009, whilst the whole world was directed to focus on the sudden unexpected death of megastar Michael Jackson, who wanted to stay forever young like his idol 'Peter Pan', but whose life was mysteriously cut short at 51 by a cocktail of medical pills, and the panhysteria that followed was unbelievable. Whilst all that commotion was going on with full world-wide media attention on him, another more significant and sinister event was happening across the Atlantic, as President Obama flew from America to see Pope Benedict XVI in the Vatican in Rome. Hurriedly and secretively, unannounced they met to sign an agreement for the so-long discussed for decades 'Sunday Law' of worship to be enforced by the head of the world police force himself, Obama. Two years later Obama signed the NDAA law giving the right to detain indefinitely any American *citizen*, who would be stripped of their citizenship under anti-terrorism laws

Obama who wears so many different hats, being mixed race Black/AfroAmerican and White (Scottish?) parentage, of Christian and Moslem backgrounds, appealing to poor African Americans and rich white middle class Americans alike, and being heterosexual, married and a father, publicly approving of same-sex 'marriages', and being the so-called first Black man to be president of USA, although records show that there were at least 7 others, less renowned before him, from early days of President Lincoln.

He professes to uphold free speech and respect human rights, has yet to fulfil his 2008 election promise to shut down the notorious Guantanomo Bay penitentiary for terrorists and terrible criminals. And his Presidential oath includes upholding the rights of American citizens to free speech and freedom of expression, including the right to worship as you wish on American soil. This after all is what the great statue of Liberty on Long Island symbolises. However that signed agreement in June three years ago, began the process that at once negates all of these freedoms for Americans.

In the scare-mongering and propaganda, following the 9/11 terrorist attacks on the twin towers of trade and commerce in 2001, and other American targets; followed by 7/7, 2005 London bombings, after the announcement that Britain had won the bid to host this year's 2012 Olympics, rightly so the governments worldwide are on panicked terrorist alert against any possible suspects, and friends of al-Qaeda. However, this jointly signed agreement between a state- government and a church-govern- ment, as symbolised in Rev 13 by the beasts and the horns, represents another dimension to the extension of who might be considered by the government agencies to be a 'terrorist'.

At present, absurd as it may seem in the UK, people who are on the suspected terrorist list include ordinary folk like those who protest against their poll/council tax, or campaigners fighting for the right to 'camp' in their protests outside key landmarks (gov- ernment or scientific strong holds, like those encamped outside St. Paul's Cathedral for years), and other less notable 'crimes' or 'dissenting' offences.

Since this agreement of 2009, 'though little is known about it, once Obama who is fighting for a second term in office this month (Sept 2012), is re-elected, it will not be long before the full importance of that action is enforced. So since Seventh Day Adventists are the Christians who worship on the Sabbath as instructed by Yahweh in His 4th Commandment, namely Saturday (sunset Friday to sunset Saturday, in accordance with original Judaism), they, if they are true SDAs will not be worshipping on the Sunday (or Lord's day as changed in 4th century), and so will be contravening and transgressing the 'Sunday law'.

These then, will become likely targets for anti-terror interventions by government official enforcers, and locked and detained, without trial for indefinite periods. This will be possible because the signed agreement also negates the 5th amendments and strips Americans of the automatic citizenship, if it is deemed they are likely or potential terrorists, and therefore they will not be entitled to the protection under the statue of Liberty or American Freedom and Justice flag, in fact they will be screwed. So persecution against Protestants will once again abound, but this time because they refuse to comply with man-made laws of Sunday worship (ie worship of the sun/pagan/devil worship)!!!

Also in Revelation 13 it talks about the second beast with its horn, bowing down and giving its authority to the first beast. Thus it is that Obama has pledged his allegiance to the Pope, head of the Vatican city, Roman Catholic church. Parallel to this is the occurrence of USA deferring to its parent/mother country Britain, unlike what has been happening since their American Independence on 4th July 1776, with Britain apparently following everything that her daughter American does,. No. Watch for signs of change that are already happening. Britain and Queen Elizabeth still rules the waves/world in her various colonial (sorry post-colonial, but entrapment trade relationships with so many countries worldwide, see earlier discussion in chapter 9 on, 'trojan' tactics of trade and aid, really being exploitrade). Greenwich Meantime still determines every other time in the world, as the origin of 24hour clock.

And of course her ancestor King Henry VIII, was the embodiment of state and church uniting and changing the laws to
suit himself. He broke away from the authority of the Vatican
and Roman Catholic church to set himself up as head of the
Church of England (Anglican), as well as being king, because
he wanted to free himself from his obligation to his deceased
brother's wife, whom he married, and marry his mistress French
Anne Boleyn, who was mother of Queen Elizabeth I, the heir
of the wrong gender (Henry wanted a son), who became the
greatest queen to rule Britain to date. There you go, apostasy,
adultery, murder by executions, and siring illegitimate children,
all in one kingly authority,- shooting down several principled
birds in one fell swoop!

And become aware of the beasts and their influences, as
described earlier in this chapter 9, the powers that control our
minds, through politics, religion, medications, media, doctrines,
music and film in the all-encompassing, pervasive, intrusive
and following you everywhere via internet on mobile phones
and apps and ipads/ipods and laptops, so NO escape and possibility of contemplating your Creator Yahweh. The image that
the beast causes the whole world to worship, developed from
the 'image that speaks' – the speak easy, or boom box, radio
transmitter, is none other than that familiar 'friend' in your living
room, or every other room you have in your home, flat screen,
small, huge, HD-ready, etc, yes you've guessed it... your TV?

What does everyone do? Sit glued to the box, every day, morning, noon and night (24hrs, never switch off, Lord help us!), that
entertains us and 'educates' us, and informs us, and CONTROLS
us through the media and advertising, and programmes elicit-
ing a diet of degrading and demeaning and debasing, images,
stories, songs, videos, you name it, they show it, (see chapter
8). And so what do we blindly do?

Monkey see, monkey do. We're losing the ability to think for ourselves anymore. Sitting there like morons, absorbing everything

we are exposed to, and yet when asked the question, what are you watching? What have you learnt? Answer 'dunno'. Not even paying attention to what's on the box. Just got it on for company, or noise, or to babysit the kids, or to fall asleep to, day or night. What is wrong with us?

Even a comedian on Edinburgh Comedy Fest(ival) joked last night on TV (6ᵗʰ /8/12), that when he felt a pain in his knee, rather than use his own judgement and common sense, he turned to the internet on his mobile phone, to find out that he had a dodgy knee! And even worse, when he went to his GP about it, instead of the doctor examining his knee, the patient found him checking on *his* internet for the answer, ie a dodgy knee. The world's gone mad, or lazy, or docile, or is on automatic pilon like robots, mindless machines, who will obey or blindly follow any command, however graphic, overt or subtle or subliminal – as in messages contained within advertising on the box!!! Wake up people! Lest you find yourselves conscripted in the 'Ben 10s alien force' /Satan's army and his royal and presidential allies, lined up to fight against the One, who has already died to save you, and has been resurrected, to one day soon return, and redeem you for His prize and reward, for that priceless and very costly sacrifice.

Who is that person? None other than Jesus Christ, the Healer and Avenger. The Great Physician and answer to all our prayers and sorrows and hurts and sufferings.

All I hope and pray, without ceasing (1 Thess 5 v 17), is that each of you decide, as I have done, to hold, no, cling onto the rock. The rock that the builders (Jewish religious leaders) rejected, that has become the capstone/ cornerstone of the Christian faith, and who will come and crush all the earthly kingdoms of Nebuchadnezzar's statue past and present (Daniel 2), and who will establish an eternal imperishable kingdom in new heaven and new earth, - the rock who is Jesus Christ. Chip of the old block. Rock stone of the Rock of Ages – Jesus the Christ, only begotten son of our Potter, our Creator, YHWH (Yahweh), who lives from before the foundation of the earth and the heavens, lives now and will still be living in an Eternity of Perfect Circles. Bless you if you do. Choose the rock. Choose Life. Choose Jesus Christ. Bless.

MY COMMISSION:-

The purpose of this book Perfect Circles is a 21st century reminder of the prophecies of the Lord Almighty. Hence all that is included in it is prophecy reiterated, with deeper revelations for the modern times. In 2012 my (DJKO) prophecy is not only as in 1990 or 1994, for Moslems and remnant Jews respectively, but for all the people, especially the Assyrians and the people in the West, to stop their sinning and wickedness, and turn back towards the Lord!!!

This day (3 Feb 2011) the Lord showed me that as prophetess, for you the people, and myself, that He has directed me to warn you all to take heed of the words of the Lord. As I warned in this chapter, and discussed elsewhere, I have been on a very hard and difficult road as prophetess. And 'I have started, so I'll finish'. I must continue through, without fear, and in honour and praise of the Lord, Most Righteous and Justified.

My preparation for this task has been life-long since being a 4 year old child, responsible and caring for younger sibling and relatives, people in the community and in my various works (for children, the elderly, the physically and mentally disabled), and through partners, children and grandchildren and friends, to be freed in my fifties to take on this greater and more challenging role as prophetess for the people.

It is no wonder that some prophets try to run away from the Lord's commission, like Jonah who tried to escape on a ship but ended up in a whale and was brought back to shore to the task he was set. It is a huge, huge responsibility. A real big, scary deal! But I too, as a disciple of Christ, and as prophetess must be fearless and even more courageous, with 'righteous indignation' (109) and a sense of Justice for the Lord, who loves us and wants to save us so we might have eternal Life. My duty is to encourage the people to listen to the Lord's warnings to 'REBUKE/ RESIST the temptations' of Satan, REPENT of wrong-doing, and to RETURN to our Father, who made us, and to whom we belong. The 3 'R's – Rebuke, Repent and Return.

Twenty two years ago, 1990, I vowed to be the Lord's willing ab'd/servant. My will is His will, and I will do it. Thus my responsibility for the people is a huge weight on my feeble shoulders, but I will gladly bear it with the help of the Holy Spirit, for Jesus bore mine and all our sins on His innocent shoulders. Can I so humble and insignificant, do less? When He has done so much for me, for us, for the love of His and our Father, whom I love and serve with all my mind, body, heart and soul? Can I refuse this commission? I think not! I *will* do what I've been asked. For my happiness, joy and peace and calmness rest in the love of the Lord. My treasure is delight in the Lord, my Saviour and Shepherd (110). I am happy and content in my commission, and have peace of mind that I am doing what is right for the Lord Most High. I am His willing and obedient ab'd, and His instrument of prophecy. I will do what He has asked of me.

For I will not be held blameless, but will be held accountable for failing or refusing to warn the people, when I have been instructed by the Most High to do so. If they continue to sin because I have not warned them, then I too, will be responsible for their deaths and the loss of their souls to damnation and Hell (111) (149). My role and duty as prophetess, is to 'chide and guide' the people back to Christ , who will forgive them and save their souls and give them eternal Life, to live in Perfect Circles of communion with Him, our Lord and Creator.

So take care, for the prophecies of the Lord do come true (151). He does not lie. He is faithful. He is Truth. He is Life. He is

Love. You have been warned. Take heed, lest you perish for-ever! Bless, DJKO.

URGENT! HURRY, HURRY!

Change your ways now and turn to the Lord!!!

Don't let: 'too late, too late' be your cry and regret.

Take the chance now whilst there is still time!

My commission is even more urgent now. Time is SHORT!!! For even now in these early months of 2011, Satan is align-ing his army of demons and people who have given their allegiance to him, and as many others as he can deceive into following him. He is getting them into position as he makes ready for his final assault on the Lord, in the battle of Armageddon.

Revelation Time reveals that our time of probation is nearly over. Don't let your cry and regret be; 'too late, woe is me! Take this chance now in this limited time. REPENT and change now!

The Lord Jesus Christ is returning soon, and too soon for some! In this final battle, whose side will you be on? I pray it will be the Lord's for your sake.

Learning of the apostle Paul's life dedication and suffering to spread Christ gospels, I am encouraged and inspired in my own endeavours. Oh my joy is to love and serve the Lord, and to endure all for His name's sake!!! My heart is bursting to over-flowing with everlasting love and happiness. Thank you so very much Jesus, and to you Most High, all laud and honour and praises and thanksgiving are due. I am eternally grateful for you choosing me to be one of your instruments to carry out your commissions. I gratefully accept, and only hope I don't disap-point, merciful Lord!

As the Spirit moves me I express these further thoughts on sex and sexuality:-

What *is* it about sex and perverted sex? - The lewdness, fornication, adultery, lust, masturbation, homosexuality, sodomy, bestiality etc?

Pit these against chastity and purity, and choosing to live as 'eunachs' for Christ's sake, ie celibacy.

Why is there this obsession with sex and perversion?

It is because the Usurper, Satan, turned his love into hate, and then became so unlovable to our Creator and Father that he was cast out of His heavenly presence. Satan, so full of self-loathing, hatred and jealousy/envy, and spite, hates the Lord and all things pertaining to His greatness and beauty and LOVE. So he hates mankind, of whom he is envious, for they now have the love (unconditionally) that once was bestowed on him, when he was a covering guardian angel of the Almighty Father in heaven (98). But Satan grew contemptuous of this love, took this blessing and privilege as though they were nothing/naught, and as if were beneath his attention, for he felt himself too important to need the love of the Father (112).

But he learnt when he was cast out of heaven, down to earth, that he was wrong. He needed our Creator's love, and badly, as he felt the coldness and aloneness and remoteness - that distance and separation, that he had brought upon himself. Envious of that love he no longer has, he spitefully does not see why mankind should have our Saviour's love either. So he masquerades and parades and flaunts sex as if it were love!!!! He masquerades sex and lust and lewd affections as though they were 'the real thing' – love. But they are NOT!

The sexual love that is needed to bind a man and woman to each other as life partners, as husband and wife in the eyes of the Lord, - He says 'let no man put asunder/separate whom 'God' has joined together as one (113) is acceptable. Remember Christ said the two become as one flesh, and so divorce is not really what was intended for a couple, but it is only permissible in certain circumstances because of the hard-headedness/stubbornness of the Jews (114). This sexual love is for the man and woman's comfort, having been banished from the comfortable living in Eden, and from the company of our Creator. It is also for procreation. He told Adam and Eve to 'be fruitful and multiply'. They were to go forth and bring children into the world. Even Abraham's seed was to multiply through Isaac and Ishmael and those 'grafted in' or 'adopted' children of 'God' in following Christ. This Christ, who lived and exercised and showed the unconditional love of our Father, our Creator, Most Highly Exalted! Merciful Jesus, give me strength to bear this!

Why then should we be obsessed with sex – lust, basic, animalistic, hormonal and emotional? Yes we need it for the above reasons, but we are different and higher than animals. We are HUMAN BEINGS! We have dominion over the animals, but we don't need to become like them, or subjected to them (ie bestial Satan!!!) We are to aspire to regain the divine love of our Father who created us, loved us as beautiful humans, as special, as beloved in whom He delighted and was well-pleased.

Adam and Eve, through being deceived, spoilt things for the rest of us, and were reduced to mere sexual love. However, our bodies are not made for sexual immorality, as if playing the harlot. We belong to the Lord as one in spirit with Him. 'For the body is the temple of the Holy Spirit, whom you have from 'God'. You are NOT your own (115). You were BOUGHT at a very high price – Jesus Christ' blood sacrifice. Therefore glorify 'God' in your body and in your spirit, which are 'God's'. In fact we are to 'flee sexual immorality' (115) (115a) apostle Paul tells us. Indeed we are to 'consecrate' ourselves and 'be holy' 'for I am the Lord, your 'God'. You shall keep all my statutes, and perform them. I am the Lord who sanctifies you'.

Jesus, who did not have sexual relationships, but loved divinely and unconditionally, came to cancel out this corrupted love, and to put us back on track to attain pure, chaste, celibate, unconditional, heavenly, divine love. That kind of love is deemed acceptable as sweet and pleasing to our Divine Ruler and Creator, our heavenly Emperor, the Lord Most High, who sits in His 7 Spirits (116), on the throne of heaven, and waits long-suffering, biding His time to *His* appointed time, known only to Him, when He will say finally:

'Enough is enough!!! Probation is over! No longer will I tolerate the Usurper ruining and destroying and stealing my people – my beautiful, beloved creations, mankind, who are to be washed and sanctified and justified and redeemed by Lord Jesus' saving blood. The people have had long enough and time enough, to repent and turn from evil, and return to Me. I AM the Almighty One!

'Now it's too late!

Now the door is shut!

Now I will send My Son

Jesus, the Victorious Conqueror

Over Satan and death,

Back to claim

His 'bride', His 'prize' -

The 'elect', the '144,000',

The remnant and redeemed –

The ones saved from evilous

Corruption and Hell,

Who chose to suffer and endure

And die for Christ's sake,

And out of love for Me, your Father,

Creator of All,

And who AM LOVE.

Now will be your time for Judgement.

Who will stand?

Whose names will be written in the Book of Life?

Will yours be among them?

REPENT! REPENT I say, before it is too late!!!

Our Father, who art in heaven, is the same yesterday, today and tomorrow.

Jesus, who comes from our Father, is also the same. Jesus is constant. He is the constant in our world of change.

Our Father has always condemned homosexuals as abomination (121). This remains constant.

Jesus said: 'drunkards, fornicators, homosexuals, and so forth, will not see heaven' (117). In clearer words – there is no place in heaven for such people.

Yet we are reminded by Jesus and our Father, that it is the SIN He hates, and not the sinner (88). For the Lord, our Father 'remembers not our transgressions' and indeed will 'blot them out' from his memory those sins of the righteous if they but repent and turn back to Him (118).

When Jesus Himself went into the inner sanctuary (119) – the holy of holies – He took the over-loaded and excessively heavy burden of ALL our sins onto His shoulders. And with His cleansing blood, His saving blood, for He is our Saviour, He blotted out our transgressions and thus removed, negated, and cancelled out all our sins.

So if we know all this, why are we putting back on the mantle/ cloak of sin? Why are we continuing to be dazzled, moreover, blinded by Satan's deceptions, and still committing sins when Jesus has already removed them from our shoulders, placed them on His own, and cleared them to zero? Why are we accumulating more? Why are we allowing ourselves, now that we know of Jesus, to continue in sinful ways? Are we that weak? Are we that wilful? Is Satan too strong for our feeble minds and bodies, that we can be easily tricked into temptations and wrong-doings?

We are not born as drunkards/ alcoholics, drug addicts etc. (Although now, because of their parents' addictions, there are babies who have these drugs imposed on them whilst still in their mothers' wombs. When these babies are born, they already suffer the effects of 'crack' cocaine, and viruses such as HIV/Aids, and other sexually transmitted diseases, or from contaminated blood transfusions.) However, we are not ordinarily born into bad habits, and our sexuality is not determined at birth. We are socialised into the ways of the world, into societies' teachings and practices, whether good or bad. Sometimes children as young as babies, have been sexually abused, and these traumatic experiences can adversely affect their development. But others, I would hope to say, the majority, develop in a natural process of maturity – hormonally, physically, mentally, and emotionally. But we are influenced by what we see and hear and know of, around us.

Habba Hotel – an internet social networking site, with digitalised characters who live in a virtual world community, where young people can meet up and design this world, and experience dating, etc. It's more sinister aspects were recently exposed (June 2012) on a TV documentary, and subsequently discussed further on channel 4 TV news interview with 4 teenagers, who had used and become addicted to the site, and were incensed that the expose' had caused the company to shut it down immediately, and so 'spoiling their fun'!!!

But this fun had begun by pre-pubescent children as young as 10 or 11 years olds being introduced to sex and encouraged to become sexually active at younger ages than they otherwise would. One teenager who'd used for almost all the 10 years! It had been operating (unsupervised, unmonitored by PG certificate ratings, or responsible internet engines or hosts of the site!!!), said within minutes of her first use of the site at age 11, she had 20 hits of, probably paedophiles, propositioning her and asking her to expose private parts of her body, via webcam!!!!! And worse still, tho' she admitted she felt uncomfortable at first, and felt it might(?) be wrong, she did it anyway, and soon became addicted to the 'friends' she met in that virtual (one step removed, 'safe' faceless, and so unable to detect and see the real danger of perverted and abominable predators!!!) .

Another girl, who'd protested loudest at its closure, said she was first introduced to sex on it, and not only had virtual dates, but had met up with 4 different girls/lesbians from there in person, face to face – bringing 'virtual to meet reality'; and increasing the likelihood of this for paedophiles to happen more easily, and undetectably!!!

The worst thing about all this is that it encourages children to lie and be secretive, furtively able to block screens from 'embarrassing' parents accidently coming into the bedroom, who would be horrified to find that their children's innocence was being snatched away from them by sexual abuse and rape made possible through this 'virtual' medium, masquerading as 'harmless' past-time, especially for more shy, isolated, less popular youngsters, whose confidence gets boosted by the 'love & affection' offered by predators!

The longest site user, now aged 23, said perhaps she was getting too old for it now, but would miss it. The young man, agreed with all the other youth comments, but added, most profoundly notably, that if he was a parent, he would NOT want his child to use that site!

Was this not how the 2, 10 year old Soham girls, 2002, Holly Wells and Jessica Chapman, with their mobile phones, who secretly sneaked out of their parents' barbecue, and ended up at the home of school caretaker, Ian Huntley, and were sexually assaulted/raped and murdered; that instigated all these national checks on suitability to work with children by Criminal Records Bureau (CRB) ???? Was not this same easily accessible media, - books, magazines, TV, films, computers, mobile phones– displaying sexually explicit and depraved, perverted, abominable, violent, murderous, men, women, children and dogs, 'acting out' fantasies! - to corrupt young minds, not yet mature enough to fully understand the dangers they are being exposed to, led into, and end up feeling and doing things, in regrettable devastation, which they then have to pay the penalty for, even though they are not mentally or emotionally mature enough to comprehend or deal with the responsibility that comes with engaging in adult behaviour???

Case in point - the 10 year old boys, Robert Thompson and Jon Venables, who in Feb 1993, abducted a 2 year old infant, Jamie Bulger, who had wandered away from his parent in a shopping centre. The boys, 'careers' in idle truancy from school, had been predatory, deliberately looking for a child victim, upon whom to inflict the brutal, horrific, sexual and sadistic things they had watched on an 18+ rated, home video, sinisterly named 'Chucky - Child's play' about a ugly-looking doll/puppet that came 'alive' and did evil things. Regrettably, that victim was infant Jamie Bulger, and having tortured him, in ways some of which were too horrific to be disclosed to the outraged public, raising the question 'were these boys 'mad or bad'?

For then it was, and still is, inconceivable and unpalatable, to accept the possibility that children could do such things deliberately -ie as 'bad', and therefore, fully culpable. They were considered and judged fully 'compos mentis', therefore being of age, and old enough to reason, and discern between right and wrong, and were therefore deemed responsible enough, and so were punished with secure imprisonment till they reached 18 - the age at which modern society deems to be the actual age of maturity, and responsibility, as an adult. They were then released and given new secret identities, by which they could try to live the rest of their lives in anonymity, out of the still outraged eye of public scrutiny. They still had a life, such as it now was.

Their victim, child Jamie Bulger, they cut short HIS life, at the tender age of 2, -still an infant! *He* is no longer able to play. And they, and we, can see that 'Chucky' was NOT child's play (innocent fun and make believe) at all, but evil seduction by ADULTS, and Satan, to corrupt and ruin children, fatally.

At their trial, then aged about 11, they showed no feelings of remorse, thereby raising my question of whether they were really 'bad', or just not mentally or emotionally mature enough to fully understand what they had gotten involved in, (led astray, right into hell's fire) and could therefore, not be fully responsible for their devastating actions.

Notably, the real culprits, the ones who produce such filth, and those who make it freely and widely available/accessible to young minds, 'were nowhere to be seen, when the shit hit the fan', and left those poor innocent,- now corrupted and ruined completely -, boys 'to face the tumultuous uproar of the world's public - our societies - alone. Where was Satan then, the instigator and instiller of bad ideas, even into innocent children? Did he stick around to defend them? No! He 'up and high tailed it' away, gleefully mocking them, and us, for successfully fooling/ tricking us into evil, and its consequences, which he spitefully, knows affronts and upsets Yahweh, who Himself, is aggrieved at our suffering and ruination. Whilst at the same time, Satan taunts Yahweh for apparently, not being able to catch up with him, to deliver His wrathful punishments so long prophesied.

But Yahweh is biding His time, and is meanwhile suffering in patient forbearance, for HIS Right time to reek His vengeance. Of THAT we can be certain! I discuss more about this case elsewhere in this book: in crimes perpetrated by man against humanity, and in this case, children. But as I stated there, and repeat here, to reinforce and drive home Yahweh's Holy Spirit's message of Truth, to make you all aware, that WE are all culpable and to be blamed for NOT caring enough about our children, or any child, to take our responsibility as educators, guardians, protectors, -mature adults,- seriously enough to ensure that NO child is exposed to any kind of corrupting, degrading, debasing, abusive or abusing, victimising or criminalising EVIL influences, that end up ruining 'innocent little children and causing them to sin' and 'denying/depriving them the chance to access 'the kingdom of heaven' that Christ' promises belongs to those who Rebuke/Resist Evil Satan, Repent of wrong doing, and Return to the Originator of LIFE, and JOY, HAPPINESS and TRUE LOVE, whose name is YAHWEH, through Christ Jesus.

And He also sternly warned: 'Woe to those responsible for causing or allowing such perpetration of evil, or obstructing children's path to freedom from sin and into paradise! Sodom and Gomorrah would fare better than these in the fate of condemnation and infernal fiery punishment that awaits them!!! Take heed! We have been warned and reproved and disciplined. Are you going to listen and take up your full responsibility as caring adults, with community spirit, to 'love one another', as Jesus and Yahweh, have and still, love us, and 'do unto others, what we would have them do to us' ie love, in truth, and for Life.

And even worse, we have the devil, prowling like a raging lion, a dragon, ready to devour us at the earliest opportunity (120)to destroy us and our relationship with our heavenly Father, that he goes around putting destructive ideas in our heads. Satan knows that homosexuality is abominable (121) to our Father and Creator, and that it is sterile and non-productive. He knows that it ultimately could lead to the reduction and annihilation of mankind. And moreover, he knows he is offending and upsetting our Father, when he instils homosexual ideas into people's minds leading them to practice it, and therefore, sin. Also causing the break-up of some marriages - that sanctified institution that Yahweh established between first man and woman, Adam and Eve. Satan is rude and disrespectful, and affronts our Father, the Lord and Creator Almighty on purpose.

But we have a saviour in Jesus Christ, who has, like our Father, delivered the Israelites from bondage/ slavery in Egypt. Jesus set us free from the bondage of sin. He won His liberty, and therefore OUR liberty from the slavery of sin, when He gave up His life and relinquished His blood on the cross at Calvary. There, when He submitted His will, gave up His I/ego/selfish concerns, and placed them under the will of His Father, our Father who resides in heaven, still, waiting for when He has had enough of man's iniquity. He is waiting until the last person has been born and lives according to His commands and has the testimony of Christ in his life and heart and mind and soul. Our Father will wait till *that* moment to send Jesus back to earth from heaven, to reclaim His own dedicated followers/ martyrs and saints – and to bring judgement upon all the peoples that ever lived, when the Books will be opened – the Book of Life, the Book of Remembrance, and the Book of Iniquities/ Transgressions/Wrong-doings or SINS.

This last is what we must be mindful of, if we want to avoid death in hell, no, the REAL and PERMANENT death – the Second death, (that is scarcely mentioned or highlighted!). THE final destination for the wicked and evil who remain unrepentant – the lake of fire and brimstone, where there is to be 'wailing and gnashing of teeth', from the pain and agony of perpetual, relentless, merciless, punishing torture and torment, perpetually forever and ever!!!! We are to resist Satan. In fact we must REBUKE him, and say: 'get behind me Satan! Leave me alone! (122).

We must REPENT of our wrong-doings, by saying we are sorry and ask for forgiveness, whilst also remembering to forgive others their wrongs to us. Finally we are to RETURN to the bosom of our heavenly Father, who waits with open and loving arms to welcome us back to His fold. For only He is the Good Shepherd (123) who cares for and loves us unconditionally always.

Then, after Armageddon, and Judgement Day is over, and the 'wheat and the tares/weeds', the good and the wicked have been separated, and the wicked destroyed. And after Satan, the false prophet and the beast have been cast into perpetual torment in the lake of fire and brimstone. The 'elect', the '144,000' will have been vindicated, set free and reclaimed and will be rewarded by being allowed into the hallowed presence of the Lord Jesus and His Father, our Father. Then He, our Creator, will once again, now reconciled to through the blood sacrifice of Jesus, be joined to His beloved mankind, now redeemed, and will walk amongst us on earth, as He did in Eden.

However, it will not be this present earth or heaven that will exist, for they will pass away into nothingness (124). It will instead be a 'new heaven and new earth, wherein lies the celestial city – the new Jerusalem, beautiful and pure, clean and bejewelled, a royal priesthood, which will live and reign with victorious Christ forever in Eternity. So not merely back to Eden, but *forward* to a perfected Eden, rebuilt anew, pure and holy.

So why wait until Christ returns in judgement? Change now and employ the 3 Rs – Rebuke, Repent and Return. There is no more time to flaff about and procrastinate, postpone or delay. It is now. The time is now to change your ways, - to change your life, so your name can be blotted out of the Book of Transgressions; that your sins be remembered no more. Instead you can have your name entered into the Holy and Sacred Book of Life.

Do you really want your life to be blessed? Really blessed? You can do all things in Christ who strengthens you, (125). Let Jesus into your life, and turn your life around.

$Y + X$ = Infinity. You and Christ will have everlasting life.

But, $Y - X = 0$. Without Christ in your life, you can be, and will have, nothing = NO eternal life.

And you know that nothing is Impossible with our Father. He can give us everything our hearts desire, if we are righteous (91). For all things work for the good, for those who love the Lord (126).

The only WAY to eternal life, to be named in the Book of Life, is through taking up your cross of trials and afflictions, even unto death, for the name sake of Jesus Christ.

So stop sinning. Restrain and curb your carnal lusts and desires, whatever they may be – promiscuity, homosexuality, addictions, vices, selfish ambitions, idol worship, abuses, whatever. Stop them. Ask Christ to come into your life to help you resist temptations. And you will be blown away by how FREE He will make you. You will then realise you don't need those crutches in your life. You will be freed from the bondage and slavery of sin. Take up Christ's Way of Life. Put the Lord our Father first in your life. Follow Christ's teachings and example. Become a disciple, not a sinner. Become free for an eternity of love and life, that is blessed, sanctified, pure and holy. We must be perfect as our heavenly Father is perfect (82), so that He will be well pleased to associate with us who are now made worthy.

We should wish to be an Enoch (127) generation, an E-generation, and not an evil generation (127a). We should want to be found wearing white robes when Christ returns - white robes that are a sign of being washed in blood for Jesus' cause, having endured trials and tribulations for His name sake. We should have a life style and character that our Lord Almighty will be pleased with. Some of us will be prophesying truths in these latter days. Get yourselves ready. Christ is returning very, very soon from now.

War is being waged against us. The battle is not over our minds. Our minds are *the* last battle grounds, in which the battle for our souls is being waged.

It is our souls that are precious. And these are what the devil is, by various means, trying to steal from our Creator.

But our Father sent Jesus to reclaim those souls of people, who follow His commandments. Those who have been tried and tested in the fiery furnace of afflictions, following Christ's lead, and who will be saved and taken back to His bosom and protective loving arms, when He is glorified and returns at the end of Time, which is not too far from now.

And now Muslims are coming to Christ (1990), and remnant Jews too (1994), and prophecy is unfolding in Egypt; and signs of the Times are quickening – famines, earthquakes, floods, disasters, climate changes, - which are the beginnings of the end. These signs indicate Christ is coming very soon.

So what does this mean for us? It means we need to keep Rebuking Satan, Repent of our wickedness, and Return to the Lord, NOW! Time is short. Turn now before probation Is over. Repent now if you want to be saved for eternal life!

This is the Age of Reason, of science of man's thinking, philosophies, religions, theologies, - his reasonings. All full of crap and bloody pie in the sky!!! Man's deluded shit, arrogantly thinking himself so important, and boasting of his mental abilities, his geniuses and ingenuities, like Satan whilst sitting in heaven (112).

But where did it come from? Where did man get his talents? Those gifts that were intended to help us better manoeuvre through this now harsh life, since expulsion from Eden? Who does man think he is? Does he really think himself better and more superior to the One who created him? Is the clay daring to question the Potter who made it? (128) Is it really?

Questions, questions, questions!

Ever inquisitive, always questioning, desiring to know everything about everything, like Satan, through his "all-seeing eye". Never satisfied. We want to know where our Creator came from? Was He created Himself, or has He always existed? Does it really matter? Will it make any difference to us and how we conceive

things? And more importantly, will it affect how we live our lives, or how we conduct ourselves?

If we have all this knowledge – of science, of history, and so forth already, and what we know thus far about creation, and Jesus Christ, and our heavenly Father Yahweh, what difference will knowing any more make? Can we not comprehend

and just accept that we are less than our Creator? We do not have His 'brain' capacity to create or even conceive what He is capable of conceiving, knowing and seeing. We are merely human beings. Can the computer be greater than its inventor? Can the clay be better than its Potter? (128). Can the creature be better than his Creator? No. Never!

So that is it. Accept this fact and humble yourself before Him, and pray that His wrath at your impudence does not consume us in the flames of hell – fire, thrown into the lake of fire and brimstone for permanent and continual punishment and torment as it will Satan, at the end of Time, and on the Final Day of Judgement. Be humble and beg clemency, so you can 'fix-up' before it is too late!!! This we *can* do if we so

choose. This Satan REFUSES to do, and so he WILL be consumed in the lake of fire and brimstone.

Man had best put on his glasses, and wipe his sodden eyes. In fact, remove the dazzling veil clouding his vision, and take several *monumental* steps back, into humility, and recognise that the buck does not stop with him. He does not have control, or the ultimate decision.

The final decision and judgement comes from the Lord,
through His hard-fought victory, won at a very expensive price
– His life's blood –for us.
And it is the Lord who is the ONLY one worthy to open the 7
seals (129)
and then have the final judgement over all of us,
separating the wheat and the tares/weeds,
the sheep and the goats,
the good and the evil,
the righteous and the wicked,
the repentant and the proud.

It will be *His* judgement, for His glory,
and in His reward will be the prized souls of the elect,
in His kingdom in the new heaven and the new earth in
Eternity.

THE FLOOD IS COMING AGAIN!!!

On December 1st 2010, I awoke from a dream telling me the flood is coming again. In my dream I saw 2 ancient Egyptian young men, scurrying away, trying to secret and hide an object deep in the vaults of possibly a temple. They were carrying a mini pyramid, between them, made of bricks, and in its centre was a sphere, transparently golden, and within which flashing lights, and colourful wriggly things and such things as I have not seen in these current times, of knowledge of such high sophistication that we in our modern progressed times cannot yet attain. We still have not been able to construct a pyramid as great and complex as those of ancient Egypt, despite our advances in technology and science.

At first I marvelled at how great must the minds of the ancient Egyptians been, if they have secreted such things that we have not been able to fathom or master ourselves yet. And I wondered why they were so frantic. For as one said to the other: 'the flood is coming'. And the other replied, 'He said He wouldn't send the flood again'. To which the other replied, 'I know, but it is coming.' I realised they were talking about the Flood in Noah's time, where the Lord, full of regret, promised not to flood the whole earth again. He gave us the rainbow as a sign of His covenant and promise to man. However, I too, pondered what this flood was that was coming, and why the Lord would break His promise.

It was only when a visiting pastor from India, pastor Ray Durairaj (140), came and gave a sermon at our Core Adventist programme this May 2011, that the Holy Spirit used him to reveal the answer to my question. That evening the devil did all in his

power to try and prevent me attending the meeting, but I did succeed, and just in time to hear the message I was destined to receive.

What or Who is that Flood that is coming? JESUS CHRIST IS THIS FLOOD.

Jesus is the living water (130). And He is the bread and water of Life (131).

When He speaks his voice is like tremulous running waters, (132).

Like a flood, Jesus' love is abundant, all-encompassing, and is boundless living waters for all who thirst and would drink of it.

The Waterfall (public domain) Like Jesus Christ the Living Fountain of Water of Life

Now we know how devastating and overpowering a flood is. The waters go everywhere and are all-encompassing. In Noah's time, when the flood came, the majority of the world was covered. There was no land spared, and no one escaped, except for 8 people – Noah, his wife and son's and their wives in the ark, - a huge ship that they had built, according to the Lord's plans.

Now whilst Noah had been building the ark, he was also preaching and exhorting the antediluvian peoples (130a) to repent and turn back to the Lord and to righteousness for 120 years! But they refused and rejected his advice and mocked him whilst he was constructing the ark for so many years. However when the ark was finished,

and he and his family and the animals entered it, and the huge door was closed, - then came a test of nerves. For 7 days no rain came. For 7 days they waited. Meantime the peoples were outside jeering and laughing at them, sneering: where is this rain, this flood that he warned them was coming? However when the rains began to fall, and the people realised that Noah had been right all along, and that this was really it, they began to panic for their lives. With a terrible fear, they begged Noah to open the door, even just for 1 hour, 1 small hour, to let them in, 1 more hour of probation, but it was TOO LATE!

For when our heavenly Father began to close that very heavy door to the ark, by His invisible hand/ forces, He closed it SLOWLY. So that there was still more time, even to the last minute, for the people to repent in that time of probation, but they failed to do so. When the door was closed tight shut, and after 7 days, the clouds opened and the rains poured and the floods came, they realised that there was no hope left for them. THEY WERE DOOMED!

How unforgiving, relentless and all- encompassing are the flood waters when they overpower an area. The waters reach everywhere. No-one can escape, unless they have a safe haven. Noah had the ark. The holy city of the New Jerusalem in the kingdom of heaven is that safe haven, - safe in the arms of Jesus.

Jesus, who is the flood due to come again, he will come reeking vengeance on those who have made our Father's people suffer and be killed since the beginning of Time, when Adam and Eve sinned in the garden of Eden. And the deceiver, Satan, the Usurper, who is the instigator of sin, will be defeated by Jesus and His angels, to be cast this time , not from heaven onto the earth as before, but from earth into Hell/Hades/the bottomless pit, and finally into the lake of fire and brimstone for eternal damnation. Not one of the unrepentant wicked shall escape this flood, who is the avenging arch angel Michael aka (also known as) Jesus Christ. (133)

This time, the evil one, who has been laughing and mocking and jeering at our Father, because he has thus far escaped due punishment, this time he will laugh no more.

When he is defeated by Jesus, and is caught and cast into the lake of fire and brimstone, where there will be weeping and wailing and gnashing of teeth (134). He will have to account for all his evil and wicked deeds. This time he will not escape. He *will* have to pay the PENALTY. No escape for him. Halleluhiah! He won't be able to harm us any more. YHWH / Eloihim has spoken (Gen1 v 3 'Let there be

light'; and there was light). It was. His word was done back then, in the Beginning, and it will be done again, even unto the end. He does not take back His word spoken in righteousness (Is. 45 v 22-25). And He will NOT give His glory to another, nor to graven images, and definitely NOT to Satan!!! (136).

Unfortunately we are not there yet, and 'sufferation a-still gwan'. For those of us who would be disciples of Jesus, there are still hard times ahead – trials and tribulations for His name sake. And at times these, like a flood, will seem overwhelming. But the Lord does not abandon the saints (psalm 37 v 28), and our sufferings will not be in vain. For finally, there will be justice for those whose 'robes have been washed white in the blood of Jesus', - those who have been martyred for their love of our

heavenly Father, and for their love of Christ. Their blood cries out 'how long, how long must we wait, for our blood to be avenged, and we be vindicated?'(135a). The Lord says He will not abandon them. He will not call back His word sworn in righteousness. He will repay! (136a). He is just waiting until the full number of their fellow saints and martyrs have been killed, is complete,(Rev 6v 11) then He will allow Christ, who would have completed His intercession in heaven's sanctuary, to come and wreak vengeance. Be warned!

EGW's Story of Redemption gives a description of what will happen at the close of probation. 'An angel with a writer's ink-horn by his side returned from the earth and reported to Jesus that his work was done, and the saints numbered and sealed. Then I saw Jesus, who had been ministering before the ark containing the ten commandments, throw down the censer. He raised His hands, and with a loud voice said: "It is done".' (Rev 10 v 6). 'Then Jesus made the solemn declaration: "He that is unjust, let him be unjust still, he that is filthy, let him be filthy still, he that is righteous, be righteous still, he that is holy, be holy still", Rev 22 v 11. Every case had been decided for life or death. While Jesus had been ministering in the sanctuary, the judgement had been going on for the righteous dead, and then for the righteous living. Christ had received His kingdom, having made the atonement for His people and blotted out their sins. The marriage of the Lamb was consummated. And the kingdom, and the greatness of the kingdom under the whole heaven, was given to Jesus and the heirs of salvation, and Jesus was to reign as King of kings and Lord of lords'.

He no longer mediated between man and Yahweh. 'The saints were living in the sight of God without an intercessor. Every case was decided, every jewel numbered.' Once Jesus stepped out from mediating, Yahweh's restraint was removed, 'and Satan had entire control of the finally impenitent. These heard the cry "Too late! Too late!! There was no one to plead to spare the sinner a little longer. No, instead 'they heard the fearful words: "It is done. It is finished." The plan of salvation had been accomplished, but few had chosen to accept it'. And the stubborn unrepentant sinners; and those who led them astray, and ministers who had not told them the truth, and had prevented others from telling them the truth, suffered ten-fold at the hands of the anguished wicked who were left behind, when Christ returned, and wreaked His vengeance. The saints, however, were protected by angels and were rejoicing in their salvation, halleluiah!!!

The Flood that is coming our way is that of terrible afflictions and destruction in punishment that our Father will command the angels of death and doom to inflict on the wicked at the end of Time, after Christ has returned the second and third times. His third Advent will be after 1,000 years of peace, the Millennium, when Satan will be bound in the bottomless pit/ hell/ desolate earth, so that he can no longer deceive the nations, (Rev 20 v 1-3). Meanwhile Jesus and the saints and Yahweh will be examining the Books and judging/ setting the punishments for the wicked, (Rev 20 v 6). When Christ returns the third time He will be bringing the new city of Jerusalem from heaven with Him, (Zechariah 14 v 1, 4, 5, 10). (See also EGW Story of Redemption chp 64-67, pps 415-433). So don't be envious of the wicked, of their evil ingenuity, their evil genius, their accolades, fame and wealth, their 'cribs' and life-styles, for their end is destruction, and their destination is Hell (psms 37 and 73).

Rather take heed of the Lord's words as He instructs us on the path to righteousness and safety. He will guide us through tests of refinement in the fiery furnace, back to His loving arms that is our refuge (psalms 23 and 91), into Life in Eternity with Him. We will be reconciled to Him in perfect communion with Him.

For the Lord does not abandon us. He loves us still, and will claim us back from Satan. He will take us under His protective wings, into life with Him and the heavenly hosts of angels in the new heaven and new earth that are to come, in His everlasting kingdom for all Eternity.

Jesus said that those who have been martyred will have their reward. They will wear His crown of glory, sit down with Him on His throne, next to the throne of our heavenly Father, in this kingdom of the new Jerusalem. But Jesus is not only the avenging angel Michael, the Flood that will wreak judgement on the wicked. He is also our safe haven. He is the ARK (of the covenant that went before Moses and the Israelites in their exodus from slavery in Egypt). He is the same yesterday, today and the future, forever in Eternity. He is the ark that abides with us, if we abide/ daily live according to His way.

Our Father walked and talked with Adam and Eve in the garden of Eden. Even after their expulsion He did not abandon them. He still communed with them; and they prayed to Him. And they brought offerings and sacrifices to the alter they made outside those very gates, where angels stood, preventing their re-entry with a

flaming sword of light (130b). Our heavenly Father walked and talked with the prophets and patriarchs of old, eg Enoch, Abraham, Moses, David, Daniel, John the Revelator, to name a few. He did not abandon us. He sent His only son, Jesus as His ambassador, to live amongst us (153).

Jesus, who is divinity in human form, lived and walked amongst us. Jesus whose name is also Immanuel, meaning 'YHWH with us', came down to us from heaven and dwelt with us. How awesome! But even before Jesus' birth, our Father already had purposed to reach out to the whole world, by extending his invitation to come to commune with Him, not only to His beloved Jews/ Israelites, but to the 'unclean' and 'defiled' Gentiles, heathens,

Moslems and the rest of humanity who did not, and do not know Him. He gave His son the name, not Joshua, which is a Jewish name, but

Jesus, which is the Greek equivalent, and means 'the Lord saves'. The name Christ from the Greek 'Christos' means 'the Anointed One' that is the Messiah. So Jesus Christ's name means 'Saviour Messiah' or 'the Anointed One who saves', (137).

Jesus Christ, therefore, saves humanity from the evil of Satan and his followers, and from their lies and injustice, and from finite death. Instead He promises us infinite life and close, living, vibrant communion with Him and the heavenly hosts, in Perfect Circles, forever and ever, Amen.

Jesus and his earthly parents were Jews, descendants from the Royal line of David, and Jesse, and Jacob/ Israel and Abraham and Adam and Eve. Yet with this name Jesus, our Father reached back in time to remember his promise and covenant with our founding fathers, to forwards to the rest of mankind, to bring them and us, to remembrance of Him. And to know of His desire to be amongst us, to fellowship with us and have our company, in fact to just be able to LOVE us, unconditionally. He sent not Joshua, but Jesus, Immanuel, to live amongst us as proof He still

desired us, and had not forgotten us. Do you know how much love that is? Can you comprehend it? Can we ever appreciate it enough? Lord save us, how marvellous and generous in spirit You are!!!

Those saved from the avenging Flood Jesus, will be folded into His loving and all-encompassing arms, into the bosom of safety, to be received into the welcoming arms of our heavenly Father, as the reconciliation that Jesus facilitated by His death on the cross, and His resurrection, will be made manifest for those saved elect. And once again our Creator will walk and commune with man - now tested and refined in the fiery furnace, even unto death to be resurrected, uncorrupted, and now immortalised - to live with Him once again in Perfect Circles. 'The tabernacle of

YHWH is with men, and He will dwell with them and they shall be His people' (154) forever, Amen.

The Flood is Jesus Christ. And how else is He described in the Bible and in hymns and songs of praise and worship? In song 'How Great is Our God', He is described as One who 'wraps Himself in Light, And (from whom) darkness tries to hide, and TREMBLES at His voice, TREMBLES at His voice!!!!

{Extract taken from the song 'How Great is our God', by Chris Tomlin, Jesse Reeves, & Ed Cash; Copyright (c) 2004 worship-together.com/songs/sixsteps Music/Kingswaysongs* & Alletrop Music^}

(And EGW Story of Redemption, p409, God's voice is like many waters, thunderous and causes an earthquake.)

Jesus' 'voice is as the sound of many waters' (Rev 1 v 12-16), that makes Satan and darkness tremble. Jesus Himself said in Matt 10 v 34-36, that He comes not to bring peace into the world, but a **sword,** that will divide up families, so that even families within the same household will be at enmity with each other, for His Name sake. (TRUE: I can testify to that in my own family).

The sword that He means is the sharp two-edged sword that proceeds out of His mouth (Rev 1 v 16; Rev 19 v 15) that strikes the nations. He is the 'lamb that has been slain' (Rev 5 v 5-7; 5 v12 -14), has risen, and is now 'worthy to be the only one to open the 7 seals', and 'is worthy to be praised'. His Name is 'Faithful and True', and is called the Word of 'God" 'On His robe and on His thigh is the name written: KING OF KINGS, AND LORD OF LORDS' (Rev 19 v 11-16).

Now obviously this does not mean Jesus has a sword for a tongue. Rather it is symbolic to represent His speech or words. For elsewhere He is called the Word (John 1 v 1). So therefore, logically it follows that as Jesus is the Living Word with a

double-edged sword for a tongue, it means His words that He speaks, coming out of His mouth, must be very sharp, and pierce or cut to the listener's heart, like a sword.

At the time he was speaking about what the cost will be of any-one who chooses to follow Him, and be His disciple. They must expect opposition from others, even friends, or within their own family, by those who are unwilling to change their comfortable, pleasure-seeking, wilful ways, in their comfort zones, and who will oppose or even try to discourage or hinder anyone who tries to be more like Christ, as being His disciple requires.

Therefore the words are not cutting, sarcastic or offensive, or deliberately wounding ie words to cause harm (like those which are evil in origin and intent). No. He means that His words admonish, reprove and correct, or chide, or encourage those who are doing wrong to desist, stop sinning, and fix-up – do bet-ter, and change for their own good. It is a rod of correction, as He rules with an iron rod (Rev 19 v 15), like a parent who loves his/ her child would say to discipline and correct erring/ bad atti-tudes or behaviour; so that the child's character and manners are reformed and improved. A mother would not let her child run head-long towards on-coming cars, nor run into a river or into the fires of hell! So she reproves and corrects before disaster strikes, and it is too late to save the child.

But those who are stubborn, headstrong and unwilling to change will construe such admonitions as 'evil' saying: 'don't repay evil with evil', as they try to cast slurs and aspersions on the speaker, rather than accept that they might be at fault, as is obvious by their own confessed retort (that they had evil intent in their actions that drew the rebuke/telling off in the first place). Whether in person, or virtual reality in cyberbullying through text or emails or phone calls at inappropriate or unsociable times, such evil has been noted in the heavenly books, and their effects have been negated, as Christ rules, and protects their victims.

So the sword is the word that reproves, corrects and disciplines (another meaning attached to disciple ie student of a Rabbi/ Teacher, is one who receives instructions/ correction and discipline, whereby to pass on this learning to others).

Who does Christ emanate from, and what does He stand for? He comes from His Father Yahweh, the Creator of All, Author and Finisher of Things, and who is ALL about TRUTH. And who cannot abide/ tolerate lies – which is why Lucifer, lying, deceiving and rebel, inciting disaffection and dissatisfaction, got kicked out of heaven. Similarly Jesus Christ stands for and was, and still is all about Truth.

So He is the sword, and His word speaks Truth. This is the sword that cuts to the quick of those who are rebellious and stubbornly refuse to repent of sins, and return to the source of Light, Life and Love – Himself. They, who prefer rather to stay in

their 'happy' deluded sins, under cover of darkness (fearing to be exposed to the light and have to face the consequences of their actions). Remember Jesus said: 'the wages of sin is death....', by which He meant the second death that comes after all, both the living and the dead, have been resurrected to face Judgement in that Great Day. And those found still unrepentant and wicked and sinful shall be cast, along with the devil, the beast and the false prophet, and Hell and Hades, into the lake of fire and brimstone – the second death, that is inescapable, permanent and terrifying. For in it will be heard the wailing and gnashing of teeth of those being punished and tormented continually, endlessly ad infinitum. No wonder Satan wants to avoid it like the plague. So much so that not even his agents in the Roman Catholic church leaders mention it at all. In fact they aggressively prevent everyone from discovering it by scaring them away from reading it in the book of Revelation! For it predicts doom and gloom and horrors, yes it does, but only for those who are wicked and who refuse to repent and reform their ways according to Christ!

But those who are Christ-like, realise the truth of joy and happiness and peace that is their portion when they read the words within it. Mike Tucker's book 'Meeting Jesus in the Book of Revelation – Taking the fear out of the Bible's scariest book' (2007, Pacific Press), can testify to this and enlighten and encourage faithful and blameless Christians, bless him. It confirms that Christ will be victorious in the end; and is already crowned gloriously 'KING OF KINGS, AND LORD OF LORDS'! Ultimately, His promised rewards, and kingdom to come will be supremely better, more beautiful, peaceful and blessed with abundance of provisions – food, water and fruits, - to sustain immortal life for Eternity in Perfect Circles.

So who is the Flood? It is Jesus with the piercing sword for a tongue, who speaks words of Truth; the Flood that those 2 ancient Egyptian young men were desperately trying to hide away their secrets and mysteries in the sphere within a mini pyramid in my dream of December 1st 2010, and by December 24th the great mystery within it revealed himself to me in a harshly whispered 'Thank you Satan' that same month. Now one and half years later, June 25th 2012, the full extent of the mystery within was revealed to me by the Living Word of Truth' s Holy Spirit of Prophecy, Christ Jesus Himself, in disclosing the secret ID of 'God', being none other than Satan!!!

Well yes, the Flood is coming, is coming and has arrived! Not as Jesus the Avenger, who is to return to earth at the end of Time. No. But before He ascended back to heaven, Jesus told His disciples He would be sending the Holy Spirit to come and help, guide and comfort them in His stead. For, He promised never to leave them or abandon them to the wicked evil one in this world. The Holy Spirit is part of the TRUE MYSTERY that is the HOLY TRINITY, - at once one with the Father Yahweh and son Jesus Christ.

Now we know that throughout history our Creator YHWH, for that is His name, has sent, and is still sending prophets to speak/ deliver His messages to a people who are still erring and straying far away from Him, hell-bent on destruction. Yahweh's Holy Spirit (one of 7, Rev 4 v 5) speaks through mortal instruments/ prophets, and as He too is of the Holy Trinity – He too stands for Truth and IS TRUTH!!!

So in 2012 – alarm bells are ringing everywhere! All are alert – on the look-out for the Return of Christ (which according to the ancient Mayan prediction earmarks this very year 2012 – as the date for the end of the world as we know it! But rather I remind you Jesus said 'of the hour, NO-ONE knows, not even the angels, or Himself the son of the Father, only YHWH knows when it will be, Mark 13 v 32-33; Matt 24 v 23-24). Well, what do the wicked and evil ones and Satan fear most? Being the originator and author of lies and deception Satan fears Christ' Return most. For, it

spells the end of his reign of terror and dominion over Yahweh's people/ the whole of humanity who belong to our Creator YHWH.

Satan has enjoyed influencing and controlling mankind in his huge web of dazzling deception, and he is no hurry to lose his power, nor does he want to meet his doom, prophesied so long ago, which is his final destination, in the less talked about second death – lake of fire and brimstone, of endless suffering and tortuous pain!!! He will have to suffer pain in multiplied strength and full measure for that which he gleefully caused millions of people and children to suffer since Adam and Eve's Fall.

But he has only enjoyed such successful influence over the whole world, because he has been allowed to deceive them again, after being released from the bottomless pit, where he was bound for 1,000 years (Rev 20 v 1-3), after he had tormented Christians the Apostasy 1260 years of the Middle Ages. Since his release he has been very active, subtle and pervasive in his deceit, regaining influence and more and more aggressively so, because he knows the hour of his doom approaches – marching relentlessly and inexorably on...

His deception is more startling because of how he has managed to get everyone onside, and to blindly accept him and all his lies, as if they were true!!! By his subtle slipping in, here and there, imperceptibly, - a little lie here and there, the 1% lie mixed in with 99%Truth, is enough corruption to lead multitudes astray down the slippery slope to perdition and hell fire, and the second death!

But he fears his deceptions being uncovered and that his true identity would be exposed. For then it all will come to an end for him. So he has done his damndest to prevent disclosure from seeping into the public domain. At the moment he reigns supreme, happy as Larry, causing ruin, corruption, chaos, and debasing and degrading and terrorising all and sundry, and mocking YHWH gleefully –even teasing and taunting his Potter, to hasten that day when He will bring His Judgement to bear, because Satan still, deluded, thinks he'll escape punishment as he has done thus far for millennia. So he is on the look-out, diligently watching for any signs or clues that Christ has Returned to come and deal with him, (whilst amassing his own army to attack Christ' own, hoping to strike first. Deluded or what!!!).

Well since after the Great Disappointment of 1844, when Christ did not return, and a new prophet emerged in 1845, teenage Ellen G White. She had the gift of the Spirit of Prophecy until her death aged 87, despite years of tremendous, life-threatening illnesses and mental and physical affliction that she and her husband endured, whilst establishing the truths and publications that founded the 7th Day Adventist Church worldwide. She understood what it meant to have prejudice and stigma directed at her from childhood impairment from an unfortunate head injury caused by a stone thrown by a child, which proved not a stumbling block since she could not therefore attend school for her education, but an opportunity for the Lord to show His mercy and power and strength in her weakness, by establishing her as one of the most prolific writers in Christianity and establishing the Sabbath-keeping SDA church.

Ellen's most important commission was delivering among other things, YHWH's 3 angel messages: (Rev 14 v 6-9)

> Angel 1 – 'Fear 'God' and give glory to Him, for the hour of His judgement has come; and worship Him who made heaven and earth, the sea and springs of water'

> Angel 2 – 'Babylon is fallen, is fallen, that great city because she has made all the nations drink of the wine of the wrath of her fornication'

> Angel 3 – 'If anyone worships the beast and his image, and receives *his* mark on his forehead or on his hand, he himself shall also drink of the wine of the wrath of 'God', which is poured out in full strength into the cup of His indignation. He shall be tormented with fire and brimstone in the presence of the holy angels and in the presence of the Lamb. And the smoke of their torment ascends forever and ever; and they have no rest day or night, who worship the beast and his image, and whoever receives the mark of his name....

Refer also to Rev 13 about the beast and his image, and especially v 16-18, where the beast causes all to worship him, and no-one can buy or sell without his mark or name or number ...which is the number of a man.

His number is 666'.

She also re-established the sacred Sabbath on its original day of worship and celebration of our Creator Yahweh, which is the same as the Jewish Saturday – from sunset Friday to sunset Saturday, as it was at the Beginning, so shall it be at the end

As well as looking forward to the second Advent /Coming, the Return of Jesus Christ.

Ellen G White (born 26 Nov 1827, died 24 July 1915) pointed out that the Holy Spirit comes to various individuals through time, and has not yet finished delivering all the messages that YHWH wants the people to hear. She foretold that there will be an 'out-pouring of the Holy Spirit in the churches in the last days before Christ returns,

and it will be a 'shaking' out, or 'weeding' out of the wicked, false people, to secure a pure and holy church of Christ's true disciples, who are Christ-like, and not fake-Christians. Whether these remain within church buildings, or in homes, or in hide-outs as in the early days, under persecution, these Christ-like disciples will bring His Truth and Light to call up those who can be saved at this 11th hour, before probation closes.

In these last days the Holy Spirit's outpouring on the churches will be as prophet Joel said in (Joel 2 v 28-31): 'I will pour out My Spirit upon all flesh. Your sons and daughters shall prophesy, and old men will dream dreams, and young men shall see

visions, even man servants and maidservants shall prophesy', as the Holy Spirit of Prophecy and Truth anoints Yahweh's chosen people from all nations and languages. And YHWH 'will show wonders in the heavens and in the earth, blood, and fire, and pillars of smoke. The sun shall be turned into darkness, and the moon into blood, before the great and the terrible day of the Lord come'. (ref E G White Patriarchs & Prophets, (1958), preface iii-iv,).

We have seen more and more evidence of this happening all over the world. Current pastors and lay preachers, preach and interpret and give clarity to the

mysterious puzzles in the Bible, especially in the Books of Daniel and Revelation, that pertain to these last days before Christ comes back in person.

Since May 1990, when the Holy Spirit started speaking His Truth through me, His willing ab'd /servant and devoted disciple of Christ, right then and there, even as the pen wrote across the page, Satan was doing all he could to try and distract and so stop me, even darting as a little red worm like a thread around the nib of my pen as I wrote. I stopped and asked the Lord if it was Him or the devil, and He replied 'the devil'. So I continued writing then, and have been doing so intermittently ever since, despite Satanic obstructions and trials and afflictions, - physically, mentally, mentally, emotionally, financially, and relationships with significant others and loved ones, yet my spirit, aided by the Holy Spirit, and Jesus as I increasingly and daily draw closer under His wings and into His bosom of safe haven, has remained strong and grows stronger in faith, to help keep me obedient, faithful and blameless till my Master calls me home or Returns in glory. Bless His Holy Name forever and ever!!!!

Nevertheless I face Satanic onslaught in all kinds of guises as the devil, panicked and livid, slapped mental illness afflictions schizophrenia, and endured psychiatric 'treatments' like ECT and 'medications' – mind-numbing and memory loss inducing drugs, that are TRANQULISERS, used on animals and humans alike!!!!, and so many physical illnesses, that have brought me near to death several times, since my premature birth. Born 2 months early, weighing but 4lbs, in 1959, so small that I fit inside a shoe box, but I needed a hernia operation on my stomach in my first week of life. Yet here I am, 53 years later, recovered from so many afflictions, and still writing and proclaiming from the rooftops, all the messages that YHWH's Holy Spirit of Prophecy & Truth have commissioned me to faithfully deliver. Incredible? No. YHWH's miracles, yes. Many of which I have experienced myself, and witnessed in others, in these contemporary times. YHWH is alive! Christ Jesus is alive!!! And is very much in the business of saving lives! Believe.

Despite Satan's ever more frantic efforts, the Lord's angels have been protecting me, and have kept Satan at bay long enough for me to continue to fulfil my commission. YHWH, the Originator of Truth, the First and the Last, Alpha and Omega, Beginning and the End, THE **Author and Finisher of Things,** *WILL* have His Say <u>and </u>the last word of Truth. He spoke and it existed. He said it, prophesied it, so it will happen. Guaranteed. So He said the Truth will out. His prophets will come out and spill the beans. YHWH's Holy Spirit has been pouring out His Truth and prophecies since 1990, and through many lay preachers, pastors, and ordinary people and even children in word, and song. People who would normally be considered as having no authority by the church – outcasts, excluded, 'mad', down and outs, single parents, children, yes even me, who amounts to all of those labels. (Joel 2 v 28-31).

As prophetess and disciple of the Lord, I must speak the Truth. I cannot be bribed, cajoled, bullied, threatened, or forced into shutting up. I must deliver the messages that YHWH has given me for His people. I will not have their blood on my hands by withholding information vital to saving their souls. I will be obedient and do my duty, for the responsibility for others is a huge one to bear, and is a deadly serious matter. So I joyfully repeat what I have been instructed to say and write and sing – words

from our Lord, delivered by His Holy Spirit, my Counsellor, Guide and Comforter, as I tread the Way of Christ, and walk closer to our Sovereign Lord and Master, YHWH. So that one day I can come into Perfect Circles in communion with Him for Eternity. This is my hope, my desire, my prayer. Amen.

Christ, the Flood, the Living Word, His Spirit of Prophecy and Truth, is not only coming, he has been coming since 1990, and is already here in 2012! For not only are Pastors, and Reverends speaking Christ' Truth, but so are children ! As the Lord YHWH showed me at the beginning of June, a few weeks ago, through the Scriptures and books and sermons and films and music, that He Himself, will teach, train, and equip His people to do His tasks, and to become worthy to be called His children –those who accept Christ, who is the Lamb who is worthy. So I by

Providence, caught a then 9 year old Brazilian boy, Jotta A.'s rendition of 'Agnus Dei' as he performed it and won the Kids got Talent 2011. The song is of the vein as Handel's famous 'Halleluiah Chorus in 'Messiah', praising the Lamb, Jesus Christ and recognising/ acknowledging and accepting His holiness and worthiness, as our Redeemer, and son of YHWH:

> 'Halleluiah! Halleluiah!!
> For the Lord, 'God', Almighty reigns....
> Halleluiah! Holy! Holy!
> Are you Lord 'God' Almighty?
>
> Worthy is the Lamb,
> Worthy is the Lamb,
> Worthy is the Lamb,
> Worthy is the Lamb,
> Amen.'

As Jesus told the Pharisees and scribes: 'have you not heard, "out of the mouth of babes and sucklings/ nursing infants you have brought perfect praise?" ' (P C chp 7 ref 95; Matt 21 v 16).

For the last 2 months (May – June 2012), Satan has been actively and aggressively and surreptitiously trying to stop me working on vol 2 of this book, Perfect Circles, as he could see me getting closer to discovering and exposing his true identity (as discussed earlier in 'who is God really?' section of this chapter. Well guess what?

Christ, as Spirit of Truth and Prophecy, is very much here in 2012. For His Holy Spirit led me to discover through books, the internet and the Book of Revelation, just who God really is, in more depth and detail than first found last year 2011, or in 1994; see earlier discussion. Suffice it to say the clue was hidden, but now exposed in the 2 lines of the song: 'Are you Lord, 'God', Almighty?' and 'Worth is the Lamb'. The two are not cotermi-nous, as we have been led to believe for centuries. As stated in earlier discussion, God is not the same as Father, Son and Holy Spirit, nor as Christ Jesus, and definitely NOT YHWH!!!

God derived from ancient Egyptian dog-god Anubis, Lord of the dead and Underworld in the After-life, has been hidden behind goddess Isis/Cleopatra's veil, in mystery for millennia, and sub-limated and incorporated into Christian religions as

'God', but he is NOT Yahweh, nor Almighty, nor worthy!!! This year, 2012, the mystery of God's identity has been exposed and is being shouted aloud, not hushed up in secret as Satan has been desperately trying to halt and cover up the exposure. So all of our traditions that have been handed down from ancient

Egypt, Greeks and Romans right into Christ and YHWH's very temple in various forms of religious practices, are pagan, and part of devil worship – Satanic!! So the Olympics, and its torch-bearers and competitions in these London 2012 games, infused with symbolism and demonic and dark scary references, as well as the torch –bearers – the

Illuminati-, who influence our entertainment industry, all are pagan in origin and hence not to be indulged.

Even our very own Queen Elizabeth (who hid her moment of anointing within a tent in the Cathedral during her inauguration ceremony in June 1953, because she said she wanted privacy – really? I would rather thought she would have shouted it from the roof tops if she were legitimate). She and her own royal family have not been of the same royal line as king David, who, like his predecessor Saul, were anointed by true prophets of the Most Sovereign Lord YHWH. So they profess to be legitimate kings and queens, they are but Pretenders, and Usurpers of the Right and Royal Heir to YHWH's throne, Jesus Christ, His son, and who alone deserves the eternal and everlasting and invincible kingdom, whose is the Rock that will bring the other kingdoms of past and present crashing to their knees, to finally recognise His right and supremacy. Selah. It will be done, for YHWH has said it, and prophets have prophesied it. YHWH and Christ and the Holy Spirits do not lie.

Unpleasant or offensive to some as it may be, I am His willing ab'd/servant and mouthpiece, and I will continue to speak/write YHWH's True words, for Rightly so, *HE* is offended and disgusted, and as our Creator and Christ our Redeemer, this is what weighs mighty with me, for HE is great and the Most Sovereign Majesty, who is to be praised, and adored, obeyed and all laud and honour given to Him by ALL and sundry, whether they like it or not. Bless HIS Holy Name, forever and ever. Christ kingdom come. Selah. For as Jesus said: 'if you continue in my word, you are truly my disciples, and you will know the truth, and the truth will make you free' (John 8 v 31). And despite all attempts and opposition, His Light and Truth, will not be snuffed out. For He (Christ) that is within me, is greater than he (Satan and his cronies) that are in the world (1 John 4 v 4). And though I am in the world, I am not of it' (John 15 v 19, John 17 v 11-15), rejecting worldly/secular values, as I daily grow to resemble the character and disposition of the Good Shepherd and Master, Christ and YHWH, much to the dismay and despising of so-called friends and family, even church 'family'. Their reactions reveal more about their evilous and unrepentant attitudes, and unwillingness to change and fix-up, than condemns me for trying to follow the good footsteps of my, and their Creator.

As I forgive them, I pray without ceasing (1 Thess 5 v 16-18) that they might yet be saved, and pulled out from the flames (of lake of fire and brimstone) (Jude 1 v 23), before it's too late, when Christ returns to close shut tight the door of probation! Wise up! It's not too late now. Take advantage of this remaining time. Seize the day and Rebuke Satan, Repent of sins/wrongdoings, and Return to our Father YHWH, through His son Christ Jesus!!!! 'Turn, turn now...why should you die?' (Ezekiel 33 v 11). Turn before there is no more time, and Time is stood still, before Armageddon and Judgement Day!

From all the prophets who have gone before, especially I learn from Isaiah, the mentor of my life; and also Malachi 4 v 1; Ezekiel, Jeremiah, apostles Paul and Peter, Mary Magdalene, and disciple of renowned good deeds Dorcas/ Tabitha (Acts 9 v 32 -42); Joan of Arc, and Ellen G White, Noah, Jonas (h), Abraham and Enoch; Moabite Ruth married Naomi's kinsmen Boaz, ancestor of shepherd boy/anointed king David, and whose root is Christ (2 Sam 7 v 8-17; Rev 5 v 5), from whom he stemmed, and who of course, is THE greatest living role model ever – Jesus the Christ, Immanuel – soon to be crushing all previous and present kingdoms – Avenger, co-Judge and co-Ruler of All and for all time! Blessed be His Holy Name forever and ever! THE Amen,

Himself, and the Flood of Truth, and Living Fountain of Waters of Life!!!

And be still and know that He is Lord YHWH! 'I will be exalted among the nations. I will be exalted in the earth!' (Psm 46 v10). 'For I AM YHWH and there is no other {God}' (Isaiah 45 v 22). He is Lord and there is no Saviour besides Him (Is. 43 v 11). Remember He, Yahweh and Christ Jesus and His & Holy Spirits (which are 7 lamps burning before the throne of YHWH, Rev 4 v 5) are One and the same in the mystery that is the Holy Trinity.

During my recent experiences since my birthday May 3rd to 12th July '12, especially since significant date 25/6/12, (see my expose of who God is, when I was shown in revelation the secret ID of God, explained in chap 9), I have learnt from YHWH's Holy Spirit, - who has been teaching me Himself the ways of a prophet and being Christ-like, - what form the Flood of Jesus Christ has taken. 2012 is not important for the end of the world as predicted by the Mayan calendar, BUT for the ARRIVAL of **Christ** as the **Spirit of Prophecy and Truth**, in the expose of the 'mystery of God' that is about to be announced by the 7th angel!!!

As cited in Rev 10 v 7, "but in the days of the sounding of the seventh angel, when he is about to sound the mystery of God would be finished, as He declared to His servants the prophets". Since Dec 24th 2010, when I had it confirmed that God is not YHWH, but Satan, as my own sister had alerted my attention to, in Dec.1994 (as I was undergoing deep mental distress of post-natal depression), and I had written

this fact in Nov 2011whilst preparing this book, which is finally due to be published this very year of 2012, PROPHECY HAS COME TRUE!!!

Satan, in fear of the prospect of his prophesied doom suddenly coming upon him quicker than he anticipated, enticed my very own 3 children to incarcerate me in a psychiatric assessment unit, Lakeside, West London, to try and shut me up and stop me from announcing his secret identity of the mystery of God, ie being himself, that serpent of old, the dragon/ beast/ devil/ former Lucifer/ now Satan!!!!

But Lord Jesus be praised!!! The drugs/ 'medication' tho' affecting my physical body, had NO lasting effect on my brain or memory, and so I can happily record the experience here, and assert that 'no weapon formed against me will prosper' (Isaiah 54 v 17) and 'I can step upon the lion and the cobra, the young lion and the serpent can I trample underfoot, and they will not harm me'; and in fact 'no plague will come near my dwelling' (psalm 91).

So 'though to me the psychiatric unit felt like I was destined for the gas chamber, right there, in the middle of the lion's den, or the fiery furnace, I, like Daniel, and Shadrach, Mishak and Abednigo (Hananiah, Mishal and Azariah in Hebrew) (Daniel 6 and 3), as from previous incarcerations in Aug 1990, and from Christmas '94 to Aug '95, to this last one end of June to mid July 2012, I can exclaim that I was protected, saved and delivered with brain unscathed! Halleluiah!!! By the hand of our Creator and Sovereign Lord YHWH, and by Christ Jesus, my best and true friend, and blessed precious Saviour, I was saved to be brought back home by the same perplexed daughters. I was undefeated and not at all down trodden, but instead, even more resolute and determined to obey my Maker and fulfil my purpose for living at all in this life!

And I can assure you, and encourage and comfort you, who desire to be more Christ-like, that psalm 23 'The Lord is my Shepherd, I shall not want...yeah 'tho' I walk through the shadow of death, I shall fear no evil, for You are with me, Your rod and Your staff comfort me'; and psalm 91, that the Lord Himself will shield me/you with His feathers, and His angels shall protect us , and YHWH's TRUTH shall be my/your shield and buckler, when you and I put on the whole armour of the Lord (Ephesians 6). For, we do not wrestle with flesh and blood (humans), but with powers and principalities of evil. And I, for one, *know* that as YHWH is for me, then who can be against me? No-one, nothing at all, (Romans 8 v 31, 37-39). Again, Isaiah 41 v 10 tells us to 'fear not, for the Lord is with us, and He will strengthen us, help us, and uphold us with the Right hand of His Righteousness'.

And I trust Him completely, and only Him (for man is fickle and like Satan can be deceitful), for Scripture says 'He who has begun a good work in you will complete it until the day of Jesus Christ, (Philippians 1 v 6). I **will** complete my commission, despite Satan and his accomplices' caprice and obstructions. **I will succeed, for Christ has won my freedom for me and my victory is already certain!** Praise the Lord!!! For His mercies are new every morning (Lamentations 3 v 23) and His grace is sufficient for me, 'for it is YHWH who works in me both to will and to do of His good pleasure' Phil 2 v 12-13; and EGW 'This day with God', 1979, p 167 date June 7th). Bless His Holy Name forever and infinitum (or as Buzz Lightyear of Toy Story would say: 'to infinity and beyond!!!').

Paul in 1 Corin 15 v 42 -57, tells how corruption and heaven are not synonymous. The corruptible cannot inherit heaven. In regard to the resurrection, 'the body sown in corruption... is raised' incorruptible...it is sown a natural body, and is raised a spiritual body....' 'It is written "the first man Adam became a living being...made from dust", but 'the last man Adam (ie Jesus) became a life-giving spirit ...who came from heaven'. Paul emphasises that we must understand that we must be righteous and right-living in the eyes of our heavenly Father, and if we are such, then we too will bear the heavenly image of Jesus, and be spiritually fit and worthy of heaven. So when the last trumpet sounds Christ's return, 'the dead in Christ' shall be resurrected first, and changed in an instant, in the twinkling of an eye, into incorruptible bodies which can then enter heaven. Death, disease and corruption are not part of heavenly living. And there is no room for them in the new heaven and new earth, the kingdom of the New Jerusalem. Halleluiah!

This is my goal. This hope and dream is what I pray and long and live for, prepared to meet even death, just as long as I see my Maker and live within His all-encompassing love and embrace of Jesus, my Saviour, for all Eternity. Is this your goal too? Is this your dream? You now know how to make this fantasy, this dream become a reality. This is only possible through our Lord and Saviour Jesus Christ, who is our hope and salvation, and who is the Flood of vengeance, justice and Love. Will you make Him your ark today?

Jesus is coming very, very soon. Probation will soon be over. The door of this ark will shut. And some of us will be like Enoch, 'translated into heaven' (127). He had such a close relationship with our Father for 300 years, that when He was ready to call him, Enoch was not permitted to die, but was 'translated' directly into heaven – he walked right in. He was just a step away from heaven. His body did not see corruption or death.

As Jesus said, 'some of you will not see death (or bodily corruption) by the time the son of Man returns'. In essence some of us will still be alive when He comes in the clouds from heaven at the end of Time, appearing larger than life. Yes those who have already died for Christ' sake will be resurrected first, and be caught up with Him in the clouds, and then those who are for Christ and still alive will join them. They will be saved in Jesus' ark, whilst the final great battle, Armageddon occurs on earth.

Take note that this battle will not merely be a physical or material one, but will be a battle that is temporal and spiritual. The great controversy will be a battle of wills and minds to claim and secure our souls. Our souls belong to our heavenly Father, but Satan tries to steal them so as he can gain victory over the Almighty One, the Creator of heaven and earth and all the universe. Such impudence!!!

But he is a fool! *You* don't have to be fooled. Satan is a deceiver, a liar, a USURPER!

But he WILL be defeated. Jesus Christ already has the victory, and paid a very high price to achieve it.

Jesus will once again come down off His throne in heaven. This time not clothed in humanity as an innocent babe. This time He comes ginormous, so everyone from east to west (138) (north to south in the globe) will see Him simultaneously, clothed in robes for vengeance, to do battle for the saved martyrs, for the last time. He will win triumphantly and spectacularly. And *everyone* will know he has come, even His accusers and crucifiers, who will be resurrected to witness His glorious return to establish His victory. He is already victorious, but His victory will be manifested at the end of Time. He *is* the Living King indeed. All bow down and praise Him! Merciful Jesus. Halleluiah!!!

WARNING! WARNING!

If after hearing the word, you ignore it, and do not heed it, Jesus said it would be worse for you. 'It would be better if you tied a rock around your neck and drowned in the sea' (139). Why? Because it would be just as though someone was given a good instruction by the Father, but he deliberately chose to disobey Him. It would be that the person did not want to do as he was told, and that he wanted to do his own thing, or go his own way. He was putting himself first, and putting his will as prominent, over his Father's will. By his own self, he was putting the 'I' in pride (140), before his heavenly Father. The precursor to 'I' as in sIn.

This disobedient person is saying in effect, to himself and his heavenly Father, who created him, the Potter who made him out of clay (128), of dust, saying: 'I am more important than You, even though it was You who made me. I am so important, and big-headed, and conceited and proud, and 'own way' that I don't see why I should listen to You. I don't see why I should obey You'. This is exactly what Lucifer thought and did as he was descending into the sIn of pride, and ended up a fallen angel, since called Satan. He disobeyed his Creator our Father, and then even worse, enticed Adam and Eve, our Father's beloved human beings, into also disobeying our Father! They so sinned, and caused death to enter Creation.

It is disobedience which Is the primary sIn, because it shows wilfulness and unwillingness to follow our Creator's laws. It ultimately indicates that you love yourself more than Him. Possibly you do not love your Creator at all! This is no gratitude or love to Him who brought you into being/existence, and breathed life into your nostrils out of His love for you. Is this how you would repay someone who loves you? Our Creator gave us laws, for our own good. He just instructed Adam and Eve to NOT eat of the tree of Knowledge of good and evil, because He is omniscient and could see into the future. He knew that evil would be detrimental to them, but He also knew that they would not keep His instruction. They would not heed His word, and so disobey Him.

This is why, knowing this, He had a solution in place, way before the problem occurred. 'In the beginning was the Word, and the Word was with "God"' (141). The Word was with our Father, the Creator in heaven, when He created the first angel, Lucifer, and other angels. He was with Him therefore, *before* Creation! It was He, who was with 'God', going over the surface of the waters of the earth, before deciding to start Creation on the planet.

The Word was and is Jesus Christ, the embodiment of Love itself, who abides in love and obedience to our heavenly Father. So if the Word was with Him at the beginning of Time, before the world was created, then Jesus was already thought about, and planned to be *THE* solution to Adam and Eve's disobedience. He would be the Saviour and Deliverer of Man from sIn and death, by his own obedience to our Father. And thereby proved his love and honour for Him, and gratitude to Him for the opportunity of life-giving creating, and life-saving delivering, as a gift to all Mankind. Jesus offered to exchange his sin-less and innocent life –blood as atonement for the guilty sins of mankind, once and for all on Calvary's cross. He did this out of love for mankind, for you and me, so that we might once again be able to be favoured, and beloved of our Father, as Adam and Eve originally were.

This history of Creation and the Great Controversy (E.G.White) – the controversy of Satan's disaffection for, and challenge to, our great and long-suffering Father, is recorded in the word, - the Bible: the Old and New Testaments of our Creator's love for us and His battles against Satan, to save us from eternal damnation in hell. The Bible testifies to our Father's original Plan A, for Adam and Eve, for humanity, and His contingency Plan B – which is the solution to their disobedience.

The Word, that is Jesus Christ, who himself lived by the word – our Father's laws and commands in the Old Testament scriptures. Jesus, who by his life example and his teachings, affirmed and confirmed his Father's laws in the Old Testament and condensed them into a New Testament. The new covenant between our Father and man, is his life-saving blood, that he willingly and obediently sacrificed for us on the cross. If he could fight against his own fears, and his will to run away from this commission (like Jonah, 142), if he could trust his heavenly Father implicitly, whom he knew loved him, what then? And because Jesus loves his Father wholeheartedly, that he could also being imbued with the Creator's love, would then extend this love, his love, to us, - his 'adopted' brothers and sisters, - who also became adopted as 'sons and daughters of the Father' (143). He submitted his will, his natural, human, bodily carnal desire for self-preservation in this life, to that of his Father's will, with whom he was at the beginning of Time, and agreed to do His bidding, however painful.

For the sins of Adam and Eve, and the rest of mankind, Jesus deliberately, solemnly and willingly, out of love, gave up his most precious life, in exchange for ours, so that we might be preserved and have eternal life. This is what you call obedience. Obedience, even unto death. This is what you call love for others.

Now, knowing all of this, - that is documented in the word, in the Living Word, Jesus, and the written word, the Bible, - knowing all of this, would you still want to reject these words you hear? Would you still disobey your heavenly Father, who created you, from dust, grew you as a seed in your mother's womb? Would you still refuse to heed and harken to the warnings that the word, spoken long ago and since, by the prophets before Jesus, Jesus himself, and those who have come since Jesus, all calling you to REPENT! Who urge you to stop doing wicked things, and say sorry for doing them, and not repeat them, and then RETURN to the waiting arms of our loving, Good Father? I can't believe it. Would you reject our Father, Himself, He who loves you so immensely?

Would you forfeit and give up your chance for salvation? Would you deny yourself the opportunity for eternal life? A life that would be spent in joy, peace and happiness, and longevity and great health, and no wars, no more tears or sadness, no poverty, or hunger, or strife, or loneliness, or anger, or abuse, or oppression, or violence, or heartaches, or death. No finality. Just infinite life..... No SEPARATION from the love and favour of our Lord and heavenly, Almighty Father and Creator of all that is around and within us (Roms 8 v 31, & v37-39). Would you give up eternal life of fellowship and warmth and communion with your Father and Creator, and fellow 'saved' human beings and angels? Knowing all this, would you? Would you really?

Then if you would, you really would deserve the punishment meted out to you when Jesus Christ returns at the end of Time. It really would be better for you to have never been born. For even Sodom and Gomorrah, Tyre and Sidon, (144) who repented after hearing the word and believed and stopped sinning, and turned back to our Father, who created them. It would as Jesus himself said: 'it would be better for you to tie a rock around your neck and drown yourself in the bottom of the sea'(139), after the fashion of self-destruction that Judas inflicted upon himself, when so distraught and wretched, from the realisation of the immensity of his betrayal of Jesus, the Living Word and our mighty Creator, he hung himself from a tree (145).

By rejecting the Word, you reject Jesus Christ, who is the light of the world. Who else will be able to save you but the Creator himself? Yet you stubbornly reject him. You reject the light that comes from him and our Father in heaven. You reject the light that belongs to the Father, who breathed the breath of life into the nostrils of Adam and Eve, and into you and me. You reject the love that He has for you and me, and all the good blessings that He has given us thus far, like Adam and Eve did in the garden of Eden, where they had everything their hearts could desire, right there at hand, all around them, originally intended for forever. But they, and we, rejected and despised and turned our noses up at all these blessings and love. They and we ungratefully looked His gift horse in the mouth, and decided it was not good enough for us.

Are we to be like the swine that had pearls cast before them (146)? Are we to be loved and blessed to no avail, to no purpose? Are you an ungrateful swine? Surely not. Or rather, would you be the seeds scattered on good fertile soil (147) (the Word), that grows and blossoms to spread the Good News, and be obedient, and thereby by the grace and mercy of our compassionate Jesus Christ, Lord and Master of All, gain a new life forever in Eternity? You must decide now, before probation is over. Please don't let it be too late.

We too must do our part. The Lord is merciful to the repentant sinner. But He also requires mercy from us to others, and values *that* more than sacrifices or tithes and offerings that are not given in love either to Him directly, or indirectly through others. Jesus called the Jewish scribes and Pharisees 'hypocrites, you brood of vipers' for demanding ritualistic observance to their man-made doctrines and laws, and encouraging young people to dishonour their mothers and fathers. He asked them: 'Why do you also transgress the commandment of 'God' because of your tradition? For 'God' commanded "Honour your father and your mother," and "He who curses father or mother, let him be put to death". But you say, "Whoever says to his father or mother, "Whatever profit you might have received from me as a gift to 'God' – then he need not honour his father or mother". Thus you have made the commandment of 'God' of no effect by your tradition. Hypocrites! ...' (Matt 15 v 1-9).

Rather sons and daughters should be attending to the needs of their parents, helping them and showing them compassion, as well as to the poor, needy, orphans, widows, the hungry, homeless, sick and imprisoned. As Jesus said 'what you do unto others, such as these, you do unto me' and thereby those are tithes and sacrifices that he values and appreciates, and will gain us entry into heaven, and eternal life. But gifts and offerings become as 'filthy rags/ menstrual rags/ blood cloths' when they are offered to the Lord, and the presenter is him- or herself offensive, because they have wickedness or unforgiveness in their hearts. How often must we forgive others? Jesus said: '70 X 7', i.e. always!!! (Matt 18 v 22).

This is why it is so important for each of us to read the Word in Bible Scriptures, with humble and contrite heart and open mind, so we can be more receptive to the teachings via the Holy Spirit and thereby draw towards taking a closer walk with YHWH, using Christ and His disciples, past, present and future as beacons of Light.

It is still not too late to repent and be saved in this 11th hour of probation, before the midnight hour strikes the return of Christ

Jesus! For as in Jesus' parable of the workers in the landowner's vineyard, those labourers who were hired last, were entitled to the same equal pay as those who had been hired earlier in the day for the same agreed fee, (Matt 20 v 1-16). To those earlier contractors who complained, the landowner replied '...Is it not lawful for me to do what I wish with my own things? Or is your eye evil because I am good? So the last will be first, and the first last. For many are called, but few are chosen.'

So don't be put off by yours or others misdemeaners. For even at this late hour probation remains open still, to all who come lately, right up to the last moment before Christ finishes interceding for us in the heavenly sanctuary, before He swears '... that there should be delay no longer' for His retributive Return (Rev 10 v 6), to have the chance of salvation, the same as those who were offered and accepted it at the beginning, and since. Those who are self-righteous, or preach their own righteousness, and not Christ' or Yahweh's; and who stubbornly and too proudly refuse to repent and bow down to the Master Potter and Creator, have only themselves to blame in this day and age, if they fall short of redemption and salvation. You need not be like them. Take this first step of many, towards your rewards promised in new heaven and new earth. Today choose Christ for Life!

Our Father YHWH /ELOIHIM' shows no partiality (148). Anyone who believes is acceptable to Him' (148a). And therefore it is understood that if you believe you will be obedient, and:-

REBUKE/RESIST Satan, REPENT of your wrong-doings, and RETURN to our heavenly Father, for we belong to Him, and NOT to that Usurper, Satan.

This message is for all who turn to Christ. For the Gentiles believed in him and were baptised by the Holy Spirit and became acceptable to our Father. So too can Muslims, remnant 'Messianic' Jews, and anyone from any other walk of life or religion, be saved, if they choose to accept Christ as their personal saviour, and walk in his footsteps and live a life-respecting, law-abiding, compassionate and love-expressing life, for the honour and glory of the Father, whom we bless with our obedience. Selah.

Again, I reiterate. My commission as prophetess DJKO, is to shout from the roof tops that 'Jesus is coming very, very soon!' Too soon for some, but hopefully not too late for others.

The Holy Spirit gives me this message to you: REBUKE! REPENT! RETURN!!!

Return your allegiance and love to its originator, our heavenly Father, for the love of Christ Jesus, who gave up *his* life's blood for *our* undeserving sakes. How will you return his love? How much do you love him? Thank you sweet, loving Jesus!!!

The devil keeps trying, almost daily, through others – my family, friends, church family members, medics and psychiatric medication and scary fears, to try and shut me up, and stop me from telling people the truth about him and who God really is.

BUT I WILL NOT SHUT UP AND PUT UP!!!!

I will not a murderer be by keeping silent (149) about what I know. By keeping silent I will deprive others of the reminders to repent, so necessary to them inheriting the whole earth, and to having life abundantly and eternally, in fellowship with our most merciful Lord.

For the Lord has saved and delivered me from death, and from the tyranny of psychiatry and other evil ones. He has given me my freedom, won by his liberty on Calvary, for our eternity with Him and our Father and the heavenly hosts and fellow Christ-like human beings.

I will not forfeit or jeopardise my future and salvation to appease the evildoers. Let it be known that our Father is not happy how things have turned out, and He, Himself, will not give up on us, His beautiful and beloved Creatures.

As a prophet and disciple of the Lord, I am required to inform others and WARN them, so that they might be saved and thereby have eternal life, as our Father originally intended.

Jesus said: 'what you have heard in secret, proclaim it from the mountain tops!!! (150). Shout it out aloud, and on all platforms, - the spoken, the written, the signed, the televisual, the internet, and the sung word. 'And do not fear those who kill the body but cannot kill the soul; rather fear Him who can destroy both body and soul', (Matt 10 v 26-28). Shout and tell all who would hear, to REPENT! Before probation is over. Before it is too late, and the pearly gates of the kingdom of heaven are shut closed tight.

I am being obedient to the Lord, in performing my commission - this book, PERFECT CIRCLES. I will willingly obey Him and continue until it is complete, when I can finally say, this work begun over 21 years ago, under inspiration of the Holy Spirit, is accomplished, and I will have proved my love and loyalty for the Lord Jesus, our Creator and heavenly Father. I hope and pray that I have faithfully transmitted what He wanted, and that I too can receive salvation and life eternal one day, on that great and marvellous day when Christ returns. This I humbly pray in all faithfulness and love.

REFERENCES chap 9

1. 'Usurpation', pp preface and p42 of E G White's Patriarch and Prophets, 1958, Review & Herald Publishing Association USA. Pacific Press Publishing Asscn. Canada. 'The great controversy between truth and error, the light and darkness, and between the power of the Creator and the attempted usurpation by the enemy of all righteousness', namely Satan the 'usurper' p42.

2a. (see also ref 31, chp 8). Laverna Patterson, 2001, History of the Church – Prophesy. www.teachinghearts.org/dre04historynotes.html, p9/51.

2b. Laverna Patterson ibid, pp 25/51 and 26/51.

3. (see ref 18, chp 2, ref 24 chp 8). Isaiah 14 v 12 -15; Is 29 v 16-17; Is. 45 v 3-10; and 2 Thess 2 v 1-12. Satan exalts himself.

4. 'devour' 1 Peter 5 v 8; see also ref 120 this chp 'roaming'.

5. Laverna Patterson ibid, pp 8/51 – 26/51.

6. Exod. 20 v 7, the 3rd commandment.

7. (see ref 77b chp7). Dr. Alan Cantwell Jnr. M.D., 2009, USA . Youtube on internet: 'The Swine Vaccination Hoax'. He exposed the use of the hepatitis D vaccine with AIDs/HIV. He discusses the Aids hoax and the Swine Flu hoax. www.QueerBlood: The Secret Aids Genocide Plot.

8. Dr. Leonard Harrowitz, Youtube: 'The Swine Flu Conspiracy Warnings' 27 April 2006. Science Publication - The Mexican Flu 2009. www.healthyworldstore.com. Harrowitz claims UK

scientists developed Mexican Flu from Euro/Asian flu strain to create a pandemic. This would be mass killing for profit, because it would generate money and private contracts for commercial publications. Created pandemics would expand their virological programmes. Hardly pro-health motives!!!

9. Whistleblower Jane Bergemeister, 2005, was trying to take the Austrian government to court for crimes against humanity. In her Youtube 'Project Camelot' interview 8/Sept/09, she exposed the government's hidden agenda – their pandemic plan for world depopulation via the Swine Flu vaccine, to allegedly prevent disease. But they would actually instigate and propel the spread of the disease. She filed criminal charges against the Austrian govt. But has been obstructed in pursuing her case, lost her job, and is currently in hiding for her safety. However she is still determined to fight on, and has international support from, not public bodies, but ordinary people. www.theflucase.com

10. 'trojan horse' tactics quoted by Dr. Cantwell ibid, 2009, exposed the Aids in small pox vaccine health cure smoke-screen. Under the auspices of the World Health Organisation (WHO) 125 million vaccines were donated to African children for small pox, but these were contaminated with Aids virus. 95 million cases contracted Aids within a year, and 75 million chil-dren died as a result. (This would explain why heretofore Aids was unknown in Africa, but suddenly out of nowhere all of Africa was now infected!)

This was a different kind of warfare, with a hidden agenda to usurp another countries' resources by stealth – hence 'Trojan horse'. For with depleted population and poverty, these African countries could not therefore afford to pay for chemical ther-apy treatments. So they had to turn to foreign countries like UK and USA, who would force them to allow them to commandeer their resources to 'pay' for the imported treatments. In fact they would be paying twice over as already paid in the 'vaccinated' deaths of their people!!! Yahweh forbad usury/making profit out of the poor, Levit 25 v 35-43: don't increase the hardship of the poor; v 43, nor impose 'rigour' on the slave.

11. Rwandan massacre, 1994, between blood relatives Hutus 80% and Tutsis 20% of pops.

12. The spread of Aids among women in USA. UK TV prog., 'Good Morning' Feb 2011.

13a. ADHD – international organisation: citizen commission for human rights (cchr –Scientology) concerned about inhumane treatments for people suffering mental health issues. Especially campaign against torturous treatments like psychosurgery (lobotomies) and ECT (electroconvulsive shock therapy), and they expose the horrors of the profit-motivated mental health agenda in 'Psychiatry: Industry of Death'.

13b. 'Rocky' David Bennett Enquiry 2005 – after Afro-Caribbean David Bennett died from being held face down in restraint by several psychiatric staff in a unit in Midlands, UK, an enquiry recommended new procedures regarding restraint; and started a 5 year programme of initiatives to improve the experiences of BME people and reduce racist discrimination. Delivering Race Equality (DRE), Time to Change (TTC), Race Equality and Cultural Capabilities (RECC) Training were amongst them, implemented through MIND, Rethink, NIMHE, and other organisations working in Mental Health. However the initiated 'Count Me In' censuses from 2005 -2010 showed increases in detentions and incarcerations for Black people, especially for men, and even more so since the introduction of Community Treatment Orders (CTOs) and Supervision Orders (S Os) in 2008/9 , up to 85% increase in some areas. (see ref 100 chp 8). Source Jayasree Kalathil, Doreen Joseph et al, 2011,

Recovery & Resilience – narratives of African, African Caribbean and South Asian women experiences of mental distress, MH Foundation, London, p 73-74.

'Serious mental illness shortens lives' – women with schizoaffective disorder have reduced life expectancy by 17.5 years, and men with schizophrenia have 14.6 shorter lives. Reasons given are a combination of factors including, social disadvantage, long term use of anti-psychotic drugs and higher risk life-styles. Source Biomedical Research Centre for Mental Health Maudsley hospital, London, in Slam, (South London and Maudsley) News, summer edition 2011, pp 12-13. Given that most Black people with a mental health condition are disproportionately given a diagnosis of schizophrenia, this is very worrying, and confirms what myself and other Black service users have claimed for years that psychiatric drugs are killing us! The vehement aggressive way the medics oppose those who want to come off psychiatric drugs, further confirms the hidden racist, and destructive agendas of those who purport to have our 'best interests' at heart! See also 'Zero Support? – Coming off psychiatric drugs' by Doreen Joseph, p 10-11, Open Mind Mental Health magazine, issue 165, March/April 2011, MIND publication, London.

14. E G White, ibid, 1958, Patriarchs and Prophets, p92.

15. Alpha & Omega, Rev. 1 v 8, v17-18; Rev 22 v 13.

16. It's not what we put in our mouths, but our evil intentions that come out that is the problem. Mark 7 v14-23.

17. Not everyone who says 'Lord, Lord' will enter heaven, - not those who do not help the needy, Matt 7 v21-27. But if you choose the difficult path - Enter by the narrow gate/door, that few can pass through, Matt 7v13-14, Luke 13 v 22-30, by putting yourself out to help the poor and visit sick and prisoners etc. you shall be deemed worthy to enter. When the son of man sits in judgement he will sort out the good from the evil, Matt 25 v 31-46, for He knows their hearts.

18. 'Panorama' BBC TV documentary 22 Dec. 2010.

19. In 2010 BBC ran a series of documentaries by teenage reporter Stacey Dooley, on child exploitation including sex work, the clothing and rug-making industries, and child soldiers. This documentary 'Kids with Guns: Stacey Dooley investigates' focused on child soldiers in war-torn Congo. www.bbc.co.uk/blogs/bbcthree/2010/10/my-experience-filming-kids-with-guns-stacey...

The eating/drinking of blood is forbidden by Yahweh, Leviticus 17 v 10-14, for the life of the creature is in it, and it is the blood that is given as atonement (price paid) for sin in animal sacrifices. Hence the significance of Jesus Christ sacrifice. His life-giving blood becomes life-saving atonement for all of our sins. The weight of the whole world's sins from time immemorial was borne on his feeble shoulders at Calvary. E G White holds that as He was the Creator at the Beginning of Time, only the sacrifice of *His* life's blood (p63, ibid P & P) could save and give hope and chance of eternal life to anyone who chooses to follow Yahweh's laws and statutes, that are for our safety and blessing. His laws are sacred for righteousness and right-living now and in Eternity. Isaiah 42 v21, 'the Lord is well-pleased for His righteousness sake'. 'The law of 'God' is as sacred as 'God' Himself' and is immutable and 'changeless' 'as Christ proved on the cross', E G White ibid, Patriarchs & Prophets, p 52 and p70.

20. blood – Leviticus 17 v 10-12, Levit. 19 v26.

21. Oscar Wilde, 1891, The Picture of Dorian Gray, publisher Ward, Lock and Co. (modern paperbacks avail.).

22. Edward V. Said, (1978) 2003, Orientalism. Penguin Classics – Penguin Books, Ltd., London, UK.

23. John 3 v16 – Yahweh gave His only begotten son, Jesus Christ, to save mankind.

24. Those who 'deny' or are ashamed of Christ, He will deny before His father, Matt 10 v 32-33. They will be damned to hell. But He will acknowledge those to His father who accept Him. Luke 12 v 6.

25. Young preacher John Davis, 19 March 2011. We are modern day Laodiceans.

26. Laodiceans were 'lukewarm' in their affections for the Lord, 'neither hot nor cold' and as such will be rejected by the Lord. Rev. 3 v 15-17.

27. Mike Tucker, 2007, Meeting Jesus in the book of Revelation, Pacific Press Publishing Association, USA.

28. ' I will spew/vomit you out', Rev. 3 v 15-17.

29. Rev 3 v 18.

30. Rev 3 v 21.

31. Jesus Christ will win in the end, for 'worthy is the Lamb to receive power and glory forever' Rev 5 v 8, v 10, v12 -13; Rev 1 v 8, 13-18. Mike Tucker ibid, Meeting Jesus in Revelation, p15 and p18. Jesus has the victory!!! Be encouraged. Be happy!!!

32. (see also ref 31 chp7). The 'wages of sin is death', Roms 6 v 23.

33. Adulterous woman... sin no more. John 8 v 3 -11.

34. Jesus calls sinners to repent; tax collector, Zaccheus, Luke 5 v 27 -32; Mark 2 v 14 -17, Matt 21 v 31 -32. Jesus hates sin, not the sinner, (see also ref 44a chp7). The Jews condemned Jesus because He associated with the despised like tax collectors and prostitutes, and lepers. But He came to heal the sick, not the so-called 'healthy/righteous', namely the hypocritical Sadducees and Pharisees.

35. Light , John 8 v 12, and John 12 v 35 -36.

36. (see also ref 81a chp7). 'Don't hide the lamp under the bushel', Matt 5 v 14 -16; city on a hill, Mark 4 v 21-23, Luke 8 v 16-18.

37. Tree known by fruit, proofs of true or false prophets, Matt 7 v 15 -20.

38. Forgiveness and forgiving, Matt 18 v 21-22; 2 Corin 2 v 5-11.

39. (see also ref 92 chp8). Criminal on cross next to Christ is forgiven, 'truly... today you will be with me in Paradise', Luke 23 v 40 -43.

40. (see 32 above), Roms 6 v 23.

41. Lot's wife turned into salt for disobedience, Gen 19 v 26.

42. Israelites' golden calf, Exod 32 v 1-35. When Moses was delayed in returning from speaking with the Lord on Mount Sinai, the Israelites made themselves a god of a golden calf from their melted jewellery. They praised and worshipped it and thanked it for bringing them out of slavery in Egypt. Moses was so angry with them on behalf of the Lord, for their disloyalty and ingratitude and idolatry that he broke the stone tablets containing the 10 commandments. Moses commanded that the wicked be killed, and some 3000, were slain by sword, and the Lord put a plague on the remainder.

43. Hell will be left in ashes, Malachi 4 v 1-2.

44. Devil was cast down from heaven to earth, Rev 12 v 9, v 4-6, v 12-17.

44a. Devil to-ing and fro-ing about the earth seeking whom he might devour 1 Peter 5 v 8. (see also ref 4, and 120).

45. Ellen Gould Herman White (lived 1827 – 1915), This Day with God, diary entry Sept 3rd, p255, pub'd 1979 by Ellen G White Estate Inc. USA. And E G White, Steps to Christ, p14 -15.

46. 2 year old Jamie Bulger tortured and murdered by 10 year olds Thompson and Venables, 1993. ' The murder of James Bulger' (Wikipedia, free encyclopaedia, April 2010). www. en.wikipedia.org/wiki/murder_of_James_Bulger.

47. Christ asks about his beautiful flock, faithful and obedient stewards, Ezekiel 34; Luke 12 v 42 –48, Matt 24 v 45 -51.

47a. 'Catalogue of cruelty': David Batty chronicles some of the most of the shocking child killings that have rocked this country in the past 60 years. In Society Guardian, 27 Jan. 2003.

www.guardian.co.uk/society/203/jan/27/childrenservices. childprotection/print;

'From Maria Colwell to Victoria Climbie: Reflections on a generation of public inquiries into child abuse', plenary paper by Professor Nigel Parton for the BASPCAN confer-ence, July 2003, (pub'd in Child Abuse Review, (2004), 13 (2), pp 80-94)

www.gptsw.net/papers/clwlclmbi.pdf

'It Must Never Happen Again' – the lessons learned from the short life of and terrible death of Baby 'P', 2009, By John McShane, pub'd John Blake, UK.

47b. Jesus said 'Suffer the little children to come unto me, for the kingdom of heaven belongs to such as these...' Matt 19 v 13-15.

47c. (see also ref 62 chp 8) 'Vengeance is mine, I will repay' says the Lord, Roms 12 v 19-20.

48. Outpouring of the Holy Spirit in last days, babes and old men etc. Will have the Spirit of Prophecy, Joel 2 v 28 -31; E G White, The Great Controversy ibid, p127 and p133; Patriarchs and Prophets ibid, introduction p iii –x.

49. 'elect persuaded to stray', Matt 24 v 24, 'for false Christs, false prophets will arise and will show great signs and wonders, so as to mislead, if possible, even the elect. Dan 11 v 34, the elect 'will be joined by many by intrigue' to lead them astray.

50. Our heavenly Father is our shield and refuge, psalm 23 and 91, and others.

51. Rev 20 v 1-3.

52. foreheads, Rev 20 v 4-6.

53. who will be around when Christ returns? (see also ref 50-52 chp 7). Rev 1 v 7, Is. 26 v 16-21, Matt 24 v 27, Matt 13 v 40-50; Matt 25 v 31-46; Matt 24 v 30.

54. 1,000 years reign, Rev 20 v6.

55. Devil's army is numerous, Rev 20 v 7-8.

56. 'Trust no man, trust 'God' (read YHWH) alone', Matt 4 v 4, where Jesus said: 'It is written: man does not live on bread alone'. YHWH even fed the Israelites in the wilderness manna from heaven, Deuteronomy 8 v3. It is not so much that man is untrustworthy, or untrusting, but 'anyone who trusts in Yahweh will never be disgraced/ dismayed', Is. 28 v 16.

Consent to 'God's promises, for your salvation by Christ, as 'anyone who believes on Him will not be put to shame', Roms 9 v33.

57. Matt 24 v 15-21.

58. Matt 24 v 22.

59. Matt 24 v 27.

60. The wicked will want to hide under rocks or in holes, Is 2 v10&v19-21; Rev20v11

61. Rev 20 v 14.

62. Luke 18 v 6-8. There will be justice for the elect, whom the Lord will avenge.

63. Rev 16 v 15.

64. Matt 25 v 13.

65. Luke 12 v 42-48.

66. Luke 12 35-40; Mark 13 v 21-37.

67. Rev 22 v 12.

68. 'Redemption draweth nigh', Luke 21 v 28.

69. Matt 24 v 31.

70. Rev 20 v 9.

71. Song 'Redemption draweth Nigh' Gordon Jensen wrote (and almost threw away because it hadn't been hard or time consuming to write), when he was 18 (in 1969), in Ontario, Canada. It has since been internationally successful with various renditions and with orchestral or other music genres anticipating the all too swift return of our Lord Jesus Christ. We are reminded, no, warned, to watch for the Signs of the Times to prepare for Christ' return.

72. Rev 20 v 9 -10, end for the wicked & lake of fire...

73. Rev 19 v 19-20, ...lake of fire and brimstone.

74. Mark 9 v 43-47.

75. Rev 19 v 21.

76. Rev 14 v 9-11.

77. Matt 24 v 51; Matt 25 v 30.

78. Rev 14 v 11.

79. Rev 19 v 19.

80. Rev 18 v 20.

81. Prodigal son, Luke 15 v 11 – 32.

82. 'Love, forgive and pray for our enemies', Matt 5 v 44-48.

83. Stockholm Syndrome: coined on Aug 23rd 1973, when two bank robbers held hostage three women and one man for five days. The hostages were strapped with dynamite and held in the bank vault until rescued. During their ordeal the captives developed unnatural affinity/'love' for their captors and even protected them from the police. They had bonded emotionally with their captors. But this type of abusive, controlling, domineering relationship existed before 1973, and unfortunately is still experienced by many victims.

84. Do good and be merciful to your enemies, Luke 6 v 27-30.

85. (see also ref 68 chp 8). Give and it will be given back to you, ie forgive! Luke 6 v 37.

86. Woe to those who cause children to sin, Matt 18 v 2-9, v 13-20.

87. Rev 13.

88. (see also ref 34 and 39 chp9, and ref 92 chp 8). Sin hated, not sinner, Matt 21 v 31-32; Luke 23 v 39-43.

89. Heal sick and call sinners to repent, Matt 9 v 12-13; Mark 2 v 17.

90. 'Come just as you are' even with all your sins, is the oft –quoted, non Biblical, Christian idea that captures the spirit of invitation Christ extends to each of us: 'Behold, I stand at the door and knock...that anyone who shall hear my voice, I will come and dine with him and he with me', Rev 3 v 20. Also Matt 18 v 12 -14, and the whole of Luke 15 encapsulates this idea, that no sinner is beyond forgiveness if he/she so chooses to repent and follow Christ back to the welcoming arms of our heavenly Father Yahweh. We don't have to wait until we feel we are perfect or worthy before we come to Jesus. He invites us to come to him and approach the throne of grace, even whilst we are yet sinners, Roms 5 v 6-11.

For He says despite our sins, which he loathes, He loves us so much that He will forgive us if we repent and return our love to Him. He Himself is the propitiation for our sins, 1 John 1 v 2. 'He bore our sins in His own body, whilst on a cross/tree, by whose stripes we are healed, so that we, having died to sin, might live for righteousness', 1 Peter 2 v 24, & Is. 53 v 4 & v11; and E G White, ibid Patriarchs and Prophets, chp 4 'The Plan of Redemption' p 63, (see my ref 19 chp 9, and ref 69a chp7). If we answer his invitation we will find peace and perfection within Him and our loving Father Yahweh. For He says 'Come to me all who labour and are heavy laden, and I will give you rest' (Matt 11 v 28), and peace eternally.

Additionally a reason why we should forgive others, show compassion so that you too may be forgiven, Matt 18 v 21-35; and there is great rejoicing in heaven when a sinner repents/ when lost sheep are found again, Luke 15 v 3 -7, Matt 18 v 12 – 14.

91. The Lord gives us the desires of our hearts, Psalm 37 v 4.

92. (see also ref 83 chp7). Matt 7 v 19-23; Luke 12 v 22-34.

93. The Beatitudes, Matt 5 v 3-12; crown of life, James 1 v 12; abide in faith, hope and love, 1 Corin 13 v 13; pursue love and spiritual gifts, 1Corin 14 v 1.

94. 1 John 2 v 15-17.

95. 'Don't be envious of the wicked... their end is death', psalm 73 v 27; & psalm 37 v 1-2.

96. The Lord is our refuge, with His protective wings, psalms of David, 23, 46, 71, 91; Is our shield, psm 3 v3, 5 v 11-12. The Lord has 'redeemed you, and called you by name. You are (his)', Is 43 v 1-3. Psm 23 'The Lord is my Shepherd, ... I shall fear no evil...'

97. (see also ref 60a chp7, ref 48 chp8), google Professor Griff, who exposed the Satanic nature of Illuminati influencing the entertainment industry.

98. (see ref a chp 8), devil as a covering cherub and guardian angel of the Lord, Ezek 28 v 13-19, where he grew vainglorious and exalted himself above the Lord; E G White ibid Patriarchs and Prophets, chp 1, p35.

98a. Satan took nearly half the angels from heaven, E G White, 'The True Story of Redemption' (1947/1980), p18, Review & Herald Publishing Assocn., Hagerstown MD 21740.

99. The Lord's Prayer, Matt 6 v 9 -13, Luke 11 v 2 -4.

100. The lord is able to reward you 'exceedingly and abundantly', Ephesians 3 v 20.

101. Ezekiel 33 v 11.

102. 'Babylon is fallen, is fallen!', Rev 14 v 8, Rev 17 v 1, Rev 18 v 2-8, v 14-21.

103. Matt 15 v 21 -28.

104. Mark 7 v 24 – 30.

105. Good Samaritan, Luke 10 v 25 -37

105a. Grateful Samaritan leper, Luke 17 v 11 -16.

106. John 4 v 1 -26.

107. John 5 v 31 -47.

108. John 19 v 19 -22.

109. Righteous indignation' - Jesus throwing out the money lenders etc from the 'den of thieves' they had turned His Father's house of prayer/temple into, Matt 21 v 12-13; Mark 11 v 15 -18; Is 56 v 7.

110. (see also ref 88 chp 8) Is 33 v 6.

111. Grave responsibility - if Ezekiel fails to warn the people, he is responsible for their deaths, Ezek 33 v 8-9; Isaiah's commission, Isaiah 6.

112. conceited Lucifer/Satan, Is 14 v 12 -15. The Lord of Hosts will bring down low the high and lofty, Is 2 v 11 – 18.

113. Let no man put asunder those whom 'God' has joined in marriage, Matt 19 v 3 – 6; Mark 10 v 5-12.

114. Divorce only permissible, on grounds of adultery, due to hardness of the Jews hearts, Matt 19 v 7 -9.

115. 'Fear not, I have redeemed you. I have called you by your name. You are mine', says the Lord, Is 43 v 1.

115a. Flee sexual immorality, 1 Corin 6 v 13 -20. 'Eunach by choice/celebate for the sake of the kingdom of heaven, Matt 19 v 12. Consecrate yourself to the Lord, Levit 20 v 7-8.

116. 7 Spirits of 'God', Rev 4 v 5.

117. Such as these will not see heaven; drunkards, fornicators/promiscuous, homosexuals, extortioners, sorcerers/magicians, idolators, cowards, murderers, liars, abominable, unbelievers, thieves, sexually immoral, Sodomites, adulterers, covetous, 1 Corin 5 v 6- 13. For theirs is the lake of fire and brimstone which is the 2nd death, Rev 21 v 8.

118. Our heavenly Father will blot out from His memory the sins of the righteous if they repent, Is 43 v 25, Is 44 v 22.

119. Jesus Himself went into the inner Sanctuary, Heb 8 v 1-2, Hebs 9 v 11, v24.

120. Devil prowling like a raging lion ready to devour...us, 1 Peter 5 v 8.

121. Homosexuals are an abomination to 'God', Leviticus 18 v 22: 'You shall not lie with a male as with a woman; it is an abomination', and 'shall be surely put to death', Levit 20 v 13; Levit 18 v23 'And you shall not lie with a beast, neither shall any woman give herself to a beast and lie with it; it is a perversion', to be 'put to death', Levit 20 v 15-16. Leviticus 18 v 9 -18, the Lord Yahweh also forbids incest, of any kind, 'it is wickedness', to be 'burned to death, so that there be no iniquity/sin amongst you', Levit 20 v 14. Don't bring any abomination into your house, lest

you be doomed to destruction like it. You shall utterly detest and abhor it, for it is an accursed thing' Deut 7 v 26. Levit 20 v 23, for 'God's wrath against sexual immorality and perversion see Roms 6, and Roms 1 v 18 -32, Roms 2 v 1 -11. For 'God' shows 'no partiality'. He will judge the good and the evil alike, no –one can escape His judgement. Jesus said watch for the Signs of the Times approaching His return: 'when you see the abomination of the desolation standing in the Holy places, that Daniel spoke about', Matt 24 v 15, Mark 13 v 14; Dan 11 v31. This is pertinent as in 2011 we saw the appointment of a homosexual priest to a high ranking office in Church of England, but was later demoted/deposed in2012, due to public protests .

122. Jesus cried 'Get behind me Satan!', rebuking Peter, Mark 8 v33; Matt 4 v 10.

123. Only the Lord is good. He is the Good Shepherd, Ezek 34. 'I am the good shepherd who lays down my life for my sheep', John 10 v11. No-one is good, except One, that is 'God', Mark 10 v 18, Luke 18 v 19.

124. 'Heaven and earth will pass away to nothingness....Behold, I make all things new', Rev 21 v1, v5.

125. You can do all things in Christ, Phil 4 v 13. All things are possible to him who believes, Mark 8 v 22-26.

126. For all things work for the good, for those who love the Lord, Roms 8 v 28.

127. Enoch, 'E' generation. Gen 5 v 18-24, Patriarch Enoch lived during the Antediluvian period before the Flood of Noah's time. After the birth of his first son at aged 65, he lived and walked and had a close communion with 'God' a further 300 years. He lived in a right-living way, righteous and humble, amidst an evil and mocking/jeering world. He was obedient to the Lord, warning and rebuking and entreating the people to repent. He looked

forward to Christ Redemption. He was privileged to see heaven in visions, and to commune with 'God' and the angels. He did not see death, but being 'but a step away' from heaven, he was 'translated' into it, and disappeared. E G White ibid, Patriarchs and Prophets, chp6, p83-89; and story of Redemption, chp 60, p 406-408.

127a 'not an evil generation', Matt 12 v 39-41 & Luke 11 v 29-30, 'This generation is a perverse/ an adulterous, evil generation; it seeks a sign, but no sign shall be given to it except the sign of Jonah. For as Jonah became a sign to the men of Nineveh, so the son of man will be to this generation', (meaning as Jonas was 3 days in the belly of the whale, so Jesus was to be 3 days in the heart of the earth after He was crucified; before He was resurrected).

128. Boastful, conceited Satan, Is 14 v 12-15. Potter/clay, (see ref 18 chp 2, ref 34 chp 8), Is 45 v 3-10, Is 28 v 14-19. Satan exalts himself as 'God', 2 Thess 2 v 1-12.

129. Jesus, our Lord and Saviour, is the only One worthy to open the 7 seals, Rev chp 5 & 6.

130. Jesus is the Living Waters, John 3 v 14.

130a. Let the thirsty come and drink of (of Jesus), out of His heart shall flow rivers of living waters, John 7 v 37-38.

Jesus, living waterfall, The Flood that is to come. Four chapters in Genesis (6-9) are devoted to the Flood. The Antediluvian people lived in wickedness in Noah's time. He was 500 years old when he had his 3 sons, and preached 120 years whilst he and his family built the Ark. It rained for 40 days and 40 nights, and the whole earth was under water for 150 days, (Gen 7 v 17& v24). Chp 8 tells that the waters did not completely subside until the 10th month, after which Noah sent out the raven, and then the dove, which successfully brought back an olive leaf, before flying off never to return. Noah lived a further 350 years after the Flood, before dying aged 950 years old. Antediluvians and Noah in E G White ibid, Patriarchs & Prophets chp 7, especially p90.

130b. Adam and Eve kept up observing the Sabbath at an altar outside the garden of Eden after their expulsion. They were prevented from re-entering Eden, and so prevented from accessing the Tree of Life for immortality, by angels, guarding with a bright light that looked like a flaming sword. E G White, ibid P & P, chp 3 p60-62, and chp 6 p80.

131. Jesus is the bread and water of Life, John 6 v 35, & v 48-51. If you are thirsty, come and drink, Rev 22 v 17.

132. Jesus' voice is like tremulous running waters,; and like thunder and many waters, Rev 1 v 15, Rev 14 v 2.

133. Avenging arch angel Michael is Jesus Christ, who fought Satan in heaven, Rev 12 v 7-9.

134. Satan to be cast into lake of fire and brimstone, where there is wailing and gnashing of teeth, Matt 13 v 49-50, Matt 13 v 37 -43, Matt 8 v 12.

135. Psalm 37 v 28, not abandoned.

135a. (see also ref 64 chp 8) the blood of saints cries out 'how long must we wait to be avenged?' Rev 6 v 9-11.

136. Isaiah 45 v 22-25; Is. 42 v 8; 43 v 10-13; 44 v 6-8; 45 v 5; 46 v 9-11; 48 v 9-11.

136a. (see also ref 62 and 67 chp 8) The Lord will repay, Roms 12 v 19-20, & Is 46 v 11. Instead of revenge, live peaceably with your enemies. Do good to evil doers, for by so doing you are heaping hot coals upon their heads, Roms 12 v 19-21, (see also ref 44b and 44c chp 7).

137. 'Saviour Messiah', Adventist Review, Sept 22, 2011, p10.

138. (see also ref 50 chp7, ref 53 chp8) 'Behold, He is coming in the clouds, and every eye shall see Him,.. even the ones who pierced Him', 1 Thess 4 v 15 -18. He shall 'appear as lightening flashes from the east to the west', Matt 24 v 27.

139. (see also ref 76 chp 8) Matt 18 v 5-6.

140. (see also ref 107 chp 8) Pastor Paul Durairaj from India, Core Adventism, London, May 2011, the 'I' in sIn.

141. 'In the beginning was the Word, and the Word was with 'God'... John 1 v 1-3.

142. Jonas/Jonah, Matt 12 v 39 - 40, Jesus refers to Jonas in the whale 3 days, represents how long He was to be entombed buried in the earth after His crucifixion, before His resurrection from the dead.

143. (see also ref 26 chp 7, ref 19 chp 8) 'adopted' or 'grafted in' children, and 'brothers and sisters' in Christ, Roms 11 v 19 -24, Roms 9 v 25-26; sons and daughters of 'God', Rev 21 v 7; adopted as children like Christ, Ephes 1 v 1-6.

144. (see also ref 75 chp 8) Sodom and Gomorrah, Tyre and Sidon, Matt 11 v 20-24; Matt 10 v 14-15.

145. Judas hung himself from a tree, Matt 27 v 3-5.

146. 'Do not give what is holy to the dogs; nor cast your pearls before swine/pigs, lest they trample them under their feet, and turn and tear you in pieces' Matt 7 v 6. Don't waste your precious things on those who will not appreciate it.

147. Parable of sower sowing seeds on fertile soil, Matt 13 v 24-30, & v 36-43; Mark 4 v 1-20.

148. The Lord 'shows no partiality, nor takes a bribe. He administers justice for the fatherless, the widow, and loves the stranger'/ sojourner/visitor, 'giving him food and clothing. Therefore love the stranger. You (Israelites) were strangers in the land of Egypt' Deut 10 v 17-18. The Israelites went from famine into Egypt under Joseph as

70 persons, and the Lord Yahweh took them out in exodus as a multitude, Deut 10 v 22. Thus fulfilling His promise to their forefather Abraham: to make his descendants as numerous as the stars in the sky, or the grains of sand on the sea shore, Gen 22 v 1-18.

148a. Anyone who believes is acceptable to 'God', see John 3 v 16-17; Blessed is he who believes and yet has not seen, John 20 v 29, John 5 v 24; he who believes has everlasting life, John 6 v 47.

149. Murderous silence - teenage preacher Chevanev Charles, London, 12 Nov 2011. Responsibility to tell others what the Lord requires of us, Ezek 33 v 8 & v 11, Isaiah 6, (see ref 111 chp 9).

150. Jesus said 'what I tell you in secret, proclaim it/ shout it from the roof tops', Matt 10 v 27.

151. Prophecies do come true, Is 37 v 26-27. 'For He says 'long ago I ordained it. In days of old I planned it. Now I have brought it to pass... that fortified cities have been made desolate and its people dismayed and put to shame...'

152. The Breakup of Yugoslavia, (Wikipedia, free encyclopaedia), www. http://en.wikipedia.org/wiki/breakup_of_Yugoslavia

Evolving ethnic and religious history of the Serbs, Croats and Bosnians, by James Mayfield, (chairman of the European Heritage Library). www.http://euroheritage.net/serbscroatsbosnians.html

The intensity of ethnic cleansing/massacres in the dissolution of Yugoslavia during the wars between 1990s and2008 horrified the Western world. The federation separated into independent states of Serbia, Bosnian Herzogovenia, Bosnia, Croatia, Albania, Macedonia, Slovenia, and Montenegro. The intense xenophobia stretched back to WWII even Nazi Germans were surprised at the intensity of allies Serbia's hatred towards Jews, Communists, Democrats and Socialists.

However racial tensions possibly had their roots in the turbulent history of invasion, occupation and independence from Western Roman Catholicism and Eastern Ottoman Turkish Moslems. After their history of establishing kingdoms began from 6th century onwards, in Slavic Russia; Croatia formed a Catholic kingdom, with neighbours Hungary, Germany and Italy. 10th century kingdom Serbia, adopted the Orthodoxy of Bulgaria and Byzantium. Bosnia and Herzegovenia became principalities in 12th century. They shared language, geography and cultural and genetic origins and heritage. These southern Slavic kingdoms built Yugoslavia 1000 years later.

From 15th to 16th centuries Ottoman Turks conquered the Balkans, including Christian Albania, the Romanian kingdoms Bulgaria, Serbia, Bosnia, southern Croatia, Greece and most of Hungary. They ruled 400 years. The Croats, Slovenes, and Hungarians escaped the ottomans by annexing themselves in marriages and political alliances to Germany and the Austrian Hapsburg empire after 1526. The various states underwent conquest and re-independence from Ottomans, Germans, Austrians during WWI and WWII. After the defeat of Hitler's Nazi Germany, and Mussolini's Fascist Italy, Yugoslavia became the battleground between competing ideologies.

152 cont'd - The less well known fact was that the Ottoman Turks were Black Moslems, of Sunni sect, from northern Africa. Travel between the two continents had been going on for centuries, but the Slavs were invaded, occupied and enslaved by the

Moors (Moorish/ Muslim Turks/ Blackamoors), and hence the term slave, that was later to afflict the whole of the African continent in the Arab and European slave trades of Black peoples during the 15th to 19th centuries. These Black Moslems were descendants of north African Tuareg, Garamantes and others, who worshipped the sun-god Amun –of the ancient Egyptian mythology, their Mystery System that the Greeks called Sophia. The Moors that invaded and ruled the Iberian Peninsula for 700 years, and brought sophistication, universities, science, maths, and metropolis to Western Spain and Portugal, are scarcely remarked and all but obliterated in the 'schizophrenic memory of the Roman Catholic Church' that took over Papal Europe, centuries later. Source: ed. Dr. Ivan van Sertima, 1992, The Golden Age of the Moor, p5, 10, 16-17, 57, 61. Transaction Publishers, New Brunswick USA, and London UK. The history of racism is deeper rooted than the Europeans will admit.

153. Matt 21 v 32 -46, Yahweh continually reaches out to have a better relationship with His people. Jesus recanted the story of a landowner who planted a vineyard, and sent his servants one after the other to enquire after it, but the people there beat and killed them. Then He sent his son, saying 'surely they will respect him', but they did likewise to him. This parable was Jesus premonition or foretelling of what the Jews had done to John the Baptist and other prophets who had preceded him, and would do to Him too, despite Him being the son of Yahweh, our living Creator!

Unfortunately for them, the Jews did not want to hear or heed His warnings, and so bear the guilt of His blood, as we do too, upon our heads, for the ransom of us guilty sinners, by one so innocent's blood. Redemption is now only possible through repentance, and acceptance of this same Jesus Christ. Yet a place is still reserved by Yahweh for even the remnant of Jews, who decide to accept Christ as their Messiah and Saviour at last. The Lord shows no partiality. Anyone who becomes a repentant sinner, and turns away from sin, with Christ' help, and reaches out to Him, is acceptable to Him as His son or daughter in Christ. He blots out all memory of our sins, cancels them, and so reconnects our desecrated 'Perfect Circles' to our Creator. Thank Him for such great mercy and love!

154. The Holy city of New Jerusalem descends from heaven, and 'behold, the tabernacle of 'God' is with men, and He shall dwell with them, and they shall be His people', Rev 21 v 2-4.

Indeed the circle will be complete – Perfect Circles.

EPILOGUE & Author's Comments:

As the hymn bids us, I will stand up for Jesus!

> "Stand up! Stand up for Jesus,
> Ye soldiers of the cross!
> Lift high His royal banner,
> It must not suffer loss.
> From victory unto victory
> His army He shall lead,
> Till every foe is vanquished
> And Christ is Lord indeed.
>
> Stand up, stand up for Jesus!
> The trumpet call obey,
> Forth to the mighty conflict
> In this His glorious day!
> Ye that are His, now serve Him
> Against unnumbered foes,
> Let courage rise with danger,
> And strength to strength oppose.
>
> Stand up, stand up for Jesus!
> Stand in His strength alone,
> The arm of flesh will fail you,

Ye dare not trust your own.
Put on the gospel armour,
Each piece put on with prayer,
Where duty calls or danger,
Be never wanting there.

Stand up, stand up for Jesus!
The strife will not be long,
This day the noise of battle,
The next the victor's song.
To him that overcometh
A crown of life shall be,

He with the King of glory
Shall reign eternally".

(song writer George Duffield – {1818 – 88}. No copyright permission needed, as too old, according to Christian Copyright Licensing International, - CCLI, 13/4/12).

Even if I am, like prophet Isaiah, a lone voice crying out in the wilderness, for our Father, against evil generations; or like Luther – who nailed the writ of proclamation against the R C church; or like Jesus – standing up against the Jewish church leaders, and was abandoned by all, even unto death, except when He cried out on the cross 'My Father, why have you forsaken me?', and instantly realised He did not abandon Him, but had allowed Him to take on the full measure of pain and death that all of mankind is under because of Satan, in order to fully appreciate and recompense and cancel out the sting of death; and re-introduce the possibility of renewed life via resurrection, into Eternity, which is attainable for those who want to follow Christ's example.

I too, as prophetess, even if I am the only one in the whole world today, even if disowned by family, friends, church, and community, I love our Father in heaven so much, and I recognise and thank Jesus for His sacrifice for me and the rest of us, and I love my children and grandchildren so much, that I am willing to endure attacks, isolation, segregation, and whatever the devil is able to throw at me, even unto death, so long as I fulfil my destiny and the tasks our Father has entrusted to me, my commission – 'Perfect Circles' – to reveal the truths about Satan in this our Revelation Time, the last days, latter days, before our loving Christ returns in glory to reclaim us from Satan.

(Quotes from Ellen G White's The Great Controversy' 1888, p 127 – about Luther – A man for his time; and in regard to prophets:(me and others yet to come?)

'To the reproaches of his enemies who taunted him with the weakness of his cause, Luther answered:

"Who knows if God has not chosen and called me, and if they ought not to fear that by despising me, they are despising God Himself? Moses was alone at the departure from Egypt; Elijah was alone in the reign of King Ahab; Isaiah alone in Jerusalem; Ezekiel alone in Babylon....God never selected as a prophet either the high priest or any other great personage, but ordinarily He chose low and *despised* men, once even the shepherd Amos. In every age, the saints have had to *reprove* the great, kings, princes, priests and wise men, *at the peril of their lives.*

I do not say that I am a prophet, but I say that they ought to fear precisely because I am alone, and they are many. I am sure of this, that the word of God is with me, and that it is not with them." (cited by EGW in p133, The Great Controversy, 1888).

P133 cont'd. Ellen White wrote 'the Reformation did not, as many suppose, end with Luther. It is to be continued to the close of the world's history... Luther had a great work to do in reflecting all the light which was to be given to the world... From that time to this, NEW light has been continually shining upon the Scriptures: And NEW truths have been constantly unfolding'.

Yes even unto me, Doreen Joseph Khadija Omowale, from May 1990 to the current times.

The importance for Perfect Circles, the meanings of my names, (given to, or chosen by,me):

Doreen — Irish Christian name, derived from Jewish Hebrew name Dorothy/ Dorothea (my mother's name).

Joseph — Irish Christian/Jewish derivative — famously Joseph the Dreamer, of techni-coloured dream coat. Joseph, beloved son of Jacob/ Israel, sold into slavery by his jealous brothers, came to the highest esteemed position in Egypt by pharaoh, and was thence able to save his family, and Israel — Abraham's blood line from famine and extinction (Gen 37 -48). Joseph was also the name of kindred descendant of shepherd boy/ king David, who married Mary, mother of our Lord Jesus Christ. (Luke 1 v26-28).

Khadija — Muslim name for the first wife of prophet Mohammed. It means to be born before her time, and is appropriate as I was born 2 months prematurely, and since age 8 have had numerous premonitions and visions in dreams.

Omowale — East African name, meaning 'back to your roots'. This was relevant to me as a British AfroCaribbean, namely getting back to Africa historically and literally, and back to Eden spiritually.

Prophetess in these latter days, living in Revelation Times... (DJKO 3/Jan/11).

My Testimony on 'God's' Gifts for Sabbath 29 Jan '11.

{Given what I've already said about the name God (backwards is dog, which is disrespectful to our Lord and Creator Almighty! and relates more to Satan) — the importance of 'what's in a name' sermon? (this chapter 9), I'd rather use how Jesus taught us to address Him – 'Our Father who is in heaven'}.

1. So I'm going to refer to 'the gifts of the Holy Spirit'.

Gifts are: wisdom, the word of knowledge, faith, healings, the performing of miracles, prophecy, discerning of spirits, different kinds of tongues (languages), the interpretation of these tongues (languages) 1 Corin 12 v 4-11; 1 Corin 12 v 29-31; Ephesians 4 v 8 & 11-13; Matt 28 v 19-20.

The Spirits' gifts are also faith, hope and love. But the greatest of these is LOVE. 1 Corin 13 v13.

2. Paul says 'pursue love, desire the Spirit's gifts, but especially that you may prophesy', 1 Corin 14 v1; for 'he who prophesies speaks edification and exhortation and comfort to men' 1 Corin 14 v 3; and so doing reproves, corrects, enhances, encourages and uplifts men. We must speak only good words that are 'necessary for edification so that 'they' may impart grace to the hearers', Ephes 4 v 29; and so teach them to live according to how Our Father, the Creator wants, so we, through Christ, might obtain eternal LIFE.

3. My gift is PROPHECY.

In Numbers 12 v 6 - 8 - the Lord said to Aaron and his wife Miriam: 'If there be a prophet among you, I, the Lord, make myself known to him in a vision. I speak to him in a dream.'

[He went on to say: 'not so to Moses' with whom He spoke 'face to face' .and who was allowed to see the burning bush, (a form of the Lord), because he was faithful, and then He reproved them for grumbling against Moses].

I have been given the gift of prophecy since I was an 8 yr old girl, which manifests itself as 'premonitions'.

My first premonition was seeing the external walls of Kew Gardens in a dream, weeks before actually visiting it on a school trip. Since then I have had countless premonitions in dreams, usually about significant events in my life, which may be about myself, or close family members, or friends,

or even famous people e.g.Spice girl Geri Halliwell just before she announced her departure from the 'girl power' group to become a UN Goodwill Ambassador on behalf of women and children (1998);

or some world event like the Asian Tsunami in Thailand (2004) that killed 200,000 people; , and the New Orleans flood disaster caused by Hurricane Katrina (2008) with unprecedented damage, killed 1,836 people and displaced a further 485,000;

- the one, because it transpired it might have been caused by man's explosions in the nearby Pacific ocean; (- News update- Dec 13th, '12, UK government allows resumption of shale fracking for gas, despite links with earthquakes/tremors in the UK. Once again 'mammon'/money/ profits takes precedence over safety of lives);

- and the other, because of the scandal of how long it took the racist president Bush to leave his golf game and send help to the victims; and the disgusting way his troops treated the Black residents, by giving life-saving preferential treatment to the white people (tourists and residents) first. As hip-hop singer Kanye West said publicly: 'Bush doesn't like Black people', to which the shamed president felt compelled to get his top Defence Secretary, black woman Condalisa Rice to refute that statement. But it was too late. The truth was exposed.

My premonitions have also been Our Father's way of warning me about people or situations, that are about to harm me, e.g when my husband suddenly started behaving in ways that made me fear him as a liability ,and as a threat to my family's security, so that I had to ask him to leave us, - (later ended in divorce). But the pressures he caused and the financial mess he left me in, forced me to overwork and overstress myself into a nervous breakdown, which the devil whom, I'd seen in a premonition some time before, had orchestrated so that I would have the mental illness schizophrenia.

This was more than a coincidence. I had a breakdown, within a month after the Holy Spirit had used me as an instrument to begin writing the book 'Perfect Circles'. This was May 1990. And the devil has been persecuting me ever since, under the tyranny and mental imprisonment of psychiatry's 'treatments' - ECT and drugs, by which he tried to kill me, or failing that, eradicate or dull my memory, so I would not continue with the book. For in it he could see the Spirit was exposing the truths about him, and of our Father, the Creator. Satan does not want everyone to know who he really is. So by having the veil he that has put over our eyes uncovered, the full extent of what a liar and deceiver he is, will be exposed in this our Revelation Time.

But *he* is not in control. The Alpha and Omega, the Beginning and the End, the Author and Finisher of things is in control. And it is He, who on 19/10 /2010 showed me in a dream, that He has vanquished the man-serpent (like Spider man's green goblin) of psychiatry (and dyslexia) - the devil's tools to suppress me for the last 21 yrs, which prevented me finishing the book Perfect Circles. The Lord has freed & liberated me to fulfil my commission - His purpose. Thank you Jesus, You are truly merciful! The Lord has preserved, saved, delivered and blessed me and mine abundantly, and been true to his word and been faithful, and forgiving and loving exceedingly. Why would I not want to fulfil his request and obey him gladly and willingly from love and gratitude? I will not cease to speak of his goodness and blessings and admonitions and warnings and callings to his love and greatness. I will do His bidding, for He is the Lord Almighty from whom all things come and whom all things and everyone owes homage and praises in highest exaltation. Halleluiahs forever!!!

As Ellen G White says:

in both Prophets and Patriarchs/ P & P, (introduction p iii - x)(my chp 9 ref 48) and The Great Controversy (where she tells us about Luther, the prophet of his time, p127 and 133),

- in these latter days before Christ's 2nd coming, there will be a great outpouring of the Holy Spirit in the churches, and not only on priests, but on ordinary, less-than -perfect people, who have the love and devotion to Christ at the centre of their hearts.

Children, old men, manservants and maidservants and more, will be 'dreaming visions' (Joel 2 v28-31; E G White ibid P & P, Introd. P iv; Acts 2 v 17-21). So that there will be many people prophesying and warning the people about the evils in this world, and admonishing them to 'fix –up' and 'take this thing seriously!!!

Jesus tells us that Satan is out to destroy us, and that our souls can only be saved from destruction if we choose to listen to the messages Christ taught us, and endure sufferings for His name sake, yet still remain faithful to Him throughout the sufferings even unto our death. This we must do, if we are to ever have a chance of eternal LIFE with Him. He warns us, and at the same time, gives us hope. This is the function of prophecy and the role and purpose of prophets/prophetesses.

Paul says: 'despise not prophesying' (1 Thess. 5 v. 19 -21); that those prophesying may be preserved blameless unto the coming/ return of the Lord (1 Thess.5 v 23) . For, they are to be tested and proved. Jesus said 'by their fruits you shall know them' ....'if they are doing good works' (Matt 7 v 20). For, we are His workmanship, created in Christ Jesus for good works, which our Father prepared beforehand, so that we should walk in them' (Ephes 2 v 10).

But note that even Jesus said: ' a prophet is honoured everywhere except in his own home town and among his friends and family' (Matt 13 v57; Luke 4 v 24 . So true -30 June '11.

As the scripture verses I've cited state quite categorically: Satan chased after the 'woman and her offspring/Child' (Mary and Jesus), Rev 12 v 4-5; and the remnant of her seed, (those who have kept the laws of the Creator – the 10 commandments- and who have the Testimony of Jesus Christ:, Rev 12 v 17). He persecuted Mary and Jesus and will also persecute those who choose to believe on Jesus and follow Him. These will be tormented and even killed by Satan.

But they will share Christ' victory that He won on the cross at Calvary, when He enters into His kingdom. They will be the 'elect' who will be 'dressed as a bride for her husband' the prize jewel, 'the new city of Jerusalem' in the New heaven and New earth, for a LIFE in Eternity with Him, the Holy Spirit and our Father in heaven, who is our Creator Almighty.

All laud and praises are due to Him!

References about the spirit of prophecy see - Acts 2 v 17 -21, v 39; 1 Corin 1 v 7; Rev 12 -17; Rev 19 v 10.

May the Lord bless you with spiritual gifts so that you may lead others to Him, in order that we and they might be saved, and attain eternal LIFE.

On the 19/10/2010 Our Creator showed me

In a dream, that He had vanquished the stranglehold of psychiatry

That for 21 years the devil held over me.

So I stand firm on my LIBERTY

From the tyranny of mental slavery

(and newly discovered dyslexia, 6/12/2010).

I have been given the clarity

To see my destiny,

To unlock the mystery of history. (completed 25/6/12, LOL!)

For Jesus Christ has set me FREE!

(discharged from psychiatry's clutches 16/11/11, and reattached summer 2012).

On His cross at Calvary.

I share His victory,

To the glory of Our Father Yahweh, our Sovereign Lord, in heaven,

Who is the Creator of us all.

Halleluiah!!!

To Him be all thanks, praises and glory,

For He is Great and Almighty!

He is The Alpha and Omega,

The Beginning and the End,

The Author and Finisher of things,

Past, Present and To Come,

By Doreen Joseph/ Khadija Omowale/Prophetess (03/Jan/11).

My Declaration of freedom

I stand firm on the victory and liberty

That Jesus Christ has won for me,

As I fulfil my destiny

To do the work of the Almighty,

Our Father in heaven.

To Him be all the glory,

Thanks, honour and praises,

For all Eternity.

DJKO (4/Jan/11)

If

Our Father

In Heaven

Yahweh & Our Creator

Is For

Me

Who can be against me?

No one,

Nothing,

At All....

(Romans 8 v 31, 37-39)

As West London, UK - born, of West Indian parents, a long memoried descendant of West African story-telling griots, who are oral historians, and having studied Latin and the Bible, I have kept the long convoluted Roman and Greek style, elongated sentences into long paragraphs. And by aid of the Holy Spirit I have used it to draw out, and explain and thus make sense of the secrets and mysteries hidden, secreted away under deception within contracted, shortened catch phrases and statements, so as to reveal YHWH's Truth and Prophecies; and to expose Satan for the real, incredible LIAR that he is.

So I apologise if my sentences are too long-winded, or too boring for you, or not 'entertaining' enough for you, or are too protracted to keep your errant mind from wandering off into any and all distractions – rather than allow yourself to really sit down, pay attention and listen, and allow yourself to absorb the messages of **love** that **YHWH** has been constantly trying to reach us with, from the Beginning of Time. And with the outstretched arms of His son **Jesus Christ**, the Messiah, our Saviour and Redeemer, who dwelt as Immanuel amongst us for a short while, and who is soon to return in person, with all-encompassing world-wide bright, shining **Light** of **LIFE**, from east to west flashing like lightening, north to south, all over this globe.

His Life –giving LIGHT is accessible to all, via His Holy Spirits, who reach out now through children like Brazilian Jotta A in praise and worship songs, through prophets –ordinary men, women and children, young and old, from humble beginnings, or with humble and contrite hearts, with no 'authorised' or 'orthodox' qualifications, other than that they happily surrender themselves, utterly and completely, in willing and obedient service and **love** to YHWH's Christ; and for the sake and love of others, and have been given YHWH's legitimate authority to preach His word. Yes, preach it to all who would be still, and want to hear, listen, and come to know, accept and **love** HIM, via His son Christ Jesus. Halleluiah! Indeed, worthy is the Lamb, who is crowned King of kings, and Lord of lords forever! Selah. (Rev 19 v 16).

When He comes back, and has victory, He will rule His eternal kingdom with an iron rod. I will hold fast to what I know 'til He returns, for, he has promised 'to he who overcomes, and keeps My (Jesus') works until the end, to him I will give power over the nations –

> "He shall rule them with a rod of iron; They, (the enemies), shall be dashed to pieces like the potter's vessels".

As I have also received from My Father; and I will give him the morning star. He who has an ear, let him hear what the Spirit says to the churches' (Rev 2 v 25-29).

So I hold firm to Jesus' promises that spur me onwards and upwards.

I cannot be bought, bribed, cajoled, flattered, threatened into forsaking our Lord's commission to 'make disciples of men', nor especially this special one of this book Perfect Circles. I have gladly vowed to fulfil my commission, and will continue until it is finished, accomplished, and is nourishing others with the spiritual food that comes by word of YHWH's Holy Spirit, until His purpose is accomplished.

So I urge you to take heed of YHWH's messages, especially to REBUKE Satan, REPENT of sins, and RETURN to our Lord, as is reiterated throughout this book, and the Bible and elsewhere. He does not speak in jest. It is for His purpose and our good. And if we want to 'be perfect as our heavenly Father is perfect', we must earn it, by choosing to follow Christ and live by His Way, and become Christ-like, and loving and forgiving and merciful, and live righteously according to YHWH's commandments as etched by His finger of fire on Moses' tablets of stone. Let not your heart be stony and stubborn. Let Jesus come in and melt your stony heart into vibrant, warm living hearts of **LOVE**! You never know, this may be your last chance for love, REAL and TRUE LOVE. Don't let this opportunity pass you by.

Here I am Lord, your messenger, still standing in your faith and love and mercy, and observing Your 7th day Sabbath. Thank you. And despite of the many Satanic and devilish obstacles and afflictions, I am even more resolute and determined to fulfil your purpose, the reason I was put on this earth at this time:- Your book showing Your Love for us, in **PERFECT CIRCLES.**

May You reign so glorious forever and ever, and from everlasting to everlasting! Selah.

This praise song written in love by pastor Clive de Silva, coincidentally in the year I was baptised SDA, 2008, encompasses my desire for others, and excited anticipated Return of Jesus Christ – His Second Advent:

'This is the Core of Adventism' (theme song, de Silva, 2008).

Lord, we are waiting now for You,
Show us what we ought to do;
Teach us what, oh Lord, is good,
Guide us to work just like we should.

Chorus: This is the core of Adventism
This is the reason that we are here,
Calling all nations and tongues
To worship the Lord in the truth and holy fear,
This is the heart of Adventism
This is the reason we are in place
Living a life that is new, a message that's true,
To prepare to see God's face,
To see God's face,
To see God's face.

We as a people must revive
To give You glory through our lives,
Lead us from darkness into light
To do what's pleasing in Your sight.

Chorus: This is the core of Adventism...
This is the church that You have raised,
To reach the world You died to save,
When You come back the second time,
Souls will be saved to joy sublime.

Chorus: This is the core of Adventism...
This is the heart of Adventism
This is the reason we are in place,

Living a life that is new, a message that's true,
To prepare to see God's face,
To see God's face,
To see God's face,
Lord we are waiting now for You...

(by permission of pastor de Silva; see http://www.YouTube.com/silvaFMmusic)

Prophetess:

I thank Jesus for the Holy Spirit,

And all that I can advise is:

Seek and you shall find.

For when I go missing

You will be listening

To the beauty of His Word –

The Truth –

Jesus Christ.

So look to Jesus,

Those who hunger and thirst

For knowledge,

And Understanding

About Truth

(Righteousness),

And you shall be satisfied (Matt. 5 v 6),

He promises you this.

Selah.

(DJKO 23/Jan/11)

Sometimes man is at enmity with our heavenly Father. Young preacher Michael Dantzie, in his sermon 'Deadly Seduction', pub'd 8th Aug, 2012, (www.thePreachingPlace.com), quotes James 4 v 4: - 'Do you not know that friendship with the world is enmity with YHWH?' For, 'the cross' that Jesus died on, 'is a REBUKE to the world!' Indeed, Jesus said you can be in the world, but like Him, not OF the world (John 8 v 23; John 15 v 19; John 17 v 11-26). In other words, do not be worldly or secular, 'experienced'or 'entertained', but be CONVICTED and CONVERTED to Jesus Christ. For, He, by the power of the Holy Spirit, is our ONLY Way to re-connect with our heavenly Father, who is constantly, yet even still today, reaching out to each and every one of us, to love us (Jerem 7 v 25; John 3 v 16), who are seeking Truth, Peace, Joy, Happiness, Love and Life, namely YHWH (Yahweh), our Creator Himself. Praise YHWH, and Live! Praise His son, Jesus Christ, and Love! Halleluiah!!! Yes even now, despite the enmity, the Holy Spirit reaches out to us, to help and guide us. My dream is that you seek the Lord Yahweh and you will be satisfied. His grace is sufficient for us (2 Cor. 12 v 9; Phil. 2 v 12-13). For He Is the Great I AM, who lives from everlasting to everlasting, Amen.

How Great Is Our God

The splendour of a King, clothed in majesty
Let all the earth rejoice
All the earth rejoice

He wraps Himself in Light, and darkness tries to hide
And trembles at His voice
Trembles at His voice

How great is our God, sing with me
How great is our God, and all will see
How great, how great is our God

`Age to age He stands
And time is in His hands
Beginning and the end
Beginning and the end

The Godhead Three in One
Father Spirit Son
The Lion and the Lamb
The Lion and the Lamb

Name above all names
Worthy of our praise
My heart will sing
How great is our God

How great is our God, sing with me
How great is our God, and all will see
How great, how great is our God.

and since Feb 2007 is the most popular worship song today (2011), and won 'Song of the year', and' worship song of the year' 2006 and 2008).

No doubt written under inspiration of the Holy Spirit,

and in the same vein as **Isaiah 40:**

Isaiah 40 extracts:

Is. 40 v 3, The voice of one crying in the wilderness: 'Prepare the way of the Lord, make straight in the desert a highway for our God...

V 10, Behold, the Lord God shall come with a strong hand, and His arm shall rule for Him; Behold, His reward is with Him, and His work before Him.

V 11, He will feed His flock, like a shepherd; He will gather the lambs with His arm. And carry them in His bosom, and gently lead those who are with young.

V 12, Who has measured the waters (seas and oceans) in the hollow of His hand, measured heaven with a span and calculated the dust of the earth in a measure? Weighed the mountains in scales, and the hills in a balance?

V 13, Who has directed the Spirit of the Lord, or as His counsellor has taught Him?

V 14, With whom did He take counsel, and who instructed Him, and taught Him in the path of justice? Who taught Him knowledge, and showed Him the way of understanding?

V 15, Behold, the nations are as a drop in a bucket, and are counted as the small dust on the scales; Look, He lifts up the isles as a very little thing,

V 16, And Lebanon's (tall trees) are not sufficient to burn, nor the beasts sufficient for a burnt offering.

V 17, All nations before Him are as nothing; and they are counted by Him less than nothing and worthless.

V 18, To whom will you liken God? Or what likeness will you compare to Him?

V 21, Have you not known? Have you not heard? Has it not been told you from the beginning? Have you not understood from the foundations of the earth?

V 22, It is He who sits above the circle of the earth. And its inhabitants are like grasshoppers; Who stretches out the heavens like a curtain, and spreads them out like a tent to dwell in.

V 23, He brings the princes to nothing; He makes the judges of the earth useless.

V 25, To whom then will you liken Me; or to whom shall I be equal? Says the Holy One.

V 26, Lift up your eyes on high, and see who has created these things, Who brings out their host (stars) by number; He calls them all by name, by the greatness of His might, and the strength of His power, not one is missing.

V 28, Have you not known? Have you not heard? The everlasting God, the Lord, the Creator of the ends of the earth, neither faints nor is weary. His understanding is unsearchable.

V 29, He gives power to the weak, and to those who have no might He increases strength...

V 31, But those who wait on the Lord shall renew their strength; they shall mount up with wings like eagles, they shall run and not be weary, they shall walk and not faint.

This is the power and greatness of the Lord of hosts, our great Redeemer and Saviour, our Wonderful Counsellor and Comforter, King of kings, Lord of lords, True Ruler, Just and Fair, the ultimate Judge and Life – giver, our Creator, Yahweh, Jesus Christ and Holy Spirit, 3 of the 7 Spirits of Love and Life itself.

He cannot be squashed into a small graven image or idol, or into one of the 3 aspects that represent Him – Father, Son or Holy Spirit. He is all of these and much, much more... He truly is great!

Give Him due respect, honour, laud and praises. Worship and thank Him, for He is worthy of our praise. His name is to be so very highly exalted forever and ever, ad infinitum. Selah. May you too be blessed for His great name's sake.

(Japanese Tea hut in a beautiful garden at Heale House, Middle Woodford, Wilts. SP4 6NT. Heale House and its 8 acres of beautiful gardens, lie beside the river Avon. Taken by unknown photographer, and is so old, that no permission license is needed to use it, April 2011).

Tree and River of Life....

(at beginning and end of humanity – Full circle)

As it was at the beginning of Creation,

So shall it be at the end for those

Who love our Sovereign Lord, our Creator.

Topical Index:

Abraham, 27, 28
- 'sacrifice of son', 27
blessed with descendants as stars, 61, 137, 376-377
- father of Jews, Moslems, Christians, 3, 4, 61, 86, 136-137
Adam and Eve – created, blessed, 16, 17, 82 -
tempted and disobedient , 16,
- exiled, regrets, 21, 83
- worshipping at altar at gate on Sabbaths, 328, 374
'Agnus Dei', 254, 340
angels, good, 5, 9
 - fallen, see demons
- angel of light, Lucifer/ Satan, 11, 96, 138
- Archangel Michael, see Jesus,
- avenging, see Jesus,
Annihilation of mankind, see destruction,
Anubis, see God - secret ID, 84, 246-262, 340-341, 344,

Apostasy, 121, 131, 184-185, 215-216, 254
Armageddon, 21, 77, 167, 227, 317
Armstrong, Louis, 14, 15, 64
Assange, Julian, see 'Davids', 52, 72
Assyria, to unite with Egypt and Israel to worship YHWH, see Egypt,

Babylon – is falling, Babel, 24, 120, 121, 160,
- corruption, financial downfall, 120, 121, 277-297,
- Nebuchadnezzar, 37, 121, 139, 253, 303
Bergemeister, Jane, see Davids, 72, 358
Beyonce, see Music industry, 87, 94, 163
Blessings & mercies from Yahweh,139,
bless the Lord – extracts, 116, 149-157 bless our persecutors, 49,

242, 367 Bread of Life, see Jesus,

CIRCLES, PERFECT, - definition of, communion, 3-6, 24

Creation, -in the Beginning, 9-15, 350

- re-creation, transformation in Christ, 44-47
- re – creation of earth and heaven, 239

CHRIST, son of man, of YHWH, 6,30,61

prophet, archangel, see Jesus, 35

Christmas - truth, 108-109

Christianity, 59, 191

Christ-like, not racist, 220, 271-275

children – abused, dom. violence, 208-213, 364-365; Victoria Climbie, Baby P, 210-212

- see paedophilia,
  - corrupted, TV, social media, Bulger, 206-208; Soham girls, 98, 278, 313,, Habba hotel, 312-313
- child soldiers, blood, gangs, 204-207
- innocent, precious, to be loved, 213,
- beloved, chosen, Israelites, 28
- adopted 'sons and daughters' of YHWH,34, obedient, faithful, blameless, 384

- son of man, of YHWH, see Jesus,

'come just as you are', CAYA, 368-369

conceit, see vaingloriousness,

CONTROVERSY, THE GREAT, 35, 82, 105

corruption of Holy Books, 135-139

Core of Adventism, 395-396

crescent moon, symbols, 129, 169-170

cross, ankh, symbols, 129, 131 David, shepherd boy/ king, of Jesse, 28; root of Messiah, house of the Lord, 329

- David and Goliath, modern day 'Davids':- Assange, Bergemeister, 52, 72; Cantwell, Harrowitz, Professor Griff, 88, 93, 358; Doreen and Neville Lawrence, 273-274;

David 'Rocky' Bennet, mental health, 359

death – introduction of, to humanity, 184, 317; - warfare, biological germ, Aids, flu, 192 - depopulation, 200

- pharmaceutical industry, 196-199
- psychiatry – 'industry of death', cchr, 145, 196-199, 359-360

- second death, lake of fire and brimstone, 122, 168, 234-239

deception, serpent Satan, Eve and Adam, of mankind, 16
- dazzling images, 6, 334

demons, fallen angels, evil spirits, 6, 11, 87, 124

Satanic, 'Harry Potter' film, 270
- debasing, degrading, degenerate, desensitising, 188-213, dehumanising, debasement of women,

destruction, of YHWH's harmonious order, 35, 82, 166
- annihilation, almost of mankind, 183, 191, 193, 201, 218, 269
- of the world, 232, 235, 316
- homosexuality, see LAWS,

disciples, of Christ, 48-60
- would-be, requirements, 49-51; ambassador's conduct, fearless, 51, 345-346
- shun material wealth, 54
- prized possessions, 40, 50, 56-60

disobedience, see obedience,

dreams – prophetic, Joseph, 160, 376, Daniel, 118, 139, Doreen J's, 50, 322, 338

Easter –truth, 107-108, 116-118
Eden, Garden of, 16; mine, 19

eternal life, Eternity, 51, 356, 389

Egypt, ancient Egyptians, 84
- helped Israelite Joseph's family of 70, 72,
- enslaved Israelites, 85 - idolatry, greatest sin, 85, 249
- Anubis, Isis, gods, ankh – cross, 84, 129
- Pharoah humbled by Moses, and crushed into obscurity, 85
- remnant to unite with Assyrians and Israelites to worship YHWH, 252, 267, Messianic Jews, 354,

Ellen G. White, prophet, Seventh Day Adventist Movement (SDA), 335-338

Enoch, translated to heaven, and E-generation, not evil -, 373

Ezekiel, see prophets,

FAITH, belief in one Creator, monotheism, YHWH, Jehovah, Allah, 3,4
- Abraham, Joseph, Moses, David, Daniel and Shadrak, Mishak and Abednigo, faithful and blameless, 393-394 financial corruption exposed, see Babylon,

Flood, of Noah's time, 23, 143, 323 - modern time, tsunamis, 101, 319

- Fountain of Life, Flood, see Jesus,
FORGIVENESS, the Lord forgives,
- Jesus forgives, - being forgiven, Mary Magdalene prostitute, Matthew tax collector, thief on cross,
- forgiving, and being healed, 223-225, 352-353, 369

Garden, see Eden,
- of Gethsemene, 50
God, 1, throughout,
- secret identity, 108, 246-262, 296, 341-342, 344
- Anubis, and other aliases of Satan, Baal, Baphomet, 95
Griff, professor, see Davids, 88, 93

Heaven, is real,
- throne of YHWH, 401-402
- where Jesus came from and returned to, and will descend from again, 325
- all of rejoices when a sinner repents, 50, 143
hell/ Hades, place of torment, Satan's and demons domain, 227, to be thrown into lake of fire and brimstone, 2nd death, 142, 227, 332
Idolatry, abominable, unforgiveable, 115-116, 142-143, 175; —— futile, Potter – clay,

golden calf, 363, 371
Illuminati, Free Masons, see music industry,
Isaiah, see prophets,
Isis, ancient Egyptian goddess, 85
Islam, prophet Muhammed, Moslems, 59, 82, 85-86,177, 319, 354, Holy Qu'ran, Tradition Hadith,
- believe Jesus as prophet only,
- descendants of Ishmael, Abraham's son, half-brothers of Israelites/ Jews,28, 86
- spiritual kin to Christ-like peoples, 161
Israel, Israelites, from Jacob, descendants of Isaac, Abraham's son, 28, chosen by YHWH, 28
- stubborn, rebellious, disobedient , 86, 161; disciplined by YHWH's agents, 85
some faithful, and remnant to unite with Egypt and Assyria to worship YHWH, (see Egypt), 252, 267, 354
JESUS, CHRIST, the Living Word, and co- Creator with YHWH and Holy Spirits, Alpha & Omega, 73, 387,
- Archangel Michael, 35

- birth, Immanuel, son of man,168, 328, 344
- prophet, the Messiah, son of YHWH, 172
- forgiving, see FORGIVENESS,
- healing, Great Physician, 303, Bread, Water/ Fountain of Life, 323, Lord of the Sabbath, 135
- raising from the dead, and raised, see resurrection,
- angry, rebuking Satan, 105, reproving religious leaders, 134-135; warning the wicked to repent, 331
- greatest LOVE, embodiment of love, 58, 245, greatest sacrifice, Saviour, 56, 61, 243, 327
- his resurrection, witnessed by others, 259,
-connecting bridge, 108,
- man's mediator, interceding in heavenly sanctuary, 325-326, 354, 379
- the spiritual Flood of Prophecy & Truth, 245-246, 322, 341, 344, 374
- second coming as Avenger and Claimant and Deliverer, 56, 142, 185, 375
- third coming, after Millennium, 327
- King of kings, Lord of lords, co-Judge, co- Ruler with YHWH, 58, 326-328

Jeremiah, see prophets,
Jerusalem, and new city of, 239, 379, 389
John the Baptist, see prophets
John, disciple/apostle, the Revelator, 328
Joseph, see dreams, 160, 376
Judaism, Jews, see Israelites,
Judas, betrayed Jesus, 141, 174
Judgement Day, & judgement, 47, 58, 234, 316-317

King Henry XVI – head of church & state, 301

Lake of fire and brimstone, see death,
LAWS of YHWH, obedience requisite, 28, 126, 171, 351
- Moses 10 commandments plus, 180
- Roman Catholic 10 commandments, 181
- sanctified Sabbath, 114
- laws broken, Sunday worship, 107
- 'Judaizing' criminalised, 106, 110-113
- forbidden/ unclean food, pork, 202
- homosexuality, same sex 'marriage', 163, sexual perversions, adultery, incest, 190-191, 307, 310-311, 371-372

- idolatry, the worst sin, see idolatry
- killing, blood, 'trojan horse', 194, 200-201, 358,361

LOVE, YHWH's, 35, 54, 59
- Christ's, see Jesus,
  - sex is NOT love, 244, 307-308
  - Stockholm syndrome, 242-243
  - TRUE love, PERFECT love, 35, 394

UNCONDITIONAL love, 35, 40, 242-243

Mammon, money, source of evil, craved, idolised, greed, 196-200, 291-293-294 - credit system new slavery, 231

marriage, - Adam and Eve first, 16, 17 sanctified, 316
  - broken, adultery, 20, 316, 371
  - abuse, domestic violence, fear, 20

Martin Luther, Protestant, reformer,382-384

Martin Luther King Jnr., civil rights leader, 52

Mary, mother of Jesus, 29, 86,120
- Mariology, 119-120

Matrix, the film, 36, 77

Michael Jackson, 'Bobby dazzler', see music industry,
- see paedophilia, child abuse,

Music industry, MTV, entertainment, Illuminati, MJ, 87-98, 94-96, 103, 105

Moses, 10, 28

Nina Simone, 'Sinnerman', 233

Noah, 23

Omnipotent, omniscient, omnipresent, omni-benevolent, YHWH, 34,

obedience, 6, 39
- disobedience, 5, 16, 39, 47

Olympics, 341

paedophilia, pederasty, child abuse, 98; - Jimmy Saville, BBC fall out, 100
- Michael Jackson, 96-98, 100-104
- Rochdale sex abuse ring, 99
- traditions - the Talmud; & China, 101
- Thailand child prostitution, 98

pharmaceutical industry, see death,

Probation, limited time, close of, 324-326, 343, 347

Prophets, as below, 265, 343
- Daniel, see dreams, 118, 345
- Ellen G White, see herself,
- Ezekiel, 370-371
- Isaiah, 375
- Jeremiah,343

- John the Baptist, 29, 39, 135
  - John the Revelator, see himself,
- Jesus Christ, see Jesus,
- Muhammed, see Islam,
- Doreen Joseph Khadija Omowale, see dreams
Psychiatry, see death,

Queen Elizabeth I, 302
Queen Elizabeth II, Jubilee, 342
- usurpation, 342

Redemption,
  - song 'Redemption draweth nigh',235-236, 379
REPENTANCE, 223-226, 310, 317-318, 351-352, 379
RESURRECTION, of the dead, 1st & 2nd resurrections, Lazarus, 47, 237, 239
  - Jesus, raised on 3rd day – MONDAY, 259, 332
Roman Catholic Church,
  - idolatry, institution of Pope as God on earth, 105-106, 118, 121
  - wealth, influence, exploitation, see mammon,
  - changed laws, see LAWS broken,
  - changed Sabbath, see LAWS broken, Sunday law, the Lord's day, 106-107, 112-113
  - Apostasy, see apostasy,

- blood on their hands,
- Crusades, Inquisitions,
- exploitation of penitent poor,
- they will be held accountable, 123, 141-142
RUTH, Moabite priestess, idolatress, converted to become ancestor of Messiah Jesus, 343

SABBATH, first established by YHWH Himself, ordinance to be kept, 13, 54, 65, 109-110
- sacred, sanctified, 82, 113, 114
- observed by Adam and Eve, 328, 374 ; & by prophets, Jesus and disciples, Jesus Lord of the Sabbath, 135
- R Catholics changed day, see LAWS broken, Sunday as Lord's day,
SACRIFICE, see Abraham's,
  - see Jesus',
  - personal sacrifice, 58-61, 245, 355
SALVATION,
Satan, Lucifer, first angel, vainglorious, proud, 11, 33, disobedient, rebel, 16, 81-104, challenger/transgressor, fallen angel, 82, 166; demon, devil, many aliases aka idol,

- Accuser, Deceiver, Usurper, 33, 83, 124-125, 144, 184, 347
- caused deaths, destroyer, 218
- secret ID of God, Anubis, 108, Santa, 250; - his punishment and final end, 142-145, 238238-239, 333

SECOND COMING/ADVENT of CHRIST, see Jesus,

Third coming of Christ, see Jesus,

Seventh Day Adventist, SDA, see Ellen G White,

Signs of the Times, 229, 235-236, 286-287, 293, 298, 301-303, 319

slavery, - Israelites, descendants of ancient Egyptians, 85, 231, 250, 266-267, 282
- London riots 2011, , looting, 228-231
- poor, Victorian work houses, 282
- credit system new slavery, see mammon

Spiritual Gifts, PROPHECY, 384-390

- spiritual fruits, - sinners repent and heaven rejoices, 50,

Suffering, count as joy for Christ, 49-53

Transformation, Jesus after resurrection, and ours by Holy Spirit, 44-47

Tree & River of Life, 14, 404

Vaingloriousness, vanity, conceit, pride, see Satan

Water /Fountain of Life, see Jesus,

warfare in heaven, 35, 82

warfare on earth, see death, and destruction,

worship, of only our Creator YHWH permitted, not of idols – idolatry, 115

YHWH, Yahweh, Creator of All, 1, and throughout book; 7 Spirits of God, 343, 371 ref 116.